CLARENDON LAW SERIES

Edited by
TONY HONORÉ AND JOSEPH RAZ

CLARENDON LAW SERIES

The Concept of Law
By H. L. A. HART

Introduction to Roman Law
By BARRY NICHOLAS

Legal Reasoning and Legal Theory
By NEIL MACCORMICK

Natural Law and Natural Rights
By JOHN G. FINNIS

The Foundations of European Community Law (2nd edition)
By T. C. HARTLEY

The Law of Property (2nd edition)
By F. H. LAWSON AND BERNARD RUDDEN

An Introduction to the Law of Torts (2nd edition)
By JOHN G. FLEMING

An introduction to Administrative Law
By PETER CANE

Conflicts of Law and Morality
By KENT GREENAWALT

Bentham and the Common Law Tradition
By GERALD J. POSTEMA

An introduction to the Law of Contract (4th edition)
By P. S. ATIYAH

The Principles of Criminal Evidence
By A. A. S. ZUCKERMAN

An Introduction to the Law of Trusts
By SIMON GARDNER

Public Law and Democracy in the United Kingdom and the United States of America

P. P. CRAIG

CLARENDON PRESS · OXFORD

This book has been printed digitally and produced in a standard design in order to ensure its continuing availability

OXFORD
UNIVERSITY PRESS

Great Clarendon Street, Oxford OX2 6DP

Oxford University Press is a department of the University of Oxford. It furthers the University's objective of excellence in research, scholarship, and education by publishing worldwide in

Oxford New York

Athens Auckland Bangkok Bogotá Buenos Aires Cape Town Chennai Dar es Salaam Delhi Florence Hong Kong Istanbul Karachi Kolkata Kuala Lumpur Madrid Melbourne Mexico City Mumbai Nairobi Paris São Paulo Singapore Taipei Tokyo Toronto Warsaw

with associated companies in Berlin Ibadan

Oxford is a registered trade mark of Oxford University Press in the UK and certain other countries

Published in the United States by Oxford University Press Inc., New York

Reprinted 2001

ISBN 0-19-825637-X

To my parents

ACKNOWLEDGEMENTS

This book has taken shape over a number of years, during which the ideas have developed and altered. I would like to thank many friends and colleagues in the United Kingdom and the United States who have found the time to read and comment upon the ideas contained in this work. I am indebted to Joseph Raz, who has provided invaluable support and guidance throughout this period, and to Neil MacCormick, who has furnished important insights on both method and substance. Other friends and colleagues who have proffered helpful advice and criticism are: Greg Alexander, Fred Aman, Jack Beatson, Denis Galligan, Leslie Green, Tony Honoré, Nicola Lacey, Pnina Lahav, Martin Loughlin, Laurence Lustgarten, David Lyons, Tom Morawetz, Morton Horwitz, Stephen Perry, and Aviam Soifer. Parts of the work were drafted while on sabbatical at Cornell Law School, which provided a congenial and stimulating environment in which to work. I have also benefited from the comments received while giving papers at Boston University, Cornell, the University of Connecticut, McGill, and Osgoode Hall. Finally, I would like to thank those at OUP who have been involved in the production of this work.

Paul Craig

CONTENTS

4. Pluralist Democracy, Groups, and Process: USA (II)

5. Pluralism, Process, and Substance: UK (I)

6. Pluralism, Process, and Substance: UK (II)

11. Participatory Democracy: The Radical View

I
INTRODUCTION

1. TWO THEMES

This is a book about constitutional and administrative law. It has two themes. The 'minor' theme is that the content and direction of both subjects are integrally related. The 'major' theme is that the nature and content of constitutional and administrative law can only be properly understood against the background political theory which a society actually espouses, or against such a background which a particular commentator believes that a society ought to espouse. Both of these ideas must be explicated more fully.

a. The 'Minor' Theme

The division between legal subjects is often problematic, contentious, or both. Dividing lines can be the product of didactic tradition, questionable conceptual classification, or outmoded societal assumptions. Where to draw the line between constitutional and administrative law may, at one time or another, have been influenced by such considerations. The division between these subjects is, however, problematic for rather different reasons. Howsoever one categorizes the material, the two areas will be integrally related in the following sense. The meaning accorded to central themes in administrative law, and the very definition of what those central themes actually are, will differ depending upon the framework of constitutional law and constitutional rights within which the administrative system subsists. The ensuing analysis will make this patently clear, but the idea can be exemplified briefly here.

Participation in administrative decision-making is a topic which has been the subject of considerable discussion within recent years.[1] The objective and incidence of such participation can, however, only be determined by placing such participatory rights within a broader constitutional framework. There is little point in incanting the idea

[1] See below, ch. 4 sec. 7, ch. 6 sec. 2.

of participation *per se*, precisely because the very objective to be attained by the development of such participatory rights will be dependent upon the type of constitutional order within which the administrative system subsists, and upon the background political theory which informs that order. Thus the purpose and incidence of participation differ, as will be seen, for those of a liberal, republican, and pluralist persuasion. A similar variance is also evident in the more particular administrative rights which are said to ensue from a participatory democracy, precisely because the content of this democratic vision has been imbued with a plethora of more specific interpretations.[2]

The interrelationship between constitutional and administrative law can also be exemplified by focusing upon the scope and direction of non-constitutional review. Opinions differ markedly on the appropriate scope for the judicial review of discretionary administrative action. Some advocate the explicit imposition of judicially fashioned substantive principles which are designed to constrain agency behaviour; others favour monitoring the process whereby the agency reached its decision in order to ensure that the views of interested parties are taken into account and that adequate reasons are given. Many approaches to judicial review assume one of these two forms,[3] although there is a considerable diversity of opinion concerning the appropriate intensity of any such review.

Both approaches are, however, founded upon, and require, a more particular constitutional vision. Those who advocate the explicit recognition of substantive principles must indicate what those principles actually are. This requires more than the general articulation of concepts such as reasonableness, proportionality, and the like. If the call for substantive principles is to be taken seriously, then this necessitates specific delineation of what that 'substance' actually entails. It demands the articulation of a particular conception of reasonableness or proportionality. This is only plausible if one addresses the constitutional rights and principles which one believes are, or should be, protected within that society. It is, therefore, impossible to determine whether an agency decision imposes an unreasonable or disproportionate burden on an individual or group without some prior vision of the normative importance of their interests, and without some view as to what trade-offs

[2] See below, chs. 10, 11.

[3] It is possible to be in favour of both of these approaches.

between interests are to be tolerated. General concepts such as reasonableness or proportionality might be adopted by those who hold differing political theories, such as market-oriented pluralists or republicans. The application of such concepts may differ markedly because of their divergent responses to the preceding valuation, and because they disagree as to the types of trade-offs which are normatively defensible.[4]

Those who favour the control of agency discretion through more process-oriented constraints are similarly dependent upon a background constitutional perspective in a double sense. On the one hand, such a perspective will furnish the rationale for this species of control. This may itself assume a variety of forms depending upon the background political theory which underpins the constitutional order. A modified pluralist may favour such controls as a mechanism for ameliorating the imbalances in the power of interest groups.[5] A modern republican may also advocate such constraint for the additional reason that it thereby serves to foster deliberation directed towards the public good, which is a central aspect of that thesis.[6] On the other hand, the underlying constitutional vision will influence the nature and type of process rights thereby accorded. Who is enabled to participate, and in what manner, will reflect substantive value judgements as to how governments should treat their citizens.[7]

b. The 'Major' Theme

The idea that the content of public law can only be properly understood against the background political theory which a society actually espouses, or against such a background which a particular commentator believes that the society ought to espouse, may not be particularly contentious or indeed novel. After all, a totalitarian society will embrace a view of public law which differs from that adopted by more democratic polities. The precise nature of the 'major' theme, and the implications thereof, must therefore be more fully elaborated.

The *nature* of the argument is as follows. Differing conceptions of

[4] See below, chs. 4, 6, 7, 8, 10.
[5] See below, ch. 4 sec. 4.
[6] See below, ch. 10 sec. 5.
[7] See below, ch. 4 sec. 7, ch. 6 sec. 2.

both constitutional and administrative law reveal themselves to be reflections of deeper controversies concerning differing conceptions of the democratic society in which we live.[8] On some occasions these controversies are framed expressly in terms of divergent views about democracy; this is exemplified by the recent debate between republicans and pluralists in the United States.[9] On other occasions it is evident that a particular doctrinal legal tradition was built upon certain central assumptions concerning the nature of democracy; thus, as will be seen, the normative foundations of the traditional model of public law in the United Kingdom are based on a specific vision of democratic ordering.[10]

The reason for the contestable interpretations accorded to the term democracy is not difficult to perceive. In negative terms it may be clear that forms of autocracy are inconsistent with a democratic society. It is, however, when it comes to the positive delineation of democracy that controversy really begins, precisely because many key issues are left unanswered by the bare articulation of that term. As Dworkin states:

> Democracy requires that officials should be elected by the people rather than chosen through inheritance or by a small group of prominent families or electors. But that abstract statement does not decide: which officials, if any, should be chosen not by the community as a whole but by sections or groups within it, how powers should be distributed among officials chosen in these different ways, how far elected officials should be permitted or required to appoint other officials to exercise some of their powers, which responsibilities should be held by elected and which by appointed officials, how long officials of either sort should serve, whether their terms of office should be fixed or subject to early termination by those who elected them, how far elected or other officials should themselves be free to change the constitutional arrangements under which officials are elected, whether a constitution should set limits to the powers of officials, so that the officials cannot themselves alter these limits and so forth.[11]

[8] It is evident from the text in the preceding paragraph that differing conceptions of public law can be reflective of differing conceptions of society which are not democratic in any sense. The present work concentrates upon divergent views of democracy, in part because this represents the main focal point of debate, and in part because of limits of space.

[9] See below, chs. 4, 10.

[10] See below, ch. 2. The reaction to this traditional model was itself cast in terms of a distinctive vision of democracy. See below, chs. 5, 6.

[11] R. Dworkin, 'What is Equality? Part 4. Political Equality', 22 *Univ. of San Francisco LR* 1, 2 (1987–8).

Particular conceptions of democracy diverge not only in relation to the nature of the participatory rights to be afforded to citizens. Proponents of these differing conceptions disagree also about the nature of rights, distributive justice, and the extent to which the state should be able to advance morally valid ideals. This disagreement may, for example, manifest itself in the recognition of distinctive rights, or in radically distinctive interpretations accorded to the same right. In this sense any discussion of democracy shades into, and becomes part of, a broader political theory which embraces complex issues such as those delineated above.

Three important *implications* follow from this for the study of public law. *First*, if public lawyers wish, expressly or impliedly, to found their interpretation of constitutional or administrative law upon such a background theory, then the meaning of that theory, must be properly understood. The complexity of this task must be appreciated. Little or no purpose is served by bland incantations of pluralist or participatory democracy, as if these were self-evident propositions from which one could extract detailed legal conclusions. The theory must be adequately comprehended in its own terms, and the normative foundations thereof must be revealed and assessed. Confusion and error abound when this is neglected. It is not possible to understand what a theory 'means' unless its normative structure is analysed; the desirability of any such theory cannot be determined unless this step is undertaken; and the cogency of critiques of a particular thesis are not plausible without engaging in such an enquiry. Thus criticisms of, for example, liberalism are often based upon mistaken assumptions as to the claims made by proponents thereof, or the results which are intended to ensue therefrom.

The preceding discussion is not based upon the presupposition that any one theory will somehow be 'perfect' in normative terms. No such claim is being made. The subsequent analysis will indicate the difficulties besetting the theories which have provided the principal focus for public lawyers. This realization does not diminish the force of the point adumbrated above. One cannot know how desirable any theory is without evaluating its normative basis; and one cannot derive any accurate conclusions for legal norms without paying close attention to the foundations of the thesis.

Nor is the previous discussion premised upon the assumption that the theory will always produce neat, determinate answers to detailed doctrinal issues or cases with which lawyers deal. Indeed, as will be seen, legal discourse often serves to sharpen the focus of theories which may have been left at a higher level of abstraction. A proper understanding of the normative foundations of the theory is, however, a *necessary* step in determining the answer to more discrete issues which arise.

When the underlying political theory has been understood, one can then proceed to the *second* stage of the enquiry, which concerns the implications of that theory for constitutional and administrative law.

This embraces a number of differing, but related, issues. The nature of the constitutional rights which are generated by a particular theory must be articulated and defended. These cannot be left at too abstract a level. As will be seen, differing background theories may well recognize a constitutional right and accord it the same name, such as freedom of speech or property, and yet imbue it with radically diverse meanings. The enquiry into the existence of constitutional rights will perforce also necessitate investigation of the conceptions of distributive justice which are contained within the rival theories. These will be of seminal importance in determining, for example, whether welfare concerns should be recognized at all, and, if so, what the constitutional status thereof should be.

The focus of administrative law which would or should exist within any such regime must also be articulated. As will become evident, the range of institutions subject to administrative control, the nature of these controls, and the meaning of administrative accountability will reflect, at one stage removed, the political theory which underpins the constitutional ordering within the state.

The articulation of the background theory, and the legal implications which are to be drawn therefrom, serve to enlighten each other in a double sense. On the one hand, either those who seek through legal doctrine to further such a theory may find that the doctrinal tools which they have chosen for the task are inadequate for its attainment, or it may transpire that they have misunderstood the thesis which they are seeking to effectuate. On the other hand, the legal enquiry may cause one to revise or refashion the background theory itself. Such theories are often left at a more abstract level. The specific implications which follow therefrom can help to enlighten us as to the meaning of these more abstract formulations and the difficulties which they can create. In this manner consideration of the detailed consequences may help to refashion the principal thesis itself.

The *third* important issue which is of relevance for the study of public law concerns the institutional implications of adopting a particular background political theory. This aspect of the enquiry has two parts.

It is necessary to investigate the role which the theory prescribes or indicates for the courts, legislatures, and other organizations within society. This enquiry is itself more complex than may seem initially apparent. Lawyers have a tendency to emphasize the judicial role as being central in attaining the preferred constitutional vision. This is too narrow a focus. Not only does it tend to place too much importance upon the power of the judiciary to orient society in a particular direction. It can also produce conceptual confusion. There is often an unspoken assumption that, if an issue is not capable of being framed as a legally enforceable constitutional right, it is therefore of no constitutional concern to lawyers. This is erroneous. One may reach the conclusion that a particular interest is incapable of being framed as a justiciable legal right, but still believe that it generates a constitutional obligation which the legislature is bound to advance. Such an obligation is of importance in itself, and may, moreover, have indirect implications for the interpretation of other legal doctrines. The discussion of the protection of welfare concerns within Rawlsian liberalism serves to exemplify the point.[12]

The institutional realization of a particular background theory may also raise broader issues concerning the socio-economic conditions which must exist if the objectives of the theory are to be advanced. The degree to which this causes difficulty will vary depending upon the nature of the theory being espoused. For example, while market-based pluralist theories can readily subsist within the existing societal framework, it is more debatable whether republican objectives can be realized without more far-reaching change.[13]

Two objections to the approach outlined in the preceding pages should be considered.

One objection is that this picture is not exhaustive of the possible approaches to public law. It does not, for example, explicitly consider the possibility of a constitutional jurisprudence founded

[12] See below, ch. 8 sec. 3b.
[13] See below, ch. 10 sec. 6.

upon the original intent of the framers of the Constitution. It could be argued that, if adopted, this would avoid the conundrum of having to choose between rival conceptions of democracy in the manner described above.

In a limited sense this objection can be conceded. This book does not set out to be a comprehensive catalogue of all possible approaches to constitutional adjudication, and the utility of such an enterprise would in any event be questionable. The rationale for not devoting space to the particular approach known variously as original intent or originalism is simply that it has been comprehensively analysed by others who have pointed out the two central difficulties with such an approach. There is the problem of divining with any degree of certainty precisely what the framers intended. There is also the more fundamental problem as to why we in the present day should be ruled by the beliefs of the framers even if they could be accurately determined.[14]

The other objection is of a different nature. Its essence is that any general theory of public law will always be flawed. Two responses to this type of objection are relevant.

First, as stated above, the approach of this book is *not* based upon the assumption that any one of the theories advanced will necessarily be perfect in normative terms, or that it will necessarily be capable of perfect institutional realization. Until the meaning of these political theories is properly explicated we are, however, in no position to make any reasoned choice between them, nor indeed are we in any position to know whether the imperfections said to reside within them are in reality objections to the theory at all, as opposed to misinterpretations of the theory by a particular commentator. For example, the cogency of the claim that 'satisfactory' constitutional law is not possible because of inherent dilemmas within liberal theory must itself be closely examined in order to assess its veracity.[15]

Secondly, it *is* a thesis of this book that some choice must be made. Agnosticism is not possible. This appears to be accepted by at least some radical critics who advocate a different background political theory to replace that of liberalism. Some species of participatory democracy is proposed as the basis of a revised polity.[16] Suggestions

[14] See below, ch. 4 n. 47.

[15] See below, ch. 9 sec. 2, ch. 11 sec. 4.

[16] See below, ch. 11.

such as this should, however, be subjected to the same careful scrutiny as any other background theory, and that is one of the tasks of this book. The normative foundations of such a theory must be examined, the implications which this theory has for public law must be assessed, and the institutional conditions for the realization of this democratic vision must be considered. Only then can any decision be made as to the desirability and plausibility of this alternative vision.

Those who purport to eschew general theorizing in favour of 'solving' more particular cases or types of dispute are faced by the following difficulties. The 'resolution' of any dispute of a constitutional nature will necessitate some interpretation of the rights which are in issue therein. This is not a self-executing process. The existence of these rights, *and* the more particular interpretations to be accorded to them, will presuppose a background theory which serves to justify the existence of that right, and the more particular meaning ascribed to it. Such an approach simply conceals this process under the guise of eschewing general theory. There is, moreover, a further difficulty with this stance. Given that the interpretive process will implicitly or explicitly require reliance on some background theory, the approach under consideration runs the risk, prevalent among lawyers, of what may be termed 'mix 'n match'. Parts of one political theory are implicitly relied upon and combined with aspects of a different theory to reach the desired results in distinctive cases. This risks distorting the very theories being implicitly relied on. The elements of a political theory are often woven together to compose a structure in which these various parts are interrelated. One element may only be included *because* of the reasoning contained in a related part of the theory. Such theories cannot easily be 'severed' by a lawyer selectively choosing the aspect which helps his interpretation within one area.

2. TWO COUNTRIES

This book deals with public law in the United Kingdom and the United States. It is not, however, a formal study in comparative law. Differences of an historical, social, economic, and political nature render such an exercise implausible. The objective is to employ the same methodology, outlined in the preceding pages, to both countries. This dual focus has required, on some occasions, a more detailed elaboration of the particular background theory and institutional structure than might otherwise have been necessary. It is hoped that readers familiar with either jurisdiction will tolerate this in order that the ensuing analysis can be understood.

There are a number of reasons for focusing on these particular countries. From the United Kingdon perspective the time seems ripe for a more theoretical appraisal of our system, and one which attempts to pursue the public law implications of a given theoretical position in some analytical detail. The defects of our traditional model of public law have often been commented upon. The theoretical assumptions underlying this model have not been fully revealed, and the construction of new schemes for constitutional ordering have been sketchy. It is hoped that the relevant chapters will add something to this debate.

The United States has a rich and sophisticated corpus of constitutional jurisprudence which provides a fertile foundation for employing the methodology adopted in this book. Notwithstanding the existence of a written Constitution, the academic literature in the United States displays continuing controversy as to the 'proper' direction of public law, and exemplifies the resort to divergent background political theories in the search for the most appropriate interpretation of constitutional and administrative law. Careful evaluation of the theories themselves, close scrutiny of the public law consequences which are drawn therefrom, and a proper understanding of the institutional conditions required for the successful implementation of any such theory, can all be fruitfully undertaken in the US context.

Although no formal comparative technique is pursued in this work, 'lessons' may well be learned by considering the results of the preceding methodology in the two jurisdictions. Lawyers in the United Kingdom have much to gain by reflecting upon the experience in the United States. At the most fundamental level this serves to remind us that the existence of a written Constitution is not the end of constitutional controversy, but rather a watershed and the beginning of contestable interpretations concerning the 'proper' direction for public law. The necessity for a clear articulation and defence of the background theory which is said to warrant a particular content for public law will be readily apparent in the following pages. Public lawyers in the United Kingdom can also learn a plethora of more particular lessons from the experience in the United States. For example, those who advocate some species of participatory democracy may gain insights from recent experimentation in the United States with these ideas.[17] The need for clarity in understanding what such a theory actually means, the public-law consequences to be drawn from it, and the institutional difficulties with its realization, will be readily apparent from the subsequent discussion.

Public lawyers in the United States will also hopefully have something to learn from the experience in the United Kingdom. At the general level this can help to be a corrective against what is sometimes the excessive judicial orientation of constitutional law in the United States. Constitutional issues tend to be defined as such, according to whether they are susceptible to constitutional review and judicial resolution. The absence of such review in the United Kingdom may have drawbacks, but it does also serve to demonstrate how both the meaning of constitutional obligations, and the notion of constitutional accountability, can embrace a wider spectrum of issues than that encapsulated by an exclusive concern with the courts. Experience in this country may also contribute insights into more particular issues. For example, the idea that a pluralist model of public law may mean something very different from the market-oriented vision in the United States can be a useful corrective to the idea that the concept of pluralism must inexorably bear the US connotation.[18]

A final word of clarification is in order. This book has not been written on the assumption that the particular theories considered are the only ones which could be proffered. They have been chosen principally because they have provided the focal point for much of the current debate concerning the scope and meaning of public law on both sides of the Atlantic. Other background theories might well be put forward. If any such construct is to be employed, then it too must be rigorously analysed. The recognition of the centrality of political theory by public lawyers is important and valuable. Bland incantations of particular democratic theories, and superficial reasoning which purports to draw specific doctrinal conclusions therefrom for public law, are of little help.

[17] See below, chs. 10, 11.
[18] See below, ch. 5.

2

DICEY: UNITARY, SELF-CORRECTING DEMOCRACY AND PUBLIC LAW

1. INTRODUCTION

All English law students learn, early in their legal education, that Parliament is sovereign. The thorny question of whether Parliament could ever bind its successors becomes one of the initial issues on which they develop their nascent legal skills. Texts, law review articles and cases are consulted in order to determine the range of possible answers to the question adumbrated.[1] What is surprising is that the reasoning used by Dicey himself is seldom examined in any detail. Much time is spent upon the analysis of case law since Dicey propounded his thesis, in order to discover whether the cases 'prove' the position one way or another. This is all the more surprising given the fact that Dicey did not utilize case law in his arguments even though there were some cases which could have been cited in support of his proposition.

The objective of this chapter is to demonstrate that the 'traditional' view of public law was integrally related to a conception of society and representative democracy held by Dicey. The role of both constitutional and administrative law was profoundly shaped by this vision, and the vision is no longer sustainable. The objective and methodology of this part of the chapter should be made apparent at the outset. Dicey's views on constitutional and administrative law have been contested by many. Some of these critiques will be considered in the course of the analysis which follows. The object is not, however, to provide a 'list' of these varying opinions which controvert or dispute Dicey's thesis. My aim is different. It is to explore the way in which Dicey's theories were

[1] For a general discussion of sovereignty, see, e.g., H. W. R. Wade, 'The Basis of Legal Sovereignty' (1955) *C.L.J.* 172; R. F. V. Heuston, *Essays in Constitutional Law* (2nd edn., 1964), ch. 4; J. D. B. Mitchell, *Constitutional Law* (2nd edn., 1968), ch. 4; G.Marshall, *Constitutional Theory* (1971), ch. 3; A. W. B. Simpson (ed.), *Oxford Essays in Jurisprudence* (1973), chs. 2, 3.

themselves explicitly premised upon certain assumptions concerning representative democracy, and the way in which it operated. It will be argued that these assumptions informed Dicey's views of both constitutional and administrative law. The enquiry is historical. The nature of Dicey's assumptions will be examined within his own historical context. It will be argued that Dicey in fact misconceived the nature of representative democracy, and that he failed to perceive certain important political developments which occurred in the late nineteenth and early twentieth centuries. The limitations of the argument which is to be presented should also be made clear at the outset. Dicey's view of, for example, constitutional law and sovereignty was not based solely upon a particular conception of representative democracy. Other factors informed this judgement. To demonstrate Dicey's error concerning his political premises does not, therefore, necessarily condemn the conclusions which he reached. No such claim is being made, nor could such a contention be sustained. It will, however, be argued that these misconceptions weakened his conclusions concerning both constitutional and administrative law.

2. SOVEREIGNTY: LEGISLATIVE OMNICOMPETENCE AND CONSTITUTIONAL LAW

It is appropriate to begin with Dicey's vision of constitutional law and sovereignty. The essential Diceyan propositions are well known.[2] Sovereignty meant that Parliament has, under the English Constitution, the right to make or unmake any law whatsoever; and further that no person or body is recognized by the law of England as having a right to override or set aside the legislation of Parliament. The structure of Dicey's argument in support of this proposition is of interest.

His chain of reasoning is eclectic. It is based in part upon the writings of previous jurists such as Blackstone and Coke,[3] partly upon examples of the exertion of parliamentary authority in the past, as exemplified by the Acts of Union, and the Septennial Act,[4]

[2] A. V. Dicey, *An Introduction to the Study of the Law of the Constitution* (10th edn., 1959), 339–40.

[3] Ibid. 41–2.

[4] Ibid. 44–5.

and partly upon instances where Parliament had exercised authority over private rights.[5] This positive side of the argument is complemented by a negative, in which Dicey dismisses other possible sources of legislative power. The monarch,[6] resolutions of either House of Parliament,[7] and the vote of parliamentary electors[8] are promptly dismissed as contenders for the legislative mantle. Judicial power is accorded little significance, and the potential for limitations of this kind is dismissed with the statement that English judges do not claim to exercise any such power.[9] Alleged legal limitations upon sovereignty derived from morality,[10] international law,[11] the prerogative,[12] and previous legislation[13] are accorded equally short shrift.

The force of the argument is empirical rather than a priori. Dicey is not principally concerned with the jurisprudential question as to whether it would be logically possible to place any limitation upon the sovereign. Although he may well be inclined to agree with Austin's[14] argument on this point, his aim is to 'prove' that Parliament is in fact such a sovereign body.[15]

To rest here would, however, be to miss certain essential elements of the Diceyan argument. His belief in the sovereign power of Parliament is not derived solely from the sources outlined above. Running throughout his thesis is a clear view about the nature of representative democracy in England at that time. The link is most evident in his discussion of Austin's view of sovereignty, and in his treatment of limits upon sovereign power.

Dicey disputes Austin's view that sovereignty resided in the king,

[5] Dicey, pp. 48–9.
[6] Ibid. 50–4.
[7] Ibid. 54–9.
[8] Ibid. 59–60.
[9] Ibid. 60–1.
[10] Ibid. 62–3.
[11] Ibid. 62–4.
[12] Ibid. 63–4.
[13] Ibid. 64–8.
[14] J. Austin, *The Province of Jurisprudence Determined*, ed. H. L. A. Hart (1955), lecture vi. There is a considerable literature on this aspect of sovereignty. Much of the literature is referred to in Lord Lloyd of Hampstead, *Introduction to Jurisprudence* (4th edn., 1979), ch. 4. See also Simpson (ed.), *Oxford Essays*.
[15] Dicey, pp. 61, 72. Dicey was perceptive when he remarked:

> Sovereignty like many of Austin's conceptions, is a generalisation drawn in the main from English law . . . In England we are accustomed to the existence of a supreme legislative body . . . This is, from a legal point of view, the true conception of a sovereign, and the ease with which the theory of absolute sovereignty has been accepted by English jurists is due to the peculiar history of English constitutional law. So far, therefore, from its being true that the sovereignty of Parliament is a deduction from abstract theories of jurisprudence, a critic would come nearer the truth who asserted that Austin's theory of sovereignty is suggested by the position of the English Parliament . . .

peers, Commons or electors, admitting that, while the electorate might justly be called politically sovereign it was mistaken to cloak it with legal sovereignty. The latter term indicated nothing more nor less than the power of law-making unrestricted by any legal limit.[16] This power resided in Parliament alone. While taking Austin to task for failing to distinguish between political and legal sovereignty, he then proceeds to point out that, under the then present political system, the exercise of the latter power should always be a reflection of the former.

> The matter indeed may be carried a little further, and we may assert that the arrangements of the constitution are now such as to ensure that the will of the electors shall by regular and constitutional means always in the end assert itself as the predominant influence in the country. But this is a political, not a legal fact. The electors can in the long run always enforce their will.[17]

The same theme is evident in the discussion of external and internal limits upon legal sovereignty.[18] For Dicey the external limit was the need to secure the support of at least a portion of the population; the internal limit was indicative of the fact that a legal sovereign would perforce be moulded by his social environment and that this would condition the type of legislation which he sought to enact. In a despotism the external and internal limits might not coincide. In a representative democracy things were otherwise.

> Where a Parliament truly represents the people, the divergence between the external and the internal limit to the exercise of sovereign power can hardly arise, or if it arises, must soon disappear. Speaking roughly, the permanent wishes of the representative portion of Parliament can hardly in the long run differ from the wishes of the English people, or at any rate of the electors; that which the majority of the House of Commons command, the majority of the English people usually desire. To prevent the divergence between the wishes of the sovereign and the wishes of subjects is in short the effect, and the only certain effect of bona fide representative government.[19]

The absence of constitutional review and the Diceyan conception of sovereignty are therefore firmly embedded within a conception of self-correcting majoritarian democracy. Representative government would necessarily produce a coincidence between the external and internal limits of sovereign power in much the same way that the

[16] Ibid. 72–3.
[17] Ibid. 73; see also p. 73 n. 1.
[18] Ibid. 76–5.
[19] Ibid. 83.

invisible hand of the market ensured a correspondence of supply and demand. A Parliament duly elected on the extended franchise represented the most authoritative expression of the will of the nation, and the exercise of public power was channelled through such a Parliament. This Parliament duly controlled the executive and therefore the affairs of the nation should be entrusted to those approved by a majority of the House. For Dicey, 'black letter' precedent and political principle formed a perfect union. All was well in the Garden of Eden. This beatific vision of legal and political harmony was to prove short-lived, and may never in reality have existed at all. This is a matter which will be considered later. The force of this vision was however indirectly reinforced by Dicey's views on the rule of law and on conventions.

The first two limbs of Dicey's rule of law will be considered more fully in the ensuing section. They are, however, also of relevance within the present context. The insistence on the predominance of the regular law and the proscription of broad discretionary power served to reinforce the authority of the established legislature. New legal norms should be created for society by the duly elected legislature, not by executive fiat. The Parliament would then operate in the manner described above: it would transform the wishes of the people into legislation and it would not enact laws which would infringe upon individual rights.

It was Dicey's third limb of the rule of law which added 'empirical' weight to the conclusions of principle which he had arrived at concerning sovereignty. The third sense of the rule of law was that in England civil liberties were the result of ordinary common-law decisions, whereas under many foreign constitutions these interests were protected by, or resulted from, general principles of the constitution.[20] Now, while Dicey admits that constitutionally guaranteed rights, backed up with adequate remedies, can be as efficacious as the common law,[21] he none the less evinces a marked preference for the latter over the former. The dislike or distrust of declarations of rights among English scholars is a notable feature of much nineteenth-century writing. It is particularly evident in the work of Bentham and the Utilitarians.[22] Dicey was much influenced by this school of thought,[23] but at base his

[20] Dicey, 195–6.

[21] Ibid. 200.

[22] See P. P. Craig, 'Bentham, Public Law and Democracy' [1989] *P.L.* 407.

[23] See A. V. Dicey, *Lectures on the Relation between Law and Public Opinion in England during the Nineteenth Century* (1905).

preference for the common law was founded on less philosophical, and more empirical grounds than those of his predecessors.[24] The common law in general furnished better protection for individual rights because constitutionally enshrined rights were often without adequate remedies and could be easily suspended.[25] Common-law protections could not be destroyed without a thoroughgoing revolution in the 'institutions and manners of the nation'.

Thus, while the twin concepts of sovereignty and the rule of law could be at odds, they could also reinforce each other. The existence of representative government ensured that the wishes of the people would coincide with those of the sovereign Parliament. There should, therefore, be no serious problems concerning civil liberties. In so far as such problems did occur, the third limb of the rule of law, the common law protection of individual rights, was at hand, which was a more effective guarantee than any constitutionally enshrined declaration of rights. Whether this aspect of the argument is in fact sustainable will be considered more fully below.[26]

A similar thematic connection can be seen between Dicey's discussion of sovereignty and conventions. For Dicey the main purpose of such conventions was to ensure that Parliament or the cabinet, which 'is indirectly appointed by Parliament', should in the long run give effect to the will of the electorate. Conventions, seen as a 'modern code of constitutional morality', indirectly secured the sovereignty of the people. Dicey's continued belief both in the self-correcting nature of democracy *and* in the power of Parliament to control the executive emerges forcefully in the following passage. Here Dicey seeks to exemplify the way in which conventions ensured electoral sovereignty.

The rule that the powers of the Crown must be exercised through Ministers who are members of one or other House of Parliament 'and who command the confidence of the House of Commons', really means, that the elective portion of the legislature in effect, though by an indirect process, appoints the executive government; and, further, that the Crown, or the Ministry, must ultimately carry out, or at any rate not contravene, the wishes of the House of Commons. But as the process of representation is nothing else than a mode by which the will of the representative body or House of Commons is made to coincide with the will of the nation, it follows that a rule which gives the appointment and control of the government mainly to the House of

[24] Valuable insights into Dicey's conception of the meaning of constitutional law are to be found in *Law of the Constitution*, pp. 1–34.

[25] Ibid. 198–201.

[26] See below, ch. 2 sec. 4b.

Commons is at bottom a rule which gives the election and control of the executive to the nation.[27]

The argument thus far has been based upon a presupposition which requires more explicit justification. In the *Law of the Constitution* Dicey speaks of representative government. It has been assumed in the foregoing discussion that he regarded the form of representative government which existed at the time he wrote as a representative democracy. A government can, of course, be representative in some degree, but not necessarily constitute a democracy. The weight of evidence, both direct and indirect, does, however, support the conclusion that Dicey believed our representative government to be a representative democracy.

Some direct textual evidence of this can be found in Dicey's other major work, *Law and Opinion.*[28] In this work Dicey defines democracy as a form of government under which sovereign power is possessed by the numerical majority of the male citizens.[29] He states that no one could doubt that by 1900[30] the English constitution had been transformed into something like a democracy. Following on from this statement, Dicey reviews the passage of the Reform Acts *up till* 1884–5, and concludes that the transition from aristocracy to democracy was 'undeniable'.[31]

Indirect evidence pointing towards the same end can be derived from the discussion of external and internal limits upon sovereign power considered above. This discussion would make little sense if Dicey was not thinking of representative democracy when talking about representative government. The contrast which he draws between despotic or monarchical government, in which there would not be a necessary coincidence between external and internal limits on sovereign power, and a representative system of government, in which such a coincidence is very likely, would collapse if the latter was not something closely approximate to a democracy. It would, of course, be possible to have a representative system of government which represented a limited portion of the nation. If the government did, however, only represent this limited segment, then the contrast

[27] *Law of the Constitution*, p. 433; the same theme pervades much of the discussion of conventions, pp. 417–38.

[28] *Lectures on the Relation between Law and Public Opinion in England during the Nineteenth Century* (1905).

[29] Ibid. 52.

[30] Ibid. 48.

[31] Ibid. 49.

which Dicey was drawing between a monarchical system and a representative system of government would simply be one of form. It would not have the substantive differences which he perceives concerning the coincidence of the external and internal limits on sovereign power. Moreover, such an interpretation of the phrase representative government simply does not fit Dicey's own language. Dicey continually refers to the fact that, under a representative government, the external and internal limits on sovereignty would coincide, and that the permanent wishes of the representative portion of Parliament would not differ from the wishes of *English people* or the *nation*.[32] This interpretation is reinforced by Dicey's analysis in *Law and Opinion*, where he expresses the same idea about the coincidence of external and internal limits, and in this context he explicitly uses the word democracy.

In respect of the influence of democracy on such laws, we can draw with some confidence one probable conclusion. We may, with high probability, assume that no law will be carried, or at any rate that no law will long remain in force, which is opposed to the wish of the people, or in other words, to the sentiment prevailing among the distinct majority of the citizens of a given country.[33]

For Dicey, the advance of democracy entailed the transference of supreme power from a single person, or a privileged or limited class, to the majority of the male citizens.[34] The process of representation as it actually operated was 'nothing else than a mode by which the will of the representative body or House of Commons is made to coincide with the will of the nation'.[35]

3. SOVEREIGNTY: LEGISLATIVE MONOPOLY AND ADMINISTRATIVE LAW

We have thus far concentrated upon Dicey's vision of constitutional law and the way in which this was founded upon a view of representative democracy. To what extent was the role of administrative law shaped by similar considerations? It will be argued that

[32] *Law of the Constitution*, pp. 83, 84.
[33] *Law and Opinion*, p. 55.
[34] Ibid. 52.
[35] *Law of the Constitution*, p. 43. This same theme is prominent throughout the discussion of conventions.

Dicey's vision of administrative law was founded upon certain assumptions about how the institutions of our representative democracy actually operated. The 'traditional' vision of administrative law which evolved rested in part upon these assumptions, and in part upon judicial discourse in the leading administrative law cases.

Sovereignty possessed a Janus-like quality. Its well-known visage, that of parliamentary omnicompetence, we have already considered. Less well known was the face of parliamentary monopoly. There was a belief, albeit not universally held, that the Commons could and did control the executive. Ministries could be made and unmade by the exercise of parliamentary will. All governmental power should be channelled through Parliament in order that it might be subject to legitimation and oversight by the Commons. This view was reinforced by the extension of the suffrage in 1867 and thereafter, which increased Parliament's sense of its own legitimacy. The demise of the nineteenth century Board system,[36] whereby a range of activities were administered by quasi-governmental agencies, bore striking testimony to the desire of the Commons to monopolize the exercise of public power.[37] The reverse side of the same coin was the development of individual ministerial responsibility and civil service anonymity. As the nineteenth century progressed, the Commons became ever more insistent upon having a minister within the House who would be answerable for all activities within his purview;[38] a corollary was that civil servants, being unelected, should no longer proffer their views on policy matters in the fashion that had been normal for a Chadwick. This belief in legislative monopoly was shared by Dicey, who assumed that the Commons did control the

[36] For a discussion of the Board system, see D. Roberts, *Victorian Origins of the British Welfare State* (1960); H. Parris, *Constitutional Bureaucracy: The Development of British Central Administration since the Eighteenth Century* (1969); N. Chester, *The English Administrative System (1780–1870)* (1981); P. P. Craig, *Administrative Law* (2nd edn., 1989), ch. 2. This theme will be considered more fully below, ch. 2 sec. 4a.

[37] There were also pressures from those who disliked the centralizing tendency inherent within some of the Boards, regarding them as an infringement of local autonomy. See J. Redlich, F. Hirst, and B. Keith-Lucas, *The History of Local Government in England* (2nd edn., 1970); D. Fraser, *Power and Authority in the Victorian City* (1979). This does not affect the point being made in the text. *If* an administrative system was to be run from the centre, then pressure would develop for the system to be more fully controlled by Parliament.

[38] See the references above, n. 36, and, also, F. M. G. Willson, 'Ministries and Boards: Some Aspects of Administrative Development since 1832' (1955) 33 *Pub. Adm.* 43.

executive and that all significant governmental power was and should be directed through Parliament. The state was unitary, with all real public power being concentrated in the duly elected Parliament. This is evident from the quotations given above and from others within Dicey's work. It is equally apparent in his discussion of the rule of law.

It was Dicey's rule of law which served to reinforce sovereignty, using that term in the second sense articulated above, parliamentary monopoly. The two main elements of Dicey's rule of law[39] possessed both a descriptive and a normative content. In descriptive terms it was assumed that the regular law predominated, that exercise of broad discretionary power was absent, and that all people were subject to the ordinary law of the realm. Public power resided with Parliament. In normative terms it was assumed that this was indeed a better system than that which existed in France, where special rules and a distinctive regime existed for public law matters.

This conception of legislative monopoly provided an appropriate framework within which to place and justify the exercise of non-constitutional review. Dicey did not consider this issue directly, other than by the assertion that the regular law predominated and was applied to the agents of government. This was in part because, as we shall see, he misconceived the scope of agency power which actually existed at the time of his writing. Notwithstanding this error, the conceptual foundation of legislative monopoly provided a fitting basis for the legitimation of judicial power which the courts were in fact exercising in the area of administrative law. The connection may be expressed as follows.

It is apparent that the execution of the legislative will may require the grant of power to a minister or administrative agency. Herein lies the modern conceptual justification for non-constitutional review. It was designed to ensure that the sovereign will of Parliament was not transgressed by those to whom such grants of power were made. If authority had been delegated to a minister to perform certain tasks upon certain conditions, the courts' function was, in the event of challenge, to check that only those tasks were performed and only where the conditions were present. If there were defects on either level, the challenged decision would be declared null. For the courts not to have intervened would have been to

[39] *Law of the Constitution*, pp. 188, 193.

accord a 'legislative' power to the minister or agency by allowing them authority in areas not specified by the real legislature, Parliament. The less well-known face of sovereignty, that of parliamentary monopoly, thus demanded an institution to *police* the boundaries which Parliament had stipulated. It was this frontier which the courts patrolled through non-constitutional review.

It would be mistaken to assume that the judiciary originally conceived of non-constitutional review in these terms. The origins of such review are complex, and are interwoven with the intricacies of the prerogative writs.[40] Moreover, the position and role of Parliament in the seventeenth century, when judicial review was emerging, differed considerably from the power and legitimacy which that body had attained by the mid-nineteenth century. The motivation behind early judicial review resided principally in the desire to ensure the predominance of the High Court over 'inferior jurisdictions', and to provide remedies to those whom the established judiciary felt had been unjustly or illegally treated by such authorities.[41] In striving to attain these objectives the courts could indeed often come into direct conflict with the legislative will. Attempts by the legislature to curb the growing power of *certiorari* by framing unambiguous privative clauses were continually circumvented by 'creative' judicial construction which preserved the power of judicial review.[42] The potential for such conflict continued into the nineteenth and twentieth centuries. Legislative attempts to preclude judicial review did not cease with the advent of the Victorian age.[43] Notwithstanding this continuing tension, the rationale for judicial review in the nineteenth century was slowly transformed, particularly in those instances where no privative

[40] See, generally, S. A. de Smith, 'The Prerogative Writs' (1951) 11 *C.L.J.* 40, and 'Wrongs and Remedies in Administrative Law' (1952) 15 *M.L.R.* 189; L. L. Jaffe and E. G. Henderson, 'Judicial Review and the Rule of Law: Historical Origins' (1956) 72 *L.Q.R.* 345; E. G. Henderson, *Foundations of English Administrative Law* (1963); A. Rubinstein, *Jurisdiction and Illegality* (1975).

[41] See, e.g., *Case of the Marshalsea* (1612) 10 Co. Rep. 68b; *Commins* v. *Massam* (1643) March N.C. 196; *R.* v. *Hide* (1647) Style 60; *Terry* v. *Huntington* (1668) Hard. 480; *R.* v. *Plowright* (1668) Hard. 480; *Fuller* v. *Fotch* (1695) Carth. 346; *Groenvelt* v. *Burwell* (1700) 1 Ld. Raym. 454.

[42] Rubinstein, *Jurisdiction and Illegality*, pp. 71–3.

[43] The most prominent and general attempt to achieve this end was the Summary Jurisdiction Act 1848. The effect of the Act was summarized by Lord Sumner in *R.* v. *Nat Bell Liquors Ltd.* [1922] 2 A.C. 128, 159, where his Lordship stated that 'The effect was not to make that which had been error, error no longer, but to remove nearly all opportunity for its detection. The face of the record "spoke" no longer; it was the inscrutable face of the sphinx.'

clause was present, and hence when there was no direct clash with legislative intent. The twin rationales for early judicial review, ensuring the predominance of the regular courts over inferior jurisdictions and the provision of remedies for those who had been unjustly or illegally treated, continued to exist. They were, however, supplemented by a growing tendency to relate the exercise of judicial power to the will of Parliament.

This was manifested in two distinct, albeit related, ways. On the one hand, the judiciary began to justify the exercise of jurisdictional control more specifically in terms of ensuring that the authority in question did not usurp or extend the area over which the legislature had granted it jurisdiction. The objective was to ensure that the agency did not assume authority to regulate behaviour or to legislate in areas outside those delegated to it by Parliament. On the other hand, the courts became more aware, in form at least, of the legitimate limits to the exercise of their judicial power. Where the jurisdictional conditions were satisfied, the courts could still exercise some control over the manner in which the consequential administrative discretion was exercised, and justify these limits by reference to implied or express legislative intent. If, subject to these constraints, the administrative agency *was* within its assigned area, then it was performing discretionary tasks allocated to it by the legislature. It was not contravening the legislative monopoly possessed by Parliament, which had chosen to delegate this function to a particular administrative authority. The courts should, therefore, be wary of substituting their view for that of the chosen agency.

These twin themes are apparent in the jurisprudence of the courts during the nineteenth and early twentieth centuries. Jurisdictional control in the nineteenth century had been characterized by two divergent lines of case law. In one group of cases, the courts adopted the view that the meaning of the prescribed jurisdictional terms was to be decided by the agency itself;[44] a distinctive set of cases took a more interventionist stance and asserted judicial authority to determine for themselves the meaning of such terms which were deemed to be collateral facts.[45] It is apparent from a reading of these cases that the judiciary involved therein adopted differing views as

[44] See, e.g., *Brittain* v. *Kinnaird* (1819) 1 B. + B. 432; *Ackerley* v. *Parkinson* (1815) 4 M.+ S. 411; *Wilson* v. *Weller* (1819) 1 B. + B. 57; *R.* v. *Justices of Cheshire* (1838) 8 Ad. + E. 398; *Cave* v. *Mountain* (1840) 1 M. + G. 257; *R.* v. *Bolton* (1841) 1 Q.B. 66; *Mould* v. *Williams* (1844) 5 Q.B. 469; *Revell* v. *Blake* (1872) 7 C.P. 300.

[45] e.g. *Bunbury* v. *Fuller* (1853) 9 Ex. 111; *R.* v. *Stimpson* (1863) 4 B. + S. 301; *Elston* v. *Rose* (1868) L.R. 4 Q.B. 4; *Ex. p. Bradlaugh* (1878) 3 Q.B.D. 509.

to the scope of power which the legislature *generally* intended to accord to an agency when the agency was assigned a task.[46]

The leading authorities which attempted to reconcile these cases focused their attention upon the divergent legislative intent which was said to attend the grant of power to the particular agencies. Thus, Lord Esher MR stated that,

> When an inferior court or tribunal or body, which has to exercise the power of deciding facts, is first established by Act of Parliament, the legislature has to consider what powers it will give that tribunal or body. It may, in effect, say that, if a certain state of facts exists and is shown to such tribunal or body before it proceeds to do certain things, it shall have jurisdiction to do such things, but not otherwise. There it is not for them conclusively to decide whether that state of facts exists, and, if they exercise the jurisdiction without its existence, what they do may be questioned, and it will be held that they have acted without jurisdiction. But there is another state of things which may exist. The legislature may entrust the tribunal or body with a jurisdiction, which includes the jurisdiction to determine whether the preliminary state of facts exists as well as the jurisdiction, on finding that it does exist, to proceed further or to do something more. . . . In the second of the two cases I have mentioned, it is an erroneous application of the formula to say that the tribunal cannot give themselves jurisdiction by wrongly deciding certain facts to exist, because the legislature gave them jurisdiction to determine all the facts, including the existence of the preliminary facts on which the further exercise of their jurisdiction depends . . . [47]

The cogency of this explanation may well be questioned.[48] Reference to the statutory grants of power in the conflicting lines of cases adumbrated above gives no indication that the results can be realistically reconciled by differences in legislative intent. The questionable nature of the reasoning did not, however, destroy the utility of the conceptual tool fashioned by Lord Esher MR. His dictum has been much quoted. Judicial intervention could be legitimated by the link with legislative intent. The courts would simply police the boundaries made manifest by the legislative grant of authority. They would prevent the administrative authority from adjudicating or making rules in areas where the real legislature, Parliament, had not accorded it authority. Sovereignty, in the sense of parliamentary monopoly in the exercise of public power, was

[46] Craig, *Administrative Law*, pp. 255–6.

[47] *R.* v. *Commissioners for Special Purposes of Income Tax* (1888) 21 Q.B.D. 313, 319. See also *Colonial Bank of Australasia* v. *Willan* (1874) L.R. 5 P.C. 417.

[48] Craig, *Administrative Law*, pp. 255–6.

thereby preserved. Judicial oversight was suffused with a greater aura of legitimacy, and the courts acquired a malleable tool through which to justify intervention with administrative behaviour.

Similar themes are evident in the judicial control of discretion. Legislative intent increasingly became the formal justification for judicial intervention, and also provided the limits to this judicial role. Where the jurisdictional conditions were satisfied, the courts would still exercise some control over the manner in which the consequential discretion was exercised. Early authorities,[49] which stated that discretion must be exercised according to the rules of reason and justice, were interpreted as containing implied conditions attached to the statutory grant of power. Control over the range of considerations which the agency could take into account, and the purposes which it could pursue, were read as applications of statutory intent.[50] Subject to these constraints, the administrative authority was master of its own proceedings. It was not arrogating to itself a power other than that expressly granted to it by Parliament. There was no contravention of the legislative monopoly of Parliament, and hence the courts should be careful of substituting their opinion for that of the agency. This theme is most systematically stated in the oft-quoted judgment of Lord Greene MR.[51]

Thus, his Lordship stated that the court was justified in intervening if the exercise of discretion was based upon considerations which the statute expressly or impliedly deemed not to be germane to the issue; or where the statute indicated that certain matters should be taken into account which the administrator ignored; or in instances where the authority made a decision which no sensible person would ever dream lay within the power of the authority.[52] The judicial role was primarily to ensure that the local authority remained within the four corners of the matters which it ought to consider. 'The power of the court to interfere in each case is not as an appellate authority to override a decision of the local authority, but as a judicial authority which is concerned, and concerned only, to see whether the local authority have contravened

[49] e.g. *Rooke's Case* (1598) 5 Co. Rep. 99b; *Hetley* v. *Boyer* (1614) Cro. Jac. 336; *Leader* v. *Moxon* (1773) 2 W.Bl. 924.

[50] e.g. *Sharp* v. *Wakefield* [1891] A.C. 173; *R.* v. *Bowman* [1898] 1 Q.B. 663; *R.* v. *Hyde* [1912] 1 K.B. 645; *Sadler* v. *Sheffield Corporation* [1924] 1 Ch. 483.

[51] *Associated Picture Houses Ltd.* v. *Wednesbury Corporation* [1948] 1 K.B. 223.

[52] Ibid. 228–29.

the law by acting in excess of the power which Parliament has confided in them.'[53]

The difficulties attendant upon this reasoning are not our immediate concern.[54] What is more apposite is the way in which the conception of the judicial role in administrative law presented above was indirectly fuelled by Dicey's account of the rule of law. Critics quickly exposed the descriptive inadequacies of Dicey's account. The existence of a plethora of administrative institutions outside the ordinary courts was indubitably a fact which Dicey had not perceived.[55] The normative aspect of Dicey's account has proven to be more resilient. One of the central tenets of this thesis, the superiority of the ordinary courts and the ordinary law over all else, continued to exert influence.[56] The ordinary courts had waged many battles with both ecclesiastical and local courts, and had emerged victorious. Dicey's contribution was to elevate this success to the level of grand constitutional principle, and to provide a platform from which the reasoning could be extended to other areas. The flexibility inherent in the concept of jurisdiction preserved the veneer that the courts were simply applying the legislative mandate, and were thereby obeying the sovereignty of Parliament. Dicey's rule of law added respectability to this exercise of power by entrenching the idea that it was natural, right, and a matter of constitutional principle that the ordinary courts should be supreme and that the ordinary law should be all pervasive. Special regimes would be frowned upon, and there was a presumption against a functionally or contextually ordered mode of interpretation which would tailor results to the needs of particular substantive areas.[57] The emphasis placed upon the ordinary courts and the ordinary law as the cornerstone of the rule of law provided ammunition for those who advocated increased judicial intervention. It was all too easy to take the conceptual step of assuming that an increase in such judicial action would further the supremacy of both the ordinary law and the ordinary courts, that this would enhance the rule of law, and

[53] *Associated Picture Houses Ltd.* v. *Wednesbury Corporation* [1948] p. 234.

[54] For a general discussion, see Craig, *Administrative Law*, pp. 281–90.

[55] H. W. Arthurs, *Without the Law: Administrative Justice and Legal Pluralism in Nineteenth Century England* (1985). See also Craig, *Administrative Law*.

[56] It pervaded the whole approach of the Committee on Ministers' Powers, Cmd. 4060 (1932).

[57] Arthurs, *Without the Law*, and 'Rethinking Administrative Law: A Slightly Dicey Business' (1979) 17 *Osgoode Hall L.J.* 1.

was therefore something to be encouraged. Such reasoning may well be a *non sequitur*, but many parts of our legal heritage have developed by processes of reasoning which are equally suspect.

It was the rule of law in the sense articulated above which also indirectly served to limit the area within which administrative law would apply. A notable feature of early administrative law, which still exercises influence, is that only those who possessed private rights in the traditional sense of a cause of action in contract, tort, property, or trust were to be allowed into the system.[58] The gateways to administrative law, whether they be natural justice, standing, or the ability to apply for relief, were barred to those who did not possess such rights. Courts acted upon the assumption that they were simply settling an ordinary private dispute in contract, tort, etc., in which one of the litigants happened to be a public body.[59] The sole judicial function was to delimit the ambit of private autonomy by demarcating the area within which the public body could legitimately operate. There is no doubt that the common-law preoccupation with traditional rights is a partial explanation of this phenomenon. However, one cannot help but think that this judicial attitude was also fuelled by the legacy of the rule of law. The idea, underlying the rule of law, that the ordinary law is being applied by the ordinary courts, sits easily with the private rights theme: the court is doing no more than applying standard notions of contract, tort, or property to cases where the defendant happens to be a public body.

The philosophy implicit within this traditional model is suspect and only partially evident. Underlying the model is an implicit dislike or distrust of the role adopted by the state which was producing this plethora of administrative institutions and agencies. The vigorous assertion of the supremacy of the ordinary law, and the protection of traditional private rights, must be seen against this setting. Control or containment of the bureaucratic organs of the state was at the centre of this philosophy.[60] The emphasis is upon

[58] Craig, *Administrative Law*, pp. 8–11; R. B. Stewart, 'The Reformation of American Administrative Law', 88 *Harv. L. Rev.* 1667 (1975). See also, e.g. *Nakkuda Ali* v. *Jayaratne* [1951] A.C. 66, on natural justice; *Pudsey Coal Gas Co.* v. *Corporation of Bradford* (1872) L.R. 15 Eq. 167; *Boyce* v. *Paddington Borough Council* [1903] 1 Ch. 109, on standing.

[59] More modern examples of this same reasoning can be found in, e.g., *Gregory* v. *Camden London Borough Council* [1966] 1 W.L.R. 899; *Gouriet* v. *Union of Post Office Workers* [1978] A.C. 435.

[60] C. Harlow and R. Rawlings, *Law and Administration* (1984), ch. 1.

the preservation of administrative power within its proper boundaries. In this endeavour external control through the courts was viewed as the main vehicle for the vindication of private autonomy. The idea that there is an interest in securing the efficacious discharge of regulatory legislation was no part of this model, except in so far as it was viewed as a natural correlative of the proper maintenance of external judicial supervision delimiting the boundaries of the legislative will.

A note of caution is, however, warranted at this juncture. It should not be assumed that the judicial objective of policing the frontiers of legislative intent, and that of protecting private autonomy, would necessarily produce the same conclusion. Such an identity of result is, of course, feasible. The judiciary could adopt the view that it was their task to demarcate these boundaries, but that only those who possessed private rights should be entitled to utilize the system. In such instances the courts would be declaring the necessity for a private right as a condition of, for example, natural justice or standing. If an individual were able to demonstrate the presence of such a right, then the court would, on the substance of the case, delimit the confines of the legislation in order to determine whether the applicant's right should be upheld.

It would be factually wrong to suppose that this identity of result always occurred. There are many instances in nineteenth- and twentieth-century case law where the judiciary have not enquired as to whether the applicant has a right, and/or where no such right, in the sense of a cause of action in contract or tort, was present.[61] The judicial desire to redress what was perceived to be a transgression of the legislative boundaries by the agency assumes prominence. This very act of judicial intervention may well result in a finding for the applicant, and, in that sense, vindicate the person's private autonomy. It would not, however, be consistent with the private rights view as adumbrated above, which required a right in the sense of a recognizable private law cause of action before the applicant could proceed at all. The judicial willingness to accept a case even in the absence of such a right was evidence of the

[61] e.g., in natural justice, see *Wood* v. *Woad* (1874) L.R. 9 Ex. 190; *Board of Education* v. *Rice* [1911] A.C. 179; in the control of discretion, see, e.g., *Galloway* v. *London Corporation* (1866) L.R. 1 H.L. 34; *Sharp* v. *Wakefield* [1891] A.C. 173; *R.* v. *Wandsworth Licensing JJ., ex p. Whitbread and Co. Ltd.* [1921] 3 K.B. 487. For a discussion of a similar theme within the law of standing, see below, nn. 62–5.

importance which the courts attached to the policing idea in and of itself; of controlling inferior jurisdictions and being the ultimate arbiters of legislative intent.

Much of the doctrinal complexity which besets nineteenth- and twentieth-century administrative law can indeed be explained as the result of the tensions which can exist between the policing idea, and adherence to a strict requirement of a private right as a pre-condition of natural justice, standing, or substantive review. The law of standing may be taken by way of example. Reflection upon the confusing nature of the case law reveals three competing themes within the jurisprudence. Some cases accorded standing expressly upon broad discretionary grounds.[62] They emphasized the willingness and desire of the courts to be able to consider the substance of the complaint and to correct agency action which transgressed the boundaries of legislative authority.[63] The policing theme assumes dominance. Other cases witness an attachment to a rigorous requirement that the applicant possesses a private right in the strict sense of a cause of action in contract or tort before being admitted to the judicial sanctuary.[64] Yet others adopt an ambivalent posture. They talk of the need for private rights, but broaden the definition of appropriate rights to encompass interests outside the traditional categories of contract or tort. Formal obeisance is paid to the private rights theme, but the predominant concern is once again with the policing function which the courts wish to perform. Within this third category should be included cases on declarations and injunctions where the courts have either ignored the requirement of a strict private right, or have interpreted the concept in an expansive fashion.[65]

[62] This was generally the case in relation to the grant of *certiorari*; see *R.* v *Thames Magistrates' Court, ex p. Greenbaum* (1957) 55 L.G.R. 129. The precise degree of interest which an applicant had to demonstrate was contested (see Craig, *Administrative Law*, pp. 349–50), but a private law right was not required.

[63] See also the early law relating to prohibition where some courts adopted the view that any person could seek the remedy, the reasoning being in part that an excess of jurisdiction by an inferior agency was a contempt against the Crown or offended against the royal prerogative, and therefore that any person should be able to inform the court of this fact; *De Haber* v. *Queen of Portugal* (1851) 17 Q.B. 171; *Worthington* v. *Jeffries* (1875) L.R. 10 C.P. 379.

[64] See, e.g., the cases in nn. 58 and 59 above. The courts would normally also allow an action if the applicant could show special damage.

[65] e.g., in the areas of declaration and injunction, see *Nicholls* v. *Tavistock Urban District Council* [1923] 2 Ch. 18; *Prescott* v. *Birmingham Corporation* [1955] Ch. 210; *Brownsea Haven Properties Ltd.* v. *Poole Corporation* [1958] Ch. 574; e.g., in the context of mandamus, see *R.* v. *Commissioners of Customs and Excise, ex p. Cook* [1970] 1 W.L.R. 450; *R.* v. *Hereford Corporation, ex p. Harrower* [1970] 1 W.L.R. 1424.

4. THE TRADITIONAL VISION OF CONSTITUTIONAL LAW: APPEARANCE AND REALITY

Having examined the foundations of the classical or traditional images of constitutional and administrative law, the important question which emerges is how accurate was this picture even at the time that it was initially depicted? This question may best be answered by considering the foundations of the constitutional and administrative arguments separately.

a. Support for the Diceyan View

There is no doubt that some support can be found for the Diceyan vision of unitary, self-correcting democracy, in which the will of the electors was expressed through Parliament, and in which Parliament controlled the government.

Thus in 1893 Lord Hartington, who had been Liberal leader in the Commons, stated:

> Parliament makes or unmakes our ministries, it revises their actions. Ministries may make peace and war but they do so at pain of instant dismissal by Parliament from office, and in affairs of internal administration the power of Parliament is equally direct. It can dismiss a Ministry if it is too extravagant or too economical; it can dismiss a Ministry because its government is too stringent or too lax. It does actually and practically in every way directly govern England, Scotland and Ireland.[66]

Courtney, writing at the turn of the century, echoes these sentiments and systematizes them. He summarizes the essentials of the Constitution in the following terms.

> First that the country must be ruled in accordance with the will of the nation; next that that will is most faithfully expressed in the result of any general election; and thirdly that the House of Commons as the embodiment of that will has a claim to predominance, at least until circumstances change so as to qualify its title as a faithful reflex of the national judgement. This principle thus recognized, that a House of Commons issuing from a general election is the most authoritative expression of the will of the nation, involves as an inevitable consequence the further principle that the

[66] Quoted in A. H. Birch, *Representative and Responsible Government* (1964), 73.

administration of public affairs and the guidance of legislation should be entrusted to persons approved by a majority of the House.[67]

Dicey, in the *Law of the Constitution*, subject to what will be said later, followed these assumptions. This is evident from the earlier discussion, and is apparent within other parts of his work. Thus we find the author stating: 'The House of Commons interferes with administrative matters, and the Ministry are in truth placed and kept in office by the House. A modern cabinet would not hold power for a week if censured by a newly elected House of Commons.'[68]

The Diceyan vision of unitary, self-correcting democracy can also be indirectly supported by examination of more structural changes in the pattern of government within the mid-nineteenth century. The decline in the Board system, alluded to above, is apposite in this context. It is common at the present time to think of new governmental functions being assigned to existing ministries or to ministries created specifically for that purpose. The term ministry may be used to denote a department of state where the power is vested in a single person who sits in one of the Houses of Parliament and is responsible to Parliament for the activities of that department. Ministerial government was not in the nineteenth century the common procedure that it has become today. The more common form of administration in the eighteenth and nineteenth centuries was the Board system.[69] Although the precise structure and powers of Boards differed from area to area, what they possessed in common was a degree of independence from direct parliamentary control.

Boards possessed a number of advantages. They allowed greater continuity of policy, being less affected by the ebbs and flows of political change. They could be more flexible to the needs of decentralized administration. Positions on Boards could be a useful form of patronage. The administrative solution provided by Boards served moreover to obviate the need for a radical expansion within the central bureaucracy itself. The latter was small, and not structured for dealing with the problems of 'mass administration' created by the reforms of the 1830s–1850s.[70] Expansion of the

67 L. Courtney, *The Working Constitution of the United Kingdom* (1901), 6.
68 *Law of the Constitution*, p. 156.
69 For a discussion of the Board system, see the materials cited above, n. 36.
70 e.g. in 1833 the Home Office had a staff of 29.

centralized bureaucracy was beset by conceptual as well as pragmatic problems. Even when social reforms were passed, their passage might not necessarily have been secured directly by the government of the day.[71] The idea that the government should bear the principal responsibility for direct administration of the enacted scheme through centralized ministries was not readily apparent. It was not conceived as the 'natural' method of administration.

The reasons for decline in the Board system were part practical and part conceptual. Ineffective management and waste could attend the passage of Board business. These pragmatic problems were not, however, the prime cause of the decline in the use of Boards. Such difficulties could well be present if the administration were to be carried out by a Ministry. The real cause of their decline was the altered constitutional position of Parliament brought about by the expansion of the franchise. As Parris states: 'The system worked well so long as boards were responsible in fact as well as in name to the King. But once the executive became primarily responsible to Parliament, the system came under strain. The result was a decline in the board pattern of administration and its supersession to a large degree by a ministerial pattern.'[72]

Parliament's sense of its own legitimacy and power, heightened by the reform in the franchise, manifested itself in a desire to control governmental action. At the least this required someone answerable in the House, a person responsible for the actions of the Board. This was particularly the case where the activities were controversial in nature. When the Poor Law Commission was created in 1834, none of the Board members could sit in Parliament. Communication was naturally extremely difficult. Parliament became frustrated due to the absence of a person who could be rendered directly answerable. The Commissioners themselves suffered through having no direct way to defend themselves against personal attack or vilification. As a result, the Commission was replaced by a ministry in 1847.[73] This

[71] e.g. the original impetus for factory legislation which regulated the hours and conditions of work therein came from Oastler, Ashley, and Sadler. It was largely due to the efforts of this group, and later of Edwin Chadwick, that the Whig government produced their own measure, which was enacted as the Factory Act 1833.

[72] *Constitutional Bureaucracy*, p. 83.

[73] See Roberts, *Victorian Origins of the British Welfare State*, p. 133; 'The Victorians' experiments in semi-independent, non-political boards reflected their fear that administrative decisions would be made the handmaid of party bias or be caught in the maelstrom of factional politics. The Poor Law Commission was the classic and tragic example of such an attempt.'

transformation sent shock waves through other areas. Various 'middle ways' were tried, one of which was to have a member of the Board with a seat in Parliament. This experiment was not a noted success, largely because the two crucial elements of the scheme were unclear: the relationship of the parliamentary member to the rest of the Board, and his relationship to Parliament. Such Boards were either converted into formal ministries, or a minister was made directly responsible for the activity of the Board. Gradually the paradigm of the modern ministry evolved. A minister running a department, and being responsible to Parliament for its actions. The correlative was the development of civil service anonymity.

The decline, albeit not demise, of the Board system afforded support to the concept of unitary, self-correcting democracy. It provided evidence of the desire and aim of the Commons to control the executive. Parliamentary control of the executive required the presence of a minister within the House. Legislative control over the executive in important areas of administration would not be feasible unless the minister could be made directly answerable for the actions of those within his purview. The assumption that legislation or rules would not be passed which were against the wishes of the majority of the electors, which was integral to the Diceyan vision, could not be sustained if important areas of policy were outside the control of Parliament.

Notwithstanding this support for the Diceyan vision of our constitutional order, the conclusions which he draws can be controverted for two reasons.

b. The Internal Coherence of Dicey's Argument

First, even if we accept the accuracy of this picture of the constitution, the conclusions concerning the lack of need for constitutional review do not, in fact, follow as self-evidently as Dicey might have us believe. The argument appears to be simple. Our system of democracy is founded upon a channel of authority flowing from the bottom upwards. The electorate choose representatives. The MPs who are elected articulate the views of those who have chosen them, and they control the executive. Legislation which might be constitutionally questionable would, therefore, not be passed, or would be repealed expeditiously.

The ambiguity in this formulation becomes apparent upon further reflection, and is indeed embedded within the quotation cited above concerning the external and internal limits on sovereignty.[74] Thus, we are told that the permanent wishes of the representative portion of Parliament can hardly differ from the wishes of the English people; that which the majority of the Commons command, the majority of the English people usually desire. The gap between these two formulations, which are juxtaposed in Dicey's text, is significant. Under the latter, it would be possible for the wishes of the majority to be faithfully translated into legislation by their elected representatives, and for this legislation to be constitutionally deleterious to the wishes of a minority. Dicey switches back and forth between these two formulations without readily appreciating the difference between them.[75]

It is not apparent how Dicey would prevent or forestall this danger of majority oppression. A possible argument would be that the 'internal limit' placed upon the parliamentary rulers would serve to ensure that the despotism of the majority did not occur. The argument would be as follows. Dicey tells us that any ruler exercises power subject to an internal limit,[76] in the sense that he would be moulded by the society in which the person lived. In a parliamentary system the majority representatives, although holding a particular view on a specific subject, would not attempt to pass legislation which would be constitutionally disadvantageous to a minority. The internal limits of that society would serve to preclude the exercise of such power. A majority might well, for example, believe fervently in Protestantism, but the pervasive spirit of toleration which constituted one facet of the internal limit within which the rulers ruled would mitigate against religious legislation which was discriminatory.

A distinctive, albeit complementary, theme can be found in Dicey's discussion of counter- and cross-currents of opinion.[77] Whether Dicey was correct in regarding legislation as the product of

[74] Dicey, *Law of the Constitution*, p. 82.

[75] Ibid. 84–5, where Dicey reverts to the earlier formulation, i.e. that representative government will produce a coincidence between the 'wishes of the sovereign and the wishes of the subjects'. The same ambiguity pervades Dicey's discussion in *Law and Opinion*, p. 55, where Dicey states that in a representative democracy no law will be carried 'which is opposed to the wish of the people, or in other words, to the sentiment prevailing among the distinct majority of the citizens of a given country'.

[76] *Law of the Constitution*, pp. 80–1.

[77] *Law and Opinion*, pp. 36–41, 311–60.

'public opinion' is not our prime concern. What is of relevance is the light which Dicey's discussion sheds upon the prospect of majority oppression. One of the themes which Dicey stresses is that 'the reigning legislative opinion has never, at any rate during the nineteenth century, exerted absolute or despotic authority'.[78] Its power is always diminished by counter-currents which are more or less directly opposed to the dominant opinion of a particular era. Such counter-currents impose a check upon the legislative action which results from those who hold the dominant faith. Thus Dicey argues that from 1830 to 1850 Benthamite liberalism was held in check by the 'restraining power' of the older Toryism,[79] and that ecclesiastical reform could not be properly understood without paying due attention to the varying counter- and cross-currents which affected its passage. Religious legislation could only be properly comprehended by appreciating that such statutes were affected by a liberalism which aimed at the establishment of religious equality, and by cross-currents of ecclesiastical opinion which desired to maintain the rights or privileges of the Established Church.[80]

Majority tyranny could, therefore, be forestalled by a combination of internal limits, coupled with counter- and cross-currents of opinion, which together would preclude legislation which was constitutionally deleterious to a particular minority. This reasoning has some plausibility. It is, however, difficult to accept that it would operate successfully in all or even the majority of instances in which minority oppression might occur. Legislation which is constitutionally suspect might well be passed because the majority perceive the 'internal limits' differently from that of the minority. They might view the specific boundaries which flow from the internal limitations distinctively from the minority who are being oppressed. Statutes may be enacted which are constitutionally questionable without the actual legislators sensing that they are controverting some societal norm which should be sacrosanct. Moreover, while the existence of counter- and cross-currents of opinion may well be undeniable, their impact upon the problem at hand is more questionable. The existence of such strains within legislative opinion might well be of impact in reducing the pace or severity of statutory change. There is,

[78] Dicey, *Law and Opinion*, p. 36.
[79] Ibid. 38.
[80] Ibid. 312.

however, no particular reason to conclude that they would prevent legislation which could be constitutionally harmful to minority interests. The presence of competing interests was, for example, a predominant theme in the formation of the US Constitution. This has not prevented the passage of legislation which is constitutionally detrimental to the interests of particular groups. The only way in which to ensure that such constitutional harm would not occur, and to link this with counter- and cross-currents of opinion, would in fact be to assume a classical form of pluralism, a society which was composed of groups competing in the political market place, in which the public interest was no more and no less than the outcome of the group exchange.[81]

An alternative line of argument which might be pursued is to return to the connection between sovereignty and the third limb of the rule of law which was considered earlier. The common law, as noted, was perceived as the best protector of individual rights. The existence of representative government served to ensure that the wishes of the people would coincide with those of the sovereign Parliament. Serious problems concerning civil liberties should, therefore, be rare. If such problems did arise, the common law was at hand to protect the harassed citizen.

This 'corrective' is too simplistic and is, upon closer examination, not borne out by Dicey's own analysis. The matter may best be approached as follows. Let us imagine that the majority within Parliament have enacted legislation which could be deemed constitutionally harmful to a minority. The internal limitation upon the exercise of sovereign power has not proven successful, and certain fundamental minority rights have been curtailed. How will the common-law protection avail these citizens, given Dicey's own doctrine of parliamentary omnicompetence? Dicey provides two responses, one of which is general in nature, the other of which is both more detailed and more particular.

The *general response* is that, where civil liberties are deduced from a constitutional document, they can be readily suspended; where, however, such rights emerged from the common law, they could not be destroyed 'without a thorough revolution in the institutions and manners of the nation'.[82] Now it may well be the case that Dicey had

[81] For a discussion of this theme within pluralism, see below, ch. 3 sec. 2b, ch. 4 sec. 1.

[82] Dicey, *Law of the Constitution*, pp. 201–02.

reason to be sceptical of continental experience with Declarations of Rights. The ephemeral quality of such documents would clearly warrant caution concerning their efficacy. The possibility of a wholesale restriction of rights, which occupies Dicey initially, is important, but does not serve to answer the conundrum posed above. A majority within Parliament may have no desire to restrict individual rights generally, either over time or over subject-matter. There may be no intent to effect any revolution in the manners or institutions of the nation. Nor need this be the effect of legislation which curtails the rights of individuals within a particular area.[83] Dicey himself admits that specific legislation could be, and had been, passed without producing the dramatic social consequences adumbrated above.[84]

The more *particular response* provided by Dicey is to be found in his detailed examination of individual freedoms which have been secured and developed by the common law.[85] The limitations of the common law become readily apparent by reflecting upon this detailed analysis. Dicey's argument within these chapters demonstrates the success which the common law can and did have in controlling the exercise of *executive* or *discretionary* power which could interfere with individual liberty. Arrest had to be founded upon statutory authority; executive fiat would not suffice. Freedom of discussion entailed the absence of any prior executive constraint; the individual could only be punished for a consequential wrong, such as libel.

Nothing within this analysis touches the situation in which *statutory* authority does exist, the effect of which is to curtail individual liberty. Thus, Dicey admits that the government can and has secured the 'statutory suspension of habeas corpus' for limited periods and for limited classes of offence.[86] The analysis of freedom

[83] To argue that *any* change which restricted such individual freedom would automatically constitute a fundamental change in the institutions and manners of the nation would be a *reductio ad absurdum*, and is not consistent with Dicey's own usage. Dicey is clearly concerned (ibid. 201–2) with state action which generally abrogates individual freedom. The whole argument is directed towards establishing that this can be more easily done where such rights are found in a written constitution rather than where they have been developed by the common law.

[84] e.g. see Dicey's discussion of the suspension of habeas corpus, where he states (ibid. 230), that the increase in the power thereby given to the executive was no trifle, but that it fell far short of the process known in foreign countries as suspending the constitutional guarantees; see also Dicey's discussion of censorship (ibid. 267–8).

[85] Ibid. chs. 5, 6, 7.

[86] Ibid. 228–37.

of speech is equally revealing. Dicey juxtaposes the position of the Press at the time he wrote to that which had prevailed hitherto. The Press in the nineteenth century were not subject to prior censorship, but were governed by the ordinary law of defamation.[87] He contrasts this with the position which had existed in the seventeenth century, where the Press were controlled by a special tribunal and were subject to regulation.[88] The discretionary system of licensing, 'which was censorship under another name', was given a statutory foundation in 1662, and remained in force until 1695. Dicey comments that:

> The passing, however, of the statute, though not a triumph of toleration, was a triumph of legality. The power of licensing depended henceforward, not on any idea of inherent executive authority, but on the statute law. The right of licensing was left in the hands of the government, but this power was regulated by the words of a statute; and, what was of more consequence, breaches of the Act could be punished only by proceedings in the ordinary courts.[89]

This quotation aptly exemplifies Dicey's detailed analysis of specific individual rights. The common law could help to limit the exercise of broad executive discretionary power which threatened such rights. The first two limbs of the rule of law would be advanced by the transformation of discretionary power into statutory form. Once the power existed in statutory form, it was sacrosanct. A statute which curtailed civil liberties was beyond the reach of the common law, except perhaps in so far as the judiciary could construe such a statute restrictively should they choose. The minority rights in the example postulated above would be equally outside the ambit of common-law protection. This result is to be expected, given the centrality which Dicey accords to parliamentary omnicompetence. If the majority within Parliament do enact legislation which is detrimental to minority interests, no sanctuary can be expected from the common law. When representative democracy proves incapable of aligning the interests of the elected representatives with the nation as a whole, so that some are constitutionally disadvantaged, the oppressed can but hope for a shift in their political fortune. Dicey's claim that constitutional protection within the United Kingdom was not only historically unfounded, but also unnecessary, is therefore

87 Dicey, *Law of the Constitution*, p. 251–2.
88 Ibid. 260–1.
89 Ibid. 268.

suspect, *even* if our democracy did operate in the manner which he postulated.

c. The Reality of Constitutional Power

The second reason why Dicey's conclusions can be contested is that this image of the working constitution was in fact flawed. Put shortly, the nineteenth century model of representative democracy contained the seeds of its own destruction. The more closely it approached perfection, the more fragile did it become. The explanation for this apparent paradox is not hard to find. Three factors were of central importance.[90]

The expansion of the franchise was of particular significance. This had increased the legitimacy of Parliament and provided substantive justification for regarding it as the authoritative expression of the will of the nation. The very need to appeal to an expanded electorate was, however, a key factor in the emergence of a more developed party system. Votes had to be won. Buying them was no longer practicable. Party organization had to be improved in order to mobilize the expanded electorate into voting for a particular party. Central organization and direction from the 'top' increased, thereby placing more power in the hands of the executive.

This tendency was furthered by the changing conception of the role of government. The idea that the government was responsible for preserving the peace, raising revenue, foreign relations and little else was undergoing a transformation. The picture of the nineteenth century as an era of *laissez-faire* was always misleading. A range of social legislation was passed during this period dealing with the poor, health, factories, and the like. The transformation which occurred was concerned, in part at least, with the role of government in the legislation which emanated from Parliament. Expansion of the suffrage necessitated not just the development of party organization to mobilize the expanded electorate. It also required promises

[90] Evidence for these changes can be found from writers who were contemporaries with Dicey; see the discussion of the works of Redlich, Ostrogorski, Maine, Bryce, and McKechnie, below, pp. 43–7; For more modern treatment of these same themes, see, e.g. S. Walkland and M. Ryle (eds.), *The Commons in the Seventies* (1977); N. Johnson, *In Search of the Constitution: Reflections on State and Society in Britain* (1977); S. Walkland (ed.), *The House of Commons in the Twentieth Century* (1979); M. Beloff and G. Peele, *The Government of the United Kingdom: Political Authority in a Changing Society* (2nd edn., 1985); H. Drucker, P. Dunleavy, A. Gamble, and G. Peele (eds.), *Developments in British Politics 2* (1986).

of legislation which would be beneficial to those accorded the vote. If at least some of these promises made to the electorate were to be carried out, the legislative process required alteration. This, in fact, occurred. The change was not sudden or immediate, but very real none the less.

The legislative process was both nationalized and centralized into the hands of the executive. Standing committees became increasingly common. Fear that increased use of such committees would transform the Commons into a legislative machine did not ultimately deter the executive from instituting procedural changes designed to facilitate the passage of legislation. Cabinet committees became more common, adding impetus to the centralization of the legislative initiative with the executive. Delegated legislation led to the same end by a different route: the legislature would accede to the passage of legislation which ultimately left a considerable residue of discretion to the executive to make further rules. Changes in the legislative process were attended by the increase in importance of the party system within Parliament. The party became the conduit for the transfer of power from the legislature to the executive. Discipline had to be tightened to ensure the passage of an enlarged governmental programme. Policy formulation became increasingly concentrated in the executive. Rarely could back-bench MPs effectively stop a measure which had executive backing.

While these factors contributed to the flow of power from the Commons to the executive, the third was the growing realization of centres of power outside Parliament which none the less exercised a formative influence on the content of government policy. The development of pluralist thought in the United Kingdom was complex and will be considered in detail later.[91] Suffice it to say for the present that the recognition of the pluralist nature of society challenged the idea that Parliament wielded a monopoly of public power.

The implications of these developments for the Diceyan vision of the constitutional order are important, but should be kept within perspective. It would be wrong to suggest that any of the changes depicted above 'invalidated' the entirety of Dicey's thesis concerning the omnipotence of Parliament. No such argument is being advanced, and no such contention could be supported. The

[91] See below, chs. 5, 6.

foundation of Dicey's views upon sovereignty was not based exclusively upon the supposed attributes of representative democracy within the United Kingdom. It was, as we have seen, a blend of two lines of thought. Part of his analysis was directed towards sustaining the factual conclusion that Parliament had, and therefore could, do anything which it wished and that there were no rivals which could disturb its all-embracing mantle. The other part of his reasoning was directed towards showing that constitutional review was unnecessary, because representative democracy was self-correcting in the sense considered above.

The implications of the constitutional developments which have just been considered were not, therefore, to destroy Dicey's picture of sovereignty. They did, however, place the conceptual justification for the absence of review under strain. The possibility of some form of constitutional adjudication could no longer so easily be dismissed as unnecessary as well as lacking any foundation in 'precedent'. The growth of executive power, and the realization that there were centres of power outside Parliament, challenged the Diceyan view of representative democracy as a self-correcting mechanism. It became apparent that there might be a greater disjunction between Dicey's external and internal limits on sovereign power than had previously been perceived. If representative democracy had in fact become oligarchic, by concentrating authority in the executive and other powerful but non-representative institutions, then it became increasingly possible that the wishes of this small group might diverge considerably from those of the majority of the electorate. This potential was augmented by a voting system which worked against minority interests and which could not infrequently return a government supported by a minority of the population.

Dicey's union between historical precedent and constitutional principle was, therefore, rendered less secure than hitherto. The conception of self-correcting representative democracy was explicitly based upon a channel of authority flowing from the bottom upwards. The MPs who were elected articulated the views of those who had chosen them, and they controlled the executive. Legislation which might be constitutionally questionable, or detrimental to significant sections of the population, would therefore not be passed, or would be quickly repealed.

The structural development explored above rendered the neat, linear pattern of this reasoning suspect. Parliament's legitimacy continued to be derived from the electorate. In this formal sense, authority could still be perceived as flowing from the bottom upwards. In substance, our constitutional system became one dominated by the top, by the executive and the party hierarchy. The people voted, the government governed, and the system began to look increasingly Schumpeterian[92] well before that classic, skeletal vision of democracy was produced. This tendency was itself exacerbated by the growing control wielded by the organized parties over the electoral agenda and the electoral process.

The legislation which emerged from the 'top down' system could no longer be certain to reflect the electorate's wishes in the simplistic self-correcting sense postulated by Dicey. The concentration of authority and power within the party hierarchy and the executive increased the likelihood that legislation could emanate from Parliament, and remain on the statute books for a considerable period of time, even though it might be contrary to the desires of many within the electorate.

At base these structural changes weakened the very contrast which Dicey drew concerning the degree of coincidence between the external and internal limits on sovereign power which could be expected to operate within a monarchy and a representative democracy. In a monarchy, the sovereign, although subject to certain internal limits, might well be able to force upon his subjects legislation which they disliked.[93] The only constraint upon such action was that the sovereign should be wary lest he transgress the external limits to his sovereign authority and provoke open resistance. A monarchical system left, however, considerable latitude to the sovereign to effectuate his personal goals which, although contrary to the desires of the people, were not sufficient to rouse them to revolt. It was this disjunction between the internal and external limits to sovereign power which the advent of representative democracy was, as we have seen, intended to cure. However, if representative democracy had become oligarchic in the manner described above, then such a disjunction became increasingly possible. The dominant group could impose its own goals, which might be contrary to the wishes of many and yet not sufficient to produce actual resistance. Representative democracy as it actually operated could, therefore, not in fact be guaranteed to prevent a

92 See below, ch. 3 sec. 2c, for a discussion of this view.

93 Dicey, *Law of the Constitution*, pp. 81–2.

divergence between the external and internal limits of sovereignty. Power wielded by an elective oligarchy, in conjunction with other powerful but non-representative institutions, might be subject to no greater constraint than that exercised by the hereditary monarch.

The difficulties with the Diceyan vision of the Constitution have not simply become apparent to later commentators. If hindsight were necessarily required in order to appreciate the arguments presented above, then this would be a factor to be taken into account in ameliorating our critique of Dicey. However, it is manifestly clear that these difficulties were perceived by a range of observers writing both before or contemporaneously with Dicey.

Thus, while Bagehot believed that the most important function of the House of Commons was as an electoral chamber, which could make and unmake ministries,[94] he was also only too aware that power did not flow in one direction only. The cabinet was the 'efficient' branch of our Constitution, and, although appointed by the Commons, it could dissolve the assembly which had created it, and appeal, if it chose, to the next. Speaking of the cabinet, Bagehot states: 'It is a creature, but it has the power of destroying its creators. It is an executive which can annihilate the legislature, as well as an executive which is the nominee of the legislature. It was made, but it can unmake; it was derivative in its origin, but it is destructive in its action.'[95]

The theme, central to Dicey, Hartington, and Courtney, that envisioned power as moving almost exclusively in one direction, from the electors via Parliament to the government was challenged by the more complex picture painted by Bagehot. Nor does Bagehot perceive representative democracy to be self-correcting in the way adumbrated by Dicey. Bagehot spends some considerable time in both the first and the second editions of the book arguing against too much democracy, and worrying about the extension of the franchise produced by the 1867 Reform Act. Unless the majority within Parliament were men of moderate sentiment, they would enact violent laws, and too much democracy would lead to the election of just such men.[96] A political combination of the lower classes, such as might be possible after 1867, would be an 'evil of the first

[94] W. Bagehot, *The English Constitution*, ed. R. H. S. Crossman (1963), 67, 150–1.
[95] Ibid. 69.
[96] Ibid. 168.

magnitude', leading to the supremacy of ignorance over knowledge.[97] Bagehot, like Marx, believed that economic class was a determining factor in the structure of government, and hence in the type of legislation which it produced.[98] Given the extension of the franchise, the evil of working class dominance could only be avoided by buying off all working-class grievances which they, the middle and upper classes, could safely concede, 'in order that they may not have to concede unwillingly some claim which would impair the safety of the country'.[99] This is hardly a vision of self-correcting representative democracy.

While Bagehot's depiction of the machinery of government cast doubt upon Dicey's assumptions, J. S. Mill undermined these foundations from a more philosophical perspective. One of the enduring themes in the writings of J. S. Mill is the fear of the tyranny of the majority, and the desire to protect minority interests. It is clear that he did not believe that some invisible hand within representative democracy would necessarily forestall the invasion of minority rights.[100]

Later commentators who were writing contemporaneously with Dicey were quick to draw upon the increased strength of party and the executive which had occurred since the 1870s.[101] Continental writers were often more astute in their depiction of political reality than were their domestic counterparts.

Redlich[102] eloquently expressed the organic connection between the passage of political sovereignty into the hands of the Commons, and the transfer of real power into the hands of the executive. The growing complexity of modern legislation had produced an executive machinery, the intricacy of which corresponded to the needs of modern society, and had led to the monopolization of the legislative initiative by the government. Ostrogorski carried the argument even further. In his innovative work[103] he set out to study the growth and

97 W. Bagehot, *The English Consitution*, 227; see also p. 247.

98 A point made by Crossman in the introduction, pp. 29–30.

99 Ibid. 278.

100 See, e.g., J. S. Mill's essay on Bentham printed in B. Parekh (ed.), *Jeremy Bentham: Ten Critical Essays* (1974), ch. 1, pp. 28–30.

101 The ensuing discussion draws on only some of the most prominent of these commentators.

102 J. Redlich, *The Procedure of the House of Commons: A Study of its History and Present Form* (1908), i, 122, 208.

103 M. Ostrogorski, *Democracy and the Organization of Political Parties*, trans. F. Clarke (1970).

power of party on the process of democratic government. The picture which he depicted was gloomy indeed. The political caucus caused the stereotyping of opinion and the obliteration of individuality. Adherence to the party creed became the avowed objective of party activists.[104] A further consequence of the dominance of the caucus was to place significant constraints upon the MP's freedom of action.[105] The diminution in the individuality of the private member was marked by the growth in power of his parliamentary leaders, who became like 'generals in command of an army'.[106] A political platform was established by the caucus, the private member was placed in the shade, and the voter came to identify more proximately with the leader and the policies propounced by the party.[107] The leader could use the power of the caucus to ensure that recalcitrant members complied with party dictates by threatening to remove the support of the caucus at the next election.[108] Yet even the leaders had to pay the price for caucus support. Legislative programmes might be forced upon them, which, left to themselves the leaders would never have adopted.[109] Whether one accepts all of Ostrogorski's reasoning and dire conclusions may well be a matter on which opinions can differ. It was somewhat paradoxical that it should be James Bryce, a lifelong friend of Dicey, who should have written the introduction to the work. While Bryce himself expresses reservations about some of the conclusions which the author draws, he does bear testimony to the importance of the topic which Ostrogorski examines.[110]

Continental writers were not, however, the only perspicacious observers of our government. Maine disparagingly described the leader of a party within a popular government as a Wire-puller.[111] Partnership, and the natural tendency for a person to take sides,[112] explained the power of the Wire-puller. The development of the party system would inevitably produce a number of deleterious consequences.[113] Policies would cease to reflect the opinions of the

[104] M. Ostrogorski, *Democracy and the Organization of Political Parties*, i. 594–5.
[105] Ibid. i. 605.
[106] Ibid. i. 607.
[107] Ibid. i. 608.
[108] Ibid. i. 609.
[109] Ibid. i. 610.
[110] Ibid. i, pp. xxxix—xlvii.
[111] H. S. Maine, *Popular Government* (1885), 30.
[112] Ibid. 31–2. And see Maine's delightful exemplification of this, p. 32: 'Once a year, large numbers of English ladies and gentlemen, who have no serious reason for preferring one University to the other, wear dark or light blue colours to signify good wishes for the success of Oxford or Cambridge in a cricket match or boat race.'
[113] Ibid. 33.

individual leader, but simply embrace the ideas which were most likely to win favour with the greatest number of voters. This Schumpeterian vision was followed by a series of acute observations. An extended suffrage, reigned over by the Wire-puller and the party system, would produce parties which were very like one another, irrespective of 'how leaders may quarrel, and partisan hate partisan'; such parties would in the long run tend to a 'mischievous form of Conservatism, and drug society with a potion compared with which Eldonine would be a salutary draught';[114] and the unfettered representative would be transformed into the instructed delegate.[115] The cabinet would become the sole source of important legislation, while Parliament would be emasculated and lose any power to initiate legislation.[116] The combination of cabinet and caucus is rendered cogent by powerful imagery. 'The old Italian toxicologists are said to have always arranged their discoveries in a series of three terms—first the poison, next the antidote, thirdly the drug which neutralized the antidote. The antidote to the fundamental infirmities of democracy was Representation, but the drug which defeats it has now been found in the Caucus.'[117]

Bryce, writing somewhat later, was equally alive to the infirmities of the traditional model. In his study of *Modern Democracies*[118] he noted the decline in the power of legislatures, and commented on the British system in which party discipline curbed the independence of the private member. Meaningful debate was prevented by procedural rules which enabled the executive to enforce a closure on legislative discourse.[119] While Bryce believed that the Commons was still at the centre of political life, he realized that the cabinet exercised real power and the caucus became an instrument of power in the hands of the party chiefs.[120] So 'modern' had Bryce become that he could restrict his discussion of the executive to questions concerning its efficiency, capability, and honesty.[121] It was only in countries where democracy was not well settled that people were still concerned about executive power; when the power of the people was established by long usage, it was unnecessary to treat the executive as a danger to democracy. Yet Bryce was far too experienced to regard democracy as self-correcting in the Diceyan

[114] H. S. Maine, *Popular Government*, 35.
[115] Ibid. 94.
[116] Ibid. 114–15.
[117] Ibid. 94.
[118] J. Bryce, *Modern Democracies* (1921).
[119] Ibid. ii. 337–8.
[120] Ibid. ii. 343.
[121] Ibid. ii. 358 ff.

sense. Thus he expressed concern about the way in which a small section of the electorate might exercise a power disproportionate to its numbers, leading to the real wishes of the electors being misrepresented;[122] he was aware of the existence of extra parliamentary groups who could wield as much power as 'all but the most outstanding Parliamentary chiefs';[123] he was alive to the dangers of pure majoritarianism, with the correlative risk to the interests of minorities; and he perceived the oligarchical[124] tendency in all organizational forms at the same time as the more famous work by Michels.[125] Other critics could well be cited.[126]

Less well known than some, but powerful in its succinct and direct approach, is the work of McKechnie.[127] Many of Dicey's fundamental assumptions were challenged. The cabinet dominated the Commons and was sovereign in any meaningful, practical sense. Democracy did not embody compromise, but implied a monopoly of power by one half of the people over the other half. 'Each party in turn is absolutely supreme, without let or hindrance.'[128] No limits existed to prevent the infringement of fundamental rights, and there was no power to balance that wielded by the central organs of government.[129] In theory all citizens had equal rights, but in practice minorities had no effective rights at all. 'There is no justification, either in reason, equity, custom or common sense for a political system which places the liberty and property, lives and honour of one half of the community absolutely and legally at the mercy of the other half.'[130] Majoritarian tyranny was the great danger of the age, and the Constitution provided no effective checks to prevent the encroachment upon minority rights.

5. THE TRADITIONAL VISION OF ADMINISTRATIVE LAW: STRAINS AND TENSIONS

We have thus far seen the weakness of the foundations upon which Dicey constructed the role to be played, or not played, by

[122] J. Bryce, *Modern Democracies* (1921), ii. 348–9.

[123] Ibid. ii. 340.

[124] Ibid. ii. 542, 546.

[125] R. Michels, *Political Parties: A Sociological Study of the Oligarchical Tendencies of Modern Democracy*, trans. E. and C. Paul (1962).

[126] See, e.g., S. Low, *The Governance of England* (1904); A. L. Lowell, *The Government of England* (1908).

[127] W. S. McKechnie, *The New Democracy and the Constitution* (1912; repr. 1971).

[128] Ibid. 24–6.

[129] Ibid. 60.

[130] Ibid. 164.

constitutional law. The implications of these developments for the role and shape of administrative law were equally profound. The conception of non-constitutional review as one in which the courts upheld the power of the Commons by policing the frontiers of the legislation became more tenuous. Legislation became the prerogative of the executive and parliamentary acquiescence was ensured by the managers of the party machine. The very form of legislation altered with broader, more open-textured grants of discretionary power to the executive, and greater use of delegated legislation.[131] The picture of the courts performing a simple demarcation role wore thin as they were faced with the need to make decisions concerning the exercise of such ministerial power. Any idea that the courts could realistically divine the appropriate scope of 'legislative' intent became more difficult to sustain. While the flexibility inherent in the concept of jurisdiction could preserve the veneer that the courts were simply applying the legislative mandate, and were thereby obeying the sovereignty of Parliament, it was an increasingly fragile mask. This fragility was highlighted by the difficulty of reconciling, or even making *ex post facto* sense of, cases decided differently upon similar fact situations.[132]

The political developments considered above also placed strain upon the idea that the courts' role was to protect private rights. The tension which could and did exist between this theme and the desire of the courts to police the boundaries of legislative intent has already been considered. The assumption that the courts were doing no more than to apply private law in a case where the defendant happened to be a public body became subject to further tension when the government began to pass the legislation which provided the foundations of the Welfare State. *Ultra vires* agency action in such areas would rarely produce an infringement of a traditional private law right which would found a cause of action in contract or tort. Judicial intervention had to be justified upon other grounds. No consistent approach emerged. The most common judicial technique was to fall back upon the policing idea, which was itself subject to the difficulties considered above. An alternative avenue was to

[131] See generally, C. T. Carr, *Delegated Legislation* (1921); C. K. Allen, *Law and Orders* (3rd edn., 1965).

[132] This is one of the themes pursued by D. M. Gordon, 'The Relation of Facts to Jurisdiction' (1929) 45 *L.Q.R.* 459; 'Observance of Law as a Condition of Jurisdiction' (1931) 47 *L.Q.R.* 386, 557; 'Jurisdictional Fact: An Answer' (1966) 82 *L.Q.R.* 515. For further comment, see Craig, *Administrative Law*, pp. 242–4.

accord an expansive interpretation to the term 'right', and to incorporate interests which would not have satisfied the traditional meaning ascribed to that concept.[133]

Moreover, the realization that the descriptive aspect of Dicey's rule of law thesis was flawed, and that administrative agencies, whether called board, commission, or tribunal, had been, in fact, dispensing administrative discretion, placed further strain upon the classical model. It could no longer be so simply maintained that Parliament actually wielded a monopoly of public power. This difficulty was compounded in those instances when it was clear that the agency was intended, for one of a variety of reasons, to have a measure of independence from either the legislature, executive, and/or the courts.[134] Challenge to these descriptive aspects of Dicey's thesis was followed by increased questioning of their normative foundations. The idea that the ordinary law, and the ordinary courts, should be supreme began to be questioned. The seemingly self-evident nature of this proposition was challenged. Changing attitudes towards the social legislation which such agencies were applying, and hence indirectly to the agencies themselves, combined with a distrust of the ordinary courts. The result was to reassess the 'natural superiority' of the ordinary law, and to reconsider the idea that administrative law should be seen as primarily directed towards control by the ordinary courts of the administrative process.

This theme is evident, albeit in varying degrees, in the work of the major public lawyers writing during the early decades of this century. It is exemplified in the work of Robson, who approached the study of administrative justice without 'any ready-made assumption that every tribunal which does not at the moment form part of the recognized system of judicature must necessarily and inevitably be arbitrary, incompetent, unsatisfactory, injurious to the freedom of the citizen and to the welfare of society'.[135] The connection between an evaluation of the agencies themselves, and the social policies which they were applying, permeates the entirety of the work. The growth of administrative law was directly connected with the extension of governmental functions; the

[133] See the discussion above, ch. 2 sec. 3 and see the material above, nn. 61–5.

[134] For a discussion of the reasons why this might occur, and the problems thereby produced, see Craig, *Administrative Law*, pp. 73–92.

[135] W. Robson, *Justice and Administrative Law: A Study of the British Constitution* (1928), xv.

progressive limitation of the rights of the individual was necessary in the interests of the health and welfare of the entire community.[136] Choices had to be made as to how these emergent schemes should be administered. Cost, speed, and flexibility were advantages attendant upon administrative agencies, as compared with the ordinary courts.[137] The preoccupation of the ordinary law with individual rights was felt by Robson to be another major disadvantage of using the 'normal' judicial machinery.

> The intense legalism of the English system of law is one of its most notable features, and one which results in a tendency to sacrifice the public welfare to private interests where the latter can lay claim to individual rights . . . It is concerned less with social righteousness than with individual rights. It tries questions of the highest social import as mere private controversies between John Doe and Richard Roe, and is so zealous to secure fair play to the individual that often it secures very little fair play to the public. Even our body of constitutional law is in the main concerned with the rights of the subject rather than with the claims of the community, or the obligations of citizenship.[138]

Robson was fully aware of the shortcomings of the tribunals which then existed, and proposed reforms.[139] He was, however, at pains to dispel the idea that the ordinary judicial process was either more 'just' or more 'neutral' than that of administrative agencies. He argued forcefully that the fear of political interference in agency decision-making was a 'bogey', unsubstantiated by empirical evidence.[140] Judicial review should be strictly confined, lest the advantages possessed by agency decision-making should be lost through the process of judicial oversight.

While other prominent public lawyers working during this period might not have accepted the entirety of the above analysis, it is equally clear that their starting-point was closer to Robson than it

[136] W. Robson, *Justice and Administrative Law: A Study of the British Constitution* (1928), 32.

[137] Ibid. 262–75.

[138] Ibid. 251–2; see also pp. 261, 275.

[139] Ibid. 275–82, 313–22.

[140] Ibid. 283, italics in the original.

> As a matter of fact, there is no evidence whatsoever which goes to show that the Administrative Tribunals now working in England are any more liable to political interference than the admittedly independent courts of law. It is as unscientific to *assume* without evidence that the former will be biased on political grounds as it would be for a fanatical believer in direct election to assume that judges will be autocratic and irresponsible merely because they are independent and largely uncontrolled by popular action.

was to Dicey. Thus, Carr criticized Dicey's tendency to regard administrative law as something alien and continental.[141] We should accept administrative agencies as 'indigenous and recognize that they have grown up with no sinister design of destroying liberty, but with a sincere desire to do the State some service'.[142] While judicial review should be preserved, the scope thereof should be carefully drawn;[143] not to do so would be to endanger the very benefits of tribunals. The 'old-fashioned' ordinary law could only realistically meet the demands of a new age by being supplemented by a system of administrative adjudication.[144] Jennings was equally concerned to demonstrate the error of Dicey's analysis.[145] Administrative law was an important branch of the law within a country where political organization was highly developed.[146] It included the legal rules relating to the civil service, local government, and the nationalized industries. From a functional perspective it incorporated the law of public health, national insurance, education, highways, and the like. These were significant state activities and the legal regime which applied thereto should be neither denied, nor treated with disdain. Jennings revealed the errors which coloured Dicey's vision of the French *droit administratif*, and adverted to the similarities between the common law and civilian systems.[147] Laski was equally critical of Dicey's reasoning, albeit for somewhat differing reasons from those considered thus far. Detailed consideration of Laski's opinions will be undertaken later.[148] For the present it may be said that, while Laski's prescriptions for administrative law differed from those of, for example, Robson, the fundamental approach was similar. The social and economic functions undertaken by the state were not matters to be viewed with alarm. They were an integral part of the state's responsibility. Controls were indeed required over the machinery which was to administer this legislation. The emphasis within Laski's analysis was, however, upon procedural checks and consultative rights, rather than upon substantive judicial oversight.[149]

[141] C. T. Carr, *Concerning English Administrative Law* (1941).
[142] Ibid. 124.
[143] Ibid. 125.
[144] Ibid. 126.
[145] I. Jennings, *The Law and the Constitution* (1933; 5th edn., 1959).
[146] Ibid. 217.
[147] Ibid. 232–6.
[148] See below, ch. 5 sec. 2.
[149] H. J. Laski, *A Grammar of Politics* (4th edn., 1938), 301, 390–7.

6. CONCLUSION

The picture of the classical model would be incomplete if we were to stop here, for it is clear that Dicey himself did realize certain of the points which undermined his own thesis. In the *Law of the Constitution* Dicey is aware of Bagehot, and appears to accept the 'reality' of Bagehot's account of relations between the cabinet and the legislature.[150] It is, however, in Dicey's *Law and Opinion*, and in the Introduction to later editions of the *Law of the Constitution*, that we see the glimmer of reality making its impression upon Dicey. The pioneering nature of, and defects in, Dicey's *Law and Opinion* are both well known. The relevance of the work for present purposes is for the light which it casts upon Dicey's perception of democracy.[151] While there are statements which continue to reflect the self-correcting view of representative democracy, there is a realization that matters may not be so simple. This is most apparent in Dicey's discussion of the debt of collectivism to Benthamism. Dicey assumed, too simplistically, that the natural tendency of Benthamism was towards *laissez-faire* and individualism.[152] He did, however, perceive that the same doctrine could be used to support increased state intervention or collectivism. If utility was to be the sole criterion by which policies and institutions were to be judged, this could, when combined with the extended suffrage, produce democratic despotism.[153] If utility demanded state intervention, which entailed for Dicey the correlative diminution in the freedom of the individual,[154] then such legislation would be duly enacted. Moreover, Dicey also perceived that the utilitarian disdain for contractarian-

[150] Dicey, *Law of the Constitution*, p. 19.

[151] Dicey, *Law and Opinion*, pp. 54, 55.

[152] Ibid., lecture VI. There is a considerable historical debate concerning the influence of Benthamite thought upon administrative development in the nineteenth century. See A. J. Taylor, *Laissez-faire and State Intervention in Nineteenth Century Britain* (1972), for a balanced account of competing views. For more detailed study, see E.Halévy, *The Growth of Philosophic Radicalism* (1928); J. B. Brebner, 'Laissez-faire and State Intervention in Nineteenth-Century Britain' (1948) 8 *Jnl. of Econ. Hist.* 61; O. MacDonagh, 'The Nineteenth-Century Revolution in Government: A Reappraisal', *Historical Journal*, 1 (1958) 52; H. Parris, 'The Nineteenth-Century Revolution in Government: A Reappraisal Reappraised', *Historical Journal*, 3 (1960) 17; W. C. Lubenow, *The Politics of Government Growth: Early Victorian Attitudes to State Intervention (1833–1848)* (1971).

[153] Dicey, *Law and Opinion*, pp. 304–5.

[154] Ibid. 308–9.

or rights-based theories deprived the individual of one possible safeguard.

For the doctrine of innate rights, logically unsound though it be, places in theory a limit upon the despotism of the majority. This doctrine is no doubt a very feeble barrier against the inroads of popular tyranny; the Declaration of the Rights of Man did not save from death one among the thousands of innocent citizens dragged before the Revolutionary Tribunal; the American Declaration of Independence, with its proclamation of the inalienable rights of Man, did not deliver a single Negro from slavery. But these celebrated documents were after all a formal acknowledgment that sovereign power cannot convert might into right. They have assuredly affected public opinion.[155]

The above quotation displays Dicey's continued belief that declarations of rights were inefficacious. Yet one also sees a realization that democracy may not be self-correcting in the sense which is central to the *Law of the Constitution*. Whether one believes that the type of social legislation which Dicey had in mind would indeed constitute democratic despotism is, of course, altogether another matter.

The shift in Dicey's opinions is further evidenced by the later editions of the two major works concerned with the constitution. The second edition of *Law and Opinion*, and the eighth edition of the *Law of the Constitution*, published a year apart, are both indicative of this alteration in long introductions. Similar themes are evident. The power of cabinet government is accepted, and much space is devoted toward the evils of the party system and the caucus. Legislation of a 'socialist' nature, such as that passed by the Liberal government of 1906, is decried and the dangers of democracy are discussed.[156] Dicey advocates the use of the referendum to curb the danger of democratic government;[157] his long and bitter battles over Ireland played a significant role in shaping his thinking in this area.[158] Dicey admits the existence of administrative discretion in England and modifies his harsh judgements concerning the French system.[159] None the less he still regarded the supremacy of the

[155] Dicey, *Law and Opinion*, p. 308.

[156] Dicey, *Law and Opinion in England* (2nd. edn., 1914), pp. lxiv–lxv, lxxxvii–lxxxix; *Introduction to the Study of the Law of the Constitution* (8th edn., 1915), pp. cxiv–cxvii.

[157] *Law of the Constitution*, (8th edn.), pp. cxv–cxvii.

[158] R. A. Cosgrove, *The Rule of Law: Albert Venn Dicey, Victorian Jurist* (1980), 106–108.

[159] *Law of the Constitution* (8th edn.), pp. lxi-lxvi. See also A. V. Dicey, 'The Development of Administrative Law in England' (1915) 31 *L.Q.R.* 148.

ordinary law as of central importance.[160] The existence of administrative institutions was still felt to be a relatively recent development and one which was to be regretted. Administrative tribunals continued to possess two inherent defects: the ordinary courts were thereby excluded, and administrative agencies were influenced by political considerations.[161]

Notwithstanding the changes of view which are apparent in these later editions, the basic texts of both works remained unaltered. It was these, and in particular the *Law of the Constitution*, which continued to exert a significant influence over constitutional and administrative law. The original text was, and is, that to which reference is still made. The realization that political and social developments had undermined many of the premises upon which Dicey had built his constitutional doctrine was never truly appreciated by the immediate successors to Dicey in the field of constitutional scholarship. They were content to draw upon Dicey's conclusions without ever evaluating the reasoning through which those conclusions were reached. Ridges adopts the Diceyan frame of parliamentary sovereignty, and borrows also the language of external and internal limits to parliamentary power.[162] Anson, while taking issue with the Austinian idea of indivisible sovereignty, accepts without question the ideal of parliamentary omnipotence.[163] Later writing has been more wide ranging in its approach. However even here the emphasis tends to be placed upon one of two questions: whether the cases, most of which are subsequent to Dicey's work, support his proposition, and/or whether it is logically possible to have a sovereign which is limited in some way.[164] This is not to deny the importance of both these lines of enquiry. It is rather to suggest that they do not, in themselves, constitute the entire subject. Dicey constructed an argument in which neither of the above issues assumed any centrality. His argument was essentially empirical, being based upon what he perceived to be constitutional historical practice, and the conditions of the democratic society in which he lived. It was by later generations challenging these

[160] *Law of the Constitution* (8th edn.), p. lxv.

[161] Dicey, *Law and Opinion*, (2nd edn.), pp. liii-xliv.

[162] E. W. Ridges, *Constitutional Law of England*, ed. S. E. Williams (3rd edn., 1922), 12–13.

[163] W. R. Anson, *Law and Custom of the Constitution*, ed. M. L. Gwyer (5th edn., 1922), 2, 7–8.

[164] See the material above, n. 1.

political and social assumptions, and postulating a different form of democratic society, that some of the most interesting new ideas concerning the role of constitutional and administrative law were to develop.

3
PLURALIST DEMOCRACY, GROUPS, AND PROCESS: USA (I)

1. INTRODUCTION

The implications which a pluralist conception of democracy will have for the shape and content of public law will be a matter on which opinion can differ. This is a consequence of the diversity of view as to what pluralism itself entails, and the extent to which pluralist doctrine has been undermined by developments within modern society. Certain predominant lines of thought can, however, be delineated. For some, the appropriate role of public law within a pluralist democracy should be confined to the protection of process values, whether this be within constitutional or administrative law. Others reject such a purely process-oriented view.[1] They regard it as both proper and inevitable that the law should be concerned with substantive rights as well as process values. Precisely which substantive rights should be protected, and to what extent, is a matter on which there is sharp disagreement. Yet others challenge the depiction of the US Constitution as a pluralist document. They argue that it in fact embodies a more republican sentiment than hitherto perceived, and that the jurisprudence of the courts is consonant with this theme.[2]

The structure of the argument within this chapter, and that which follows, should be made apparent at the outset. First, the meaning and nature of pluralist democracy will be examined. This is in itself a complex enquiry, since diverse strands of thought have been encompassed under the label 'pluralism'. Secondly, it will be argued that three distinctive models of pluralism can be identified. The descriptive and normative aspects of these models will be revealed, and the implications which they have for constitutional adjudication will be assessed. Thirdly, attention will be focused upon administrative law. The pluralist vision of democracy suggests, as will be

[1] e.g. L. H. Tribe, *Constitutional Choices* (1985), ch. 2.

[2] See below, ch. 10 sec. 4. See also C. R. Sunstein, 'Interest Groups in American Public Law', 38 *Stan. L. Rev.* 29 (1985).

seen below, that central themes of administrative law should be delegation of power, and interest representation within administrative decision-making. The extent to which these objects have been fostered will be considered. The difficulties and dysfunctional consequences which are said to beset pursuit of these themes will be examined, and the interconnection between a process-oriented conception of constitutional and administrative law will be explored.

2. PLURALIST THOUGHT IN THE UNITED STATES

a. *Madison: Pluralist or not?*

One element of pluralist thought is said to be evident at the very inception of the US Constitution. It finds expression in the Madisonian concept of democracy, which had an influence upon the Constitution itself. Whether the Constitution should be regarded as a pluralist document is, however, a strongly contested issue, which will be considered in more detail when we evaluate the republican reading of the federalist argument.[3] For the present a brief summary of the pluralist reading of the Constitution and the objections thereto will be considered.

For Madison it was axiomatic that any individual or group of individuals would tyrannize others unless restrained in some manner.[4] The view of man inherent in this hypothesis is Hobbesian in character. Man pursues his own desires, one of which is the desire for power over other individuals because of the benefits which can accrue to him from such control. The Madisonian strategy to forestall the occurrence of this danger was, however, markedly different. To ensure the existence of a non-tyrannical republic, the accumulation of all legislative, judicial, and executive powers within the same hands was to be avoided. It was this which was to provide the basis from which many of the checks and balances which are characteristic of the US Constitution have developed. Separation of governmental power was not the only condition for a non-tyrannical

[3] See below, ch. 10 secs. 3, 4.

[4] Many of the following arguments are to be found in *Federalist*, No. 10; see C. Rossiter (ed.), *The Federalist Papers* (1961). For comment, see R. A. Dahl, *A Preface to Democratic Theory* (1956), ch. 1; R. W. Krouse, 'Classical Images of Democracy in America: Madison and Tocqueville', in G. Duncan (ed.), *Democratic Theory and Practice* (1983), ch. 5; Sunstein, 'Interest Groups', p. 29.

republic. The other was to prevent factions acting adversely to the rights of other citizens or to the aggregate interests of the community. Minority factions could be outvoted. The possibility of a majority faction presented greater difficulty. The response was to broaden the franchise. A majority faction was less likely to exist, and less likely to act as a unity, the more extended and diverse were the interests of the electorate. In a pluralistic society a majority would lack stability, thereby reducing the threat to minority interests. Madisonian democracy stressed balance and the separation of powers, the avoidance of powerful faction, and competition between interests.

It would, however, be mistaken, or at the least an oversimplification, to regard Madisonian democracy as a pure blueprint for a pluralist society within which interest groups bargained for their own selfish private interests. In the words of Sunstein:

> Madison willingly abandoned the classical republican understanding that citizens generally should participate directly in the processes of government. Far from being a threat to freedom, a large republic could help to guarantee it. At the same time, Madison's understanding was sharply distinct from that of the modern pluralists. He hoped that national representatives, operating above the fray, would be able to disentangle themselves from local pressures and deliberate on and bring about something like an objective public good. Those representatives would have the virtue associated with classical republican citizens.[5]

It would be misconceived to view the subsequent development of US pluralist thought as an inevitable, or even direct, consequence of Madisonian democracy. There are, as will become apparent, significant differences in both emphasis and content between the pluralism of Madison and that of later writers.

b. Modern Pluralism

It was the work of Bentley which provided the focal point for the development of modern pluralist thought in the United States.[6] The

[5] Sunstein, 'Interest Groups', p. 42. Sunstein argues that the structural provisions of the Constitution attempted to foster 'public-spirited representation, to provide safeguards in its absence, and to ensure an important measure of popular control', (p. 43; see also pp. 44–5). This view is not uncontroversial. For a more general discussion, see below, ch. 10 secs. 3, 4.

[6] A. F. Bentley, *The Process of Government* (1908; repr. 1949).

work first appeared in 1908, and, as noted in the introduction to a later issue, it was initially much cited but little read. One suspects that this may be true even now. Bentley's aim was very different from that of the British pluralists. There was no monistic state to be dethroned in the United States.[7] The objective was to fashion a tool through which to examine social processes. Bentley thus devoted the first part of the work to a critique of other criteria which have been used to explain social development, attacking the views that ideas[8] or feelings[9] provided an adequate explanation.

How then should we explain social development? The raw material of government, and of all decision, was activity. This activity was interconnected. Explanations of decisions could not, therefore, be found solely in law reports, statutes, constitutional conventions and the like. One had to look behind the façade to perceive the reality within. Only by looking at the formative influences upon regulation, administration, or adjudication could the process of government be comprehended.[10] How could such activity be measured?[11] Feelings and ideas could not be calibrated. The key was group activity. All individuals belonged to a variety of groups. The interplay between these groups became the touchstone for understanding society.

> The great task in the study of any form of social life is the analysis of these groups. It is much more than classification, as that term is ordinarily used. When the groups are adequately stated, everything is stated. When I say everything I mean everything. The complete description will mean the complete science, in the study of social phenomena, as in any other field. There will be no more room for 'animistic' causes here than there.[12]

An important corollary of Bentley's pluralistic vision was that there was no objective public interest in politics. Any interest was merely a group interest.[13] It could be accorded no higher status than that.[14] To talk of objective good or objective utility in politics was 'like the undiscovered and unsuspected gold under the mountain, a social nullity'.[15] Claims that a societal interest as a whole mandated a particular course of action were equally vacuous. Even 'murder'

[7] For a discussion of this aspect of pluralism, see below, ch. 5 sec. 2.
[8] *The Process of Government*, pp. 136–53.
[9] Ibid. 169–70.
[10] Ibid. 176–80.
[11] Ibid. 200–2.
[12] Ibid. 208–9.
[13] Ibid. 211; see also Bentley's criticism of Marx, pp. 465–8.
[14] Ibid., chs. 13–16.
[15] Ibid. 213.

could be condoned if it was supported by powerful interests, as in the case of railroad operation or sweat-shops.[16] The balance of group pressure *was* the existing state of society.[17] Laws could not be classified into those which were directed towards evil, and those which were conducive to the public welfare. Any such categorization was tendentious, unsupportable, and a reflection of the pre-existing disposition of the commentator.[18] It followed that log-rolling should not be regarded as a term of opprobrium; it was the characteristic type of legislative process.[19] To condemn it presupposed a pure public spirit which should guide legislators; an atmosphere of Jovian calm in which they would decide upon what was best for the whole people. This was illusory. Legislation was trading, the adjustment of interests, and nothing more.[20] Justice and truth were made and maintained by group pressures.[21]

The absence of any objective criterion of good, truth, justice, or welfare within society was implicitly based upon certain premises. Philosophical scepticism pervaded the political discourse. The pluralist theme, that the result of group interaction produced a natural equilibrium, was simply a corollary of this reasoning. The conclusion of group interaction *represented* the public welfare. Usage of the phrase natural equilibrium reflected the absence of any other criterion through which to measure the public good. The very language used reinforced this theme through its own potent imagery. Equilibrium connoted harmony. It was indicative of balance. Natural equilibrium suggested a self-generating impetus. The analogy with market forces and economics was evident; it added weight to the view that the social sciences could be reduced to one discipline, or one mode of thought.

A considerable literature concerning groups and the political process ensued. An important ambivalence permeated the apparent uniformity of this approach. The relationship between groups and the public interest was viewed in differing ways. The nuances which are apparent within pluralist literature can be exemplified by briefly comparing the work of Earl Latham and Truman.

Earl Latham began his study with orthodox pluralist rhetoric.[22] Congress could not be understood as 'a mere 'bill-bearing and

[16] *The Process of Government*, p. 221.
[17] Ibid. 259–60.
[18] Ibid. 288.
[19] Ibid. 369.
[20] Ibid. 370–1.
[21] Ibid. 447.
[22] E. Latham, *The Group Basis of Politics* (1952).

resolution-breeding institution'.[23] It was merely one official group which functioned in an environment of groups, official and unofficial. Public policy was the equilibrium reached in this struggle at any given moment. The legislative vote on any issue was a direct reflection of the balance of power among these competing groups.[24] Thus far all was normal. At other points within his study Earl Latham, however, argued that the role of the state was not necessarily confined to a few policing functions where the intersecting groups touched upon each other; it was not limited to being a referee in a group conflict.[25] It was established to promote normative goals, 'as custodian of the consensus', and to help formulate those goals. The legislature was not, therefore, an inert cash register confined to ringing up the additions and withdrawals of strength.[26] Legislatures, although groups, possessed a sense of identity which unofficial groups had to recognize if they were to represent their members effectively.

Truman's[27] analysis was equally pluralist in its orientation. Political groups were one, albeit specialized, form of interest group. The essential features of such a group were similar to those of non-political groups.[28] Governmental decisions had to be viewed as group interaction.[29] An all-embracing public interest, distinctive from the interests of particular groups, did not exist.[30] An association might try to enlist the 'public interest' in support of its claim,[31] but this was no more than a publicity ploy through which to increase the attractiveness of its demands.[32]

A more perfect testament to pure Bentleyan pluralism would be difficult to imagine.[33] Close inspection reveals that even Truman qualified this pristine vision. Political equilibrium would not necessarily result from group competition. The stability and viability of the political process were dependent upon overlapping membership and the presence of potential interest groups. A normal person would be a member of a variety of interest groups which cut across each other. This would tend to obviate the possibility of

[23] *The Group Basis of Politics*. p. vii.
[24] Ibid. 36.
[25] Ibid. 14.
[26] Ibid. 37.
[27] D. B. Truman, *The Governmental Process* (1951).
[28] Ibid., pt. I.
[29] See also ibid., pt. II.
[30] Ibid. 50–1.
[31] Ibid. 358–9.
[32] Ibid. 51.
[33] Even the existence of traditions such as civil liberties were explained in terms of potential interest groups; ibid. 51–2.

irreconcilable conflict between groups.[34] The ever present likelihood of new groups emerging, should their interests be too neglected by the status quo, in itself ensured that the existence of these interests would exert a minimum of influence.[35] However, Truman accepted that the stabilizing effect of overlapping membership would be seriously impaired if groups operated within narrowly defined social classes.[36] The organized, class-based groups might gain a monopoly of access to government, and the claims of excluded groups could assume an explosive character.[37] Truman may not have believed in the idea of a separate public interest. He was, however, aware that group interaction would not necessarily produce a stable, political equilibrium.

The differences of emphasis which were apparent between the US pluralists should not conceal the similarities in their approach. As the volume of pluralistic literature grew, so the ever fine line between description and prescription was erased. Pluralism became an integral part of US ideology. Nicholls captures this transition.

> Pluralism became not only an account of what is, but an outline of what ought to be. A free society, as opposed to totalitarianism, is characterised, and is protected, by the existence of semi-autonomous groups with overlapping membership; there is thus no single centre of power, no monolithic body, attempting to impose upon the country some total way of life, but rather a benevolent umpire ensuring that all groups are able to have a foot in the political door.[38]

The work of Robert Dahl was influential in reinforcing this general conclusion. Dahl was no simple defender of the status quo.[39] He was fully aware that groups wielded unequal power, and that access to the governmental process was unbalanced. Notwithstanding these caveats, the general conclusion which he reached in the 1950s was that all active and legitimate groups in the population would be able to make themselves heard at some crucial stage in the process of decision. Control over the eventual outcome of decisions might be unevenly distributed. Some measure of access was, however, available to all, and that was 'no mean thing in a political system'.[40]

[34] *The Governmental Process*, pp. 508, 510.
[35] Ibid. 512.
[36] Ibid. 520–3.
[37] Ibid. 523.
[38] D. Nicholls, *Three Varieties of Pluralism* (1974), 25.
[39] *A Preface to Democratic Theory*, (1956).
[40] Ibid. 150. Dahl's opinions have altered over the last twenty-five years. His recent work strikes a less optimistic chord; R. A. Dahl, *Dilemmas of Pluralist Democracy* (1982). For a discussion of these later views, see below, ch. 3 sec. 2c.

Support for the Bentleyan conception of pluralism has emerged more recently in the work of 'public-choice' theorists, who utilize market analogies systematically in order to predict the behaviour of 'political markets'. Public choice theorists differ in degree on important issues within their own conceptual framework. While the literature has become technically complex, some idea of the central themes is, however, necessary for an understanding of modern pluralism.

The methodology of public choice is economics. The subject-matter is the same as that of more traditional political science, *inter alia* the role of the state, the behaviour of bureaucracy, the explanation of voting patterns, the ascription of rights, and the effective discharge of public policy. As with any other part of economic or political discourse, there are both descriptive or positive and normative aspects of public choice theory. The division between the two is no more easily sustainable within this area than it is within others which we have discussed.[41] With this caveat firmly in mind let us begin by focusing upon the positive aspects of public choice, and attempt to reveal the normative assumptions underlying this discourse.

One of the seminal works is that of Buchanan and Tullock.[42] The object was to analyse some of the traditional topics of political science through economic spectacles. Their work was not specifically directed towards issues such as the division of power, or judicial review. The emphasis was rather at one stage removed. It was to analyse the 'calculus of the rational individual when faced with questions of constitutional choice'.[43] What types of decision-making rules would the rational individual choose? The form of analysis adopted in answering this question was 'methodological individualism'. Human beings were conceived as the only ultimate choice-makers in determining group as well as private action. The authors contrast this 'methodological individualism' with 'individualism' as a norm for organizing social activity. The former merely postulated that political choices would be made by an individual's choice between competing alternatives; no position needed to be taken concerning the ultimate goals which directed his choice.[44] The latter

[41] See, e.g., J. M. Buchanan, 'Comment', 18 *J.L.E.* 903, 904 (1975).
[42] J. M. Buchanan and G. Tullock, *The Calculus of Consent* (1962; repr. 1965).
[43] Ibid., p. vi.
[44] Ibid., p. vii.

required the acceptance of certain value criteria. Buchanan and Tullock emphasized that their commitment was to the former, claiming that this would make their analysis free of the normative connotations which beset the latter. Thus all that was required was to ascribe centrality of position to the rational individual. Whether the individual based his or her decision on narrowly egoistic or hedonistic grounds, or whether altruism played a prominent role, was not essential for the analysis.[45]

Methodological individualism did, however, entail the rejection of two other conceptions of the state. On the one hand, it necessitated denial of any organic view of the state, such as that posited by German political philosophers. As a corollary, the authors also repudiated any idea of a 'general will', in the sense of a conception of the public interest which was distinctive from the separate interests of the individuals who comprised the community. The 'grail-like' search for the public interest was a quest for the non-existent.[46] On the other hand, conceptions of the state which were based upon the exploitation of a ruled by a ruling class were also dismissed. Marxist conceptions of the state and it would seem, extreme versions of élite theory, were both rejected.[47]

The connection between Bentleyan pluralism and public choice can now be understood. Although Buchanan and Tullock stress methodological individualism as the foundation of their study, they explicitly support Bentley's vision of the political process.[48] This might at first sight seem odd, given that the latter highlights the group basis of politics. Any paradox is, however, apparent rather than real. Buchanan and Tullock explicitly state that the word 'group' could be substituted for the word 'individual' without altering the substance of their analysis. The explanation for this is not hard to find, and resides in the identical thematic assumptions which provide the foundation for the work of Buchanan, Tullock, and Bentley. For Bentley, the individual was a rational maximizer of his own self-interest. Groups were simply the *organizational form* through which this self-interest was made manifest. Each group pursued its own goals, and the public interest was nothing more than the outcome of this pluralist intergroup competition. The same thesis pervaded the work of Buchanan and Tullock. The utility-maximizing individual occupied the political stage. No conception of

45 *The Calculus of Consent*, pp. 3–4, 14.

46 Ibid. 12.

47 Ibid. 12–13.

48 Ibid. 9, 285–286.

the public-interest separate from the results of individual choice, whether expressed by individuals as such or through groups, was attainable.[49]

The thematic connection mentioned above provided the basis from which public choice theorists gave positive support to Bentleyan pluralism. The economic analysis of the public choice theorists, 'scientific' and 'empirical' in its approach, would furnish the hard evidence to sustain Bentley's perception of how the political universe functioned. Thus we find Buchanan and Tullock repeatedly stating that, while most political theorists had failed to perceive the value of economic analysis within the political arena, Bentley and Truman had been on the right track.[50] The job simply required more finely tuned tools. What, then, did the use of these more finely tuned tools reveal? The outline of what is a complex argument may be presented as follows.

First, the authors argue that use of economic criteria will reveal when an individual will choose to undertake action collectively rather than privately.[51] Collective action becomes a means of reducing the external costs which are imposed on an individual through purely private or voluntary action. These 'external costs' have to be balanced against the 'decision-making costs' which an individual will incur as a result of his own participation in an organized activity. The authors describe these two types of cost as the cost of social interdependence. The minimization of these interdependence costs is the primary objective in deciding upon the appropriate method of taking decisions. More specifically, the choice between voluntary action, individual or co-operative, and collective political action will depend upon the relative costs of social interdependence. Collective political action will only be chosen where these costs are lower than if the activity had been privately ordered,[52] whether individually or co-operatively.[53]

Secondly, the choice of whether to proceed by collective political action will be partially dependent upon the costs of decision-making thereby entailed. Requirements of unanimity, special majorities, or simple majority will produce different answers to this calculation.[54] Thus a majority voting rule, as opposed to one requiring unanimity,

[49] *The Calculus of Consent*, pp. 32.
[50] Ibid., e.g. pp. 20 n. 2, 22 n. 39, 32.
[51] Ibid. 43–8.
[52] Ibid. 57–60.
[53] Ibid. 60–2.
[54] Ibid., ch. 6 and pp. 207–8.

might expedite decision-making, but it would increase the likelihood that the outcome of such a vote would itself impose external costs on the individual in the form of a decision which he disliked.[55]

Thirdly, the fact that collective political decisions are taken over a period of time necessarily generates vote-trading or log-rolling. Buchanan and Tullock thus affirm Bentley's assertions.[56] Each individual's vote possesses an economic value for which a market will develop, as in the case of any other commodity. The mutual and reciprocal recognition of the value of votes as between the decision-makers will be conducive to implicit trade, as manifested in log-rolling. Such trade is inevitable, and of value in indirectly allowing individuals to express the strength of their utility preferences.[57] Condemnation of such behaviour simply reflects the belief that voting should be based upon some non-economic ground, or upon a generalized conception of the public interest. Sound economic reasons may, however, exist for restricting the incidence or manner of vote trading.[58]

Finally, the fact that much political pressure and log-rolling is exerted through the medium of pressure groups should come as no surprise. The emergence of such groups can itself be explained in economic terms.[59] As the size of the public sector grew, and as the expansion increasingly took the form of collective decisions which have a differential impact upon separate groups of the population, so further investment aimed at securing these differential gains by political means became more attractive. Buchanan and Tullock do not, however, subscribe to a simple thesis of pluralistic equilibrium as the result of intergroup competition. It is the very prospect of differential benefits flowing from collective activity which attracts the interest group.[60] How to reduce the external costs flowing from such behaviour was one of the important areas for further study.

Buchanan's and Tullock's work was, as stated, one of the

[55] *The Calculus of Consent*, pp. 89–90, 109.

[56] Ibid. 122–4; See also p. 123 n. 4, quoting Bentley with approval.

[57] Ibid. 125–30, 209; see, generally ch. 10.

[58] Ibid. 280. In systems of majority rule possession of the vote can be used to impose external costs on others. This problem is itself much debated in public choice: D. Mueller, *Public Choice* (1979), 50–2.

[59] Buchanan and Tullock, *The Calculus of Consent*, pp. 286–7.

[60] Ibid. 291–2, 294, either by endorsing statutes which give benefits to certain groups but impose the costs on all, or through legislation giving benefits to all, which imposes the cost on a few.

important early studies developing public choice theory.[61] It has been followed by a large volume of technical literature[62] dealing with an extensive array of topics which have traditionally been regarded as the preserve of political science.[63] The potential application of this work has, not surprisingly, been drawn upon by those interested in law and economics.[64] The Bentleyan vision of pluralism has, however, been strongly challenged, and it is to this challenge that we must now turn.

c. *Élitism, Behaviouralism, and Élite Pluralism*

Pluralism had scarcely become a fully articulated political doctrine before critics began to appear. Indeed, as will become apparent, the seeds of one line of criticism were sown almost contemporaneously with the emergence of pluralist thought itself. The relevance of such thought for legal doctrine cannot be properly appreciated without adequate consideration of these rival theories. It is to one of the oldest of these competing doctrines that we turn first, élite theory.

Élite theory has its modern origins in the writings of Mosca, Michels, and Pareto in the early part of this century.[65] The central core of the thesis propounded by what may be termed the classical élite theorists is, in essence, simple. Decisions within any society will always be made by a minority of the population, who will dominate the majority. The explanations for this dominance varied considerably. For Mosca it was the possession of some quality or value which

[61] G. Stigler, 'The Theory of Economic Regulation', 2 *Bell J. of Econ. & Mgnt. Sci.* 3 (1971), was also particularly influential.

[62] Mueller, *Public Choice*, provides a good general introduction to the literature. See also R. E. McCormick and R. D. Tollison, *Politicians, Legislation and the Economy: An Inquiry into the Interest-Group Theory of Government* (1981); I.McLean, *Public Choice: An Introduction* (1987).

[63] G. Tullock, *The Politics of Bureaucracy* (1965); W. A. Niskanen, *Bureaucracy and Representative Government* (1971). See, more generally, A. Downs, *An Economic Theory of Democracy* (1957); M. Olson, *The Logic of Collective Action: Public Goods and the Theory of Groups* (1965). For incisive comment, see B. Barry, *Sociologists, Economics and Democracy* (1970).

[64] R. Posner, 'Economics, Politics and the Reading of Statutes and the Constitution', 49 *U. Chi. L. Rev.* 263 (1982); W. Landes and R. Posner, 'The Independent Judiciary in an Interest-Group Perspective', 18 *J.L.E.* 875 (1975). See also F. H. Easterbrook, 'Foreword: The Court and the Economic System' 98 *Harv. L. Rev.* 4 (1984); J. R. Macey, 'Promoting Public-Regarding Legislation through Statutory Interpretation: An Interest Group Model' 86 *Col. L. Rev.* 223 (1986).

[65] For general discussion, see H. K. Girvetz, *Democracy and Elitism* (1967); G. Parry, *Political Elites* (1969).

was highly regarded by members of that society, coupled with the ability of the élite to organize itself into a closely knit group, thereby allowing it to wield disproportionate power.[66] The cohesiveness and consciousness of the élite were, however, accorded less significance in Mosca's later work, which becomes closer to a vision of élite pluralism.[67] For Michels the inner logic of organisations was of central importance.[68] It was this which provided the foundation for the 'iron law of oligarchy'. The existence of organized society resulted in concentration of power. Michels's succinct formulation, 'who says organization, says oligarchy', is the precise encapsulation of this reasoning. For Pareto the cause of élite power was more complex, but equally inexorable.[69] An oligarchy would always dominate in fact, irrespective of the governmental form. The existence of universal suffrage and representative democracy provided no exception. Popular representation was a fiction, and 'poppycock grinds no flour'.

All three writers emphasized the scientific nature of their enquiry. Truth and moral judgement belonged to another realm of discourse, the existence of oligarchy being 'beyond good and evil'.[70] Such statements should serve as a tocsin bell. The writers protest too much. A recurring theme of political science has been the discovery of the ideological content beneath the descriptive veneer. The élitists' claim to be ideologically neutral has been contested both in terms of their methodology and in their interpretation of the factual data.[71]

Mosca, Michels and Pareto were European. The full impact of élite theory in the United States was only felt when it was adopted by US political scientists. The work of Wright Mills proved to be particularly influential.[72] His central thesis was that, within that particular epoch, a power élite controlled the economic, political, and military domains. The top of the power system in the United States was much more unified, and the bottom more fragmented,

[66] G. Mosca, *The Ruling Class* (1939 edn.), 50, 53.

[67] Parry, *Political Elites*, pp. 40–2.

[68] R. Michels, *Political Parties: A Sociological Study of the Oligarchical Tendencies of Modern Democracy*, trans. E. and C. Paul (1962).

[69] V. Pareto, *The Mind and Society*, trans. A. Livingston (1935).

[70] See, e.g., Michels, *Political Parties*, pp. 50–7, 333–56; Pareto, *The Mind and Society*, p. 6.

[71] Parry, *Political Elites*, pp. 25–6.

[72] C. W. Mills, *The Power Elite* (1956). See also J. Burnham, *The Managerial Revolution* (1942); A. A. Berle, *Power without Property* (1959); T. R. Dye and L. H. Zeigler, *The Irony of Democracy* (7th edn., 1987).

than had been commonly supposed. The pluralist thesis was attacked. There was no natural balance of competing interests which resulted in equilibrium. Inequality in group power undermined this ideal. Moreover the very expression of the vision was itself tendentious, implicitly idealizing the status quo as satisfactory. The élite did not have to justify their power since the very basis of the system was a denial that such power existed. An explicitly conservative ideology was not required. The accumulation of this authority was deemed legitimate, the consequence of a natural balancing within society.[73]

A complex debate has ensued between defenders of the pluralist model, and proponents of élite theory. This debate is still current and has two principal strands. *On the one hand*, there have been empirical studies designed to show who makes the important decisions within a particular area. Are policies in fact made by an élite or do they result from some more pluralistic process of intergroup competition? The work of Floyd Hunter[74] and of Dahl[75] respectively exemplify élitist and pluralistic interpretations of such data. The methodology and conclusions of both studies have been challenged.[76] Later years have witnessed the burgeoning of an increasingly sophisticated series of empirical studies designed to remedy the deficiencies of the earlier works.[77] The results are difficult to summarize, but certain conclusions do emerge. The degree to which communities may be described as élitist or pluralist has been found to vary. However, the overall degree of citizen participation was found to be low, and the sense of being alienated from the community was one important factor which influenced the readiness to play a more active role. Subtle shifts in the meaning of the terms under debate have exacerbated the problem of interpretation. As Presthus states, sociologists have found monopoly and called it élitism, whereas political scientists have found oligopoly but

[73] Mills, *The Power Elite*, pp. 242, 246, 259–61. Wright Mills modified his views in later work. For perceptive comment, see P. Bachrach, *The Theory of Democratic Elitism: A Critique* (1967), 55–9.

[74] F. Hunter, *Community Power Structure* (1958).

[75] R. A. Dahl, *Who Governs?* (1961); *Polyarchy: Participation and Opposition* (197).

[76] e.g. Parry, *Political Elites*, pp. 108–9; E. E. Schattschneider, *The Semi-Sovereign People: A Realist's View of Democracy in America* (1960); P. Bachrach and M. S. Baratz, 'Two Faces of Power', in W. E. Connolly (ed.), *The Bias of Pluralism* (1969), ch. 3.

[77] R. Agger, D. Goldrich, and B. Swanson, *The Rulers and the Ruled* (1964); R. Presthus, *Men at the Top* (1964).

defined it in more honorific terms as pluralism, even though very small numbers participate in group competition.[78]

On the other hand, there have been 'behavioural' studies purporting to demonstrate that citizen participation in political activity is low, that society is perforce governed by the interested and involved élite, and that too much participation would be disruptive and detrimental. Subscribers to this line of argument, which has obvious relevance for participation in administrative decision-making, present it with varying nuances, but the work of Almond and Verba is reasonably representative.[79]

The authors argued that society required a balance between active and inactive citizens.[80] It was wrong to suggest that a democracy would necessarily work better in proportion to the degree of active individual involvement in the governmental process.[81] Political activity was but one part of a citizen's concerns, and this was usually an unimportant part. Most individuals did not possess the knowledge, expertise, or interest to become involved in political affairs. The necessary investment of time to acquire these skills would be irrational in economic terms. Moreover, if individuals did become too enmeshed in such affairs, the business of government would become impossible. The optimum balance was, therefore, one in which the élite carried on the business of government, but were responsive to the demands of the non-élite.[82]

This balance was difficult to attain. The necessities of government required the citizen to hand over power to the elite to enable it to rule. This entailed passivity and deference by the individual. Yet the élite must remain responsive to the non-élite, since this was an integral element of a democratic society.[83] Reality and perception had to co-exist in complex harmony for this balance to be struck. The citizen had to believe that he could influence events if he so chose, provided that he did not attempt to exercise this power with any force or frequency.[84] The governing élite had to believe that this power was capable of being exercised if they were to remain responsive, even if in most instances they could bet short odds on apathy.[85]

[78] *Men at the Top*, pp. 430–1. See also Parry, *Political Elites*, ch. 5.
[79] G. A. Almond and S. Verba, *The Civic Culture* (1965).
[80] Ibid., ch. 13.
[81] Ibid. 338–9.
[82] Ibid. 340, 341.
[83] Ibid. 343.
[84] Ibid. 346.
[85] Ibid. 352.

This ghostly ritual between reality and perception required yet more manipulation if it was to remain stable. Fine tuning was of the essence. The citizen must maintain some emotional involvement in the overall political process. Loyalty devoid of any commitment was a hollow vessel. Too intense an emotional attachment was equally dangerous. It could upset the balance between citizen activity and passivity; it could foster 'mass, messianic movements that lead to democratic instability'.[86] A similar balance had to be maintained between consensus and cleavage in order for democracy to operate. Democratic politics assumed differences of view, and, in that sense, cleavage. This had, however, to be kept within bounds. An overarching consensus had to exist for the system to continue, and some important relationships had to be considered outside the political arena.[87]

The behavioural thesis has, not surprisingly, been challenged both directly and indirectly. The more *direct* critique has concentrated upon revealing the normative assumptions underlying the collation and interpretation of the 'facts'. What one writer has termed an ideology of empirical conservatism[88] permeates the arguments adumbrated above. The assumption behind the behavioural thesis is that Anglo-American political arrangements are satisfactory, and that other political systems should be judged by how closely they conform to this ideal type. Balance in all things assumes centrality. Caution is the byword. Intemperate behaviour is frowned upon. An excess of zeal is treated like a *faux pas* in a Victorian drawing-room. It is not quite the done thing. The winds of change would barely susurrate in such a political system. The dreams of incumbent élites would be fulfilled. They would continue to set the boundaries of the political agenda, and control the range of the 'realizable' options. Should any among the non-élite manage to penetrate this barrier, and to question the fundamentals on which the realizable options are founded, the élite can demand that they speak in more hushed tones. The etiquette of the library combines with the moderation and formality of the Victorian drawing-room. Politics becomes

86 G. A. Almond and S. Verba, *The Civic Culture* (1965). 354–5.

87 Ibid. 357–9. See also B. Berelson *et al.*, *Voting* (1954); S. Lipset, *Political Man* (1960); L. W. Milbrath, *Political Participation: How and Why do People get Involved in Politics?* (1965).

88 D. Kavanagh, 'Political Behaviour and Political Participation', in G. Parry (ed.), *Participation in Politics* (1971), 117.

a ritualized manœuvre over carefully defined, safe territory.[89]

The *indirect* challenge to the behavioural thesis concentrates on the assumptions concerning democracy which underlie the behavioural argument. A Schumpeterian vision of democracy pervades the work of the writers considered above. Schumpeter rejected what he alleged to be the traditional eighteenth century meaning of democracy.[90] He defined this as: the institutional arrangement for arriving at political decisions, which realizes the common good by making the people itself decide issues through the election of individuals who are to carry out its will. Schumpeter dismissed this conception of democracy as unworkable.[91] His own now famous definition of democracy was: the institutional arrangement for arriving at political decisions in which individuals acquire the power to decide by means of a competitive struggle for the people's vote.[92]

Schumpeter's analysis provided the broad frame of legitimacy within which élite theorists and behaviouralists reasoned. It was a 'top down' conception of democracy. The people chose, but the government then governed. Political leaders devised the package to be offered to the electorate. It was they who breathed life into the, as yet, latent demands of particular groups. The electoral will was manufactured in ways analogous to that of a commercial product. Political action was not the business of the ordinary people. Such a conception of democracy provided the appropriate base for the analysis of élite theorists and the behaviouralists. Not only could they argue that people did not engage in political activity and that encouraging such behaviour could produce deleterious consequences. They could also contend that political participation of this type was not an integral element of democracy. It should, therefore, come as no surprise that the Schumpeterian picture of democracy forms the background for the work of these writers.[93] Schumpeter's view has,

[89] Critics have also directly challenged the ascription of cause and effect presented by the behavioural school; e.g. do people abjure from participation because of disinterest or because they feel helpless? See Kavanagh, 'Political Behaviour'. See also C. Pateman, *Participation and Democratic Theory* (1970); Bachrach, *The Theory of Democratic Elitism*.

[90] J. Schumpeter, *Capitalism, Socialism and Democracy* (1942).

[91] He argued, *inter alia*, that the people could never agree on the common good in sufficiently precise terms to provide answers to particular problems.

[92] *Capitalism, Socialism, and Democracy*, p. 269.

[93] See, e.g., Lipset, *Political Man*, p. 45; Milbrath, *Political Participation*, pp. 144–5, 149; Almond and Verba, *The Civic Culture*, p. 342. See also the views of G. Sartori, *Democratic Theory* (1942), 125–27; W. Kornhauser, *The Politics of Mass Society* (1960), 230, 235–6.

as we shall see, been challenged both in its own terms, and for its misinterpretation of 'classical' democratic theory.[94]

The starkness of the original debate between pluralists and élitists has been ameliorated by modifications in the positions of protagonists on both sides. This is not to suggest that the divide has disappeared. It is, however, to suggest that increasing shades of grey now characterize a picture which was once painted in more distinctive tones. Truman has significantly modified his previous vision of pluralist society.[95]

Dahl's later work does not present as stark a contrast with his own earlier writing as is apparent in the case of Truman. Nor has it developed along the same thematic lines as Truman. It has, however, altered significantly in its emphasis. As we have already seen, Dahl's earlier studies, while recognizing imperfections in the US system, professed a quiet satisfaction with the pluralist society which he analysed. Dahl never believed in some simple, self-executing Bentleyan vision of pluralism. None the less there is still the overriding faith in the opportunity for political action being available to all.[96]

A more cautionary, and less sanguine, note emerges in Dahl's recent work. Independent organizations are still regarded as desirable to prevent domination, to create mutual control, and to facilitate the running of large-scale democracy.[97] Élite theorists are still criticized for underestimating the strength of tendencies towards political autonomy within the organizational universe.[98] However, while Dahl continues to deny a conspiratorial, cohesive élite thesis, he is fully aware of the perils of élite domination within a particular organization. Indeed he recognizes the force of Michels's point that to foster independence between organizations can generate élite control within a particular institution.[99] Equally important is Dahl's recognition of the defects of pluralist democracy. The optimism of the earlier work is replaced by a more troubled tone.[100] Independent organizations can stabilize political inequalities, deform the civic consciousness, distort the public agenda, and alienate or appropriate final control over public functions. Gone is any hint that pluralism necessarily entails the absence of a public interest

94 See below, ch. 3 sec. 2d.

95 D. B. Truman, 'The American System in Crisis', *Pol. Sc. Quart.* 481–97 (Dec. 1959). For critical comment, see Bachrach, *The Theory of Democratic Elitism*, pp. 52–4.

96 R. A. Dahl and C. E. Lindblom, *Politics, Economics and Welfare* (1953).

97 *Dilemmas of Pluralist Democracy*, pp. 31–40.

98 Ibid. 33.

99 Ibid. 36.

100 Ibid 40–54.

divorced from that of particular interest groups. Gone is the notion that pluralism can realistically be viewed solely in process terms.

Notwithstanding Dahl's continued critique of the classical élite theorists, his own reformulated position comes close to one of élite pluralism. Competing groups, each dominated by a small élite, command the political arena. At times he goes even further. While he denies the inevitability of cohesive élite control, he recognizes that contingent political conditions can engender something approximating to this. Thus, in democratic countries where there are relatively low barriers to organizational autonomy, such organizations will tend to exist around the most salient cleavages in society. This organizational pattern can persist over time, and the institutions will become habituated to a certain type of accommodation *inter se.*[101] Thereafter, none will seriously seek to destroy the other.

> Although such a system is sometimes said to be in equilibrium, it would be more accurate to say that among the major organized interests there is mutual accommodation or detente. When this happens, organized pluralism is a stabilizing force that is highly conservative in the face of demands for innovative structural change. Each of the major organized forces in a country prevents the others from making changes that might seriously damage its perceived interests. As a consequence, structural reforms that would significantly and rapidly redistribute control, status, income, wealth and other resources are impossible to achieve—unless, ironically, they are made at the expense of the unorganized. In this way, a powerful social force that in authoritarian countries carriers with it the unmistakable odor of revolution can in democratic countries strongly reinforce the status quo.[102]

The impetus towards a narrowing of the gap between élite theorists and pluralists is not explicable solely in terms of individual figures altering their views. Research studies have indubitably had an impact. While controversy continues to rage over methodology, and over interpretation, the general tenor of the more recent research has added force to the softening of polarized positions. Leaving aside the normative implications to be drawn from this work, the thrust of the empirical findings has been to narrow the focus of debate. Many groups will be controlled by the active, interested few. In that sense society may be said to be élitist, or relatively élitist. The key issue then becomes one of deciding

[101] *Dilemmas of Pluralist Democracy*, p. 42. [102] Ibid. 43.

whether to depict society in terms of élite pluralism or élitism. The former postulates conflict and competition between the élites who dominate the groups. The latter assumes a greater degree of cohesiveness and consciousness among the leaders. Debate will doubtless continue as to which of these bears a closer relationship to reality.

d. The Critique of Pluralism and Élite Pluralism

Whichever of these labels is accepted will not radically affect the nature of the more recent attack upon pluralism. Three themes are predominant within this literature. First, there is a challenge to the premises on which traditional pluralism is based. Inequality of group power and the 'biased' nature of political decisions are stressed. Secondly, the reformulation of pluralism into élite pluralism is attacked. The Schumpeterian democratic foundations of élite pluralism are questioned. Thirdly, a democratic vision for the future is suggested. Some espouse a form of participatory democracy. Others see the future in terms of the reinvigoration of democratic society from the 'top', by strengthening and building upon the powers of the centre.

These themes are evident, albeit in varying degrees, in the work of a number of writers. Bachrach is critical of élitism.[103] He contrasts élite theory with democratic theory. The latter entails both results and process. The public interest comes to be measured not just by the soundness of the decisions which are reached, but also by the degree of public participation accorded in reaching them. Élitists, or those who talk of democratic élitism, conceive of democracy solely as a method for choosing those who are to govern. This Schumpeterian vision excludes any consideration of the inherent value of participation as a means of enhancing the development of the individual.[104] It also presumes a narrow definition of 'political' by concentrating upon the choice of government. Arguments for the expansion of democracy in the industrial sphere are indirectly pre-empted by definitional fiat. Elite power within non-governmental institutions, while acknowledged, is deemed to be an exercise of private authority.[105] A willingness to conceive of democracy in participatory,

[103] *The Theory of Democratic Elitism,* pp. 3, 5.

[104] Ibid. 94–5.

[105] Ibid. 97, 102, where Bachrach points out the inconsistencies in the definition of the political arena which characterize the thought of élite theorists.

developmental terms, and to adopt a broader view of the political arena, is required.

The conclusions reached by Bottomore are similar, although the reasoning differs. [106] He criticizes the views of the classical élite theorists, concerning the emergence, development, and change of the dominant class.[107] Bottomore is also critical of claims that the resultant élite comprise a cohesive, conscious group. Competition between élites represents a more accurate picture of society.[108] This empirical hypothesis is then clothed with legitimacy by market-orientated conceptions of democracy, such as those of Schumpeter or Downs, which depict democracy in economic terms. Competition for the peoples' vote, and the choice of policies which will maximize 'political profit', validate élite pluralism.[109]

Bottomore contests the assumptions concerning democracy provided by Schumpeter, Downs, and others.[110] Nineteenth-century democratic theorists would not have conceived of inter-party competition as the ultimate point of democratic progress. Democracy was envisioned in more dynamic terms, as a movement towards 'an ideal condition of society in which men would be fully self-governing', even though this might never be attained in reality. The static concept of democracy, encapsulated in the periodic choice of government, was a later development. The emergence of one-party states, whether of a fascist or communist form, lent credence to this narrow, static vision. Bottomore, like Bachrach, also stresses the interconnection between developmental democracy within government, and participation in other decision-making spheres.[111]

The misconstruction of 'classical' democratic theory is also one of the predominant themes in Pateman's work.[112] Her argument is that much modern democratic theory is premised upon a mythical conception of classical democracy.[113] Schumpeter's definition was, as we have seen, derived from his critique of 'classical democracy'. Pateman's argument is that Schumpeter's interpretation of 'classical democracy' was defective. Schumpeter never 'named names'; he never explicitly revealed who was supposed to be the standard-bearer of this outdated theory. Assuming that he had Rousseau, J. S. Mill,

[106] T. Bottomore, *Elites and Society* (1964).
[107] Ibid., ch. 3.
[108] Ibid. 84.
[109] Ibid. 106–7.
[110] Ibid. 110.
[111] Ibid. 115.
[112] *Participation and Democratic Theory*. See also G. Duncan and S. Lukes, 'The New Democracy', *Political Studies*, 11 (1963), 156–77.
[113] Pateman, *Participation and Democratic Theory*, p. 17.

James Mill, and Bentham in mind, Pateman has little difficulty in demonstrating that these theorists cannot possibly be treated as a unity. Their perception of, for example, the objectives of democracy, and the role of participation therein, differ radically, particularly as between the first and last two members of the above quartet. Equally important is the conclusion that none of these theorists, treated individually, could realistically fit the paradigm of classical democracy as defined by Schumpeter.[114] By artificially fusing and misinterpreting the views of the earlier theorists, Schumpeter provided support for his own, much narrower, definition, which was then adopted by later writers. This step was crucial in circumscribing the focus of debate.[115] No longer was it necessary to consider whether the people influenced actual decisions or participated in the political process. This was not the essence of democracy. The chosen leaders framed the actual policies, and the peoples' participatory role was exhausted by the act of voting. Any interrelationship between political and industrial democracy was foreclosed.

Other writers share in some of the criticisms of pluralism advanced above, but prefer solutions aimed at reinvigorating the 'top', rather than fostering participation from the 'bottom'. Kariel[116] focuses upon the dilemma presented by a constitutional system which works towards the fragmentation of power, while the technological system fosters its consolidation.[117] Corporate oligarchies control the industrial sphere, faced by equally oligarchic groupings which dominate the labour market.[118] A fragmented government, faced with an economic system which is decreasingly pluralist, will often simply approve bargains which are struck by unrepresentative private interests.[119] The main impetus behind pluralism, a desire to uphold the dignity of the individual, is undermined by an economic and political system which operates against individualism.[120] Dispersal of power no longer has the talismanic qualities which it was once thought to possess. By way of contrast to the writers discussed above, the prospect for the future

[114] Ibid. 17–21, ch. 2.

[115] See also W. E. Connolly, 'The Challenge to Pluralist Theory', in W. E. Connolly (ed.), *The Bias of Pluralism* (1969), ch. 1; D. Miller, 'The Competitive Model of Democracy', in G. Duncan (ed.), *Democratic Theory and Practice* (1983), ch. 9.

[116] H. Kariel, *The Decline of American Pluralism* (1961).

[117] Ibid. 3.

[118] Ibid. 25, 48, 67.

[119] Ibid. 88–90.

[120] Ibid. 179.

was to build upon the power of central government. Only in this way could individual rights be adequately protected. The state must possess the power to 'frustrate those private arrangements which, masquerading as healthy pluralism, tend to stratify and congeal society, to freeze markets, and to control individuals'.[121]

Lowi has advanced an equally strident attack upon pluralist ideology.[122] He criticizes pluralism for the way in which it strips government of legitimacy and renders planning skeletal; for its creation of vested privilege and its inherently conservative tendencies. Legitimacy is jeopardized by the pluralist insistence on the unity of government and society. The pluralist belief in the natural harmony of group competition, and the consequential automatic political society, could not tolerate the separateness of government.[123] As government came to be viewed as nothing more than another set of competing interest groups, so its legitimacy and the coercive power which it wielded was placed in question. Administration and planning are rendered more difficult by the pluralist insistence on incrementalism. The relatively minor alterations in policy allowed by incremental decision-making narrow the range of any change around some pre-existing equilibrium which is presupposed to be good or just.[124] More critical movements in policy which are imposed from the 'top', as opposed to bargained for from the 'bottom', are regarded as both unjustified and unsatisfactory. New privileged groups are created. Organizations do not compete equally in the political market-place. Large interest groups which operate at the level of national politics exercise a disproportionate amount of power.[125] This is augmented by the oligarchic tendency of power concentration within the organizations themselves, creating a situation in which the few wield inordinate amounts of influence. Not surprisingly the resultant status quo is one which is highly conservative and resistant to change.[126] Alliances form both between groups, and between groups and organs of government. Rules of the game emerge which formalize both political competition and political alliance. New radical developments which threaten to upset the orderliness of these arrangements are strongly opposed.

[121] *The Decline of American Pluralism*. p. 271; see also pp. 226, 275, 277.

[122] T. J. Lowi, *The End of Liberalism: Ideology, Policy and the Crisis of Public Authority* (1969).

[123] Ibid. 48.

[124] Ibid. 50–1.

[125] Ibid. 88, 294–5.

[126] Ibid. 90.

The pluralist insistence on bargain favours the *ad hoc* solution and the consequential exercise of administrative discretion. Justice within such a discretionary system becomes impossible.[127]

We shall have occasion to consider Lowi's suggestions[128] at a later stage.[129] It is, however, now time to consider the nature of a pluralist conception of constitutional law in the light of the preceding discussion. What conclusions will be drawn for both the shape and content of constitutional law if one believes that a pluralist conception of democracy should be its organizing rationale?

[127] *The End of Liberalism*, pp 289–91.

[128] Ibid. 297–8, 299–303.

[129] See below, ch. 4 sec. 7a, See also, T. J. Lowi, *The End of Liberalism: The Second Republic of the United States* (2nd edn., 1979). The most significant alteration is the addition of ch. 10, in which Lowi depicts the United States as being in a state of permanent receivership.

4

4. PLURALIST DEMOCRACY, GROUPS, AND PROCESS: USA (II)

It is clear that the choice of a particular conception of democracy will itself reflect certain normative judgements on the part of the observer.[1] There will be those who, for example, argue vigorously for a form of republicanism and for a species of participatory democracy. This theme will be considered more fully at a later stage.[2] What is of more immediate concern is that there are significant differences of opinion even *within* pluralism. The choice between these competing visions will itself reflect important value judgements, and the preferred option will have significant repercussions for the shape and content of constitutional review. Three such visions can be delineated.

1. MODEL ONE: THE PUBLIC-CHOICE MODEL

a. A Summary

The traditional pluralist vision is that derived from Bentley, Truman, and, more recently, from the public-choice theorists. This can be summarized 'thematically' in the following way. First, emphasis is placed upon the political market, which functions similarly to the ordinary economic market. Legislation is a product which will be 'produced' by the legislature in response to demand from the 'consumers', who vote and who exercise influence on the legislature. *Homo economicus* who inhabits the ordinary market-place also inhabits the political arena and behaves in much the same way, operating so as to maximize his own individual preferences.[3] Groups emerge because this is often the most efficient organizational form in which gains can be won from the legislature. Group interaction thus characterizes political society, and entry and exit from the political

[1] R. Dworkin, 'The Forum of Principle', 56 *N.Y.U.L. Rev.* 469, 502 (1981).
[2] See below, chs. 10, 11.
[3] e.g. G. Brennan and J. M. Buchanan, *The Reason of Rules* (1985), ch. 4.

market are relatively easy. There is no conception of the public interest which is truly separate from the preferences of individuals within society. Much (some would say all) intervention by the state on distributive grounds is itself no more and no less than a reflection of the current power alignments between groups within society. These groups will seek to maximize their own position. Either they can do so by, for example, producing their goods more efficiently and hence reaping greater profits; or they can attain the same financial goal by winning special treatment from the legislature in the form of subsidies, preferential tax rates, etc.

Secondly, the role of the state within this pluralist vision should be narrowly confined for two related reasons. On the one hand, it is argued that the ordinary 'private market' is often 'better' at reaching the optimally efficient solution than is the political market. Even when there is some species of ordinary market failure, the problem may well be exacerbated rather than cured by governmental regulatory intervention. Moreover, much legislative intervention is regarded as a 'front' to mask wealth-transfer and rent-seeking behaviour by particular interest groups. On the other hand, the role of the state should be limited because governmental intervention via redistributive policies may well be 'illegitimate'. Such legislative action can infringe individual entitlements.[4]

b. *Constitutional Implications of the First Model*

The present model has two principal implications for constitutional law. First, it affects the way in which statutes are constitutionally reviewed by the courts. The precise nature of this effect is, however, disputed because of a tension within the theory itself. On the one hand, it has been argued that the present model is indicative of the fallacy of invalidating legislation on the ground that it is not rationally related to a proper legislative purpose. Interest groups can and should be able to influence the legislative outcome, and it cannot therefore be correct to invalidate legislation just because it was procured by such a group.[5] This would, however, be the effect of

[4] e.g. ibid., chs. 6–8; J. M. Buchanan, *Liberty, Market and State: Political Economy in the 1980s* (1986), chs. 12, 13, 15, 22, 23; J. M. Buchanan, *The Limits of Liberty: Between Anarchy and Leviathan* (1975). See below, ch. 4 sec. 1c, for further discussion of this point.

[5] e.g. R. Posner, 'Economics, Politics and the Reading of Statutes and the Constitution', 49 *U. Chi. L. Rev.* 263 (1982).

rationality review, since 'legislation passed on behalf of an interest group typically will flunk any test of rationality other than pure self-interest'.[6] The courts should in other words recognize that much legislation is the successful product of interest-group pressure on the legislature; such legislation should not be invalidated on the mistaken assumption that this is an abnormal or unnatural event. The independence of the judiciary itself has been explained by arguing that this fosters the durability of interest-group deals by endowing such deals with greater durability. A court which was dependent upon the current legislature might be inclined to overturn a bargain reached by interest groups within a prior legislative period, and hence to reduce the value of such deals.[7]

On the other hand, there is a more cautionary note in the literature which seeks to deter the making of legislation, or to increase the cost of doing so. Interest-group pressure by those who seek to maximize their own preferences is accepted as 'typical' legislative action. However, such legislation may amount to an unwarranted and inefficient wealth-transferring exercise. The costs of engaging in legislative activity should, therefore, be increased to reduce its incidence. Features of constitutional design such as the separation of powers are said to be useful devices towards this end.[8]

The second major implication of the public-choice pluralist model for constitutional law has a different focus. The objective of limiting the scope of legislative action has been touched upon above. An important facet of this argument is that certain economic distributive decisions should be taken away from the ordinary processes of majoritarian democracy. They should be constitutionalized.

> The general conclusion to be derived from this analysis is that majority rule is at best a highly imperfect means of pursuing distributive justice. Majority rule either generates cycles (that is, is basically distributionally indeterminate) or, when appropriately restricted, generates a specific pattern of transfers that is perversely responsive to normatively relevant changes (say, to changes in the income of the poorest).

[6] 'Economics, Politics and the Reading of Statutes', p. 285. Cf. F. I. Michelman, 'Politics and Values or What's Really Wrong with Rationality Review?', 13 *Creighton L. Rev.* 487, 503–6 (1979).

[7] W. Landes and R. Posner, 'The Independent Judiciary in an Interest-Group Perspective', 18 *J.L.E.* 875, 877–9 (1975).

[8] e.g. J. R. Macey, 'Promoting Public-Regarding Legislation through Statutory Interpretation: An Interest Group Model', 86 *Col. L. Rev.* 223 (1986), and 'Transaction Costs and the Normative Elements of the Public Choice Model: An Application to Constitutional Theory', 74 *Virg. L. Rev.* 471 (1988).

All this suggests the possibility of lifting the determination of the redistributive or transfer budget out of the jurisdiction of in-period majoritarian politics and making it a matter of explicit constitutional compact.[9]

The desire to place a constitutional limit upon distributive transfers is an increasingly prominent feature in the public-choice literature.[10] The basis of this claim is best discussed within the critical evaluation which follows.

c. *The Public-Choice Model: A Critique*

It is evident from the preceding analysis that the public-choice model of pluralist society has both descriptive and normative elements. Critical evaluation of this model can best proceed by considering these aspects separately, although some overlap between the two may be inevitable.

The *descriptive validity* of the public-choice model is itself dependent upon the 'correctness' of a number of differing, albeit connected, claims. The individual is said to behave in the same way in the political and the economic market; the behaviour which characterizes both spheres is that the individual seeks to maximize his personal preferences; players in political and economic markets are therefore seeking the same profit-maximizing goals; and private markets on the whole are the more 'disciplined forum' for ensuring efficiency, thereby avoiding the wasteful rent-seeking behaviour which marks out much of the produce from political markets. The correctness of these descriptive presumptions is far from self-evident. Space precludes a thorough discussion of this issue, but closer analysis of two of the previous descriptive propositions reveals their contentious nature.

The assumption that the individual behaves in the political arena in a similar manner to the way in which he behaves in the market-place is not descriptively self-evident. This is normally asserted rather than demonstrated in any convincing fashion. Even if the assumption is accepted, this still leaves open the issue of how market-place behaviour itself should be viewed. Differing formulations are apparent. At one extreme is the view that individuals and

[9] Brennan and Buchanan, *The Reason of Rules*, p. 132; see also pp. 127–31, 134–50.

[10] e.g. ibid; Buchanan, *Liberty, Market and State*, chs. 15, 16, 23, 24; Buchanan, *Freedom in Constitutional Contract* (1978).

elected officials seek to maximize a fairly specific wealth function. At the other extreme is the 'non-falsifiable' view, which seeks to incorporate all ideological and other variables within an individual's utility function. Behaviour and motivation are flattened and reduced to an 'economic calculus', which often amounts to little more than the tautological observation that people who understand the consequences of their actions 'will do things that make them as well off as they can possibly be'.[11]

The connected claims that much legislation is directed at rent-seeking, and that the consequential regulatory regime will often not produce any general benefit to the public are also problematic. The essential idea behind this argument is relatively simple. Economic rent is the return earned by a factor of production in excess of marginal production costs.[12] One of the paradigms of a rent-seeking interest group would be a set of producers who would like to form a cartel, but who do not trust each other or who cannot police the operation. The group then moves to the political market-place to persuade government to grant it some monopolistic status, thereby achieving through legislation what it could not do privately. Consumer surplus is transferred to the group of producers. Public-choice theorists accept that not all legislation can be characterized in this fashion. They do none the less argue that much regulatory activity is either ineffective, or is a front for rent-seeking activity which benefits a particular group in the above manner. It is, however, only through detailed analysis of particular regulatory regimes that one can determine whether these claims are substantiated, and the conclusions which have been drawn by public-choice theorists have been contested by others.[13]

The normative validity of the public-choice model requires separate treatment. In order to assess the normative argument its essential elements must be presented more fully than hitherto. First, the basis

[11] M. Kelman, 'On Democracy-Bashing: A Skeptical Look at the Theoretical and "Empirical" Practice of the Public Choice Movement', 74 *Virg. L. Rev.* 199, 206, 217 (1988).

[12] A factor of production will need to earn a certain amount in its present use in order to prevent it from being transferred to another use. These sums are often termed transfer earnings, and economic rent is the excess which that factor actually earns over the former amount. In essence the argument about rent-seeking is that interest groups will attempt to use legislation to gain extra returns on factors of production which they would not otherwise be able to earn under market conditions.

[13] e.g. Kelman, 'On Democracy-Bashing'.

of the normative position is described as contractarian.[14] Just conduct consists of behaviour that does not violate rules 'to which one has given prior consent',[15] and it is this consensus which performs the basic normative function. A rule is fair if the players agree to it; players do not agree to the rule because it is fair.[16] This contractarian position is viewed as non-consequentialist and deontological. Evaluation is directed towards rules or processes rather than to any end state or result.[17]

Secondly, it is clear that the nature of the voluntary consensus is therefore of central importance. Ordinary market exchanges are perceived as voluntary exchanges set against an initial distribution of endowments; and politics are viewed as a 'complex many-person system of exchanges or contracts'.[18] However, as public-choice theorists readily concede, there must be some prior assignment of 'who has what rights to do what with what, when and to whom' before any normative decision can be reached as to the justice of the final outcome.[19] Two elements are crucial in determining the nature of the voluntary consensus. On the one hand, the voluntary nature of an agreement is not vitiated by inequality in the bargaining strengths of the parties, or their relative income position. Only duress narrowly defined will suffice.[20] On the other hand, a broad notion of desert serves to legitimate an individual's entitlement to goods obtained in the political or economic market-place. An individual's distributive share in the societal sum of available goods will be determined by choice, luck, effort, and birth. Differential holdings which result from the first three of these are regarded as perfectly acceptable; there is 'no legitimate argument for regarding such differentials as being unfair or unjust'.[21] Differences which result from birth are prima facie treated as unjust. They do warrant state action to redress such inequalities through tax transfers, publicly financed education, and the like.[22] However, such distributive exercises based upon contingent differences in birth appear to be narrowly confined. Inheritance of money from a rich parent does justify state intervention.[23] Other contingent differences which flow

[14] e.g. Brennan and Buchanan, *The Reason of Rules*, p. 19. See also the material above, n. 4.

[15] Ibid. 97–8.

[16] Buchanan, *Liberty, Market and State*, p. 126.

[17] Brennan and Buchanan, *The Reason of Rules*, p. 45.

[18] Ibid. 24–5.

[19] Ibid. 26.

[20] Ibid. 102.

[21] Buchanan, *Libery, Market and State*, pp. 128–9.

[22] Ibid. 129, 130, 132–5.

[23] Ibid. 133.

from birth are treated distinctively. Thus the distribution of natural capacities and talents is characterized as a matter of 'luck in the draw of history', which does not require distributive redress.[24] Only a limited amount of state action to alter the results reached voluntarily within the political or economic market is, therefore, justified.

Thirdly, even where state action is regarded as justified, public-choice theorists evince a strong preference for constitutionalizing any such transfers. If the decisions on handicapping and transfers are left to be determined through unconstrained majoritarian politics then decisions will be reached on shorter time horizons than for comparable behaviour within private markets. These decisions may lead to 'traps', in the sense that they produce results desired by no person or group in the community.[25]

Three comments can be made on the preceding analysis. The first is *methodological*. Public-choice theorists stress the distinctive nature of their contractarian vision. This is founded upon methodological individualism; all sources of value, however divergent, merit consideration, because they are values held by individuals.[26] It is the consensus reached between individuals on certain rules which provides the normative foundation for the distribution of goods within society. The non-contractarian position is characterized as one in which some conception of the public good is postulated, and this is presumed to have an external existence 'outside the values of the person who is expressing himself through his choice behaviour'.[27] The *objective* and *external* nature of the good being sought is contrasted with the *subjective* nature of the ends *internally* conceived which are said to characterize the contractarian vision.[28]

The distinction between deontological and teleological theories is well known,[29] but the way in which this distinction is employed by public-choice theorists distorts the mode of analysis which charac-

[24] Buchanan, *Liberty, Market and State*, pp. 141, 151. The treatment of differences which flow from birth is not always clear. On some occasions, birth is taken to cover inheritance, capacities, talents, etc. On others, capacities and talents are treated in the manner discussed in the text.

[25] Brennan and Buchanan, *The Reason of Rules*, pp. 82, 96; Buchanan, *Liberty, Market and State*, pp. 132–3.

[26] e.g. J. M. Buchanan and G. Tullock, *The Calculus of Consent* (1962; repr. 1965), 3–4, 12, 13; Brennan and Buchanan, *The Reason of Rules*, p. 21; Buchanan, *Liberty, Market and State*, pp. 249–50.

[27] Brennan and Buchanan, *The Reason of Rules*, p. 37.

[28] Ibid. 37–45.

[29] For more extensive discussion, see below, ch. 8.

terizes the former type of theory by over-simplifying it. The objective is to derive a framework of rules which forms the basic structure of society, and to demonstrate that individuals would agree to the rules thus delineated.[30] In order to prevent individuals from structuring the rules so as to benefit those who have the same attributes as themselves, some device such as a Rawlsian veil of ignorance is employed which hides knowledge of these attributes from those who are deciding upon the rules for the basic structure. Public-choice theorists tend to employ a related idea which they term the veil of uncertainty.[31] The nature of the rules which would be chosen will be considered below. However, the process of choice which takes place at this abstract level is only imperfectly described as 'subjective' and 'internal'. The representative individuals who engage in this choice process are attempting to find rules on which agreement would be reached. It could be argued that any input into this decision-making process is subjective and internal, but this simply uses those terms in a non-falsifiable and misleading way. If, for example, those deciding upon the rules agree that liberty of conscience should be constitutionally protected, they are not doing so because the individuals necessarily subjectively and internally value such a liberty, in the same way that an individual may, with the veil of ignorance or uncertainty lifted, subjectively and internally value ice cream or baseball. In order to substantiate the inclusion of such a liberty within the most basic rules, then recourse will have to be made to reasoning which is external to the preferences of any particular individual. The very existence of the veil of ignorance, or even the veil of uncertainty, serves to ensure that, when deciding on the most basic rules for society, the rules which are chosen are not dependent on any particular group's subjective vision. At this abstract level the distinction between the subjective and objective basis of the values becomes difficult to maintain. The reasoning remains ostensibly subjective, but only in that it is in some sense based upon assumptions as to what people generally value, and what therefore they would agree upon.[32] Even subjectivity at this general level is difficult to sustain. Thus some of the criticism of Rawls's conception

[30] The nature of this process is considered more fully below, ch. 8.

[31] See Brennan and Buchanan, *The Reason of Rules*, pp. 28–31, 139.

[32] In fact the reasoning is far more complex than might be suggested by this sentence. For an examination of this within the Rawlsian model, see below, ch. 8 sec. 2.

of justice has been to argue either that his depiction of what people generally value is inaccurate, or that it is imbued with a hidden, objective sense of what is valuable, which is contestable.[33]

The second comment relates to the *behaviour* of those who operate the system, particularly the legislators themselves. Let us imagine that certain rules have been agreed upon to regulate the distribution of goods within society; let us imagine also that these rules include, *inter alia*, some element of economic redistribution. The legislature will, therefore, have to devise policies to attain these goals. The enactment of such legislation may be regarded as an example of what Rawls terms imperfect procedural justice: the desired outcome is identified, but there may be no certain way in which this can be attained.[34] Thus the objective would be to devise policies to achieve redistributive aims which are contained in the basic structural rules of the system, but there may be no certainty that this objective will always be attained in fact, because people may well disagree as to the best way to reach this goal. It is, however, clear that the legislators have an obligation to attempt to effectuate the desired objective.[35] Such an obligation is not consistent in *normative* terms with a vision of politics which seeks to legitimate legislation on the basis of intergroup bargain *per se*. If the basis of the system is abiding by rules to which one has given prior consent, then more abstract agreed rules govern the behaviour of players within the system. People have agreed to a basic structure which contains some element of redistribution; they do not, therefore, countenance legislative behaviour pursuant to this basic structure which seeks to legitimate distribution on a narrow, group exchange. As Rawls states, having emphasized that legislation is an instance of imperfect procedural justice: 'A just constitution must rely to some extent on citizens and legislators adopting a wider view and exercising good judgement in applying the principles of justice. There seems to be no way of allowing them to take a narrow or group interested stand point and then regulating the process so that it leads to a just outcome.'[36]

The third comment relates to the *content* of the rules which would be voluntarily agreed upon. There are two issues to be considered.

[33] See below, ch. 8 sec. 2c.
[34] J. Rawls, *A Theory of Justice* (Oxford, 1973), 85–6.
[35] Ibid. 342–50.
[36] Ibid. 360; See also pp. 197, 493.

On the one hand, the place of traditional civil liberties within any such scheme is not entirely clear. The main thrust of the public-choice normative argument is to provide a foundation for constitutionally limiting the extent to which the state should be allowed to intervene in the wealth-distributive process. It is unclear whether such theorists would constitutionally protect civil liberties, and if so why; and it is also unclear whether they would assign such liberties a Rawlsian-style lexical priority and prevent them from being infringed by pursuit of policies designed to ensure greater economic equality.[37] The types of arguments which a contractarian would advance to justify the constitutional protection of civil liberties within the basic structure are complex, as will be seen later.[38] It is not at all readily apparent that such arguments would be accepted by contractarians of the public-choice school. This is particularly so, given their reluctance to accept any reasoning which seeks to derive such rights, from an 'external and objective perspective', and given their belief in politics as an exchange process.[39] Some minimal but important constitutional protections could be envisioned in order to ensure that the current majority does not, for example, abolish the electoral process in order to establish itself in power permanently. This would preclude politics as an exchange process from operating, in the sense that changing preferences could no longer meaningfully be registered. It is, however, more difficult to see why other traditional civil liberties should be given the same constitutional protection or priority.

On the other hand, the reasons which are given to justify the content of the rules which would be agreed upon are contentious. This is of crucial importance to the normative public-choice argument. The force of the normative argument for constitutional limitation upon the state's ability to engage in a wealth-distributive process is derived, in part at least, from the presupposition that such activity may well infringe individuals' entitlements. Such entitlements are themselves perforce derived from the more abstract rules which would be voluntarily agreed upon by those operating behind the veil of ignorance or the veil of uncertainty. The nature of the

[37] References are made to Rawls's first principle of justice. However, this is often part of an argument which seeks to use that principle in order to buttress an argument for the constitutional limitation of wealth distribution by the state; e.g. Buchanan, *Liberty, Market and State*, pp. 165–77.

[38] See below, ch. 8 secs. 2, 3.

[39] Cf. Brennan and Buchanan, *The Reason of Rules*, p. 37 n. 2.

reasoning which is designed to buttress these claims has been considered above. However, the two central reasons which are put forward are far from self-evident. The argument that the voluntary nature of any agreement is not vitiated by differences in income or economic inequality raises the controversial and complex issue of the relationship between liberties and the worth of liberties.[40] The assumption that rewards gained from choice, luck, and effort should necessarily be retained by the individual is not as morally self-evident as public-choice theorists would lead one to believe.[41] The argument that contingent differences resulting from birth, which produce varying capacities and talents, can be regarded as a matter of luck in the draw of history, with the consequence that individuals should be entitled to retain the rewards therefrom, is not self-evident at all. An extensive philosophical literature surrounds this issue, and even those who support an individual's ability to retain such rewards do not generally base their arguments upon any analogy with luck.[42]

2. MODEL TWO AND MODEL THREE: A SUMMARY

The second model can be termed *modified pluralism*. It stems from the critique of traditional pluralist doctrine considered above.[43] The precise form of this challenge differs, but certain predominant themes can none the less be identified. Group power is highly concentrated, within both the corporate and the labour markets. The political agenda is controlled or constrained by these major power groupings. Political change tends to be incremental, and is based upon some pre-existing equilibrium, which is presupposed to be good or just. The status quo is resistant to major shifts in policy. Groups representing certain interests may be effectively excluded from the political process as a result of the natural accommodation which attends the bargains struck by more powerful groups. A theory of constitutional review which attempts to alleviate these ills of pluralist democracy will have to address social and economic concerns of a substantive nature. The reasons for this will

40 See below, ch. 8 secs. 2, 3.
41 See below, ch. 8 secs. 2, 3b.
42 See below, ch. 8 secs. 2, 3.
43 See above, ch. 3 secs. 2c, d.

be identified below. The important point to stress at the outset is that such a theory based upon this conception of pluralist democracy would not begin with the assumption that the sole judicial concern should be with process.

The third model of pluralist democracy can be termed the *process model*.[44] It attempts to steer a course between Scylla and Charybdis. The weaknesses of traditional pluralist doctrine are recognized. The danger of power concentration, and the possibility that particular groups would permanently lose out in the pluralist competitive struggle, are accepted. Constitutional review is legitimated as the corrective, partial at least, for this pluralist imbalance. However, the proponent of this view might wish to limit, or purport to limit, review to process issues. The rationale for this limitation might vary. It might be argued that the corrective for this type of pluralist imbalance naturally directed constitutional review towards process considerations. It might be contended that these limitations should exist for reasons of judicial competence, the judiciary being unsuited to passing judgement on substantive issues. It might be established that the constitutional document itself only served to protect process and not substance. A combination of all three arguments might be used.

The contrasting implications of models two and three can be highlighted by focusing on Ely's work.

3. ELY AND CONSTITUTIONAL LAW

a. *The Theory*

Few topics have aroused as much controversy in the US literature as the Supreme Court's power of constitutional review. Opinions differ markedly both as to the justification for the existence of such a power, and as to the form which such a power should assume. One theory of judicial review which has received considerable attention has been propounded by John Hart Ely. His conception of review is of particular interest because of its connection with the pluralist model of democratic society adumbrated above.

To understand Ely's thesis, the structure of his argument must be

[44] The public-choice model also purports to be about process, but there are, as will become apparent, significant differences between model one and model three.

made clear. Ely begins by distinguishing between two approaches to constitutional adjudication, 'interpretivism' and 'non-interpretivism'.[45] The former is taken to represent the view that, when judges decide constitutional issues, they should confine themselves to enforcing norms which are either stated or clearly implicit in the Constitution. The non-interpretivist view asserts that it will be necessary and legitimate for the courts to proceed beyond the Constitution, and to enforce norms which are not discoverable within the four corners of the document itself.

Ely then draws a further distinction between two forms of interpretivism. Clause-bound interpretivism, the narrower of the two formulations, dictates that the prescriptions within the Constitution should be interpreted primarily from their language, together with any aid which legislative history can provide, but without the help of principles or policies external to the Constitution. A broader form of interpretivism is based upon the premiss that it is not possible to interpret certain constitutional phrases solely from their language or from the legislative history. Aid must, on this view, be sought from outside the founding document. What distinguishes this from a non-interpretivist approach is that the theory which supplies the required content is to be derived from the 'general themes of the entire constitutional document and not from source entirely beyond its four corners'.[46]

Ely rejects a clause-bound interpretivism as being unworkable.[47] Certain provisions of the Constitution cannot be interpreted solely upon the basis of their language coupled with aid from legislative history.

He also rejects the non-interpretivist approach. Put more accurately, he takes issue with, and dismisses, a variety of views which, although distinctive, all accept that the courts should enforce norms not discoverable within the Constitution itself. Those who have advocated the view that the courts should endorse substantive fundamental values are taken to task. A plethora of such approaches are set up and promptly demolished. Thus the belief that the

[45] J. H. Ely, *Democracy and Distrust: A Theory of Judicial Review* (1980), 1–2, 12–13.

[46] Ibid. 12.

[47] Ibid., ch. 2. See also G. C. MacCallum, 'Legislative Intent', 75 *Yale L.J.* 754 (1966); P. Brest, 'The Misconceived Quest for the Original Understanding', 60 *Boston U.L. Rev.* 204 (1980); Dworkin, 'The Forum of Principle', p. 469; D. Lyons, 'Constitutional Interpretation and Original Meaning', 4 *Social Philosophy and Policy*, 75 (1986).

Supreme Court should be applying its own values to measure constitutional legitimacy is attacked,[48] as is the opinion that natural law provides the repository of principles against which constitutional adjudication should be measured.[49] Wechsler's conception of neutral principles[50] is said to be of limited utility, since an attachment to such neutrality leaves two central issues unanswered:[51] the substantive content of the principles, and the method by which the Court derives the values embodied therein.[52] An appeal to moral and political philosophy is found equally wanting.[53] Failure to agree on what the fundamental principles of moral philosophy actually are, particularly with the degree of specificity required for adjudication, bedevils this criterion.

The invitation to judges seems clear: seek constitutional values in—that is overrule political officials on the basis of—the writings of good contemporary moral philosophers. Rawls's book *is* fine. But how are judges to react to Dworkin's invitation when almost all the commentators on Rawls's work have expressed reservations about his conclusions? The Constitution may follow the flag, but is it really supposed to keep up with the *New York Review of Books?*[54]

Having rejected both clause-bound interpretivism, and non-interpretivism, Ely proceeds to articulate his own theory of judicial review.[55] He advocates a 'participation-oriented, representation-reinforcing' approach to judicial review.[56] The argument is, in essence, as follows. The provisions of the Constitution are not primarily concerned to buttress substantive values; the choice of

[48] Ely, *Democracy and Distrust*, pp. 44–8.

[49] Ibid. 48–54.

[50] H. Wechsler, 'Toward Neutral Principles of Constitutional Law', 73 *Harv. L. Rev.* 1 (1959).

[51] Ely, *Democracy and Distrust*, pp. 54–5.

[52] See also J. G. Deutsch, 'Neutrality, Legitimacy, and the Supreme Court: Some Intersections between Law and Political Science', 20 *Stan. L. Rev.* 169 (1968); R. H. Bork, 'Neutral Principles and Some First Amendment Problems', 47 *Ind. L.J.* 1 (1971).

[53] Ely, *Democracy and Distrust*, pp. 56–60.

[54] Ibid. 58; italics in the original. Similar criticisms are levelled at those who wish the court to have recourse to conventional morality when deciding cases; ibid. 65, 67. Ely takes a number of writers to task within this section, including A. M. Bickel, *The Least Dangerous Branch* (1962); H. H. Wellington, 'Common Law Rules and Constitutional Double Standards: Some Notes on Adjudication', 83 *Yale L.J.* 221 (1973); M. Perry, 'Substantive Due Process Revisited: Reflections on (and beyond) Recent Cases', 71 *Nw. U.L. Rev.* 417 (1977).

[55] Ely, *Democracy and Distrust*, chs. 4–6.

[56] Ibid. 87.

such values is left almost entirely to the ordinary political process. The Constitution is principally concerned with process in a double sense. Certain provisions are directed towards procedural fairness in the resolution of individual disputes, what Ely calls process writ small. Others are aimed at process writ large, with ensuring broad participation in the processes of government. This latter form of process is itself subdivided. On the one hand, there are constitutional provisions and judicial decisions which are designed both to secure and to clear the channels of political change. Constitutional terms and court decisions dealing with political expression, association, and voting rights fall within this category. On the other hand, there are aspects of the Constitution combined with judicial interpretation which attempt to correct certain types of discrimination.

Ely adduces support for his thesis from the Constitution itself and judicial interpretations thereof. He is, however, at pains to stress that his theory is consonant with the fundamental tenets of representative democracy in the United States. Ely recognizes that republican sentiments pervaded the original discussions from which the Constitution emanated. He argues however, that the predominant theme underlying the constitutional document was pluralist. 'The original Constitution's more pervasive strategy, however, can be loosely styled a strategy of pluralism, one of structuring the government, and to a limited extent society generally, so that a variety of voices would be guaranteed their say and no majority coalition could dominate.'[57]

As society developed in the United States, the pluralistic nature of decision-making became more pronounced.[58] Any idea that 'the people' were joined by a homogeneity of interest was discarded. The two limbs of Ely's 'process writ large' find their own conceptual link within this pluralist vision. The protection of process rights, whether they be of speech, association, or voting, was designed to ensure that people or groups could partake in the bargaining process characteristic of pluralist democracy. The link between pluralism and the protection of minority rights is less immediately obvious, but equally central. Given that society was composed of a plurality of interests, provision had to be made to prevent the elected representatives from severing the interests of the majority from those of the minority.[59] A refusal to represent a minority could not be countenanced. Nor

[57] Ely, *Democracy and Distrust*, p. 80; see also pp. 78–9.

[58] Ibid. 83–5.

[59] Ibid. 82, 84, 103.

could a situation in which, although technically enfranchized, a group found itself in a disadvantageous position for a long period and hence susceptible to discriminatory treatment. Such groups might, as Ely states, just as well be disenfranchized.[60]

The interconnection between the two parts of Ely's scheme should be made explicit. The emphasis within the first limb, clearing the channels of political change, focuses primarily upon the elective process itself. The concern with a revival of the non-delegation doctrine reflects a further commitment that the legislature should legislate. Attention within the second limb, facilitating the representation of minorities, is directed to the *results* of the elective and legislative process; to ensuring that those elected are prevented from passing certain types of legislation which can be harmful to those on the losing side of the pluralist process. Inequalities generated by the elective process itself are, on this view, alleviated by precluding certain types of legislation which might discriminate against the losers, the 'outs'.

Constitutional review exists, therefore, to clear the channels of political change, and to facilitate the representation of minority interests. Clearing the channels of political change involves, for Ely, judicial review to ensure freedom of speech, publication, and political association. These are integral to the function of 'an open and effective democratic process'.[61] The right to vote qualifies on the same terms: 'unblocking stoppages in the democratic process is what judicial review ought to be about', and denial of voting rights is the quintessential stoppage.[62] Speech, association and voting must be reviewed because we cannot leave it to the 'ins' to decide, directly or indirectly, who stays 'out'.[63] The choice of representative is only part of Ely's concern. He is equally anxious to ensure that those chosen do what they have been chosen to do, in this instance legislate. Thus he favours putting more teeth into the non-delegation doctrine in order to force those elected to articulate their ends with greater specificity, and to prevent the delegation of unstructured discretion to administrators.[64]

When Ely comes to his second theme, facilitating the representation

[60] Ely, *Democracy and Distrust*, p. 84.
[61] Ibid. 103.
[62] Ibid. 117.
[63] Ibid. 106, 120.
[64] Ibid. 131–5. For a more detailed discussion of the non-delegation doctrine, see S. G. Breyer and R. B. Stewart, *Administrative Law and Regulatory Policy: Problems, Text and Cases* (2nd edn., 1985), 68–95.

of minorities, he recognizes some of the criticisms which have been voiced against traditional pluralist doctrine. The inequalities which can exist between competing groups and the oligarchic nature of power concentration are admitted.[65] His second theme is directed towards countering these imbalances. The corrective is once again process-oriented in appearance at least.[66] Thus it is argued that the Equal Protection Clause cannot be held to mean that everyone is entitled to equal treatment by every law; the purpose of much law is to secure differential treatment for different groups. Nor, Ely argues, can the Constitution be read as imposing a particular distributional pattern of wealth within society. Ely contends that: 'The constitutionality of most distributions thus cannot be determined simply by looking to see who ended up with what, but rather can be approached intelligibly only by attending to the process that brought about the distribution in question—by what Robert Nozick has called a "historical" (as opposed to an "end result") approach.'[67]

The distribution of benefits that were not essential to political participation, or were not explicitly guaranteed by the language of the Constitution, would only be subject to constitutional attack if there were a malfunction in the process by which such benefits were distributed. The discussion thereafter is directed towards the way in which judicial concern with legislative motivation and the doctrine of suspect classification can counter the defective distributional process. For Ely, the two issues are related. The special scrutiny afforded to suspect classifications is a mechanism for buttressing the attack provided by motivation analysis.[68] The concern for 'discrete and insular minorities' has, for Ely, its rationale in the protection which it thereby affords to those who will constantly be on the losing side of the pluralist bargaining process.[69] Its ultimate aim is to preclude legislative classifications which will be both harmful to that group, and discreditable in constitutional terms.[70]

[65] Ely, *Democracy and Distrust*, p. 125. Thus, e.g., Ely cites, at p. 242 n. 4, P. Bachrach, *The Theory of Democratic Elitism: A Critique* (1967), and E. E. Schattschneider, *The Semi-Sovereign People: A Realist's View of Democracy in America* (1960). For a discussion of this, and other similar literature, see above, ch. 3 sec. 2d.

[66] For a discussion of whether the corrective really is process-based, see below, ch. 4 sec. 3b.

[67] *Democracy and Distrust*, p. 136.

[68] Ibid. 145. For a general discussion of equal protection, see J. E. Nowak, R. D.Rotunda, and J. Nelson Young, *Constitutional Law* (3rd edn., 1986), ch. 14.

[69] *Democracy and Distrust*, p. 151.

[70] Ibid. 152.

What Ely therefore presents to us is a constitutional theory constructed from the perceived attributes of US democracy. The preclusion of substantive review is founded upon the assumption that such value judgements are for the legislature, *and* that there is no satisfactory criterion on which the court can intervene. The consequential emphasis upon process values is justified by envisioning the court as the corrective for the blocks or imbalances which can arise within such a pluralist system; this is said to have the additional benefit of restricting intervention to those areas where judicial expertise is particularly strong, as is the case in the context of process rights.[71]

b. The Substance within Process

The most prominent type of criticism which has been levelled at Ely is that no ostensibly process-based theory can in fact avoid making substantive value judgements. One version of this criticism has been advanced by Tribe.[72] Having argued that, contrary to Ely, certain of the Constitution's express provisions *are* substantive in nature, he contends that even allegedly procedural norms necessitate substantive choices. Thus, the very fact that the Constitution enshrines certain provisions concerned with process writ small, or adjudicative process, as well as process writ large, or representative process, necessitates a choice between the two. The decision whether a person is entitled to be heard as a litigant or as a voter requires a substantive theory which can serve as a criterion to determine how the government can categorize people.[73] Determining what kind of participation the Constitution demands will perforce entail consideration of the nature of the interest at stake, and its importance in the life of a particular individual.[74] Even when the decision has been made as to what type of process a person should be entitled to, further substantive questions will arise concerning the content of the chosen form of process. For example, if we decide that representative process is appropriate within a particular context, we will then have to determine who should be allowed to participate through the vote.

[71] *Democracy and Distrust*, p. 101–2.

[72] L. H. Tribe, 'The Puzzling Persistence of Process-Based Constitutional Theories', 89 *Yale L.J.* 1063 (1980).

[73] Ibid. 1068.

[74] Ibid. 1069.

This will entail substantive value judgements concerning the nature of a political community.[75]

The focus upon minority representation requires a similar exercise in substantive evaluation. Not all groups which lose out in the political struggle can thereby be regarded as a discrete and insular minority deserving of special protection. Something more is required. Criteria such as discreteness or immutability fail, in and of themselves, to provide the solution. 'Any constitutional distinction between laws burdening homosexuals and laws burdening exhibitionists, between laws burdening Catholics and laws burdening pickpockets, must depend on a substantive theory of which groups are exercising fundamental rights and which are not.'[76]

Brest has criticized Ely's thesis on not dissimilar grounds.[77] He regards constitutional adjudication which is directed towards fundamental values, and that which is focused upon process and representation, as Siamese twins. Most instances of representation-reinforcing review demand value judgements which are not different in kind from those required when adjudicating upon fundamental values. Alternatively, the claims in cases concerning fundamental values are often directly translatable into representation-reinforcing claims.[78]

Dworkin's critique of Ely begins at a more abstract level.[79] He questions Ely's assumption that democracy is necessarily solely concerned with process, and denies that there is any consensus as to what constitutes democracy. The Supreme Court would therefore have to develop its own conception of democracy, and to consider what constitutes a good argument for one conception rather than another.[80] In making this choice, the Court would have to select between an input and an output case for democracy. The former envisions democracy as a method of allocating political power between the people and the officials they elect, or between the people themselves; such a democracy is not, however, judged by the wisdom of the legislation which will be produced. The latter regards

[75] Tribe, 'The Puzzling Persistence', p. 1071.

[76] Ibid. 1076.

[77] P. Brest, 'The Substance of Process', 42 *Ohio St. L.J.* 131 (1981).

[78] Ibid. 140. A collection of critical essays on Ely can be found in the same volume. See, e.g., M. J. Perry, 'Interpretivism, Freedom of Expression, and Equal Protection', 42 *Ohio St. L.J.* 261 (1981).

[79] 'The Forum of Principle' p. 469.

[80] Ibid. 502, 504.

the outcome of the democratic process as the primary reason for its establishment. Utilitarian conceptions of democracy are, in this sense, outcome-based. The justification for democracy resides in the fact that the substantive decisions which are thereby produced will maximize utility. It is therefore only if the Court can rely on an input case for democracy that it can avoid making the substantive choices which Ely's theory demands.[81] Much of the ensuing part of Dworkin's analysis is directed towards showing that a purely input case for democracy is not readily sustainable.[82]

4. THE SECOND MODEL AND THE FOCUS OF CONSTITUTIONAL REVIEW

Which of the particular conceptions of pluralist democracy does Ely employ? It is clear that he does not adhere to the traditional model of pluralism adumbrated by Bentley. Ely recognizes that pluralism is not naturally self-correcting,[83] and is critical of those legal writers who continue to invoke pluralist rhetoric in its 'original unqualified form'.[84]

The interesting and important question is, therefore, the choice between the second and the third conceptions of pluralist democracy. An initial reading of Ely's thesis, and much of the rhetoric contained therein, might lead one to suspect that he was adopting the second model of pluralism.[85] If this were the case, then Ely's thesis would be untenable. It is worth dwelling on the reasons why this is so, since only by doing so can the viability of the third model of pluralism be evaluated. A theory of constitutional review which was premised upon the second conception of pluralist democracy

[81] Dworkin, 'The Forum of Principle', pp. 503–4.

[82] For further criticism of Ely, see M. V. Tushnet, 'Darkness on the Edge of Town: The Contributions of John Hart Ely to Constitutional Theory', 89 *Yale L.J.* 1037 (1980).

[83] *Democracy and Distrust*, pp. 80–1, 135–6.

[84] Ibid. 242, n. 4.

[85] Much of the discussion within Ely's work is based upon the hypothesis that there are defects in the traditional model of pluralist democracy, and that the alleviation of these defects provides the rationale for constitutional review. This provides the core of Ely's argument when he is developing his own theory of review; ibid. 77–88. The idea that such review is justified when the political market malfunctions and when groups are in danger of being persistent losers in the pluralist bazaar is a recurring theme throughout the book; see, e.g., pp. 103, 151, 152.

would *not begin* with the assumption that the focus was to be solely upon process issues. An understanding of the pluralist literature which underlies this second model will reveal why substantive social and economic issues would also have to be addressed. I am at present making no claim as to whether such issues should therefore be regarded as constitutional in nature. This is a complex question which will be touched on here and addressed more fully later. The present aim is more limited. It is to enquire whether one can coherently construct a theory of constitutional review which is designed to alleviate the ills of pluralist democracy as perceived by this second model, without addressing such social and economic concerns. The substance of the argument is that this is not plausible. There are four reasons why an exclusive concern with process would fail to achieve its objective.

First, inequalities in the electoral process will persist which cannot be corrected by clearing the channels of political change. Even when these channels have been cleared in the most pristine fashion, by giving due attention to speech, association, voting, etc. *who* is elected, and *what* views they represent, will be reflective of pre-existing inequalities between power groups within society. Some will be over- and some will be under-represented.[86] Paying attention to the formal attributes of speech, voting, and association will, as stated above, be necessary to clear the channels of political change. They will, in no sense, be sufficient. Persistent inequalities undermine the claim that, by focusing attention on speech, voting, etc., we are thereby clearing the channels of the political process.

Ely does perceive this problem. The brief response is to fall back upon considerations of administrability.[87] He argues that one person, one vote is the only workable standard which a court can adopt. Differing degrees of influence might be wielded by different groups within a particular electoral district, but it would be impossible for a court to investigate these variable power alignments, and then to make decisions concerning appropriate weighted voting rights.

There are two possible responses to this argument. One would be to accept it, and to accept also that this thereby demonstrates the

[86] See the discussion, above ch. 3 secs. 2c, d. The extent to which traditional pluralist doctrine really did place emphasis upon the groups being of equal strength is itself a contentious issue; see R. A. Dahl, *Dilemmas of Pluralist Democracy* (1982), 207–9.

[87] Ely, *Democracy and Distrust*, pp. 123–5.

limits of legal correctives for pluralist imbalance. Viewed in this light, Ely's response is no more than an admission of the argument presented above, coupled with an argument that this is all that can be done through legal means. It does not alter the underlying fact that such a legal clearing of the channels of political change will be at best only partial. No judicial cleansing of the Augean stables can be expected.

The other response to Ely's argument would be that it begs the question. Ely's thesis is, as we have seen, founded upon the premiss that constitutional review is justified because of its curative effect upon blocks and imbalances in US representative democracy. The *assumption* is then made that this concentrates our attention upon process issues.[88] Democracy is conceived, in part, as a method of choice, and the first half of Ely's thesis, concerned with clearing the channels of political change, is directed towards ensuring that all can express their choice through meetings, speaking, the vote, etc. Yet the very selection of these issues as the ones which are pertinent to democratic choice reflects presuppositions which can be questioned. If, as the literature would seem to indicate,[89] pluralist disequilibrium is caused as much by inequality of social and economic power as by any formal limitation upon speech, voting, or association, why are only the latter regarded as integral to the political clearing process and not the former? To respond that the Constitution does not protect the former, but only the latter, will not do. Even accepting that this might for the sake of argument be true,[90] all that it would demonstrate is that the manner of correcting pluralist block or imbalance was constitutionally constrained. It would not somehow prove that the constitutionally perceived

88 See further Ely's discussion (ibid. 136), where he states that the proper scope of review for laws touching upon presumptive constitutional entitlements is that they cannot be denied without compelling reason. The provision of benefits, 'goods, rights, exemptions or whatever', that are not essential to political participation *or* are not explicitly guaranteed by the Constitution can only be reviewed if there is malfunction in the process whereby the distribution was effected. Ely furnishes no explicit justification as to why social and economic factors should not be regarded as, in his own language, essential to political participation.

89 See above, ch. 3 secs. 2c, d.

90 Whether the Constitution could, and/or should, be read to protect such social and economic interests is a complex issue. It would certainly not be an impossible construction of certain constitutional provisions; see e.g. C. R. Sunstein, 'Interest Groups in American Public Law', 38 *Stan. L. Rev.* 29, 72–3 (1985). This theme will be considered in more detail when the third model of pluralist democracy is considered; see below ch. 4 sec. 5.

manner of correction focused attention upon the only, or even the most, important cause of such blocks.

The second reason why Ely's thesis is likely to be of limited efficacy relates to the second limb of his theory, facilitating the representation of minority interests. Ely's desire to avoid substantive constitutional adjudication leads him to restrict the ambit of the second limb of his theory and to exclude groups which those critical of pluralist theory would argue require protection. The recognition of the inequality between groups which characterizes much of this critical writing also suggests those who are likely to lose out in the uneven struggle. The 'list' causes no surprise: ethnic groups, aliens, homosexuals, and the poor all figure prominently. While Ely might be willing to countenance the use of doctrinal techniques, such as legislative motivation and suspect classification, to counter legislation which deleteriously treats aliens, racial groups, or homosexuals, the poor are largely excluded.

> failures to provide the poor with one or another good or service, insensitive as they may often seem to some of us, do not generally result from a sadistic desire to keep the miserable in their state of misery, or a stereotypical generalization about their characteristics, but rather from a reluctance to raise the taxes needed to support such expenditures—and at all events they will be susceptible to immediate translation into such constitutionally innocent terms. A theory of suspicious classification will thus be of only occasional assistance to the poor, since their problems are not often problems of classification to begin with.[91]

This exclusion of the poor is all the more important because if we have to choose one element above all others which has destroyed the pluralist myth of an automatic society, it is disparities in wealth and power which would emerge at the top, or proximate thereto.[92] Such differences, and the divergences in power which follow, have sullied

[91] *Democracy and Distrust*, p. 162. For a general discussion of the motivations behind central legislative decision-making, see, e.g., D. R. Mayhew, *Congress: The Electoral Connection* (1974) and M. P. Fiorina, *Congress; Keystone of the Washington Establishment* (1977), where considerable emphasis is placed upon the desire of Congressmen to be re-elected as an explanation for legislative behaviour. Other writers such as R. F. Fenno, *Congressmen in Committees* (1973), and R. D. Arnold, *Congress and Bureaucracy: A Theory of Influence* (1979), lay stress on the desire for re-election, achieving influence within the legislature, and promoting public policy. See also A. Maass, *Congress and the Common Good* (1983); G. C. Jacobson, *The Politics of Congressional Elections* (1983); P. Woll, *Congress* (1985).

[92] See above, ch. 3 secs. 2c, d. See also R. D. Parker, 'The Past of Constitutional Theory—and its Future', 42 *Ohio St. L.J.* 223 (1981).

the pluralist vision of beatific harmony. It is the poor who are among the closest to the picture of the eternal losers in the perennial political competition. The absence of sadism on the part of those who inflict the defeat makes it none the less real. Ely cannot admit the poor into his scheme because to do so would be to render untenable his claim to exclude substantive considerations from constitutional review. The basis of this claim is, as we have seen, dubious.[93] While Ely continues to restrict the conception of discrete and insular minority to groups distinguished by race or origin, he can at least try to maintain the impression of being non-substantive. Once consider admitting the poor and the veneer wears increasingly thin. Indeed it may well be the case that the very focus upon 'discrete and insular minorities' no longer adequately describes those who will be the eternal losers in the pluralist bazaar. As Ackerman has stated:

> Long after discrete and insular minorities have gained strong representation at the pluralist bargaining table, there will remain many other groups who fail to achieve influence remotely proportionate to their numbers: groups that are discrete and diffuse (like women), or anonymous and somewhat insular (like homosexuals), or *both* diffuse and anonymous (like the victims of poverty). If we are to treat *Carolene* as something more than a tired formula, constitutional lawyers must develop paradigms that detail the systematic disadvantages that undermine our system's legitimacy in dealing with the grievances of these diffuse or anonymous groups.[94]

There is a third difficulty with Ely's theory which is related to the second. The inequalities in social and economic power which are not removed through clearing the electoral process itself will only be partially ameliorated by paying attention to minorities in the legislation which results from the elective process. This is in part because of the point made above, the refusal to characterize certain types of group as discrete and insular minorities. It results also because of an asymmetry which is not readily apparent from Ely's own analysis. His approach is dependent upon the existence of legislation which categorizes people in certain ways. What it leaves almost untouched is the negative side of the coin, the absence of legislation. A constant theme which permeates the criticism of classical pluralist doctrine is the control over the political agenda

[93] See above, ch. 4 sec. 3b.

[94] B. Ackerman, 'Beyond *Carolene Products*', 98 *Harv. L. Rev.* 713, 742 (1985); italics in the original.

wielded by the major power groupings, the conservative tendencies which follow from mutual accommodation by these organizations, and the pressures against anything other than minor incremental change.[95]

The significance of this line of criticism is that those who are under-represented because of persistent inequalities in the electoral process itself, are likely to suffer as much from the absence of legislation paying attention to their needs, as from legislation which is harmful to them in a positive sense. Focusing upon legislative motivation and its handmaiden, suspect classification is of little or no help in these instances. Ely's techniques remain in abeyance, for the legislators' sheet is blank.

A response to the two preceding arguments might take the following form. Ely has already clearly stated what the second limb of his thesis is *not* meant to connote.[96] Facilitating the representation of minorities requires neither that all be treated equally by every law, nor that the Constitution be interpreted as requiring a particular distributional pattern against which to judge the allocation of benefits to determine their constitutionality. The constitutionality of distributions could therefore only be determined not by seeing 'who ended up with what', but by attending to the process that brought about the particular distribution. Hence the concentration on legislative motivation and suspect classifications. The court cannot pass any judgment in the absence of legislation which might benefit an under-represented group, or which disadvantages the poor, either because this might amount to enforcing a particular distributional pattern, or because there would be no basis on which to determine whether this absence of legislation could offend Ely's own process formula.

Such an argument is flawed. We should keep in the forefront of our mind that Ely's own process theory is designed to relate particular provisions of the Constitution to the needs of representative democracy within which that Constitution subsists. That is its principal rationale. Clearing blocks in the process of political change, and ensuring that technically enfranchized minorities are not systematically disadvantaged, comprise its working parts. Now,

[95] e.g. Schattschneider, *The Semi-Sovereign People*; P. Bachrach and M. S. Baratz, 'Two Faces of Power', reprinted in W. E. Connolly (ed.), *The Bias of Pluralism* (1969), ch. 3.

[96] *Democracy and Distrust*, pp. 135–6.

in deciding what constitutes such systematic disadvantage it would of course be possible to proceed by way of definitional fiat, and to proclaim that only actual legislation which falls foul of Ely's process criteria is to count as such harm. This would be, however, to ignore the extensive evidence describing how the absence of legislation can produce the same effect. If the theory cannot assimilate the problem of systematic minority harm flowing from the absence of legislative benefit or from legislation which disadvantages the poor, then the theory is correspondingly weakened. It might be argued that the Constitution precludes an investigation into this type of issue. This would not alter the response provided above. The existence of such constitutional constraints, were they to exist, would not prove that a significant element of pluralist imbalance was not the result of the inequalities previously considered. It would simply weaken the tools at the disposal of one minded to construct a theory which regarded the infirmities of the pluralist process as the prime organizing rationale for constitutional review. Whether in fact the Constitution does impose such constraints will be considered more fully when examining the third conception of pluralist democracy.

The final reason why Ely's theory is likely to be of limited effectiveness is, in one sense, a correlative and extension of the third. Even when those within power and those who support them do wish to attain positive ends, legislation may not be their chosen route. Classical pluralist doctrine may have many faults. Proponents of this doctrine, such as Bentley, did, however, perceive two matters of lasting significance. The 'political world' could not be equated with that of government in the narrow formal sense of that term, and the fact that government could attain its goals in a variety of ways.[97] Put shortly, the 'ins' have a variety of tools at their disposal for excluding the 'outs'. Informal understandings, contract, executive directive, and obstruction are all potential weapons in the armoury. They are, however, more difficult to attack. Their very informality may well render them less apparent than if the same objects had been encapsulated within legislation. The utility of the devices which Ely advocates to redress, alleviate, or correct the inequalities in pluralism will be of limited effectiveness when faced with this pattern of political decision-making. Moreover, the reinvigoration of

[97] A. F. Bentley, *The Process of Government* (1908; repr. 1949); D. B. Truman, *The Governmental Process* (1951). This is not denied by more recent critical literature on pluralism.

the non-delegation doctrine, which is also espoused by Ely,[98] could exacerbate the difficulty presented above. If the legislature were to feel unduly constrained by the obligation to articulate standards, one response would be to pursue these goals by other, less visual, means.

What the preceding discussion has sought to show is that the very desire to keep review 'clean' demonstrates the limited role which it can play in combating the dilemmas of modern pluralism. The image of the autonomous self-correcting political society was emasculated by the realization of the imperfect bargaining which characterized the political market. These imperfections were themselves largely the result of substantive economic and social inequality. Process-based review can remain aloof from such issues. It can so define its component parts as to exclude many of these matters. Let us, however, not be too sanguine that such a theory will be the panacea for the ills of pluralist society. Constitutional review based upon the second model of pluralist democracy would not, therefore, begin with the assumption that this foundation focused attention upon process. It might well be accepted that limitations should be placed upon such review because certain issues were felt to be unsuited to judicial resolution. However, as will be seen,[99] the notion of judicial competence is itself a complex one, which requires more detailed analysis than that provided by Ely.

5. THE VIABILITY OF THE THIRD MODEL

If, therefore, Ely intends to construct a theory of constitutional review which is founded upon the second conception of pluralist democracy, the enterprise will not be a noted success. The central question to which we should now turn concerns the viability of the third vision of pluralist democracy and constitutional review adumbrated above.

In approaching this issue the thematic structure of Ely's thesis should be made clear. Ely's own constitutional philosophy follows his critique of the interpretivists. It is the search for a species of constitutional adjudication which does not require the judicial imposition of fundamental values. He finds the kernel of his

[98] *Democracy and Distrust*, pp. 131–4.
[99] See below, ch. 4 sec. 5.

philosophy applied in the decisions of the Warren Court,[100] which he argues were primarily concerned with process in the double sense outlined above. These decisions of the Warren Court era were, Ely argues, themselves foreshadowed by Justice Stone's famous footnote in the *Carolene Products* case.[101]

The justification for this process-oriented approach then unfolds. Three interconnected themes can be delineated. The primary theme is that this is consonant with the democratic philosophy which pervades the Constitution.[102] While Ely recognizes that republican sentiments did influence the reasoning of the framers, he argues that the predominant philosophy was pluralist. It is this philosophy which provides the foundation for the two limbs of his thesis. The consequential attention placed upon process is said to possess the additional benefit of preserving substantive political decisions for the elected legislature. The secondary theme is that the provisions of the Constitution are, notwithstanding much opinion to the contrary, in fact concerned with process and not substance.[103] The picture is completed by the addition of a third theme which is concerned with judicial competence;[104] judges are more suited to dealing with matters of process as opposed to substance. The tenor of Ely's theory is encapsulated in the following quotation.

> The approach to constitutional adjudication recommended here is akin to what might be called an 'antitrust' as opposed to a 'regulatory' orientation to economic affairs—rather than dictate substantive results it intervenes only when the 'market', in our case the political market, is systemically malfunctioning . . . Our government cannot fairly be said to be 'malfunctioning' simply because it sometimes generates outcomes with which we disagree . . . In a representative democracy value determinations are to be made by our elected representatives, and if in fact most of us disapprove we can vote them out of office. Malfunction occurs when the *process* is

[100] *Democracy and Distrust*, pp. 73–5.

[101] *United States* v. *Carolene Products Co.* 304 U.S. 144, 152–3 n. 4 (1938), where Justice Stone suggests, *inter alia*, that prejudice against discrete and insular minorities may be a special condition, which tends seriously to curtail the operation of the political processes which are ordinarily to be relied on to protect minorities, and which may therefore call for a correspondingly more searching judicial inquiry of legislation. For a recent evaluation of the *Carolene* case which argues that the footnote does not direct attention towards process, see L. Brilmayer, '*Carolene*, Conflicts and the Fate of the "Inside-Outsider"', 134 *U. Pa. L. Rev.* 1291 (1986).

[102] Ely, *Democracy and Distrust*, pp. 77–88.

[103] Ibid. 88–101.

[104] Ibid. 102.

undeserving of trust, when (1) the ins are choking off the channels of political change to ensure that they will stay in and the outs will stay out, or (2) though no one is actually denied a voice or vote representatives beholden to an effective majority are systematically disadvantaging some minority out of simple hostility or a prejudiced refusal to recognize commonalities of interest, and thereby denying that minority the protection afforded other groups by a representative system.[105]

The difficulties with this third conception of pluralism and constitutional review become apparent upon closer inspection of its working parts. Ely utilizes concepts drawn from pluralist political theory and political science. This literature is clear that any rigid divorce between political, social, and economic concerns is not sustainable. In so far as the channels of political change are blocked, and in so far as certain minorities do represent the eternal losers, this literature would indicate that substantive social and economic concerns are equally important as those which are apparently process-related. Four responses are possible.

A first reply might assume the following form. It could be argued that the provisions of the Constitution do not allow such considerations to be taken into account. The formal attributes of speech, voting, and association might well be protected, but the 'value' which these rights might in fact have for those within society are not accorded similar constitutional concern.[106] It might be contended in the same vein, that the equal protection clause does not institutionalize any particular distributional pattern, but is only concerned to ensure equal concern and respect in the design of institutions which govern society.[107] The general thrust of this response would therefore be to argue that not all the problems which beset pluralist democracy can be assumed to be constitutional in nature.

Ely does not develop this type of argument in any detail, and the problem is not so easily resolved. The distinction drawn by Rawls, and Dworkin's idea of equal concern and respect, are both themselves part of more complex political theories which will be

[105] Ely, *Democracy and Distrust*, 102–3; italics in the original.

[106] Cf. Rawls, *A Theory of Justice*, pp. 204–5. See below ch. 8 sec. 3a (ii), for a discussion of this idea within Rawls's own theory. Ely does not appear to adopt this idea explicitly, although it may be regarded as implicit in some parts of his analysis.

[107] Ely, *Democracy and Distrust*, p. 82, does suggest this approach, quoting R. Dworkin, *Taking Rights Seriously* (1977), 180. One may find the idea of equal concern and respect appealing. The question is whether it makes sense, given Ely's concern to alleviate the problems of pluralist democracy.

considered hereafter. They cannot simply be severed from such settings and applied within a different theory.[108] Whatever one believes about these ideas, the relevant issue is their suitability and effect *given* Ely's own theory. This is based on intervention when the political market is systemically malfunctioning. If the Rawlsian and Dworkinian themes are taken to mean that issues of social and economic power cannot be constitutionally challenged, then, as the preceding analysis demonstrates, review will play only a tangential role in performing the very task which serves to justify its existence. The court is to wage a battle for the 'outs', having been told to exclude the principal factors which place groups in that position.

A second response might draw upon the analogy with antitrust, as is apparent from the quotation cited above. The contention is that antitrust will apply only when there is a malfunction within the ordinary market-place, but that it will not dictate a particular substantive result. Clearing the channels of the political market-place can thus be similarly process-based. This argument misconceives both *how* and *when* antitrust operates. The rules of antitrust will become applicable when there has been a determination of some market failure which results in, for example, monopolization or cartelization.[109] In arriving at the decision whether market failure has occurred, the law of antitrust will consider the substance of the matter in the following sense. It will examine the evidence to determine whether companies did in fact collude. The apparently innocent form of an agreement will not be conclusive. An analogous approach is evident in relation to issues of market power.[110] The courts will consider structural indicia of monopoly. They will also take account of behavioural factors, such as whether the defendant brought certain pressure to bear upon recalcitrant corporations. It might, therefore, in a general sense, be said that antitrust polices the process within the private market.[111] To conclude from this general

[108] e.g. (a) the Rawlsian distinction is applied within a theory which *does* afford protection to substantive rights; it is problematic even within such a theory. (b) Rawls *does* now accept that the worth of *political liberties* should be enshrined in the principles of justice; see below, ch. 8 sec. 3a (ii).

[109] See, generally, L. A. Sullivan, *Antitrust* (1977), chs. 3, 4; P. Areeda, *Antitrust Analysis* (3rd edn., 1981); R. A. Posner and F. H. Easterbrook, *Antitrust* (2nd edn., 1981); E. T. Sullivan and H. Hovenkamp, *Antitrust Law, Policy and Procedure* (1984), ch. 4; H. Hovenkamp, *Economics and Federal Antitrust Law* (1985), ch. 4.

[110] See, e.g., Sullivan and Hovenkamp, *Antitrust Law, Policy and Procedure*, ch. 6; Sullivan, *Antitrust*, ch. 2; Hovenkamp, *Economics and Federal Antitrust Law*, chs. 5, 6.

[111] The precise requirements for a violation of s. 2 of the Sherman Act are still

statement that antitrust is, therefore, about process is erroneous.[112] In deciding whether a malfunction has occurred, the courts will consider the substantive social and economic power wielded by the protagonists. The antitrust analogy, applied to political markets, would suggest that, in deciding on *whether* a malfunction existed, all the facts should be considered, not just those which could ostensibly be regarded as relating to process. One would need to consider, for example, not just whether a group possessed the formal rights to speech, voting and association. One would need to decide whether the action of another group, possessed of significant political power, was acting so as to exclude the former group, in whole or in part, from the political market-place. The relative social and economic power of the respective groups would be in the forefront of such an enquiry.

A third reply which Ely might proffer is that it is necessary to restrict the meaning of systemic malfunction to issues which are process-based, in appearance at least, because of the perceived dangers of engaging in substantive review. This latter form of review would, it is argued, inevitably draw the judiciary into making distributional decisions as to 'who ended up with what'.[113] Hence Ely's insistence on Nozick's 'historical' as opposed to 'end result' approach.

This justification for the interpretation accorded to systemic malfunction is, upon closer examination, no more convincing than that derived from the antitrust analogy. The root of the difficulty resides in an ambiguity as to the meaning of the word substance. Let us assume for the sake of argument that the Constitution cannot be read as incorporating any particular distributional pattern, and in

contentious for two interconnected reasons; (a) courts have used different tests at different times; (b) even when successive courts have adopted the same test, the interpretation placed upon that test when applied to the facts of a case may vary significantly. See above, n. 110. The leading authorities are: *United States* v. *Aluminum Co. of America* 148 F. 2d 416 (2d Cir. 1945); *United States* v. *United Shoe Machinery Corp.* 110 F. Supp. 295 (D. Mass. 1953), *aff'd per curiam*, 347 U.S. 521 (1954); *United States* v. *Grinnell Corp.* 384 U.S. 563 (1966); *Berkey Photo, Inc.* v. *Eastman Kodak Co.* 603 F. 2d 263 (2d Cir. 1979), *cert. denied*, 444 U.S. 1093 (1980); *Aspen Skiing Co.* v. *Aspen Highlands Skiing Corp.* 105 S.Ct. 2847 (1985).

[112] Precisely which types of behaviour by a firm possessed of monopoly power should be enjoined is a matter which continues to divide courts and commentators alike; e.g. whether the leasing system adopted by United Shoe, above n. 111, should have been regarded as exclusionary is a debatable issue.

[113] Ely, *Democracy and Distrust*, p. 136.

this sense precludes substantive review. The word substance as employed here refers to the distributional content of the actual legislation which emanates from Congress. For the sake of clarity this may be termed direct substantive review.

Let us assume also that we still wish to incorporate within our theory of constitutional review a method of protecting those who will be the eternal losers in the pluralist bazaar. We apply the name discrete and insular minority to such a group. This requires a determination as to which groups should be accorded this appellation. The substantive evaluation is not in this instance aimed directly at some appropriate or ideal distributional pattern which legislation should achieve. It is not, therefore, direct constitutional review in the sense adumbrated above. To engage in any protection for minorities will none the less entail not only a judgement concerning the rights of that particular group.[114] It will also require an evaluation of the relative social and economic power which such a group wields. Any decision as to whether for example blacks or women are likely to be eternal losers in the pluralist bazaar will necessitate a complex determination as to the place of such groups within society, and of the power which they exercise. Ely's own detailed analysis of equal protection in fact evidences the necessity for such an enquiry.[115]

Ely's interpretation of systemic malfunction as applied to the equal protection clause may well, therefore, avoid direct substantive review based upon distributional considerations. It cannot, however, escape the more indirect form of substantive judgement considered above. The relationship between these two species of substantive review is itself more complex than might seem initially apparent. One may not be condemning specific legislation directly upon the basis of some ideal distributional pattern. One is none the less opening up such legislation to closer scrutiny upon the basis of, *inter alia*, distributional considerations which affect the position of that group within society at the time the contested legislation is promulgated.[116] One may not, therefore be engaging directly in

[114] In the sense articulated by Tribe, 'The Puzzling Persistence', and Brest, 'The Substance of Process'.

[115] See, e.g. the discussion of race (*Democracy and Distrust*, pp. 151–4), and of women (pp. 164–9), where his reasoning and conclusions are permeated by such assumptions.

[116] Ely hints at this in passing when he states, in parentheses, that the 'distributional pattern can provide powerful evidence' concerning the process by which benefits are distributed in a particular instance; ibid. 136.

decisions as to 'who should end up with what' from a particular piece of legislation which is under review; in this sense, direct substantive review upon distributional criteria can be avoided. One cannot, however, avoid taking account of *past* distributional patterns in the very determination of whether a particular group is a discrete and insular minority.

Ely's justification for his interpretation of systemic malfunction as applied to the second limb of his thesis is, therefore, weakened in the following sense. The object is to provide aid to those who, although technically enfranchized, will be 'permanently' on the losing side in the pluralist bazaar, for reasons which are constitutionally discreditable.[117] Ely's approach may succeed in avoiding direct substantive review, in the sense adumbrated above. Substantive judgements will none the less be entailed in the very decision as to which groups should be categorized as discrete and insular minorities, and therefore which pieces of legislation should be subject to special scrutiny. The types of substantive social and economic considerations which would be in the forefront of the enquiry on the second model of pluralist democracy considered above have been excluded from the front door only to reappear at the back.[118]

A final response to the argument presented above[119] might assume the following form. It might be argued that the limited scope of constitutional review is justified for reasons of judicial competence. The contention would be that the judiciary are more suited to resolving issues which are related to process because they have expertise in this area, and also because in doing so the courts are not thereby trespassing upon areas which should be regarded as within the legislative domain. It is clear, as we have seen, that judicial competence is a factor which features within Ely's own analysis.[120]

[117] Ely, *Democracy and Distrust*, 152.

[118] The line between direct and indirect substantive review may be rendered more tenuous by the recognition of the 'feedback loop' which connects the two. The very decision to evaluate, *inter alia*, past distributional patterns in determining whether a group is likely to be an eternal loser in the pluralist bargain, and to review legislation which affects such groups more closely, will necessarily affect the chances of survival of the particular piece of legislation which is under scrutiny. The court may not be enforcing some ideal distributional pattern when considering this legislation. It will none the less be engaging in some 'distributional vision', in the sense that the particular statute would never have been reviewed at all, had not the court decided, *inter alia* upon social and economic grounds, that the group in question was likely to be a permanent loser in the pluralist bazaar.

[119] See above, p. 108.

[120] *Democracy and Distrust*, pp. 88, 102.

This response fails, however, to provide the requisite justification for the theory of constitutional review actually espoused by Ely. The obvious difficulty with the response is the overlap between process and substance which has been encountered throughout the previous discussion. One cannot assume that the judiciary possess some special expertise in such matters of 'process', as if all that were being considered were the technical rules of the adversary process in a criminal trial. Difficult and contestable substantive judgements concerning the nature of a political community will be involved.

There is also a less evident, but equally important, difficulty with this response. Whatever one may believe about judicial competence as such, one thing is clear. A conception of the proper role for the judiciary cannot by some magical technique of 'relation back' alter the nature of pluralist democracy, nor can it change the nature of the problems which beset such a system. A particular conception of the appropriate role for the judiciary cannot somehow justify the argument that a system of constitutional review founded upon the ills of pluralist democracy would concentrate our *initial* attention upon process. An exponent of the *second* model of pluralist democracy might well argue that a system of review designed to address the ills of pluralism would, at the outset, have to address a whole range of social, economic, and political factors, including those related to substance as well as process. Such an advocate might well then recognize limits to the enterprise flowing from a perception of the appropriate role for the judiciary. The precise nature of those limits might well be controversial. This is, however, very different from an argument which seeks to maintain that there is a neat fit between the problems of pluralist democracy, and the proper role for the judiciary.[121] To invoke the word process as if it were the self-evident answer to both issues is to present a symmetry which is apparent not real.

6. PLURALISM AND PROCESS: THE DILEMMA

The descriptive and normative difficulties which attend the public-choice model have been considered above. The model of constitutional adjudication advanced by Ely is intended to address and

[121] Ibid. 87–8.

alleviate deficiencies arising within pluralist democracy. The perfection of this design is, however, hampered by two obstacles.

On the one hand, the recognition that important value choices lie behind a particular conception of pluralist democracy, and are also embedded within ostensibly procedural norms, challenges the value-free claims of the enterprise. If no objective criterion exists from which such judgements can be made, what entitles the judiciary to engage in such value judgements when they emerge in the context of evaluating process? Any attempt to distinguish between the type of value judgements which underpin process, and those which relate to other fundamental values, is itself beset by the difficulty of drawing the line between the two.

On the other hand, there is the realization that a conception of constitutional review which is restricted, in theory at least, to process will prove of limited utility in alleviating the deficiencies of pluralism. The closer one comes to eradicating such blocks or imbalances, the less tenable does it become to pretend that review is based upon process. In this respect Ely's jibe against fundamental-rights theorists rebounds upon his own thesis. He criticizes such theories for many reasons, one of which is that the very choice of issues which are deemed to be fundamental reflects middle-class values, such as expression, education, academic freedom, and the like. 'But watch most fundamental-rights theorists start edging toward the door when someone mentions jobs, food or housing: those are important, sure, but they aren't *fundamental*.'[122]

Yet he fails to perceive the applicability of the same type of critique against his own thesis. Given that the traditional model of pluralism does not work in pristine fashion, the very elaboration of devices to cure these defects necessitates a prior decision as to the most potent causes of the breakdown. That decision is not self-evident or value free. Ely's thesis, by excluding many instances of social and economic inequality in the electoral process itself or in the legislation which ensues thereafter, is susceptible to the same type of criticism which he levels at others. He assumes that systemic malfunction within the political market serves to concentrate our attention upon issues such as freedom of speech and association, as if it were self-evident that these were the most important and exclusive causes of pluralist imbalance.

[122] *Democracy and Distrust*, p. 59; italics in the original.

How far social and economic distributional concerns should be a matter for constitutional adjudication is a complex question which will be considered in more detail hereafter. Such concerns are ruled out of bounds by the ostensible concentration on process. The paradox resides in the constraints imposed by this apparent concentration on process. We can pretend that we are ameliorating the ills of pluralism. But then we can, as Alice said, pretend anything. The danger may well reside in what we find if we confront reality. As Unger states:

> If it turned out that the irremediable disadvantages that trigger the application of generality-correcting equal protection were widespread, one of two disturbing conclusions would follow. The judiciary would have to assume ever greater responsibilities to revise the results of legislation and to transform, through such review, the structure of power in society. . . . Alternatively—and far more plausibly, given the constraints upon judicial power—the judiciary might simply refuse to acknowledge or correct the irremediable disadvantages. These disadvantages would then accumulate or rigidify, and produce a long sequel of subversive effects upon the claims of the established order to allegiance and of the underlying conception to credibility.[123]

One further paradox merits brief mention. Not only will an exclusive concern with process fail to redress the problems of pluralism. Pluralist theory itself undermines or weakens the classic case against the judiciary undertaking substantive review. Modern pluralist thought is not only based on the conception that groups within the normal political process will bargain to reach a substantive decision. It challenges the previously accepted orthodoxy that the formal legislature wields a monopoly of public power. Important policy decisions are seen as emanating from interest groups outside the process of government, working with whichever part of the legislative process is most likely to be supportive of its goals.[124] The results may be cloaked with some scintilla of formal legitimacy by being presented for legislative approval. Whether they even achieve this will be dependent upon the precise method by

[123] R. M. Unger, 'The Critical Legal Studies Movement', 96 *Harv. L. Rev.* 563, 608–9 (1983).

[124] See, e.g. Bentley, *The Process of Government*, chs. 13–15, 18, 19; Truman, *The Governmental Process*, chs. 3, 4, 11, 12, 13; H. Kariel, *The Decline of American Pluralism* (1961), 47–8; T. J. Lowi, *The End of Liberalism: Ideology, Policy, and the Crisis of Public Authority* (1969), 48, 49, 84, 90.

which public policy is implemented in a particular area. This is not to say that the traditional organs of representative government lack any real power. That would be nonsense. The point is rather that pluralist theory stresses the continuum between state and society, the interplay between representative and non-representative institutions, and the very real power possessed by the latter.

This, of course, does not serve to justify the court rendering substantive value judgements. Two wrongs do not make a right. Bickel addressed this point forcefully some time ago:[125] the recognition that some non-representative institutions make political decisions does not in itself justify adding the court to that list. This may well be true. Yet the very realization that unelected, non-representative institutions do share in the exercise of public power should at least cause us to reflect a little further.

The standard objection to substantive constitutional review is that it replaces a value judgement made by the elected, responsible legislature with one given by the unelected judiciary. A key assumption is, therefore, that legislatures possess a monopoly of power over public decision-making. Representative democracy is presumed to be unitary. If, in fact, society is characterized by a dispersion of power, if some substantive value judgements are made by non-representative institutions, should we then be so concerned with the court exercising a similar power? Should we be so intent upon cleansing review of all judgements about substance, in order to restrict it to the unsullied, virginal sphere of process?[126]

7. ADMINISTRATIVE LAW

a. Pluralism, Delegation, and Interest Representation

The purpose and direction of administrative law is a topic which is much debated. Should the 'meaning' of administrative law be

[125] *The Least Dangerous Branch*, pp. 18–20. Bickel's attempt to distinguish between the political power wielded by groups and that of the judiciary when and if it exercises substantive review is not, however, very convincing. Thus, e.g., 'admirals and generals' are said to be responsible to officials who are themselves elected and 'through whom the line runs directly to a majority'. When such non-elected personnel do make policy they do so only in an interstitial fashion; ibid. 19–20. Few today would be as certain as Bickel on either of these issues; cf. A. S. Miller, *The Modern Corporate State: Private Governments and the American Constitution* (1976). See also Ely, *Democracy and Distrust*, p. 67.

[126] It is, e.g., not certain that judicial review is more 'final' than are other decisions

sought in substantive judicial review, internal agency controls, rule-making, or some combination of these and other devices which are at our disposal? A pluralist conception of democracy, with its emphasis upon group bargain, places stress upon process considerations. It favours delegation of power as a method of more finely accommodating such bargains between competing groups. It also fosters interest representation with the object of ensuring that those affected by agency decisions will be able to participate in their formulation. What is of interest, in the light of the preceding discussion, is the extent to which the courts have not only fostered such process rights, but have also felt the need for more substantive forms of judicial control. The infirmities of pluralism may indicate that, while process rights are a necessary element of administrative law, they are not sufficient; that more substantive judicial control is necessary in order to guard against the danger of overpowering faction. This will be explored later in this section. For the present let us turn to a consideration of delegation. Lowi captures the essential connection between delegation and pluralism.

Too much law would obviously be intolerable to scientific pluralist theory. In a vitally important sense, *value-free political science is logically committed to the norm of delegation of power because delegation of power is the self-fulfilling mechanism of prediction in modern political science.* Clear statutes that reduce pluralistic bargaining also reduce drastically the possibility of scientific treatment of government as simply part of the bundle of bargaining processes and multiple power structures.[127]

In the complex modern world a tension is created. On the one hand, it may be felt that certain activities require control or regulation. On the other, the inner thrust of pluralism indicates that authority should emerge from individual bargains for it to prove acceptable. Broad delegations of power to administrative agencies before which interested parties compete and bargain become the mechanism whereby this tension is eased.

Lowi provides us with an interesting developmental analysis of delegation and the administrative process. His theme is that with

reached with non-representative institutions; see H. H. Wellington, 'The Nature of Judicial Review', 91 *Yale L.J.* 486 (1982). Moreover, judicial decisions are at least more open to public scrutiny compared to the covert bargains characteristic of pluralist society.

[127] *The End of Liberalism*, p. 127; italics in the original. The emphasis upon delegation of power is also evident in the work of the UK pluralists; see below, ch. 5 secs. 2, 4.

the passage of time empowering legislation has sanctioned ever broader, more open textured grants of authority to the administrative agencies.[128] Certain aspects of Lowi's analysis may well be questioned.[129] Differences of opinion on the developmental detail should not, however, cloud the importance of the central point. Delegation fits the logic of pluralist thought. If activities must be regulated, they should be regulated through bargaining, through group participation in agency decision-making. The decentralization of decision-making fostered by delegation facilitates this end. Delegation in broad, open-textured terms enhances it still further by providing nothing but the minimum of central guidance to curb the policy-making which results from the bargains struck by the parties themselves. Congress rests content with this state of affairs. Its tacit approval, and its refusal to fill out the interstices of legislation with more specific standards, are explicable because less troublesome than the alternative. Specification of standards means making a judgement. Making a judgement may mean making an enemy of those who disapprove of one's choice. Much easier to pass the buck to the administrative agency. Even better if, in doing so, one can claim to be furthering the process of democratic decision-making. The tacit approval of Congress is itself buttressed by that of the courts as manifested by the moribund nature of the non-delegation doctrine. Earlier decisions, striking down legislation which did not articulate with sufficient specificity the standards to be applied by the administrative agency, have been largely ignored.[130] It will be interesting to see whether hints of a revival in this area are developed in the future.[131] For the most part the courts have focused their attention in a different direction. They have nurtured the second of the twin elements of pluralist non-constitutional review, interest representation.

Interest representation may be seen in operation at different

[128] *The End of Liberalism*, pp. 133–41. See also R. M. Unger, *Law in Modern Society* (1976).

[129] His description of the early antitrust legislation is too sanguine. It was less concrete than Lowi maintains. See R. H. Bork, 'The Rule of Reason and the Per Se Concept: Price Fixing and Market Division I', 74 *Yale L.J.* 774 (1965), and 'The Rule of Reason and the Per Se Concept: Price Fixing and Market Division II', 75 *Yale L.J.* 373 (1966).

[130] *A.L.A. Schechter Poultry Corp.* v. *United States* 295 U.S. 495 (1935); *Panama Refining Co.* v. *Ryan* 293 U.S. 388 (1935). See Breyer and Stewart, *Administrative Law and Regulatory Policy*, pp. 68–95.

[131] *Industrial Union Department, AFL-CIO* v. *American Petroleum Institute* 448 U.S. 607 (1980); *American Textile Mfrs. Institute* v. *Donovan* 452 U.S. 490 (1981).

points in the legal system in the United States.[132] Five may be briefly reviewed here. Firstly, the courts have expanded the class of interests which have been entitled to participate in agency decision-making. Due process will protect the individual deleteriously affected by the refusal to grant that person certain benefits, or one who is the subject of enforcement action.[133] A person may, however, wish to intervene in agency proceedings which have already begun in order to ensure that a certain viewpoint is taken into account, or to stimulate agency action which would not otherwise take place. The ability to do so is of importance to a pluralist conception of non-constitutional review. If review is to function as a means for ensuring that a broad range of interests is enabled to bargain and compete in a decentralized, surrogate, political process, then the ability to intervene in agency proceedings, or to awaken the comatose into action, is vital. Statutory provisions vary on this issue.[134] The courts have none the less recently adopted a liberal approach to claims for intervention by interested parties, arguing that such interveners play a valuable role in representing certain aspects of the public interest.[135]

A second, and related, way in which judicial concern with public participation has manifested itself has been through the expansion of standing to seek judicial review of agency action.[136] Courts have explicitly linked the scope of intervention before the agency itself, and the scope of standing to seek judicial review.[137] Commentators

[132] For general discussion, see, D. L. Shapiro, 'Some Thoughts on Intervention before Courts, Agencies, and Arbitrators' 81 *Harv. L. Rev.* 721 (1968); R. C. Cramton, 'The Why, Where and How of Broadened Public Participation in the Administrative Process', 60 *Geo. L.J.* 525 (1971–2), and 'A Comment on Trial-Type Hearings in Nuclear Power Plant Siting' 58 *Va. L. Rev.* 585 (1972); E. Gellhorn, 'Public Participation in Administrative Proceedings', 81 *Yale L.J.* 359 (1971–2); J. L. Sax, "The (Unhappy) Truth about NEPA', 26 *Okl. L. Rev.* 239 (1973); R. B. Stewart, 'The Reformation of American Administrative Law', 88 *Harv. L. Rev.* 1667 (1975) Breyer and Stewart, *Administrative Law and Regulatory Policy*, ch. 10.

[133] For the general scope of the due process doctrine see Breyer and Stewart, *Administrative Law and Regulatory Policy*, ch. 7.

[134] In brief: (a) statutes dealing with specific agencies may have specific provisions on intervention; (b) other statutes are silent; (c) agency rules or discretion may determine intervention rights; (d) The Administrative Procedure Act 1946 allows an interested person to appear in certain cases, but also allows exclusion if time or the public interest so requires; s. 5(b), 5 U.S.C. 544(c).

[135] *The National Welfare Rights Organization* v. *Finch* 429 F. 2d 725, 736–8 (D.C. Circ. 1970); *Office of Communication of the United Church of Christ* v. *F.C.C. (Church of Christ I)* 359 F. 2d 994, 1003–4 (D.C. Circ. 1966).

[136] Stewart, 'The Reformation of American Administrative Law', pp. 1723–48.

[137] E.g. *Finch*, above, n. 135.

have endorsed this connection.[138] It is not therefore surprising to find that the expansion of standing to seek judicial review has been caused by similar considerations to those which have prompted increased intervention rights before the agency itself. The law relating to standing had traditionally been narrowly circumscribed and bore analogy to the earlier approach to due process. Standing was posited upon the possession of a private law right, or something closely proximate thereto. Both were infected with the same conception of administrative law, the protection of private autonomy, and the correlative settling of a private dispute which the individual had with the government. It is not surprising that this increasingly unrealistic façade began to crumble in both areas. The precise metes and bounds of standing cannot be considered here. At a general level,[139] the transformation of standing has strengthened the impression that the object of administrative law is not just the protection of private autonomy, but includes also the accommodation of a broader range of associated and collective interests which are concerned with the direction of agency action.

Public participation directed towards the initiation of agency action represents the third way in which interest representation has been enhanced. This is of importance because there may be no proceedings in which the individual or the group can intervene. Willingness on the part of the courts to review prosecutorial or enforcement discretion provides an important element in ensuring the representation of interested parties. It is of special significance because the failure to initiate agency action may well be the result of mutual accommodation between powerful interest groups and the agency itself. This would be threatened by the 'interference' of protagonists who hold diverse views. One need not go so far as saying that an agency has been captured by its main clients. Imbalance in the pluralist process may well be more subtle than the tendentious verb 'capture' would connote. A way of considering problems may develop in which the agency perceives issues through blinkers; in which the advantages and disadvantages of certain action are unconsciously thought of in terms of the major client groups; and into which it becomes increasingly difficult to inject new

[138] Breyer and Stewart, *Administrative Law and Regulatory Policy*, pp. 1194–5. For a contrary view, see L. L. Jaffe, *Judicial Control of Administrative Action* (1965), 524–6.

[139] For detailed consideration, see Stewart, 'The Reformation of American Administrative Law', pp. 1723–48; C. A. Wright, *Law of Federal Courts* (4th edn., 1983), 53–84.

data. The courts have rejected arguments that the prosecutorial discretion was wholly unreviewable.[140] The importance of these developments is shown by Stewart.

> By affording all affected interests with a recognized stake in agency policy the right to demand and participate in such procedures, *Medical Committee*, *Ruckelshaus*, and the cases following them facilitate effective judicial review of asserted agency laxity or bias. When the agency has clearly failed to protect the beneficiaries of the administrative scheme, courts have gone so far as to mandate appropriate enforcement measures. . . . Where the agency has already initiated enforcement proceedings, courts have, in selected cases, scrutinized settlements of these proceedings. The judges have thus begun to assume the ultimate protection of the collective social interests which administrative schemes were designed to secure.[141]

The fourth device through which the courts have furthered public participation in agency decision-making is a corollary of those adumbrated above. Ability to intervene in agency proceedings, or to initiate agency action, would be of little value if the agency could simply go through the motions of listening to the intervener's arguments without according them any real weight. A necessary adjunct, therefore, to the rights of intervention or initiation is that the agency accords adequate consideration to the opinions presented to it.[142] The courts have responded by demanding that administrators do just that. A similar concern to ensure that the administrator grants more than formal obeisance to the arguments presented by contending groups is also evident in the more rigorous attitude towards review in the hard-look doctrine,[143] and in recent interpretations of the arbitrary and capricious standard. Under

[140] Stewart, 'The Reformation of American Administrative Law', pp. 1752–6; Breyer and Stewart, *Administrative Law and Regulatory Policy*, pp. 1200–11 R. B. Stewart and C. R. Sunstein, 'Public Programs and Private Rights', 95 *Harv. L. Rev.* 1193 (1982); *Medical Committee for Human Rights* v. *SEC* 432 F. 2d 654 (D.C. Circ. 1970), vacated as moot, 404 U.S. 403 (1972); *Environmental Defense Fund* v. *Ruckelshaus* 439 F. 2d 584 (D.C. Circ. 1971). For later cases, see, Breyer and Stewart, *Administrative Law and Regulatory Policy*, pp. 1208–10.

[141] 'The Reformation of American Administrative Law', pp. 1755–6.

[142] 'The Reformation of American Administrative Law', pp. 1756–60; Breyer and Stewart, *Administrative Law and Regulatory Policy*, pp. 1211–15; *Office of Communication of United Church of Christ* v. *FCC (Church of Christ II)* 425 F. 2d 543 (D.C. Circ. 1969). Cf. C. S. Diver, 'Policymaking Paradigms in Administrative Law', 95 *Harv. L. Rev.* 393, 422–5 (1981), who argues that increased participatory rights can be at odds with other doctrinal tools which are aimed at ensuring that an agency adopts a comprehensive, considered analysis of the problem assigned to it.

[143] For a discussion of the hard-look doctrine, see Breyer and Stewart, *Administrative Law and Regulatory Policy*, pp. 341–71.

these tests the courts will insist upon reasoned decisions, ensure that relevant factors are taken into account, and assess whether the agency's conclusion is consonant with the evidence presented.[144] The appropriate standard or intensity of such review is a complex matter, and the Supreme Court now appears to be advocating less intensive review than that postulated above.[145] Judicial competence to evaluate technical evidence is one such issue which has divided the judiciary. The dangers of judicial substitution of judgement presents another facet of the problem. The relationship of review to pluralism presents a third. On one view, provided that the agency is open to interested groups and gives some adequate consideration to the contending views, the result should stand. The interplay of group interests represents the public interest, and the courts have exhausted their legitimate role. On another view more is required. Even if the process is open to all who are concerned, there may be a danger of Madisonian faction distorting the agency outcome from that intended in the original legislation. The possibility of substantive controls to supplement process rights, a theme which was developed at the outset of this section, has been defended by Sunstein.

> Reviewing courts are attempting to ensure that the agency has not merely responded to political pressure but that it is instead deliberating in order to identify and implement the public values that should control the controversy. A principal concern is that without the procedural and substantive requirements of the hard-look doctrine, the governing values may be subverted in the enforcement process through the domination of powerful private groups.[146]

[144] See e.g. *Motor Vehicle Manufacturers Assn.* v. *State Farm Mutual Automobile Ins. Co.* 463 U.S. 29, 42–3 (1983), where the court adopted a broad view of arbitrary and capricious. Cf. *Baltimore Gas and Electric Co.* v. *Natural Resources Defense Council* 462 U.S. 87 (1983), where a narrower reading is given to the same phrase. The broader interpretation of the *State Farm* case bears analogy to the broader view of unreasonableness within UK law; see P .P. Craig, *Administrative Law* (2nd edn., 1989), 300–3.

[145] For general discussion prior to *Chevron*, see Breyer and Stewart, *Administrative Law and Regulatory Policy*, pp. 350–4, 1213–15. The less intensive attitude to review emerges in *Chevron, U.S.A., Inc.* v. *Natural Resources Defense Council, Inc.* 467 U.S. 837, 842–3 (1984). See also the materials cited in n. 146 below.

[146] 'Interest Groups', pp. 29, 63; C. R. Sunstein, 'Deregulation and the Hard-Look Doctrine' (1983) *Sup. Ct. Rev.* 177. The following are also of relevance; R. B. Stewart, 'Regulation, Innovation and Administrative Law: A Conceptual Framework', 69 *Calif. L. Rev.* 1256 (1981); P. J. Harter, 'Negotiating Regulations: A Cure for Malaise', 71 *Geo. L.J.* 1 (1982); Diver, 'Policymaking Paradigms in Administrative Law' (1981); A. C. Aman, 'Administrative Law in a Global Era: Progress, Deregulatory Change, and the Rise of the Administrative Presidency', 73 *Cornell L. Rev.* 1101 (1988); C. R. Farina, 'Statutory Interpretation and the Balance of Power in the Administrative State', 89 *Col. L. Rev.* 452 (1989).

The final method of fostering interest representation is in some ways the most general.[147] This is to be found in those requirements of the Administrative Procedure Act 1946 which apply to rulemaking. The APA provides for two basic types of rule-making. Notice and comment rule-making requires the agency to publish a general notice of the proposed rule in the Federal Register, specifying the time and place of the rule-making proceedings, the legal authority relied upon for their issuance, and the content of the proposed rules.[148] Interested parties are allowed to submit written comments, and, at the discretion of the agency, to have the opportunity for oral argument. The notice and comment procedure is subject to a number of important exceptions.[149] The second main type of rule-making procedure to be found in the APA is more formal. It operates when the relevant statute provides that rules should be made on the record after opportunity for agency hearing. The more formal nature of the enquiry normally includes the taking of evidence through adversary trial-like proceedings by a hearing officer or administrative law judge, an initial decision made upon the basis of this evidence, followed by the opportunity for an appeal on the basis of the record composed by the original decision-maker.[150] Only where rule-making is of this type does an exclusive evidentiary record exist which can then be reviewed by the court. The ambit of formal rule-making has, however, been curtailed by the Supreme Court.[151] The two species of rule-making adumbrated above have been supplemented by a third. This has taken the form of a hybrid procedure, requiring more than the notice and comment procedure, but less than formal rule-making. Courts have built upon the provisions of the APA concerned with notice and comment, transforming these into 'paper hearings' in certain areas.[152] These modifications have

[147] See below, ch. 10 secs. 3, 4, 5, for a consideration of the republican attitude to interest groups.

[148] 5 U.S.C. 553. See, generally, Breyer and Stewart, *Administrative Law and Regulatory Policy*, ch. 5.

[149] There are two types of limit: (a) certain substantive areas such as welfare and government contracts, are excluded; (b) certain types of rules, such as interpretive rules, are also not covered.

[150] 5 U.S.C. 556, 557; Breyer and Stewart, *Administrative Law and Regulatory Policy*, pp. 567–8.

[151] *United States* v. *Florida East Coast Ry. Co.* 410 U.S. 224 (1973). For discussion, see Breyer and Stewart, *Administrative Law and Regulatory Policy*, pp. 569–82.

[152] Breyer and Stewart, *Administrative Law and Regulatory Policy*, pp. 597–8, 603–4. See, more generally, ibid. 592–604.

been complemented by statutory changes requiring a similar intermediate-style rule-making procedure in particular areas.[153] The development of hybrid rule-making has, however, been blunted, if not halted, by a Supreme Court decision disapproving of the judicial imposition of procedures additional to those required by the APA.[154]

The movement of US law towards greater interest representation has, therefore, not been entirely uniform in pace or direction.[155] While the courts have expanded initiation and intervention rights in agency adjudicatory proceedings, recent trends in the rule-making context have been more ambivalent. Supreme Court decisions which have limited the scope or content of rule-making procedures may not have been primarily motivated by a desire to limit interest representation. That has, however, been one of the indirect results of, for example, the limitation placed upon hybrid rule-making.

b. Pluralism and Administrative Law: Criticism and Uncertainty

The pluralist conception of administrative law has not been immune from criticism. Like the pluralist vision of constitutional law, it has come under fire from a number of different directions. Two may be identified here.

First, there are those who wish to see a revival of the non-delegation doctrine in order to enforce greater specificity in the articulation of congressional standards. This call has emanated from a number of writers who are not necessarily uniform in their own beliefs. We have already seen that Ely advocates a newly invigorated non-delegation doctrine.[156] Judge Skelly Wright has articulated a similar view.[157] A more strident opponent of the pluralist ethic, Lowi,[158] is in agreement with both Ely and Judge Skelly Wright on

[153] Breyer and Stewart, *Administrative Law and Regulatory Policy*, pp. 604–7.

[154] *Vermont Yankee Nuclear Power Corp.* v. *Natural Resources Defense Council* 435 U.S. 519 (1978). For comment see R. B. Stewart, 'Vermont Yankee and the Evolution of Administrative Procedure', 91 *Harv. L. Rev.* 1805 (1978); C. Byse, 'Vermont Yankee and the Evolution of Administrative Procedure: A Somewhat Different View', 91 *Harv. L. Rev.* 1823 (1978); S. G. Breyer, 'Vermont Yankee and the Courts' Role in the Nuclear Power Controversy', 91 *Harv. L. Rev.* 1833 (1978).

[155] Breyer and Stewart, *Administrative Law and Reegulatory Policy*, pp. 1199–200. For the interrelationship between interest representation, freedom of information, and laws requiring that agencies deliberate in public, see ibid. 1228–59.

[156] *Democracy and Distrust*, pp. 131–3.

[157] Judge Skelly Wright, 'Beyond Discretionary Justice', 81 *Yale L.J.* 575, 584–5 (1972). See also the cases cited above nn. 130, 131.

[158] *The End of Liberalism* (1969), 154–5, 298.

this issue. He vehemently opposes the bargaining which characterizes agency decision-making, castigates open-textured grants of discretionary power, and wishes the rule of law to be restored by giving renewed attention to the non-delegation doctrine.

There is little doubt that the doctrine could be revived to the extent that the courts could curtail very broad, open-textured delegations of power. There is, however, equally little doubt that there are real limitations to the efficacy of this device. It may be difficult to specify the standards to be applied in a novel area of regulatory policy. The judiciary may, as Stewart has pointed out,[159] not be in a good position to assess whether the degree of specification of standards given in the statute represents the best obtainable at that moment. The divide between abdication of legislative responsibility and the limits imposed by the lack of congressional knowledge may be exceedingly difficult to draw.

How successful a revival of the non-delegation doctrine could be depends moreover on the precise nature of the objective. Such a revival could, subject to the limitations noted above, go some way to increasing the relative strength and responsibility of the elected government at the expense of political bargaining at the agency level. To assume that it can do more is misplaced. Lowi places great emphasis on the doctrine, but it would do little to redress the disadvantages which he ascribes to interest-group pluralism. His own indictment of this political credo replicates the essence of his argument which we addressed earlier: the inability to plan, the inability of a non-rule-based system to achieve justice, the corruption of democratic formalism, the fact that group competition is not self-correcting and that it is characterized by inequality in the political and economic power of the protagonists.[160]

Breathing life into the non-delegation doctrine might have some impact upon the incremental nature of decision-making which is integral to pluralist analysis. There is none the less little evidence to suggest that central decision-making as a whole would not remain incremental in nature.[161] A range of constraints upon governmental freedom of action, including budgetary limits and the relatively small room for manœuvre imposed by past decisions, combines to

[159] 'The Reformation of American Administrative Law', p. 1696.

[160] See above, ch. 3 sec. 2d.

[161] On decision-making, see H. Simon, *Administrative Behaviour* (2nd edn , 1957); D.Braybrooke and C. E. Lindblom, *A Strategy of Decision* (1963); A. G. McGrew and M. J. Wilson (eds.), *Decisionmaking, Approaches and Analysis* (1982).

limit radical, systematic shifts in public policy. It is, moreover, unclear how far rejuvenation of the non-delegation doctrine, or any other of Lowi's proposals, would correct the fundamental defects of pluralism which he sees flowing from group inequality.

Legislation itself would still result from a combination of bargaining and compromise within the legislature, coupled with the application of group pressure from outside. Bargaining within the legislature would itself still be the result of an elective process in which groups competed unequally, and hence imperfectly. Parent legislation will be just as beset by the problems of which Lowi speaks as will the 'surrogate legislation' arrived at by bargaining before an agency. The accommodation of competing groups is not more self-correcting at congressional than agency level. In certain respects a reinvigoration of the non-delegation doctrine may exacerbate the problem. By increasing the concentration of power at the national level, it is likely to augment the influence of large organizations,[162] and to reinforce the imperfect nature of the group competition, since it is the powerful groups which will be better able to muster the resources to apply pressure on the national forum.

Lowi also argues that renewed emphasis upon the non-delegation doctrine should be buttressed by agency formulation of rules. Davis has been the leading exponent of the idea that agencies should be encouraged to structure and confine their discretion through the formulation of rules.[163] There may be significant advantages to this

[162] On interest-group pressure, see, e.g., T. J. Lowi (ed.), *Legislative Politics U.S.A.* (3rd edn., 1973), pts. 4, 5; S. J. Makielski, *Pressure Politics in America* (1980); D. S. Ippolito and T. G. Walker, *Political Parties, Interest Groups and Public Policy: Group Influence in American Politics* (1980); G. K. Wilson, *Interest Groups in the United States* (1981); I. McLean, *Dealing in Votes* (1982); G. Wootton, *Interest Groups, Policy and Politics in America* (1985). The precise degree of influence wielded by pressure groups at the national level is difficult to estimate. Two issues become interwoven. First, there is the definitional issue, as to what constitutes an exercise of influence, pressure, or power. The relative importance of overt pressure, the ability of groups to set the agenda, non-decisions, and the structural limitations placed upon actors in the political world continue to be debated by those within the field. Secondly, there is the more 'empirical' issue as to the evidence of lobbying activities and the like by various interest groups at the national level. The trend in the last decade appears to be towards increased organization by pressure groups at this level, caused partly at least by the need for business to defend its interests against consumer and environmental groups. See Wilson, *Interest Groups in the United States*, pp. 130–46.

[163] K. C. Davies, *Discretionary Justice: A Preliminary Inquiry* (1969). A large literature has developed on this topic: see, e.g., D. L. Shapiro, 'The Choice of Rulemaking or Adjudication in the Development of Administrative Policy', 78 *Harv. L. Rev.* 921 (1965); J. L. Jowell, *Law and Bureaucracy* (1975); D. J. Galligan, 'The Nature and Function of Policy within Discretionary Power' [1976] *P.L.* 332; R. Baldwin and

approach. Formal justice, in the sense of treating like cases alike, will be enhanced. Review may be facilitated by rendering the agency policy choices more apparent, and it may be easier for individuals to predict the results of their actions. The limitations of this technique must, however, be borne in mind. It may be difficult for a court to decide whether an agency has structured its discretion to the optimum degree. The policy which the agency is pursuing may not yet be ripe for rule formulation, and too precipitate an insistence upon rule-making may rob the agency of flexibility.

Moreover, in so far as agency rule-making is viewed as a cure for the ills of interest-group pluralism, it suffers from similar defects to the non-delegation argument. The rules which emerge will be based upon group participation through one of the techniques adumbrated above. Given the substantive inequalities which beset interest-group pluralism, it is not immediately evident why these will be alleviated through paying greater attention to rule-making. Addressing the form through which agency policy is expressed will not self-evidently cure or correct agency bias towards certain types of interest. It may indeed be exacerbated by being enshrined in rules.

A possible response would be to contend that there is a closer link between the formal justice secured through rule-making and the substantive inequalities spoken of above. The argument would be that rule-making would render the agency policy more explicit, and that review could enforce adequate consideration of all interests in the formulation of that policy. While this might occur, a number of factors limit the probability of the suggested connection. Agency bias may not be evident from the face of the rule. It may be more subtle or indirect, as for example in Selznick's study of the TVA.[164] Even where such imbalance is evident, judicial review framed in terms of adequacy of consideration may be of limited impact. The problem facing unrepresented groups is often that they lack the resources or cohesiveness to present a case against that advocated by their more powerful adversaries. If the object is, therefore, to redress the disequilibrium in the pluralist bargaining process, it will have to begin several stages further back. Moreover, in so far as such review can have any curative effect, this technique is not restricted to

K. Hawkins, 'Discretionary Justice: Davis Reconsidered' [1984] *P.L.* 570. See also the material above, n. 162; Stewart, 'The Reformation of American Administrative Law', pp. 1698–702.

[164] P. Selznick, *T.V.A. and the Grass Roots: A Study in the Sociology of Formal Organization* (1949).

agency policy articulated through rules. Courts are capable of using this device when reviewing agency decisions which result from adjudication.

The second main thematic challenge to the pluralist conception of administrative law has emerged from writers who question both the desirability and efficacy of interest representation as an organizing rationale for the subject. Two principal obstacles have been explored in the literature.[165] On the one hand, there are the difficulties of defining an interest, and of securing the adequate representation of affected interests. On the other hand, there are certain disadvantageous consequences which are said to flow from increased participatory rights. These include cost, delay, increased formality of procedure, and the questionable impact of such participatory rights upon the quality of decisions.[166]

The implicit thrust of these criticisms is important, and should be made explicit. At base they question the role of process rights in a pluralist democracy. Ely's thesis was, as we have seen, attempting to sustain the argument that process should be regarded as both a necessary and sufficient basis for constitutional law. The tenor of the arguments presented above was that this vision was defective. Process might well be conceived as a necessary facet of constitutional law, but it could not be regarded as sufficient. The critique of interest representation is of especial concern because it implicitly asks to what extent process rights are a necessary aspect of pluralist democracy as it operates at the level of administrative law. Let us, therefore, examine the two objections raised above.

How do we define an interest and how do we ensure that those who wish to voice their views are accorded an opportunity to do so? How do we prevent the more powerful lobbies from wielding coercive influence?[167] This is perhaps the central conceptual problem with increased participatory rights.

This problem undoubtedly exists. What is surprising is the very fact that commentators should ever have expected otherwise. If we are to regard such participation as a surrogate or complement to the normal political processes of representation and legitimation, why

[165] The seminal article is by Stewart, 'The Reformation of American Administrative Law'. Reference to other important articles will be found above, n. 132.

[166] A more radical attack will be explored below, ch. 11 sec. 4b. For an example of such an attack, see G. E. Frug, 'The Ideology of Bureaucracy in American Law', 97 *Harv. L. Rev.* 1276 (1984).

[167] Stewart, 'The Reformation of American Administrative Law', pp. 1762–70.

should we expect the problems which are apparent for the parent not also to affect the offspring? The literature concerning elections, legislating, and executive decision-making at the central level is replete with references to the effects of interest groups on these processes, the way in which certain channels of representative government are short-circuited or biased towards certain interests, and the difficulties of controlling and equalizing group power.[168] It is an endemic problem at all levels of decision-making within representative democracies. This is not to say that all legislation can be viewed simply as the outcome of conflicting group pressure. Nor is it to maintain that the obstacle of securing the adequate representation of affected interests is somehow made less difficult by being more widespread; the generality of a problem does not dilute or dissolve it.

However, the recognition of the broader context is of importance. Discussion is too often premised upon an implicit idealized conception of the way in which the democratic process operates in other parts of our political system. The problems of participation in administrative law are then juxtaposed to this rose-tinted vision. If the problems of ensuring the parity of group power, or the definition of an interest, are felt to rule out interest representation as one method of controlling and legitimating decision-making within administrative agencies, what is the effect of these problems upon the legitimacy of national decision-making? Do the imperfections of the child not also taint the parent? If we are willing to persevere with these processes, despite their imperfections, should the existence of similar problems at the administrative level sound the death-knell of participation within this area? When answering this question, a narrow perspective which is based upon a rigid dichotomy between administrative and constitutional decision-making can only seriously distort our vision. The very reason for the problem is that agencies are making decisions of a legislative nature, directly through rule-making or indirectly through adjudication. The exigencies of the modern state necessitate this, and will continue to do so even if the non-delegation doctrine were to be given a shot of

[168] See the materials above, nn. 124, 162. This is a theme which permeates the work of writers such as Bentley, Truman, Earl Latham, Dahl, Lowi, Bachrach, Presthus, Wright Mills, Floyd Hunter, Connolly, and many others. These authors might well however, as we have seen, disagree on many other issues, including, e.g., the extent of such influence, the degree of power concentration within particular areas, and the corrective for such disequilibrium.

adrenalin.[169] Viewed in this light a central issue becomes the feasibility of complementing or replicating the central representative process with some species of process before the agency itself. A pristine definition of an 'interest' or the 'perfect' representation of all interests may well not be possible, at *whichever* level of the decision-making process one is focusing upon.

What would be the consequence if, notwithstanding the argument presented above, we decide to pursue the game no further? We make a decision that, because of the conceptual objections, interest representation should not be regarded as an important aspect of administrative law in a pluralist democracy. Perfection is regarded as a chimera, the game is ended, and we desert the field of play.

This is, of course, an option. It is, however, only an option in a limited sense. We may desert the field, but the game will not thereby come to an end. All that will have happened is that we will have signalled our unwillingness to play any role in determining which interests should be represented in the decision-making process. Play will, however, continue. What form will it take? Different scenarios are possible. In some contexts the decision-makers may be enlightened and do their best to ensure the adequate representation of affected interests; in others they may consider the views of limited 'client' groups; in yet other areas they may proceed in a more autocratic fashion, consulting with few, if any, of those who are affected by their action.

A decision by 'us' to abstain is none the less a decision for being negative. To say that interest representation has 'failed' does not, therefore, somehow magically mean that it ceases to be of central importance to the decision-making process which characterizes administration. If lawyers believe that intervention within the game should cease, they implicitly countenance the disposition of interests presently considered by the agency, and refuse to accede to the requests of other groups who may wish their views to be heard. Powerful lobbies will continue to press their claims. A decline in

[169] Even if the non-delegation were to be revived in the way which Ely, Lowi , and Chief Justice Rehnquist so desire, this might ameliorate the problem but would not dispel it. Clearer articulation of standards would not remove the necessity for creative agency legislation on complex issues which the more finely tuned legislative dictates did not and could not resolve: e.g. such issues might not have been apparent; they might have been apparent but lack of experience might preclude any firm guidance from the legislature; the initial legislative standards, howsoever tightly drawn, might provide scant guidance on the resolution of a specific matter.

judicial concern for participation may well have only a marginal impact upon these groups. Their position might, in fact, be improved in so far as judicial abstinence facilitates the exercise of influence in more covert fashion. The losers in the process are more likely to be those groups who, without judicial support, may wield insufficient power to ensure that their views are taken into consideration.

Deserting the field of play may have another more indirect consequence. It is precisely because the problem of participation is one which permeates decision-making at all levels of society that we must realize that choices made within one area may well have an effect in other contexts. Studies have shown some connection between participation in governmental and non-governmental spheres.[170] While one cannot automatically assume that the converse will hold true, there is a reasonable likelihood that, if individuals are excluded from participating in governmental decision-making, this will have a negative effect upon participation in other contexts. If the democratic nature of the system is Schumpeterian, and depends solely upon the national arrangements for voting, the choice of representatives, and the resultant competition between them, then this link would be either unimportant or contested.[171] The same conclusion would follow if one adopted the behavioural thesis outlined earlier.[172] If, however, one takes a broader view and regards participation in many differing facets of life as integral to the maintenance of a truly democratic polity, then the effect of denying participation in one area upon the efficacy of its operation in another is not a matter which can be overlooked.

In summary, the problem of securing the adequate representation of interests, and of defining an interest, is a real one. It is, however, a problem which permeates all levels of decision-making within society, not just those which administrative lawyers customarily investigate. Perfection will not be attained.[173] To pretend that the

[170] See Pateman, *Participation and Democratic Theory* (1970); Bachrach, *The Theory of Democratic Elitism* (1967); Bottomore, *Elites and Society* (1964).

[171] For a discussion of the Schumpeterian view of democracy, and the connection between this view and the work of élite theorists and behaviouralists, see above, ch. 3 sec. 2c.

[172] See above, ch. 3 secs. 2c, d.

[173] For recent efforts, both judicial and statutory, to provide some measure of funding assistance to particular individuals or groups, see Breyer and Stewart, *Administrative Law and Regulatory Policy*, pp. 1216–27.

problem will disappear if lawyers cease to pay attention to it is mistaken. To do nothing is implicitly to accept the range of interests presently considered by the decision-maker. This will be likely to favour the more powerful lobbies, and may well have disadvantageous side-effects on participation in other parts of society.

The second principal objection to interest representation is that various disadvantageous or dysfunctional consequences are said to attend increased participatory rights.[174] These consequences vary. Decision-making may become protracted, since the decision-maker feels wary of excluding any participant who may have something to say which is of arguable relevance to the matter at hand. Compromises are rendered more difficult because of the large number of parties involved, and this can lead to the process becoming over judicialized and formal. Rule-making is rendered more problematic because the scope of interests to be considered tends to highlight the *ad hoc*, polycentric nature of the issue. The quality of the resultant decisions becomes difficult to calculate precisely because each of these decisions emerges from a complex one-off assessment which may be impossible to apply to other similar fact situations. Moreover, the grant of increased participatory rights may do little to alter the substantive inequalities of group power to which the agency is subject. The agency will, in other words, still remain subject to considerable pressure from powerful organized interests to arrive at a decision which is acceptable to their own aims.

The likelihood of some of these suggested consequences may be questioned, and will in any event be dependent upon the type of subject-matter which is in issue. For example, the argument that increased participatory rights would lead to recourse to more formal types of decision-making, and prevent informal negotiated compromise, is debatable. In some areas it could lead to the realization that formal adversarial–adjudicatory styles of procedures, which might be suited to bipartite disputes, are inappropriate to the resolution of more variegated multipartite problems. These procedures could then be modified or replaced by procedural norms which are more akin to mediation or arbitration.[175]

[174] Stewart, 'The Reformation of American Administrative Law', pp. 1770–81; Sax, 'The (Unhappy) Truth about NEPA', who argues that participatory rights can simply be a way for the agency to 'package' and 'sell' its own proposals.

[175] L. L. Fuller, 'Mediation: Its Forms and Functions', 44 S. *Cal. L. Rev.* 305 (1971), and 'The Forms and Limits of Adjudication', 92 *Harv. L. Rev.* 353 (1978); M.

The contention that expansion of participatory rights will necessarily slow down decision-making is not as self-evident as it appears at first sight. It is not clear that a form of mediation based upon a wider spectrum of views would always be more protracted than a more formal bipartite adversarial process. There is, moreover, a facet of speed which is not often considered. Even if the restriction of participatory rights were to expedite the initial decision, it must surely be the ultimate success of the administrative scheme with which we are concerned. Our conclusions concerning speed would, therefore, have to include an assessment of the extent to which the exclusion of certain interest groups from the original decision produced delays at other stages of the administrative process.[176] These could take many forms. The most obvious manifestation would be increased challenge to the scheme, or decisions made thereunder, by those who were not afforded any participatory rights. Less obvious, but equally important, might be passive resistance by those upon whom the efficacy of the scheme depends. Last, but by no means least, is the fact that the very substance of the policy might well be improved by allowing interested parties to proffer their views.

There is, moreover, a more fundamental point at stake. Even when such consequences do ensue, they cannot unequivocally be stated to be dysfunctional or deleterious to the decision-making process. Speed and the possibility of rule-making as opposed to *ad hoc* discretion are aspects of the decision-making process. Even where interest representation does place such consequences at risk, to conclude that this process is less good, deleterious, or some other epithet is partly to beg the question at issue. *If* the only way to achieve speed, negotiated compromise, or rules *were* to mean the

A. Eisenberg, 'Participation, Responsiveness and the Consultative Process', 92 *Harv. L. Rev.* 410 (1978); R. A. Macdonald, 'Judicial Review and Procedural Fairness in Administrative Law: II' (1980–1), 26 *McGill L.J.* 1.

[176] Lawyers are prone to think of the problems of bureaucracies in somewhat segmented, self-contained terms. The desirability of taking a broad view of the administrative process is important when considering the question of participation and delay. Modern organization theory which stresses a systems-analysis approach to bureaucracy emphasizes the interconnection between the inputs and outputs of administrative decision-making. One important output is the reception afforded to the rules by those whom they affect. See, e.g., P. J. O. Self, *Administrative Theories and Politics: An Inquiry into the Structure and Process of Modern Government* (2nd edn., 1977); J. Bourn, *Management in Central and Local Government* (1979). See also R. G. S. Brown and D. R. Steel, *The Administrative Process in Britain* (2nd edn., 1979).

exclusion of group interests whose views we believe to be prima facie relevant, then we would be faced with a difficult decision. The determination whether to admit these groups, even though this produced the consequences mentioned above, would be dependent upon a substantive value judgement as to the relative worth of these different goals.

c. *Pluralism and Administrative Law: Some Reflections*

The picture of a pluralist society populated by equal competing groups which bargain between themselves, and which are automatically self-correcting, no longer reflects reality. The previous analysis has shown how this vision has been shattered by, *inter alia*, the oligarchic and unequal nature of group competition. Whether the result should be more correctly depicted as élitism or élite pluralism is a matter on which debate continues.

Some of the implications of these developments for administrative law have been considered above. Given the existence of this modified form of pluralist democracy, the key question, as we have seen, is the appropriate focus for administrative law. The difficulties of reviving the non-delegation doctrine, and the equivocal benefits that would thereby be secured, have already been considered. Interest representation, although not without difficulty, should be of continuing relevance, even though the classical pluralist vision has been destroyed. It should be regarded as a presumptively necessary, if not sufficient, facet of administrative law.

The change from classical pluralism to élite pluralism[177] has affected all tiers of decision-making. In the foreseeable future, Congress will continue to find it necessary to delegate decisions upon legislative matters to administrative institutions, even if the non-delegation doctrine were to be revitalized. Whether 'legislation' occurs at the congressional or agency level may well be fortuitous. The opportunity for democratic input at the latter stage can be a valuable complement or surrogate for the centralized processes of representative democracy. We should be mindful of the inequalities of group power which exist, and aware of the élite pluralist nature of the participation which occurs before agencies. We should, however, also realize that these traits characterize decision-making at other levels within society. To correct these imbalances, whether on the

[177] See above, ch. 3 sec. 2c, for a discussion of this theme.

constitutional or administrative plane, would require substantive policies designed to redress the causes of these imperfections. Process will never in this sense be sufficient. It should, however, continue to be presumptively necessary. The transformation from classical pluralism to élite pluralism or élitism has increased rather than diminished this need. The very fact that political activity tends to be the preserve of the few should lead us to pause before declaring that the law should have no role to play in aiding those interests which do desire to participate.

The presumption may be displaced or the extent of such participation may be curtailed if circumstances warrant. It may, for example, be felt that participation in areas of mass administrative justice can be both impracticable and ineffective.[178] Increased attention to the internal organizational pattern of the agency, with the prophylactic aim of avoiding error and improving the quality of decision-making, may be perceived as a more profitable line of enquiry. The administrative 'map' is far too complex to be susceptible to one uniform approach. The relationship between interest representation and other tools at the disposal of administrative law will vary with the particular substantive area which is under consideration. This theme will be developed in more detail at a later stage.[179] Suffice it to say for now that our perception of that relationship will depend upon a clear articulation of the aims which the area is designed to serve. Differing perceptions as to the nature of these aims will produce varied prescriptions as to the correct package of such tools to be utilized in any one area. In this sense, neither interest representation nor any other single tool can provide *the* rationale for the entire subject-matter of administrative law.

The recognition of this fact should not, however, lead us to overreact in the opposing direction. The realization that interest representation has limits, that it cannot be applied universally, should not lead to the conclusion that it has been a failure. Society

[178] J. L. Mashaw, *Bureaucratic Justice* (1983); Breyer and Stewart, *Administrative Law and Regulatory Policy*, pp. 836–51; Diver, 'Policymaking Paradigms in Administrative Law', pp. 422–5.

[179] See below, ch. 6 secs. 2d, e. For more extensive development of this theme, see P. P. Craig, 'Discretionary Power in Modern Administration', in M. Bullinger (ed.), *Verwaltungsermessen im modernen Staat* (1986), 79–111. See also the discussion by Shapiro, Cramton, Gellhorn, and Stewart, above, n. 132, all of whom, albeit with differing degrees of emphasis, suggest that the scope of participatory rights should be determined upon functional criteria.

remains pluralistic, even in the form of élite pluralism. Many of the important insights of pluralism, including a more realistic conception of 'governing' institutions and an appreciation of the way in which policy evolves, continue to have lasting significance, notwithstanding doctrinal deficiencies which have been subsequently revealed. To deny that process rights still provide an important technique at our disposal is to controvert the reality of these insights. It is to revert to a unitary conception of democracy in which the assumption is that important policy decisions are made only by the formal machinery of centralised government. The citizen's process rights are exhausted by the vote and its ancillary attributes. Governments then govern directly, or indirectly through agencies. The individual is quiescent and the shadows of Schumpeter and the behaviouralists cast their pale light across the political stage.

5
PLURALISM, PROCESS, AND SUBSTANCE: UK (I)

1. INTRODUCTION

A benefit which is claimed to inhere in an unwritten constitution is its flexibility. The British genius for the *ad hoc* and the informal finds its ultimate manifestation in our ability to mould constitutional development to the needs of the present. Doctrine and abstract theorizing can be the preserve of others. We can trust to pragmatism and good sense. Such qualities have enabled us to avoid severe civil turmoil for over three hundred years. The nature of our constitutional constructs have been subtly transformed during this period, accommodating the shift from monarchical to parliamentary power. Other less dramatic changes can be met by the continuing adaptation of our constitutional norms.

This vision of constitutional order is not devoid of truth. The Constitution has proven capable of assimilating significant changes in the political balance of power. The vision is none the less a serious distortion of reality. To maintain that our constitutional law has kept pace with the developments of the last one hundred years is naïve. The reasons for this disjunction between established constitutional norms and political reality are not immediately evident. One important reason might reside in the very unwritten nature of the Constitution itself. This attribute might well, in a paradoxical sense, provide a partial explanation for our constitutional torpor. While unwritten constitutions are, in theory at least, easily altered, this can also lead to indeterminacy. It prompts searching enquiries as to the content of this malleable beast.[1] Such enquiries can cause unease, particularly when the answer is not at all immediately evident. It is small wonder then that we should heave a sigh of relief when a Dicey happens along to set us all straight. The domain of constitutional law is etched clearly, and demarcated from that of troublesome disciplines such as politics.[2] Our satisfaction is heightened when we

[1] This can, of course, occur even when the constitution is written.

[2] See A. V. Dicey, *An Introduction to the Study of the Law of the Constitution* (10th edn., 1959), ch. 1, in which Dicey outlines his perception of the 'true nature' of constitutional law.

realize that the content of the constitutional order accords so well with what we believe ought to be the case. Parliament sits like a colossus above the unitary political system. Its sovereignty dominates. Parliament is the repository of all public power and is also capable of any legal action. The inadequacy of the Diceyan thesis has already been considered. What should replace this vision is less immediately obvious. The analysis within this and the subsequent chapter will proceed in the following manner.

First, there will be an examination of the pluralist challenge to Dicey's unitary conception of democracy. There are a number of differing interpretations of pluralist democracy within the United Kingdom. It will, however, be argued that two principal types of pluralism can none the less be distinguished and that both of these are distinctive from the 'pure pluralism' which has subsisted in the United States. Both models of pluralism begin from similar descriptive foundations as to how power is exercised in modern society. The prescriptive conclusions which are drawn therefrom are, however, radically different, and both visions are beset by fundamental inner tensions. On the one hand, there is a vision of pluralism stressing group power, group rights and obligations, decentralization, and the interconnection between economic and political liberty, the latter requiring governmental intervention in order to secure such liberties for the individual. The early UK pluralists exemplify this line of thought. This approach was always subject to an inner tension between the desire for decentralization, and the existence of the requisite central authority to enable the economic objectives to be fulfilled. On the other hand, there is a more market-based conception of pluralist democracy which is apparent in some of the recent literature, and in governmental policy within the late 1970s and the 1980s. This second species of pluralist democracy acknowledges the existence of group power which constrains and shapes governmental action, hence its pluralist connotation. The connection between economic and political liberty is, however, conceived in different terms from that of the early pluralists. The market is viewed as the best 'arbitrator' of economic issues, and direct governmental regulation thereof is perceived as necessary only when there is market failure, the existence of which is closely defined. The sphere of legitimate governmental action is, therefore, drawn more narrowly. This second type of pluralism is also subject to inner tensions. The thesis may well be pluralist in admitting the existence of group power which constrains governmental action, and, albeit more controversially, by devolving decision-making in some areas to the market. In certain important respects it has, however, produced a more powerful, centralized conception of government. The fulfilment of those objectives which *do* remain within the sphere of the government may require increased control over other areas of decision-making within society, such as that of local authorities. Negotiations between the government and other power groupings within the state will be tightly circumscribed so that they do not jeopardize the primary goals which remain within the government's direct purview. There is, moreover, an authoritarian element which is present within current conservative philosophy which serves further to enhance the power of the centre.

Secondly, the consequences which should ensue for both administrative and constitutional law from an albeit imperfect pluralist democracy will be considered. It is clear that the nature of these consequences will alter depending upon which of the two preceding variants is adopted. To incant the phrase 'pluralist democracy' as if it furnished a self-evident answer is necessarily incomplete. There may be agreement that Dicey's unitary conception of the state was descriptively misconceived. There may be consensus on the existence of group power which shapes governmental behaviour. The prescriptive step, which entails drawing out the consequences concerning the nature of the state and its interrelationship with group power, will be more controversial.

The initial focus will be upon the development of process, and the way in which an understanding of pluralist democracy can enlighten us as to the appropriate ways in which process rights can be developed. It should be made clear at the outset that the object is not to argue that such process rights can be regarded as sufficient within public law. The value judgements which underlie the very determination of process rights have been considered in the previous chapter, as has the difficulty of sustaining any purely process-oriented conception of public law. The realization that such value judgements permeate any discussion of avowedly procedural norms will be reinforced in the discussion which follows. It will be argued that any such development of procedural rights will be accompanied, directly or indirectly, by increased attention to oversight of the substantive decisions made by those who come within the purview of public law. The way in which the two principal types of pluralism affect the development of such process rights will be considered in the course of the analysis.

Thirdly, it will be argued that the nature of the value judgements which underlie both procedural and substantive intervention cannot be deduced or inferred simply by invoking ideas of pluralist democracy *per se*. The place of procedural and substantive rights within such a view of democracy must be seen as part of a broader political theory which embraces an understanding of the nature of rights themselves. Only then can we adequately comprehend the way in which the value judgements underlying such rights are made, and the role which a particular conception of democracy plays in their formulation. The differing conclusions which the two principal variants of pluralist democracy produce will be analysed within this framework.

2. EARLY PLURALIST THOUGHT

The development of pluralist thought in the United Kingdom was eclectic, and the content of the resulting thesis differed markedly between pluralists. The unifying theme beneath this eclecticism was a challenge to the monistic theory of legal and political sovereignty inherent in the nineteenth-century models of representative democracy.[3] This conception of the state can be traced back considerably further, and finds its most forceful expression in the work of Hobbes. The fear of internal anarchy entailed the necessary absence of any intermediary power structures.[4] The individual and the state faced each other across a bare plain. Speaking of matters which weaken the commonwealth, Hobbes states:

> Another infirmity of a commonwealth is the immoderate greatness of a town, when it is able to furnish out of its own circuit, the number, and expense of a great army: as also the great number of corporations; which are as it were many lesser commonwealths in the bowels of a greater, like worms in the entrails of a natural man. To which may be added, the liberty of

[3] See, generally, D. Nicholls, *Three Varieties of Pluralism* (1974), and *The Pluralist State* (1975); G. D. Carson, *Group Theories of Politics* (1978); S. Ehrlich, *Pluralism On and Off Course* (1982).

[4] This is a point made by H. J. Laski, *The Foundations of Sovereignty* (1921), 13, 27, 28–9; E. Barker, *Reflections on Government* (1942), 142–4.

disputing against absolute power by pretending to political prudence; which though bred for the most part in the lees of the people, yet animated by false doctrines, are perpetually meddling with the fundamental laws, to the molestation of the commonwealth; like the little worms, which physicians call *ascarides*.[5]

It was Austin who 'cleansed' this conception of the absolute, monistic sovereign.[6] It was his analytical discourse which purported to demonstrate logically the indissoluble and illimitable nature of sovereign power. Dicey added the finishing touch. There would be a natural congruence between the legal and political sovereign, between Parliament and the people. Fear was misplaced. What had been erected in fear of anarchy could now be preserved as the foundation of harmony.[7]

The analysis of the pluralists brought disorder to this convivial harmony. Maitland spearheaded one avenue of attack, having been influenced by the work of Von Gierke.[8] The state and corporations were both, in reality, species of the same genus. The former might be 'a highly peculiar group unit', but no immeasurable gulf should be placed between it and other groups. In so far as writers imputed a real will to the state, could this be denied to other types of association to which man belonged, and to which he might feel a greater affiliation?[9] A book on English Fellowship law could well be written, which would embrace the many and varied associations to which Englishmen owe allegiance.[10] Group personality should not be seen as a purely legal phenomenon. If the law said that it did not exist where as a matter of moral sentiments it did exist, then the lawmaker would incur 'the penalty ordained for those who ignorantly or wilfully say the thing that is not'.[11] English law had

[5] T. Hobbes, *Leviathan*, ed. M. Oakeshott (1960), 218.

[6] J. Austin, *The Province of Jurisprudence Determined*, ed. H. L. A. Hart (1955), lecture vi.

[7] For a discussion of this theme in Dicey's work, see above, ch. 2.

[8] F. W. Maitland, introduction to O. Von Gierke, *Political Theories of the Middle Ages* (1900). The main aim of Von Gierke's work had been to resurrect the indigenous elements of German law, and to extirpate the alien influences of Roman law doctrine. Part of his argument was that the individual and the state did not comprise the entirety of society. Other bodies, such as towns, guilds, and associations, possessed an autonomy which should be respected. cf. A. Jacobson, 'The Private Use of Public Authority: Sovereignty and Associations in the Common Law', 29 *Buffalo L. Rev.* 599 (1980).

[9] Maitland, introduction to Von Gierke, *Political Theories*, p.xi.

[10] Ibid., p. xxvii.

[11] F. W. Maitland, *Collected Papers* (1911), iii. 314.

only succeeded in avoiding many of the difficulties attendant upon the existence of associations by the device of the trust.[12] It was only the 'hard exterior shell provided by the trust' which served to conceal the inadequacy of our theoretical constructs.[13]

Barker's analogous but distinctive challenge to the unitary state has more overt implications for public law. The importance of groups is complemented by a division between state and society. This distinction was a characteristic trait of the pluralists. It stands in stark contrast to the unitary thesis which provided the foundation for much of the earlier analysis. The argument for such a distinction emerges with force and clarity in the work of Barker.

> There is a vision which has often haunted human thought—the vision of the one and only organization: the vision of the total State which is all and everything, and includes all and every purpose . . . But if we adopt this vision of unity, we only achieve a deep disunity. It is not only that the individual may rise insurgent against an excessive claim. It is also a matter of other and rival societies arising, based on some rival principle, whether of religious faith or economic doctrine, which either claim to be franchises or immunities, exempt from the State, or aspire to dethrone it and take its place as the one total organization. The State which is all and everything is a State which always invites negation.[14]

The distinctiveness of state and society was reinforced by temporal perspectives. Society preceded the state. Voluntary activity between groups was the material on which 'there is stamped the form of the state'.[15] The state was a national society which had transformed itself into a juridical organization by virtue of the legal act of creating a constitution. Yet the transformation of society into state did not mean that society had perished, nor that it had turned the entirety of itself into that form. Both the development *and* the liberty of the individual were expressed not only through the state, but also in the social groups which constituted the substance of society.[16] The individual owed loyalties to the state and to groups with which he was affiliated. These could exist in harmony or could conflict. This problem could not be solved by enthroning one

[12] Maitland, *Collected Papers*, p. 321.
[13] Ibid. 379; see also pp. 367–8.
[14] *Reflections on Government*, pp. 20–1.
[15] E. Barker, introduction to O. Von Gierke, *Natural Law and the Theory of Society (1500–1800)* (1950), i. 23.
[16] Barker, *Reflections on Government*, p. 22.

loyalty.[17] Such unity would only be purchased at the cost of confusion. The freedom of the group was not absolute. It was bounded by the liberties of the individual, of other groups, and of the state itself.[18] Group liberty did not imply the existence of a second state which was to be a rival of the existing state. It entailed the existence of social groups distinctive from, and complementary to, the state.[19]

Laski developed a similar thematic attack in more detail. He bore testimony to the work of both Figgis[20] and Maitland. Laski's views on pluralism developed considerably during the course of his life. His original vision of pluralism is to be found in a trilogy which he published between 1917 and 1921.[21] Similar ideas pervade all these works. Three major themes can be detected.

First, Laski attacked the monistic theory of the state. He, like Barker, emphasized that this conception of the state was born of an age of crisis. The supremacy of the state, articulated in differing ways by Bodin, Hobbes, and Hegel, was designed to preserve the state from fragmentation.[22] The threat to the continued existence of the state might come from religious warfare, internal civil unrest, or external threat. The response was uniform: to assert the supremacy of the state over all other institutions. Lawyers provided conceptual support for supremacy by developing the notion of unlimited sovereignty.[23] This centralization and idealization of the state was both ethically inadequate and administratively incomplete.[24] The state was a pluralistic universe, inhabited by a variety of self-governing groups to whom individuals owed allegiance. They were part of the state, but could not be reduced to a unity.[25] The state was not the creator of all rights, and must seek justification through the consequences of its actions.[26] It had no special claim to pre-eminence.

[17] Barker, *Reflections on Government*, p. 23.

[18] Ibid. 23, 24.

[19] Barker was, however, concerned over the dangers attendant upon the Germanic doctrine of the personality of groups; introduction to von Gierke, *Natural Law*, p. lxxxv.

[20] J. N. Figgis, *Churches in the Modern State* (1913).

[21] H. J. Laski, *Studies in the Problem of Sovereignty* (1917); *Authority in the Modern State* (1919); *Foundations*.

[22] *Foundations*, pp. 233–4; *Studies*, ch. 1.

[23] *Foundations*, pp. 235–6.

[24] Ibid. 240.

[25] Ibid. 168–9. See also *Studies*, pp. 272–4.

[26] *Foundations*, p. 170.

The only demands upon our allegiance were those of what we deem to be right conduct.[27]

Secondly, the pluralist view of the state entailed decentralization. Centralization of power impeded the balance of associations which was the safeguard of liberty.[28] Concentration of power stifled creativity. Only through developing a 'federal' structure within a state would there be sufficient centres in which the enterprise and abilities of people could be enlisted.[29]

Thirdly, political pluralism could not be considered in isolation. The distribution of economic power within society was of crucial importance. Concentration of economic power could render the political personality of the average citizen ineffective.[30] The industrial worker might well possess the suffrage; but he was enmeshed in a system which deprived its use of any fundamental meaning. Political liberty was inextricably linked with economic equality.[31] Greater equalization of economic power and the extension of democracy to industry were both necessary if real political freedom was to be attained.[32]

Laski modified his views in his later work.[33] He continued to endorse a pluralistic conception of the state, and renewed his attack on the monistic vision of writers from Hobbes to Austin.[34] The artificiality of Dicey's distinction between legal and political sovereignty was included in this analysis.[35] However, while society as a complex whole was pluralistic, the unified power of the state was made monistic by the fact that it possessed the coercive power to ensure that its will was obeyed. Laski still believed in the disjunction between state and society. The state was no more entitled to allegiance than any other association 'on grounds of ethical right or political wisdom'.[36] The allegiance of the individual towards the group, the sovereignty of these groups within their assigned spheres, and the essentially federal nature of political society are recurring themes throughout this later work.[37]

27 *Foundations*, p. 245.

28 Ibid. 86.

29 Ibid. 87; see also pp. 52, 54, 66, 242.

30 Ibid., p. ix.

31 Ibid. 76–7.

32 Ibid. 84. See the connections between this reasoning and that of republican theorists, below, ch. 10.

33 e.g. H. J. Laski, *A Grammar of Politics* (4th edn., 1938), p. xi.

34 Ibid. 45–6.

35 Ibid. 50–5.

36 Ibid., p. xi.

37 Ibid. 60, 61, 67, 68, 71; Laski does, however, move away from the idea that groups were real persons.

The weakness which he perceived in pluralism was that it did not sufficiently take account of the state as an expression of class relations. Only if the state claimed that sovereignty was indivisible could it define and control the legal postulates of society.[38] If the state were to cease to be sovereign, it could no longer give effect to those class-based purposes. Pluralism became, therefore, part of a larger purpose. The objective of the pluralist must be a classless society, in which there would be no need for supreme coercive power.

Laski's allegiance to the Labour party and his own developing political ideas were of importance in this shift in his thinking. His work, even in its later period, is, however, of more general importance for an understanding of pluralist thought. While other writers of the pluralist 'school' might not endorse the particular political vision advanced by Laski, many none the less subscribed to the more general theme concerning an interconnection between political, social, and economic democracy.

Barker, for example, is more sanguine than Laski about the prospects of pluralist democracy in a society pervaded by inequality of wealth. Nor does Barker accept the thesis that legislation will inevitably be class based. He does, however, devote considerable attention to the stress which disparity in economic wealth places upon pluralism, and he does not confine democracy to mere process values.[39] If equality in thought and action is to have substance and content, there must be some equality in means. Pure equality in this domain may be impossible, but a steady reduction in inequality should be the objective.[40] Democratization of the workplace was advocated as a further mechanism whereby economic inequality could be indirectly alleviated. Lindsay pursued a similar theme. If the sense of economic cleavage was greater than that of common nationality, or if there were permanent social minorities, a healthy democracy was impossible. Where a minority could not turn itself into a majority, voting became merely 'a process of counting heads to save the trouble of breaking them'.[41] Democracy within non-political associations was vital as part of the training towards a larger citizenship. The scale of political government might mean

[38] *A Grammar of Politics*, p. xii.
[39] *Reflections on Government*, pp. 106–17, ch. 6.
[40] Ibid. 418.
[41] A. D. Lindsay, *The Essentials of Democracy* (1929), 49.

that it was impossible to render it truly representative. However, the existence of a vigorous non-political democratic life could facilitate the harmonization and co-ordination of public opinion by the political arm of government.[42]

The attack upon the unitary state was also an integral part of the Fabians' work. The interrelationship between political pluralism, economic power, and democracy within associations is manifest in their approach. Discussion of the pluralist traits within their work is none the less difficult. Their views as a whole altered over time, and there were also internal disagreements within the group. The gradual transformation of society by democratic and peaceful means was one of the central tenets of the Fabian philosophy. Gradual reform would move towards the socialization of land and capital. Parliament should be modified, and greater use should be made of the varying forms of social activity. Stress was placed upon municipal reforms, and decentralization.[43]

The early work of the Fabians was criticized for ignoring the role which trade unions, co-operative movements, and other vocational organizations could play. Modifications to the central themes of Fabian policy occurred towards the end of the nineteenth century. This period saw the publication of works on the co-operative movement, trade unionism, and industrial democracy by the ever-prolific Webbs. Decentralization continued to provide an important pluralist element within their philosophy. Their plans for central government were founded upon a distinction between groups with social interests, those with economic interests, and groups with interests in the whole. The corollary was that Parliament should be divided into two parts: there would be a Political and a Social Parliament, and the House of Lords would be abolished. The functional dichotomy drawn by the Webbs was strongly criticized by Laski.[44] He emphasized the continuum between social, economic, and political policy. To imagine that these issues could be separated was wholly unrealistic.[45]

[42] The work of both Barker and Lindsay is also of relevance for a developmental conception of democracy which will be considered in chs. 10 and 11.

[43] Ehrlich, *Pluralism On and Off Course*, p. 49.

[44] *A Grammar of Politics*, pp. 335–40.

[45] Functional representation of a differing type was also important to the work of Cole, who was criticized by Laski for the impractical nature of his proposals; ibid. 82–5, 439–40, 444–6. Cole's work is difficult to summarize, partly because it was unclear, and partly because he shifted position so often; see Nicholls, *The Pluralist State*, p. 79.

It is evident from the preceding discussion that the views of the pluralists were not uniform. To attempt to impose unity upon such diversity would be to force a Procrustean frame upon unwilling recipients. Some summary of the main themes may none the less be helpful.

Two such themes appear explicitly or implicitly within this literature. First, there was the challenge to the monistic theory of the state which had characterized much of the theorizing of the nineteenth century and earlier periods. This vision of the state was questioned in both descriptive and normative terms. From a descriptive perspective pluralist writers pointed to the very real constraints which associations or groups imposed upon the freedom of state action. This was reinforced by the normative argument which manifested itself in the distinction drawn between state and society. The state was not the origin or fount of all rights which existed within society. Groups existed and had rights even before the evolution of the state. Individuals often owed a prior allegiance to such associations. The evolution of the idea that groups were real, or had a real personality, became one embodiment of this theme, although it was not shared by all pluralist writers.

A second theme is to be found in the interconnection between political pluralism and broader issues of social and economic policy. Political pluralism, with its attendant ideas of decentralization, group autonomy, and diversified spheres of activity, was seen as but one important part of a larger picture. The constraints which social and economic conditions could place upon the attainment of political goals was a constant subject of discussion. Opinions differed markedly. Laski, Cole, Barker, Lindsay, and the Fabians had divergent views. None, however, doubted the relevance of the question.

An important consequence followed from the acknowledgement of this interrelationship. It is a consequence to which we shall return in more detail later, but warrants mention here. There is little, if any, evidence that the pluralists believed that the interplay of group pressures would, in and of itself, produce a natural equilibrium, or that the public interest was simply the result of such group interaction. Pluralism was conceived neither as being self-correcting, nor as being concerned solely with what we might term process values. Process was a necessary, but not sufficient, condition of pluralism. The implications that this was to have for the shape of public law will be considered in due course.[46]

[46] See below, ch. 6.

3. THE CORPORATIST CHALLENGE

A plethora of meanings have been ascribed to corporatism, as the ensuing discussion will make apparent. One central thrust of corporatism is a denial of the pluralist thesis that decisions result from the interaction of a series of relatively autonomous voluntary groups, the membership of which overlaps. The premiss is that a dominant group will exist within a particular area, which will itself represent and articulate the demands of other interest groups within the same sphere.[47] In this important sense corporatism is founded upon an élitist perception of the political universe. Corporatist theory does not, however, necessarily postulate that these dominant groups, or peak organizations, will exercise a cohesive or conscious uniformity in behaviour. One, influential, definition of corporatism has been advanced by Schmitter.

> Corporatism can be defined as a system of interest representation in which the constituent units are organized into a limited number of singular, compulsory, non-competitive, hierarchically ordered and functionally differentiated categories, recognized or licensed (if not created) by the state and granted a deliberate representational monopoly within their respective categories in exchange for observing certain controls on their selection of leaders and articulation of demands and supports.[48]

Schmitter fully admits that corporatism has been used to describe a broad range of ideologies, including organic theories of the state and fascist authoritarianism.[49] The definition proffered above is an attempt to escape from this ideological morass, and to depict corporatism as one type of interest representation which can subsist in systems which have a differing ideological base. Schmitter does, however, draw a further, important division between societal and state corporatism.[50] This reflects both the rationale for the development of corporatism,

[47] Cf. M. L. Harrison (ed.), *Corporatism and the Welfare State* (1984), 7–8.

[48] P. C. Schmitter, 'Still the Century of Corporatism', in P. C. Schmitter and G. Lehmbruch (eds.), *Trends toward Corporatist Intermediation* (1979), 13. Pluralism, by way of contrast, is characterized by a system of interest representation in which the groups are multiple, competitive, and non-hierarchically ordered; where no particular group is licensed by the state; and no one group enjoys a monopoly of representational status with the government; ibid. 15. Cf. Harrison, *Corporation and the Welfare State*, pp. 9–10.

[49] 'Still the Century of Corporatism', p. 9.

[50] Ibid. 20–2.

and also its mode of operation once established. Societal corporatism was to be found in political systems in which there were relatively autonomous, multilayered territorial units; open electoral processes; party competition, and some degree of ideological heterogeneity. An advanced, post-liberal capitalist society would develop this species of corporatism. State corporatism was evident in political systems in which territorial units were tightly subordinated to central bureaucratic power; elections were either non-existent or plebiscitary; a one-party system predominated, or the party system was weak; and ideological conformity was imposed upon the populace. This second form of corporatism would be found in the 'antiliberal, delayed capitalist, authoritarian, neomercantilist state'.

It is, however, with societal corporatism that we shall be predominately concerned. What then was the cause of this type of interest representation? What prompted the transition from a pluralistic polity to one of a corporatist nature? The most fundamental reason[51] resided in the basic needs of 'capitalism to reproduce the conditions for its existence', and to continue to accumulate further resources. This somewhat cryptic formulation requires explanation. The modern state is required to undertake a wide range of activities in order to correct defects in, or problems arising from, the operation of the capitalist system. Governments are forced to juggle with goals such as full employment, economic growth, the resolution of labour conflict, the regulation of trade cycles, the prevention of inflation, and the provision of safe working conditions. The pursuit of these objectives necessitates discussion and collaboration with major interest groups. These groups are brought into a consultative role with the government. They help to shape governmental policy, and their own objectives are themselves fashioned or constrained by the same process. Peak organizations attain their monopoly of representation for a number of reasons. The government perceives obvious benefits in dealing with one bargaining agent. A relationship of trust can be built up, an understanding of the rules of the game, and an assuredness that the organization will promote an agreed policy amongst the relevant 'constituency'. Industrial concentration and economies of scale provide further impetus towards the emergence of a particular interest group which will speak or bargain for the whole.[52]

[51] 'Still the Century of Corporatism', p. 24.

[52] See also P. C. Schmitter, 'Modes of Interest Intermediation and Models of

A general analysis of corporatism as it operates within the United Kingdom has been advanced by Cawson.[53] His central thesis is that a dualism pervades the economy, and that this has generated a distinctive pattern of relationships between firms and the state.[54] Traditional ideas of a competitive market now only have real meaning within part of the economy. This competitive market sector has been overlaid by a corporate sector. Concentration and centralization within industry confer a degree of power over the market, and over the firms within the competitive section. The repositories of power within the corporate sector develop close and symbiotic links with the state in order to consolidate and expand their authority. Government responds in its capacity as manager of the economy, in order to effectuate the complex set of policies which this role demands.

The analysis of the dual structure of the economy, therefore, has its counterpart in politics.[55] Pressure groups are not fluid and competitive, but 'hierarchical, stratified and inegalitarian'. A mutually dependent bargaining relationship emerges between government and the corporate sector, in which favourable policies are traded for co-operation and expertise. Representation and intervention become fused. State power is fragmented as a result of the bargaining and negotiation between organs of government and particular peak organizations. This dispersal of governmental power is further enhanced by the delegation of policy implementation. Cawson therefore views the operation of corporatism as distinctive from a system in which there is centralized bureaucratic control.[56]

Considerable diversity of opinion continues to exist at the theoretical level concerning the reasons for the growth of the corporate state,[57] and the relationship between peak organizations

Societal Change in Western Europe', in Schmitter and Lehmbruch (eds.), *Trends toward Corporatist Intermediation*, ch. 3. The following are also of relevance: R. M. Unger, *Law in Modern Society* (1976); J. Habermas, *Legitimation Crisis*, trans. T. McCarthy (1976); C. Offe, *Contradictions of the Welfare State*, ed. J. Keane (1984).

[53] A. Cawson, *Corporatism and Welfare* (1982).

[54] Ibid. 15–20.

[55] Ibid. 37–41.

[56] Ibid. 52, 65–6. The results which Cawson associates with a corporatist mode of intervention may, however, be questioned; ibid. 67. For a distinctive, though not unrelated, view of corporatism, see A. Shonfield, *Modern Capitalism: The Changing Balance of Public and Private Power* (1965), 161–2, 231.

[57] See, e.g., L. Panitch, 'The Development of Corporatism in Liberal Democracies', in Schmitter and Lehmbruch (eds.), *Trends toward Corporatist Intermediation*, ch. 5; B. Jessop, 'Corporatism, Parliamentarism, and Social Democracy', ibid., ch. 7.

and the government therein.[58] More specific empirical evidence for, or application of, corporatist theory in the United Kingdom can be found in a variety of contexts. The work of political scientists, theorists, and historians provides a rich corpus of information, even if the conclusions drawn therefrom may be contested. This may be so even where the particular writer did not express himself in overtly corporatist language.

For example, Finer's work on the lobby would not normally be regarded as a principal 'text' of corporatism, yet much of the reasoning therein is more consistent with corporatism than with traditional pluralism.[59] Thus Finer stresses the reciprocal need which brings the lobby and the government together. The government needs the lobby partly for the information which it can provide, and partly because it may require active help in the administration of the policy. Consultation is facilitated when the organizations are few and highly representative. The representational monopoly which a peak organization may well possess is a recurring theme in Finer's work. A close and closed relationship can exist between the department and one dominant group spokesman.[60] The organization which seeks to engage in such 'fraternal' ties with the department must earn its position. Misuse of confidence or sharp practice will sunder this bond. The transition from a close alliance to a closed one can be all too easy.[61]

The consequences which ensue from such closed relationships are important. The negotiated conclusions reached between department and group exclude both the wider public and Parliament. Once a deal is struck and supported by the executive there is little that the House of Commons can achieve.[62] Executive dominance combines with the inexpert and uninformed nature of Commons' criticism to

[58] R. J. Harrison, *Pluralism and Corporatism* (1980); O. Newman, *The Challenge of Corporatism* (1981); J. Simmie, *Power, Property and Corporatism: The Political Sociology of Planning* (1981); P. C. Schmitter and G. Lehmbruch, *Patterns of Corporatist Policy-Making* (1982); R.King (ed.), *Capital and Politics* (1983); Harrison (ed.), *Corporatism and the Welfare State*; J. H. Goldthorpe (ed.), *Order and Conflict in Contemporary Capitalism* (1984); W. Streeck and P. C. Schmitter (eds.), *Private Interest Government: Beyond Market and State* (1985); A. Cawson, *Corporatism and Political Theory* (1986); P. Birkenshaw, I. Harden and N. Lewis, *Government by Moonlight: The Hybrid Parts of the State* (1990).

[59] S. E. Finer, *Anonymous Empire* (2nd edn., 1966).

[60] Ibid. 36.

[61] See, e.g., the discussion of the monopoly position secured by the National Farmers Union; ibid. 38.

[62] Ibid. 42.

assure success of the preordained package. The closed relationship also affects the overall strategy of the lobby. Attainment of this representational monopoly, and exclusive access to the department, becomes the goal of pressure groups. The closer that this ideal comes to realization, the less inclined is the lobby to bother with the ordinary parliamentary machinery. A quiet word behind closed doors is to be preferred to the clamour of the political market-place.[63] This reasoning fits comfortably into corporatist thought, even though this might not be the case for all aspects of the work.

A more explicitly corporatist historical perspective has been provided by Middlemas.[64] He argues that for a period after the First World War, until at least the mid-1960s, a major theme of government was crisis avoidance. The elevation of unions and employers' associations to a new status played an integral part in attaining this goal. They became governing institutions: bodies which undertook functions devolved on them by government, while sharing at least some of the assumptions about the national interest held by government. New 'estates of the realm' were thereby created, which were committed to co-operation with the state, notwithstanding their opposition to particular governments.[65] Middlemas uses the term corporate bias to describe the effects of these developments upon decision-making within society.[66] The underlying consensual view of the national interest which predominated between the government and other governing institutions necessarily reduced the power of interests which were excluded. A secondary consequence was to blur the lines of class conflict and social cleavage. The emergence of this corporate bias was not explicable solely in terms of economic factors. It was not simply a response of government to the needs of economic planning. It had a political substance in its own right, but should not be perceived as entailing a particular ideology.[67] Notwithstanding the differences of terminology, the views of Middlemas have affinity with those of both Schmitter and Cawson. Thus Middlemas agrees with Schmitter's definition of corporatism given above, with the qualification that government only rarely achieves the degree of control over the governing institutions suggested by Schmitter's formulation. He also accepts Cawson's theme of a dual state, in which competition is confined to the groups which remain

[63] Ibid. 43.
[64] K. Middlemas, *Politics in Industrial Society* (1979).
[65] Ibid. 372–3.
[66] Ibid. 374–5.
[67] Ibid. 378–80.

outside the sanctified boundaries of collaboration with the government.[68]

4. THE FREE MARKET, THE STRONG STATE, AND MODERN PLURALISM

It is readily apparent that Conservative governmental policy has been at odds with certain aspects of early pluralist thought and with certain elements of corporatism. The central themes of this policy must be explored in order that the implications thereof for public law can be duly appreciated.

'Thatcherism' is a word currently employed by many of those writing within this field. It is, however, important to realize that the term can be used in a variety of ways.

> Firstly, one could abandon 'Thatcherism' as an analytical term and just define concepts and study topics without referring to it. Secondly, one could treat uses of 'Thatcherism' as a topic for analysis in their own right without committing oneself to an independent definition. These represent the agnostic approaches. Some positive definitions could also be given. Among such definitions four broad approaches stand out. Thus, thirdly, one could define 'Thatcherism' in terms of Thatcher's personal qualities. Fourthly, one could examine 'Thatcherism' in terms of the Thatcher style of political leadership. Fifthly, one could define 'Thatcherism' in terms of the policies pursued by the Conservative Party under Thatcher, and, sixthly, one could define it more broadly in terms of the changing strategic line of the Conservative Party as organized under the Thatcher leadership.[69]

The present analysis will focus upon the policies actually pursued by the Thatcher government. Two themes are apparent within these policies: the preference for free-market solutions to micro- and macro-economic problems, and the need for a strong state in order, *inter alia*, to implement these developments. These themes will be analysed in turn.

The preference for market-based solutions to economic problems

[68] Ibid. 382–3. For interesting discussion as to the role, or non-role, of corporatism in the United States, see Shonfield, *Modern Capitalism*, pp. 309–10; R. Salisbury, 'Why no Corporatism in America?', in Schmitter and Lehmbruch (eds.), *Trends toward Corporatist Intermediation*, ch. 8; A. S. Miller, *The Modern Corporate State: Private Governments and the American Constitution* (1976).

[69] B. Jessop, K. Bonnett, S. Bromley, and T. Ling, *Thatcherism* (1988), 5.

is not in itself a simple one-dimensional approach to the task of managing the economy. A variety of more specific theories contest the arena. Notwithstanding this diversity, certain central themes can be identified. The first is the rejection of Keynesian macro-economic management, and a preference for 'sound money' based upon monetarism.[70] Secondly, there is a distrust of governmental regulatory control of certain sectors of the economy, particularly those concerned with allocative choices. While economic theory might be correct in asserting that intervention might be required in order to correct market failure, the actual areas in which such intervention is felt to be warranted are narrowly drawn. The market is still felt to be the most efficient mechanism for allocating resources. Even if there might be areas where the market is prone to failure, this did not necessarily warrant state intervention, because governmental failure is felt to be even more likely than market failure. There are two reasons for this.[71] On the one hand, the 'vote market' is inherently inflationary in a way in which the 'real market' is not. In the electoral market the consumer can buy/vote for the most expensive products/policies; the politicians will have an incentive to produce more expensive products/policies because these will sell better than cheaper alternatives, even though the medium- and longer-term result might be inflationary and disadvantageous. On the other hand, the bureaucracies which administer these policies are not subject to the normal constraints of the market and have a tendency, which some claimed to be inexorable, to expand their sphere of influence. The cost of government will rise, and politicians will not be able to maintain detailed control over the operations of bureaucracies. The conclusions of this aspect of governmental policy are patent. It has resulted in the privatization of nationalized industries and the deregulation of certain areas of the economy. It has led to increasing emphasis upon the use of market disciplines in diverse areas of society, ranging from the procurement policies of local authorities to education, and from the structure of planning law to transport policy. The distrust of democracy as a method of determining and aggregating individual choices, and the inherently inflationary nature of such mechanisms, are, as we have

[70] A. Gamble, *The Free Economy and the Strong State* (1988), 39–45; D. Marquand, 'The Paradoxes of Thatcherism', in R. Skidelsky (ed.), *Thatcherism* (1988), 162.

[71] Marquand, 'The Paradoxes of Thatcherism', pp. 162–3.

seen,[72] part of the public-choice philosophy. A third element in the preference for market-based solutions has come from libertarian philosophers such as Nozick, who has argued against the moral acceptability of attempts by the state to engage in redistributive policies.

The second of the two themes adumbrated above, the need for the strong state, is a more complex phenomenon. Two elements must be distinguished. On the one hand, a strong state may be required in order to enable the free-market regime to be 'installed'. A strong central authority may be needed to unravel the 'coils of social democracy and welfarism which have fastened around the free economy'.[73] It may be required in order to defeat those who, directly or indirectly, are seen to oppose the new policies, such as local authorities who were said to pursue economic policies which were inconsistent with the current state policy. A strong state may also be needed to police the market regime in order, at the least, to maintain formal equality between economic agents, and, more controversially, to suppress private forms of coercion, or discrimination.[74]

On the other hand, a strong state has been advocated for reasons which do not relate directly to the establishment of a free market. This conservative or authoritarian aspect of 'new-right' thought does not always sit easily with all aspects of the free market philosophy. As Gamble states:

> A free economy is seen as a prop for a strong state instead of the other way round. The authority of the state is all important and no principles or policy goals, such as the sanctity of individual rights or the need to maximize economic efficiency, can be allowed to override it. The task of the state is to ensure that authority is upheld throughout society because this is the basis on which its own authority rests. Private property is an important bulwark of social authority and it is for this reason that a free economy must be preserved.[75]

While this conservative element in new-right thought is still suspicious of certain aspects of free-market capitalism, it is even more distrustful of collectivist state intervention. Such intervention

[72] See above, ch. 3.

[73] Gamble, *The Free Economy*, p. 32; D. Kavanagh, *Thatcherism and British Politics: The End of Consensus?* (1987), ch. 4.

[74] Gamble, *The Free Economy*, p. 33; A. Gamble, 'The Political Economy of Freedom', in R. Levitas (ed.), *The Ideology of the New Right* (1986), ch. 1.

[75] Gamble, *The Free Economy*, p. 35.

undermines traditional property rights, fosters special interest groups which weaken the established governmental order, overburdens the state, and erodes those institutions, such as the family, on which the state depends for its own support.[76] While neo-conservatives may, therefore, distrust collectivist state intervention, their beliefs are not easily accommodated with their neo-liberal 'partners'. Thus, whereas neo-liberals endorse the values of the individual, freedom of choice, market society, *laissez-faire* and minimal government, neo-conservatives espouse doctrines which enshrine strong government, social authoritarianism, disciplined society, hierarchy, and the nation.[77]

The presence of a 'strong state' clearly limits the pluralistic nature of societal ordering. However, society is still perceived to be pluralistic *within* the bounds allowed by the authority at the centre. There are two complementary reasons for this characterization.

First, the *result* of the preference for the 'free economy' is that market-based pluralism becomes the dominant species of decision-making within many areas. The distrust of democracy and bureaucracy as methods of decision-making reflects central themes within the public-choice philosophy considered above.[78] Governmental and bureaucratic powers should be limited, because they will result in more deleterious decisions than those reached by the market; governmental failure is regarded as more prevalent than market failure. The constitutional focus is upon ways to prevent the government from engaging in wealth-distributive exercises. Policy choices and planning decisions which would previously have been made by government are devolved to the market. The overall direction and indeed existence of services is rendered subject to 'consumer sovereignty'. Political choice becomes a species of market choice best undertaken by the market itself. This is said to represent the ultimate in pluralistic decentralization, and to be far less prone to the forms of rent-seeking behaviour which are said to characterize much legislative intervention.

Secondly, the *initiation* and *shaping* of the policy which emerges is itself conceived to be the result of pluralistic interplay of group

[76] See, e.g., R. Scruton, *The Meaning of Conservatism* (2nd edn., 1984); M. Cowling (ed.), *Conservative Essays* (1978).

[77] A. Belsey, 'The New Right, Social Order and Civil Liberties', in Levitas (ed.), *The Ideology of the New Right*, pp. 172–3.

[78] See ch. 3 sec. 2b, ch. 4 sec. 1.

pressures. Thus, for example, Richardson and Jordan[79] argue that it is this interplay of group pressure which is the dominating feature of the policy process in the United Kingdom and that decision-making is 'incremental' rather than 'rational'.[80] Official organizations such as government departments, quangos, or nationalized industries are treated as group actors in the same way as more traditional groups such as the CBI and the TUC. Decision-making within government is characterized by competition between departments, and the very scope of choices is shaped by external client groups which are ranged like 'battalions' behind their respective departments. Policy options do not reside with a triumvirate of Parliament, cabinet, and the electorate, but rather with the cabinet, departments, and pressure groups. Even if the Conservative approach towards decision-making has moved away from the tripartite form of corporatism, there is abundant evidence of the existence of continuing group pressure on policy-making, and of the continuing power of dominant groups within this process.[81]

The connection between the two limbs of the modern pluralist thesis can be presented as follows. First, writers such as Richardson and Jordan draw heavily upon the market-oriented thesis espoused by Bentley and Truman in the United States.[82] If politics is viewed as the result of a competitive struggle analogous to that of the ordinary market-place, then it provides support for those who argue that the ordinary market-place might indeed be a 'better' decision-maker, unless the area is one which should be specifically preserved within the governmental sphere. Secondly, such writers also furnish support for the idea that central control over those areas which do remain within the government's purview will be facilitated by narrowing down the sphere in which the government tries to exercise direct authority. Governmental 'overload' can be alleviated by devolving certain decisions to the market.

[79] J. J. Richardson and A. G. Jordan, *Governing under Pressure* (1985). See also A.Potter, *Organized Groups in British National Politics* (1961); G. C. Moodie and G.Studdert-Kennedy, *Opinions, Publics and Pressure Groups* (1970); R. H. Kimber and J. J. Richardson, *Pressure Groups in Britain: A Reader* (1974).

[80] Richardson and Jordan, *Governing under Pressure*, pp. 18–24.

[81] See, generally, Cawson, *Corporatism and Political Theory*. And see also J.Vickers and G. Yarrow, *Privatization: An Economic Analysis* (1988), for specific examples of the influence of major corporate groups on the privatization process; Birkenshaw, Harden and Lewis, *Government by Moonlight*.

[82] See above, ch. 3 sec. 2b.

5. CONCLUSION

The realization that the state is not unitary in the sense presupposed by Dicey, and that it should in some way be regarded as pluralist, only takes us so far. Different conclusions are consonant with this realization. It is possible to build a socialist orientation on to this pluralist base, as is exemplified by the work of some early pluralists. A more market-oriented conception of the state is also feasible. This serves to reinforce the point made at the outset of this chapter. A conception of democracy will, implicitly or explicitly, be part of a broader political theory which must embrace, *inter alia*, a conception of rights and distributive justice. The implications which a pluralist conception of democracy might have for public law in the United Kingdom can now be examined.

6
PLURALISM, PROCESS, AND SUBSTANCE: UK (II)

1. INTRODUCTION

This chapter will, as indicated previously,[1] be concerned with the consequences which should ensue for both constitutional and administrative law from a pluralist conception of democracy. It is readily apparent that the nature of these consequences will differ depending upon which of the two variants considered in the preceding chapter is adopted. To incant the phrase 'pluralist democracy' as if it furnished a self-evident answer is necessarily incomplete. There may be agreement that Dicey's unitary conception of the state was misconceived descriptively, and that its prescriptive foundation was unconvincing even within its own terms.[2] There may be some consensus on the existence of group power which shapes governmental behaviour. The prescriptive step, which entails drawing out the consequences concerning the nature of the state and its interrelationship with group power, will be more controversial. Two main issues will be discussed within this chapter.

First, the development of process rights within constitutional and administrative law will be considered, and the interrelationship between such process rights and pluralist democracy will be analysed. The objective is not to contend that such process rights can be regarded as sufficient within public law. The previous discussion has revealed the difficulties of sustaining any purely process-related conception of public law,[3] and the realization that substantive value judgements underlie any consideration of avowedly procedural norms will be reinforced in the discussion which follows. The ways in which the two principal types of pluralism affect the development of such process rights will be considered in the course of the analysis.

Secondly, the nature of rights within a pluralist democracy, at

[1] See above, ch. 5 sec. 1.
[2] See above, ch. 2, ch. 5 secs. 2, 3.
[3] See above, ch. 4 secs. 3, 4, 5.

both the constitutional and administrative levels, will be discussed. It will be argued that the place of both procedural and substantive rights within such a view of democracy must be seen as part of a broader political theory which embraces an understanding of the nature of rights themselves. Only then can one adequately comprehend the way in which the value judgements underlying such rights are made, and the role which a particular conception of democracy plays in their formulation. The differing conclusions which the two principal variants of pluralist democracy produce will be analysed within this framework.

The following chapter will consider the arguments currently advanced for constitutional reform. The nature of the interpretive difficulties which would be encountered if we were to adopt a Bill of Rights will be analysed, and these will be related to the differing conceptions of democracy considered in this and the previous chapter. The discussion of constitutional reform will also cover the broader issues concerning possible devolution or independence for Scotland and Wales, and the impact of membership of the EC.

2. PLURALISM AND PROCESS

a. *Participation and the Common Law*

One can begin by surveying the extent to which the common law at present fosters participation in the administrative process. It is a trite proposition that natural justice is, in one sense, inevitably about the representation of interests, in that it tells us who should be allowed to participate in the decision-making process by the grant of a hearing prior to the reaching of a decision. This does not in itself take us very far, because a legal system may simply say that only those who have legal rights in a narrow sense are entitled to be represented. The liberalization of the requirements of natural justice has undoubtedly extended some process requirements to interests which would in Hohfeldian terms be regarded as privileges.[4] The key question is, however, the extent to which this liberalization has

[4] P. P. Craig, *Administrative Law* (2nd edn., 1989), ch. 7. The courts have, however, on occasion, reintroduced the same type distinction, albeit under a different name; ibid. 206–7. Cf. W.W. Van Alstyne, 'The Demise of the Right-Privilege Distinction in Constitutional Law', 81 *Harv. L. Rev.* 1439 (1968).

facilitated the development of interest representation or participatory rights. A short answer would be, not much.

Notwithstanding the broadening of the rules of natural justice, categorization of function still continues to play some role in determining whether a particular applicant should be entitled to protection. The most apposite example of this is that the courts have held that these rules do not in general apply to legislative functions. Rule-making, whether by a minister, fringe organization, or local authority, is therefore still generally regarded as outside the realm of natural justice.[5] There are certain exceptions or limitations to this basic proposition. Thus, it seems to be the case that, where a public body has established a rule on which a particular individual or group has relied, it may have to grant a hearing to those who are affected by the change,[6] and the individual may be entitled to insist that the policy is actually followed in relation to him. Moreover, if an individual has in the past enjoyed a benefit which he could legitimately expect to continue, he may be entitled to a statement of reasons for the change of position, and an opportunity to be consulted thereon.[7] There is also authority that an applicant should be informed of what the rule or policy entails, the rationale being that otherwise there would be no effective way to challenge it.[8] There are, in addition, certain instances in which the legislature prescribes consultation prior to the making of a rule, and the courts have shown themselves to be adept at ensuring that this obligation is fulfilled.[9] That these limitations or exceptions exist does not alter the force of the general principle outlined above: the common law provides no general obligation to consult or to take into account the views of those who are affected prior to the making of a rule. Natural justice or fairness afford no protection in such instances.

The development of procedural due process has therefore not been used as a pedestal from which to advance a broader concept of

[5] *Bates* v. *Lord Hailsham* [1972] 1 W.L.R. 1373. See M. Asimow, 'Delegated Legislation: United States and United Kingdom' (1983) 3 *O.J.L.S.* 253, for a comparison of rule-making in the two countries.

[6] *R.* v. *Liverpool Corporation, ex p. Liverpool Taxi Fleet Operators' Association* [1972] 2 Q.B. 299; *Attorney-General of Hong Kong* v. *Ng Yuen Shiu* [1983] 2 A.C. 629; R. v. *Secretary of State for the Home Department, ex p. Ruddock* [1987] 1 W.L.R. 1482.

[7] *R.* v. *Secretary of State for the Home Department, ex p. Khan* [1985] 1 All E.R. 40; *Council of Civil Service Unions* v. *Minister for the Civil Service* [1985] A.C. 374, 408–9.

[8] *R.* v. *Port of London Authority, ex p. Kynoch* [1919] 1 K.B. 176, 184; *R.* v. *Criminal Injuries Compensation Board, ex p. Ince* [1973] 1 W.L.R. 1334, 1344, 1345.

[9] See, e.g., *May* v. *Beattie* [1927] 3 K.B. 353; *Rollo* v. *Minister of Town and Country*

participation.[10] Nor have other legal doctrines been used to achieve indirectly what the courts appear unwilling to advance directly. Thus, the concept of relevancy could be used as the basis from which to advance a doctrine of interest representation. This has not, however, occurred. Relevancy has normally been used to demarcate the types of issue which an administrator must consider, and not the range of interests which should be consulted.[11] Even when the term has been used in this latter sense, there is scant evidence to suggest that the courts view this as a method of ensuring participation in the process of decision-making.

The criteria for standing have recently been liberalized, but the rules are still in a state of flux.[12] While certain restrictive conditions from the past have been swept away, the scope of the new rules is unclear. If the rules of *locus standi* were to be developed to allow something approximating towards a citizen action, this would provide some support for a broader concept of participation. Standing is, however, concerned with participation before the court, and not before the institution which made the rule or decision which is being challenged.[13]

b. Participation: Two Arguments for the Status Quo

It might be contended that the general approach of the common law is correct in circumscribing the availability of such participatory rights. Two complementary arguments might be adduced towards

Planning [1948] 1 All E.R. 13; *Sinfield* v. *London Transport Executive* [1970] Ch. 550; *Agricultural, Horticultural and Forestry Industry Training Board* v. *Aylesbury Mushrooms Ltd.* [1972] 1 W.L.R. 190; *Powley* v. *ACAS* [1978] I.C.R. 123. See also A. D. Jergesen, 'The Legal Requirement of Consultation' [1978] *P.L.* 290.

[10] See also the relative absence of meaningful participatory rights in areas such as (a) television franchises: N. Lewis, 'IBA Programme Contract Awards' [1975] *P.L.* 317; D. C. Hague, W. J. M. MacKenzie, and A. Barker (eds.), *Public Policy and Private Interests: The Institutions of Compromise* (1975), ch. 7; (b) planning: J. P. W. B. McAuslan, *The Ideologies of Planning Law* (1980).

[11] S. A. de Smith, *Judicial Review of Administrative Action* (4th edn., 1980), 339–43; Craig, *Administrative Law*, pp. 281–5.

[12] The leading decision is *R.* v. *Inland Revenue Commissioners, ex p. National Federation of Self Employed and Small Businesses Ltd.* [1982] A.C. 617. The ambiguities in the case are discussed in P. Cane, 'Standing, Legality, and the Limits of Public Law' [1981] *P.L.* 322; Craig, *Administrative Law*, pp. 359–63, 368–70.

[13] See, however, above, ch. 4 sec. 7a, where the argument is made that there should be a connection between standing and intervention rights before the agency itself. For comment in the UK context, see Craig, *Administrative Law*, p. 376.

this end. It could be argued that, if Parliament wishes to impose an obligation to consult, it could so specify in the enabling legislation as it has done in certain instances. There is, therefore, no warrant in the courts intervening where the legislature has declined to tread. This argument would be reinforced by a second, the essence of which is that there are existing checks on rule-making and that, in practice, the forces of pluralism will in any event ensure the adequacy of group consultation. Common-law intervention would, therefore, be not only unwarranted but unnecessary. These arguments will be addressed in turn.

Reasoning which derives its authority from general statements concerning legislative intent or parliamentary omission should be viewed with caution. A concealed premiss underlying the argument is that the parliamentary process operates in such a way that, on each occasion on which legislation is enacted, the question as to whether consultation in the rule-making process should be required will be carefully considered; that the advantages and disadvantages of the inclusion of such an obligation will be carefully weighed and the appropriate conclusion will be reached. There is little warrant for this assumption. The inclusion of such a requirement, or consideration of whether such a requirement should be included, is much more likely to reflect the existence of an articulate, relatively homogenous interest group, which brings pressure to bear in order to ensure that any future rule-making will be dependent upon prior consultation with those it represents.[14]

The argument from legislative intent is, moreover, weakened in a less obvious manner. It is predicated upon the assumption that the particular institution would, in fact, be making rules, or acting in some fashion which could render consultation desirable. This assumption does not accord with the facts. In many instances a bureaucracy, particularly one which is dealing with large numbers of claims, will make rules as a mechanism for expediting its disposition of business. There may be no specific mandate in the legislation which enables it to do so, but it is a natural habit for a

[14] A public-choice theorist might argue that, as legislation is a bargain, the courts should not intervene to procure terms for one party which that party was not strong enough to secure for himself. This conclusion is dependent upon accepting the premisses of this theory, and on agreeing that a particular statute should be viewed as a bargain rather than being designed to serve the public interest. See above, ch. 4 sec. 1.

bureaucracy to conduct its affairs in this manner.[15] In these areas the legislature may not even have addressed its mind to the question of whether consultation should be required as an adjunct of the rule-making process.[16]

The argument derived from legislative intent may, as we have seen above, be reinforced by the contention that further judicial reinforcement of participatory rights is unnecessary. This contention itself has two limbs. One aspect of the argument is that existing parliamentary controls over rule-making are effective; the other is that *de facto* consultation between government and affected groups will, in any event, occur, and that this renders more formally structured participatory rights otiose. These arguments will be addressed in turn.

The weaknesses of legislative scrutiny cannot be developed here. They have been well documented by other writers.[17] Control on the floor of the House is extremely limited, and the committee system designed to supplement this control has been hampered by the restricted nature of its powers. Many rules will not even be reviewed by Parliament at all, because they do not come within the ambit of the legislation.[18] The Statutory Instruments Act 1946 is framed in formal terms. It covers powers to be exercised by Orders in Council, and powers conferred on a Minister of the Crown which are

[15] See, e.g., H. Parris, *Constitutional Bureaucracy : The Development of British Central Administration since the Eighteenth Century* (1969), 193; Craig, *Administrative Law*, pp. 188–95.

[16] A further argument against the view that the absence of a statutory requirement to consult should be taken to be conclusive is that it is not easy to reconcile this with the general law on natural justice. One common explanation for the requirement of natural justice is that the court is supplying the omission of the legislature. If this is the justification for the imposition of procedural protection in cases concerned with adjudication, it becomes more difficult to argue that procedural due process should not apply to rule-making unless the legislature has explicitly so enacted. One might contend that there are essential differences between rule-making and adjudication which warrant procedural process in the one instance, but not the other. This is, however, a separate argument, and one which would have to be assessed in its own terms. See below, ch. 6 sec. 2d, for an exploration of this theme.

[17] J. Beatson, 'Legislative Control of Administrative Rulemaking: Lessons from the British Experience', 12 *Corn. I.L.J.* 199 (1979); A. Beith, 'Prayers Unanswered: A Jaundiced View of the Parliamentary Scrutiny of Statutory Instruments' (1981) 34 *Parliamentary Affairs*, 165; Craig, *Administrative Law*, pp. 179–82; R. Baldwin and J. Houghton, 'Circular Arguments: The Status and Legitimacy of Administrative Rules' [1986] *P.L.* 239; G. Ganz, *Quasi-Legislation: Recent Developments in Secondary Legislation* (1987).

[18] Craig, *Administrative Law*, pp. 178–9.

expressed to be exercisable by statutory instrument. Reliance upon a formal definition may well avoid awkward or intractable difficulties attendant upon a substantive definition. Such solutions always have a price. In this instance the price is the exclusion from the coverage of the Act of many rules which may in substance be legislative.

What then of the other aspect of the argument outlined above? Does not the literature on pluralist policy-making indicate forcefully that affected interests will be afforded participatory rights in practice? Do not the plethora of advisory boards, commissions, and the like reinforce this conclusion? A superficial understanding of pluralism or élite pluralism might suggest this conclusion. A more considered appreciation of pluralist democracy reveals the inadequacies of this argument.

Pluralism might well indicate the impact which non-elected groups can and do have upon the policy-making process. It might serve to dispel the illusion that Parliament is the sole repository of public power. It does not, without more, tell us whether this will occur in all areas of the administrative process. There is ample evidence for the continued existence of rules which are dispositive of a person's case, which may well be unpublished and the result of no consultation. The limitations of the empirical literature on pluralism should also be borne in mind. Even where this literature demonstrates that groups are consulted, this does not tell us whether the types of groups which are thereby consulted adequately cover the range of affected interests. Studies may demonstrate that this is so within a particular area. They may also, as we have seen, indicate that representative status is accorded to the select few.[19] The views of Sir Douglas Wass, who has had many years of experience within the central bureaucracy, are particularly apposite in this context.[20] He notes the tendency of departments to 'mark' certain pressure groups, to the exclusion of other groups, and of less organized interests.[21] Pluralism as an empirical phenomenon would lead one to expect group pressure upon the administrative process. The criticisms and qualifications of pluralism which were considered in this and the previous chapter would cause one to suspect that group

[19] See above, ch.3 sec. 2c, ch. 4 sec.7.

[20] Sir D. Wass, *Government and the Governed* (1984), 104–5.

[21] Wass believes that the political influence of such groups can only be checked by more, not less, popular involvement in decision-making; ibid. 106–8. See also J. Vickers and G. Yarrow, *Privatization: An Economic Analysis* (1988), for the influence of powerful firms on the privatization process.

pressure would be uneven. Whether it would now be more correct to depict decision-making as élite pluralist, or corporatist is more debatable.[22] The answer may vary depending upon the nature of the substantive area, and the attitude of the government in power. What is readily apparent is that arguments from the undeniable existence of participation, to the sufficiency thereof, are simplistic. Factual evidence that groups can influence policy is no basis for asserting that an adequate range of interests will be consulted. The early pluralists saw nothing inconsistent in recognising group power, *and* advocating the express acknowledgement of consultation rights.[23]

c. Participation, Constitutional Structure, and Pluralism

The arguments adduced in support of the proposition that the law should not play any greater role than at present in fostering interest representation have been found wanting. This does not, in itself, make the case for a change in our legal rules. The status quo may rest on uncertain foundation, but, as with many areas of life, some more positive reasons are required before thoughts of reform will be taken seriously. A fact which is being increasingly perceived by administrative lawyers is that reasons for change in their own area may well be connected with broader issues of constitutional law and constitutional design.[24] The argument which will be presented within this section exemplifies this connection. It can be summarized in the following manner. Our approach to participation within administrative law continues to be coloured by a unitary conception of the constitution. It is only by revealing the inadequacies of this unitary view that we can begin to make a principled decision as to the role which participation should play within society.

The foundation of this unitary view is a concept which we have encountered before. It is the less-well-known face of sovereignty, that of legislative monopoly.[25] The presupposition is that Parliament is either the direct initiator or the controller of all that emerges

[22] See above, ch.3 sec.2c, ch.5 secs. 2, 3.

[23] e.g. H.J. Laski, *A Grammer of Politics* (4th edn., 1938), 80–2, 133, 246, 270, 324–6, 380–4; E. Barker, *Reflections on Government* (1942), 225–6, 250–1.

[24] J. P. W. B. McAuslan and J. McEldowney (eds.), *Law, Legitimacy and the Constitution* (1985); J.L. Jowell and D. Oliver (eds.), *The Changing Constitution* (2nd edn., 1989); I. Harden and N. Lewis, *The Noble Lie: The British Constitution and the Rule of Law* (1986).

[25] See above, ch.2 sec. 3.

formally as legislation. Ministers are accountable to, and controlled by, Parliament. Policy issues underlying legislation or delegated legislation will have been considered by Parliament.[26] Governmental agencies will be controlled by and accountable to Parliament through the relevant minister.[27] A natural correlative of this conception of legislative monopoly is that a duality in the meaning of the term 'legislative' is concealed. Norms which emerge with the formal seal of Act of Parliament or statutory instrument are the sole qualifiers as legislation. Parliament controls or initiates the passage of such norms and thus the fundamental tenets of representative democracy are preserved. The realization that there are rules of a legislative character which may be substantively indistinguishable from those actually passed by Parliament, but which are not subject to parliamentary control, cannot be squarely faced without undermining the very conception of legislative monopoly.

If Parliament really did still exercise the degree of control ascribed to it, if it did possess this legislative monopoly, initiating or controlling the passage of legislation, and if the only norms of a legislative character which regulated our lives were those emerging as a statute or delegated legislation, then all might be well. There would be little need for any further participation in this Illyria. The problem is immediately apparent: our constitutional structure does not conform to such an idyllic vision. Constitutional conventions should be founded upon some measure of empirical evidence. If our theoretical constructs depart too much from reality, they risk becoming at best empty vessels; at worst they serve as invalid premises for the development of more particular rules of conduct. Few can seriously maintain that the picture of power and legislative monopoly ascribed to Parliament accords with reality. A more accurate portrayal of our political system would highlight two

[26] e.g. objectors to new motorways who have attempted to question the need for these roads have been prevented from doing so on the hypothesis that policy questions will have been decided by Parliament even though the Commons may not have debated the policy; and see the unitary conception of contractual capacity contained in *Town Investments Ltd.* v. *Department of the Environment* [1978] A.C. 359. See also *Nottinghamshire County Council* v. *Secretary of State for the Environment* [1986] A.C. 40.

[27] e.g. *Laker Airways Ltd.* v. *Department of Transport* [1977] Q.B. 643, and the criticism of the reasoning therein by R. Baldwin, 'A British Independent Regulatory Agency and the "Skytrain" Decision' [1978] *P.L.* 57. On a more general level, the presupposition that Parliament either initiates or controls all that emerges as legislation goes some way to explain the absence of any developed legal conceptual structure within which to consider quangos; Craig, *Administrative Law*, pp. 90,92.

themes, both of which have direct relevance to the issue of participation: the growth in the power of the executive, and the increasingly complex nature of public decision-making. The former undermines the ideal of parliamentary power, and thereby places the value of primary participation, in the form of the vote, in its true perspective. The latter challenges both the ideal of parliamentary power and the legislative monopoly of Parliament. In doing so, it thereby raises the question of whether other forms of participation are warranted.

The growth in the power of the executive has already been considered in a previous chapter.[28] By the early decades of this century the legislative process was already being both nationalized and centralized into the hands of the executive. Whether one now chooses to regard our political process as adversarial or oligarchic, the implications for participation are equally profound. At its most extreme, one commentator has described our system as elective autocracy.[29] The most basic act of participation is the vote, and elective autocracy provides this minimum form of participation for all. It is, however, only a minimum form of communication operating once every four or five years. The voters' own MP will have precious little input or control over the parliamentary process, which will be firmly in the hands of the executive. One need not necessarily go as far as this and yet still agree that the vote as a mechanism by which, through one's chosen MP, one participates in the process of government falls sadly short of an ideal contained in the 'golden age' of Parliament model. If the demise of real parliamentary power minimizes the participation resulting from the vote, the increasingly complex nature of government action both reinforces this and provides more positive support for other forms of participation. It is to this second theme that we now turn.

The last ten years have witnessed the emergence of a growing literature concerned with the problems attendant upon the existence of a large number of institutions which exercise governmental responsibility but which do not conform to the departmental norm.

[28] See above, ch. 2 sec. 4c. For modern treatment, see, e.g., S. Walkland and M. Ryle (eds.), *The Commons in the Seventies* (1977); N. Johnson, *In Search of the Constitution: Reflections on State and Society in Britain* (1977); S. Walkland (ed.), *The House of Commons in the Twentieth Century* (1979); M. Beloff and G. Peele, *The Government of the United Kingdom: Political Authority in a Changing Society* (2nd edn., 1985); H. Drucker, P. Dunleavy, A. Gamble, and G. Peele (eds.), *Developments in British Politics 2* (1986).

[29] J. Lucas, *Democracy and Participation* (1976).

Such institutions are not new. They have been inhabitants of our governmental landscape for a considerable period of time.[30] In the nineteenth century, at least in the first half thereof, it was the norm to allocate areas of governmental responsibility to such bodies. Decline in the Board system resulted from the assertion of parliamentary supremacy. Parliament wished to exercise a degree of control over the activities of Boards which their institutional structure rendered difficult. The result was the absorption of a number of Boards into new Ministries.

While the number of such bodies declined, the general category has never disappeared. Governmental agencies of one form or another, which did not conform to the ordinary departmental norm, continued to exist. The post-war period has witnessed a rapid expansion in these institutions. A plethora of such organizations now exist, with a bewildering variety of name, structure, and personnel. The rationale for their creation has been equally varied. Some have been established to allow greater expertise to be focused upon a particular task, others to foster greater public participation within the organization itself. The desire to set governmental functions apart from ordinary party-political pressures, or to ensure greater fairness in the allocation of resources in which the government has a direct interest, provides further reasons for their creation. Overlapping with these reasons is a more general desire to maintain some cohesion in the traditional Whitehall bureaucracy and to hive off certain specialized tasks to particular institutions.[31] The number of such organizations will increase as a result of the government's decision to restructure the Civil Service and to utilize agencies to implement major policy initiatives which have been decided upon by the executive and bureaucracy.[32]

Quangos or fringe organizations are not the only reason for the

[30] D. Roberts, *Victorian Origins of the British Welfare State* (1960); Parris, *Constitutional Bureaucracy*; D. Fraser, *Evolution of the British Welfare State* (1973); N. Chester, *The English Administrative System (1780–1870)* (1981); H. Arthurs, *Without the Law: Administrative Justice and Legal Pluralism in Nineteenth Century England* (1985).

[31] For general discussion, see Report on Non-Departmental Public Bodies, Cmnd. 7797 (1980); Hague, Mackenzie, and Barker (eds.), *Public Policy and Private Interests: The Institutions of Compromise*; A. Barker (ed.), *Quangos in Britain* (1982); R. Baldwin and C. McCrudden, *Regulation and Public Law* (1987). For a more radical explanation than those set out in the text, see, e.g., A. Cawson and P. Saunders, 'Corporatism, Competitive Politics and Class Struggle', in R. King (ed.), *Capital and Politics* (1983).

[32] R. Baldwin, 'The Next Steps: Ministerial Responsibility and Government by Agency' (1988) 51 *M.L.R.* 622.

increasingly complex nature of governmental action in our society. Government contracting presents another facet of the same problem. Corporations which are, in formal legal terms, private may have a substantial input into the policy-making process.[33] While we can try to preserve strict constitutional theory by maintaining that such organizations are simply concerned with the means of fulfilling clearly articulated governmental policy, this may bear little relation to reality. Means and ends are not easily separated, and only the most sanguine observer would seriously suggest that the role of the private corporation is limited to the mechanism for effectuating goals which have already been defined by the traditional political processes.

What are the implications of these developments and what light do they shed on the question of participation?[34] The presence of such organizations challenges the ideal of the legislative monopoly of Parliament, the idea that Parliament controls or initiates all legislation, *and* that only those rules formally stamped as an Act of Parliament or delegated legislation are of concern in a representative democracy. The presence of fringe organizations questions this presupposition in two ways, both of which have direct implications for participation.

First, in relation to certain types of fringe organizations, the traditional devices of the 'golden-age' model do not work even in theory. Fringe organizations can be accommodated within our standard constitutional theory by accepting that they will be held accountable to Parliament either through the responsible minister, and/or through direct supervision by, for example, a select committee. What is apparent is that such premises run counter to the very reasons for the creation of certain fringe organizations. Some of these institutions will be established in order positively to secure a degree of independence from the normal party political processes. Decision-making divorced from the standard depart-

[33] B. L. Smith and D. C. Hague (eds.), *The Dilemma of Accountability in Modern Government* (1971); C. Turpin, *Government Contracts* (1972); J. L. Jowell, 'Bargaining in Development Control' (1977) *J.P.L.* 414, and 'Limits of Law in Urban Planning' (1977) *C.L.P.* 63; T. C. Daintith, 'Regulation by Contract: The New Prerogative' (1979) *C.L.P.* 41.

[34] Participation within such bodies can give rise to problems of patronage: see N. Johnson, 'Editorial: Quangos and the Structure of British Government' (1979) 57 *Pub. Adm.* 379; A. Davies, 'Patronage and Quasi-Government: Some Proposals for Reform', in A. Barker (ed.), *Quangos in Britain*, ch. 10.

mental norm is the aim.[35] In such areas it would be contradictory to insist upon the methods of accountability dictated by traditional constitutional doctrine.[36]

Secondly, while our traditional constitutional model encounters theoretical obstacles when applied to certain fringe organizations, the practical difficulties which lie in its path are no less severe. Ensuring effective ministerial accountability for those fringe organizations which are not intended to be independent in the sense articulated above is subject to all the normal difficulties attendant upon that doctrine. These are then exacerbated by the fact that the institution is not part of the normal departmental structure. Direct parliamentary supervision through one of the remodelled select committees may hold out some hope of more effective scrutiny. However, as Johnson has said,[37] the impact of such committees will probably be highly selective unless they are equipped with staff and resources on a scale not contemplated thus far.

While traditional forms of accountability may be subject to constraint in this area, this does not mean that other forms of control and accountability may not be available. There may be financial controls, and guidelines laid down in the enabling legislation. Monitoring the decisions reached by the organization is a further possibility.

Participation in the decision-making process can be another valuable device. We are accustomed to thinking of accountability in its traditional sense, from the 'top', from Parliament. The limitations, both theoretical and practical, of this technique have already been addressed. Accountability need not, however, be seen exclusively in this way; a different but important method of accountability may come from the 'bottom', from participation of those affected in the decision-making or rule-making processes of a particular institution. The existence of impediments to the traditional form of accountability from the 'top' does not necessarily preclude parti-

[35] Some control may be exercised e.g., through financial checks, and/or through the provision of guidelines in the empowering legislation. This does not affect the point being made in the text.

[36] See Johnson, 'Editorial', and D. Keeling, 'Beyond Ministerial Departments: Mapping the Administrative Terrain: Quasi-Governmental Agencies' (1976) 54 *Pub. Adm.* 161, for a discussion of the differing meanings of control and accountability.

[37] Johnson, 'Editorial'; N. Johnson, 'Accountability, Control and Complexity: Moving beyond Ministerial Responsibility', in A. Barker (ed.), *Quangos in Britain*, ch. 12. For more general comment, see G. Drewry (ed.), *The New Select Committees: A Study of the 1979 Reforms* (1985).

cipation in the decision-making process from the 'bottom'. Thus, for example, the fact that we justifiably wish the allocation of media licences, or funds for the arts, to be dispensed free from party bias does not in any sense import the conclusion that interested parties should not be enabled to participate or air their views.

It is, of course, true that this type of accountability from the 'bottom' is different from the traditional concept. To accept that it is different is not, however, to suggest that one should be the sole bearer of the citizens' interest. The traditional concept rests ultimately on the idea that, in a representative democracy, decisions of a governmental nature should reside with the elected representative, directly or indirectly. This ideal has, as we have seen, come under increasing strain. The growth of executive power over the legislature has rendered the first limb of the 'golden-age' model, that Parliament wields real power, outdated. The consequence has been to reduce the importance of the citizens' primary participation, in the form of the vote, to a minimum.[38] This very growth in executive power, coupled with the increasingly complex nature of governmental institutions, challenges the second limb of that model, that of legislative monopoly. When we attempt to apply traditional notions of accountability, we encounter theoretical and practical difficulties of the type mentioned above. A greater regard for consultation in the process of rule-making can constitute a valuable form of secondary participation for the citizen in government. This applies as much to rule-making by the executive as to that by fringe organizations.[39]

Secondary participation in the sense adumbrated above should, of course, not be regarded as the panacea for all ills. The discussion of the conceptual and pragmatic difficulties which attend participatory rights in the United States is of relevance here also.[40] Problems of

[38] A major alteration of our voting system, such as the introduction of proportional representation, could have some effect upon executive–legislative relationships. It would be likely to weaken the dominance of the single party in power because that party would often have to rely on the support of other smaller groupings to retain its majority.

[39] The Rules Publication Act 1893, now repealed, is of interest in this respect. The Act imposed a duty on those making statutory rules (defined in s. 1(4)) to publish the rules in forty days before finalizing the rule. Public bodies, which were not defined by the legislation, were then able to make representations to the rule-making authority. The legislation primarily applied to those rules which were required to be laid before Parliament, but which were not actually subject to real parliamentary scrutiny, because they were operative immediately. Consultation with at least some interested parties was, therefore, seen to be a way of validating and controlling the enactment of such rules in the absence of parliamentary supervision.

[40] See above, ch. 4 sec. 7b.

defining an interest, and of securing the adequate representation of affected interests, are endemic whenever such rights are accorded, even though their precise form may vary from country to country. The same is true concerning problems of cost and delay. However, if the generic nature of the problems experienced in the United States is apposite, so too are the rejoinders and qualifications to those problems considered above. We shall return to this issue once again at a later state. Before doing so, a separate, albeit connected, argument in favour of participation will be addressed.

d. Participation: Voting, Rule-Making, and Adjudication

Participation is obviously not a one dimensional concept, and political participation even less so. Although not free from difficulty, the meaning used by Parry will be adopted here. Political participation is the taking part in the formulation, passage, or implementation of public policies.[41] It is evident that political participation can take many forms. At one end of the spectrum there is the formalized vote. Voting[42] is obviously not the only mode of participation. Studies have dissected the decision-making process, indicating the varying political roles which are played between the inception of a project and the attainment of the final decision.[43] Formalized adjudication represents yet another avenue through which an individual can participate in the political process.

Viewing participation in the above manner prompts an interesting and important enquiry. Our legal rules at present protect both 'ends' of the spectrum, but treat the middle ground as no man's land. Formalized participation both through the vote or through adjudication, is legally protected.[44] Intermediate forms of participation, in, for example, rule-making by quasi-governmental agencies, are not afforded analogous treatment in the absence of specific

[41] G. Parry, 'The Idea of Political Participation', in G. Parry (ed.), *Participation in Politics* (1972), ch. 1.

[42] What voting system should be preferred is itself a complex question; see, e.g., S. E. Finer (ed.), *Adversary Politics and Electoral Reform* (1975); V. Bogdanor, *The People and the Party System* (1981); P. Dunleavy and C. T. Husbands, *British Democracy at the Crossroads: Voting and Party Competition in the 1980s* (1985).

[43] See Parry, 'The Idea of Political Participation'; R. L. Nuttall, E. K. Scheuch, and C. Gordon, 'On the Structure of Influence', in T. N. Clark (ed.), *Community Structure and Decision Making: Comparative Analysis* (1968), 349–80.

[44] For protection of participation through adjudication, see Craig, *Administrative Law*, ch. 7; for protection through the vote, see H. Rawlings, *Law and the Electoral Process* (1988). This is not to claim that such protection is perfect.

statutory provisions. The remainder of this section will be devoted to considering the cogency of this position. Three reasons can be advanced to suggest that the present position is unsatisfactory.

First, the rationale for dividing the legally protected forms of participation into only two categories, those of litigant and of voter, is defective, being based upon an inadequate and simplistic theory. Rule application in an adjudicative context is held to warrant the requisites of procedural rectitude. Rule-making of a legislative nature is said to be different. No individual is a 'litigant', and participation is ensured, if at all, through the vote. Rule-making will be validated by the normal legislative process, and no further attention need be given to participation. The consequence is that the method by which the government chooses to deal with individuals becomes dispositive of their procedural rights. If it opts for an individualized form of adjudication, then the courts will activate the common-law procedural safeguards; if it chooses to treat citizens as a group, through the enactment of a rule, then the common law will abjure from supplying the omission of the legislature. The courts have been dormant, anaesthetized by the mention of the word legislative.[45] That the result may render procedural protection haphazard, and subject to fine distinctions between what is legislative and what is not, is itself objectionable. This point will be returned to below. What is equally important is that the reasoning fails to convince on a more theoretical level.

What *form* of participation an individual should be entitled to—the right to be heard as a litigant, the right to be counted as a voter, or some intermediate right to participate in the rule-making process—is, as Tribe has argued,[46] itself necessarily premised upon a substantive theory. The decision as to which kind of participation is warranted demands analysis, not only of the effectiveness of the different processes, but also of the importance of the interest which is being affected; and that in itself is dependent upon a substantive theory of values and of rights. Our law concerning process is perforce based upon a substantive theory, but it is one which is defective. The premiss is a rigid dichotomy between adjudication and rule-making in which due process is regarded as essential in the

[45] This is subject to the qualifications contained in the more recent case law on legitimate expectations considered above, ch. 6 sec. 2a.

[46] L. H. Tribe, 'The Puzzling Persistence of Process-Based Constitutional Theories', 89 *Yale L.J.* 1063 (1980). For discussion of this point in the US context, see above ch. 4 sec. 3b.

former in order, *inter alia*, to comply with the dictates of formal justice. No such obligation attends the latter; participation will be adequately ensured through the vote. What is more, the government's choice as to which avenue it should follow will be conclusive. It is clear that the concept of participation through the vote has become etiolated, and our law will remain seriously inadequate if it continues to be based upon a theoretical construct which so ill accords with reality. Important interests are dealt with through the promulgation of rules which the primary legislature cannot effectively control, and which demand a higher degree of participation than allowed by the vote. What is needed is a substantive theory which will recognize the possibility of a category intermediate between participation as litigant and participation as a voter. Only then will our law of process be equipped to meet the realities of modern government.[47]

A second reason why our present law may be regarded as unsatisfactory has been touched upon already. Distinctions between legislative and adjudicative action may be no easier to draw than those between, for example, judicial and administrative or administrative and executive action. Many cases may, although they arise as bipartite disputes, have broader multipartite implications.[48] The judicial focus may be directed towards, not just the resolution of a completed set of past events, but the modification of conduct in the future. Decisions reached by a public body through the medium of adjudication may entail broad issues of social and political choice which are indistinguishable from a legislative act. The distinction

[47] In general, participatory rights in rule-making in the United States are the creation of statute, see S. G. Breyer and R. B. Stewart, *Administrative Law and Regulatory Policy: Problems, Text and Cases* (2nd edn., 1985), ch. 5. The Constitution does not normally require due process in such cases: *Bi-Metallic Investment Co.* v. *State Board of Equalization* 239 U.S. 441 (1915), and compare to *Londoner* v. *Denver* 210 U.S. 373 (1908). However, some courts have read certain regulatory statutes broadly, and have maximized the opportunity for hearing rights in legislative type cases: see, e.g., *The National Welfare Rights Organization* v. *Finch* 429 F. 2d 725 (D.C. Cir. 1970); *Environmental Defense Fund, Inc.* v. *Ruckelshaus* 439 F. 2d 584 (D.C. Cir. 1971). The reasoning in such cases comes close to the courts supplying the omission of the legislature; see C. R. Sunstein, 'Interest Groups in American Public Law', 38 *Stan. L. Rev.* 29, 67–8 (1985). For more general discussion, see above, ch. 4 sec. 7a.

[48] A. Chayes, 'The Role of the Judge in Public Law Litigation', 89 *Harv. L. Rev.* 1281 (1976). The multipartite implications of adjudicatory decisions can emerge, directly or indirectly, within varying stages of administrative law; see, e.g., the way in which they arise in the choice between rule-making and adjudication as a method of advancing agency policy; Breyer and Stewart, *Administrative Law and Regulatory Policy*, pp. 397–415, 466–90.

between legislative and adjudicative action is further blurred by the grant of broad discretionary powers to administrators. These may be concretized, either through the medium of individualized adjudication, or through the enactment of rules, or the one may follow the other. The former may have legislative effects every bit as real as the latter.[49]

Two consequences follow. On the one hand, it means that the problems of interest representation, of ensuring both that those interested in the suit do have a chance to make representations, and that the litigant presenting the case adequately represents future interests, may often be present even when the issue arises formally as adjudication.[50] We retain, however, a concept of adjudication in which the only interested parties are normally the actual litigants, a model which may well fit much private law adjudication, but is less suited to the subject-matter of public law. On the other hand, because we are still wedded to the idea that action of an overtly legislative nature generally carries no participatory rights, we refuse to countenance any interest representation when the general norm-creating nature of the action is made explicit. We seek to preserve our classical ideas of adjudication, and refuse to admit participatory rights in rule-making, partly at least because to do otherwise would be to admit the unthinkable, that public bodies external to Parliament make decisions of a broadly legislative nature. The force of our constitutional convention makes its presence felt once again.

The third and final reason why our present law may be open to question is that the very justifications for process rights in the context of adjudication bear some analogy to the reasons afforded for political participation in non-adjudicative contexts.

Justifications for due process in adjudication vary. One rationale emphasizes the connection between procedural due process and the substantive justice of the final outcome. Procedural deficiencies can undermine public confidence in the fairness of the proceedings, and render the substantive decision unreliable in the sense that an error is more likely to occur in the absence of procedural safeguards.[51]

Another justification often given for due process in an adjudicative

[49] See, generally, D. J. Galligan, *Discretionary Powers: A Legal Study of Official Discretion* (1986).

[50] Craig, *Administrative Law*, pp. 373–4; J. Vining, *Legal Identity* (1978), 20–5.

[51] See, e.g., D. Resnick, 'Due Process and Procedural Justice', in J. R. Pennock and J. W. Chapman (eds), *Due Process: Nomos 18* (1977), 217; Resnick accepts that there are non-instrumental justifications for due process, pp. 217–18.

context is that formal justice and the rule of law are thereby enhanced. The principles of natural justice encapsulated in the twin precepts of 'hear the other side' and 'let no man be a judge in his own cause' guarantee, as Hart has said, impartiality and objectivity.[52] Formal justice demands the regular and impartial administration of public rules, what Rawls terms 'justice as regularity'.[53] This contains a number of elements. The actions required by the law should be of a kind which men can reasonably be expected to do and to avoid. Like cases should be treated alike. Laws should be open, clear, and prospective.[54] Natural justice is a further such precept, designed to ensure that the legal order will be impartially and regularly maintained.[55]

A further rationale for due process views it as a condition for the moral acceptability of those institutions that allow some people to control the lives of others. Procedural due process is seen as playing a role in protecting human dignity by ensuring that the individual is told why he is being treated unfavourably, and by enabling him to take part in that decision. In serving these ends, the system is thereby responsive to demands for participation and revelation.[56] At its most fundamental, a right to be heard is regarded as integral to being a person. The very horror of the Kafkaesque world resides in the fact that the individual is caught up in a seemingly inexorable train of events over which he has no control and for which there is no explanation. The dehumanizing quality of the experience rapidly becomes evident.

Many reasons have been given for advocating political participation in contexts other than adjudication. Underlying these variants lie two more general theories, one of which has been termed instrumental, the other developmental.[57] Instrumental theories, as the nomenclature would suggest, regard political participation as a mechanism for achieving a particular goal, which may be to prevent

[52] H. L. A. Hart, *The Concept of Law* (1961), 156, 202.

[53] J. Rawls, *A Theory of Justice* (Oxford, 1973), 235.

[54] J. Lucas, *The Principles of Politics* (1966), 106–23; J. Raz, 'The Rule of Law and its Virtue' (1977) 93 *L.Q.R.* 195.

[55] Rawls, *A Theory of Justice*, pp. 238–9.

[56] F. I. Michelman, 'Formal and Associational Aims in Procedural Due Process', in Pennock and Chapman (eds.), *Due Process: Nomos 18*, ch. 4; R. B. Saphire, 'Specifying Due Process Values: Toward a More Responsive Approach to Procedural Protection', 127 *U. Pa. L. Rev.* 111 (1978); J. L. Mashaw, *Due Process in the Administrative State* (1985), chs. 4–7.

[57] Parry, 'The Idea of Political Participation'.

tyranny or to counter excessive bureaucracy. Since the individual is regarded as the best judge of his own interests, this implies that he ought to have the chance to exercise his preferences. While practical necessity requires that the actual process of government should be carried out by a limited number, these should be responsive to the wider populace through consultation.[58]

There is a proximate connection between the instrumental theory of participation and the rationale for due process which is based upon a link between process rights and the substantive justice of the final outcome. Participation in non-adjudicative contexts, such as rule-making, may help both to prevent the use of rule-making power in a way which is substantively arbitrary, and also increase the likelihood that the chosen rule will effectuate its avowed purpose.[59] This is not to say that it will always be a success. The same may, however, be true of due process in an adjudicative context. The desired link between due process and the substantive justice of the final outcome may not be evident or may not operate in a particular area.

Developmental theories of participation have a different emphasis from those of an instrumental character. The benefit of participation does not reside wholly in its tendency to prevent arbitrary government. An ability to participate in decision-making is regarded as part of the broader development of the individual, both morally and politically. This theme has considerable pedigree.[60] The developmental theme can be found in the Aristotelian view of politics. The citizen finds his true realization through participation in political life. John Stuart Mill wrote in a similar vein.[61] He extolled the virtues and desirability of participation; only thereby would individuals develop their capacities to the full. The ability to organize one's life would be enhanced, and the very process of participation would be educative by forcing one to take into account the interests of others when deciding upon a course of action. Elements of the developmental approach can also be found in the

[58] An instrumental perspective does not, however, dictate one particular form of political society; ibid. 22–6.

[59] Even behaviouralists can advocate participation as a method of ensuring that élites remain responsive to a wider populace; e.g. L. W. Milbrath, *Political Participation: How and Why do People get Involved in Politics?* (1965), 144.

[60] See below, ch. 10.

[61] J.S. Mill, *Utilitarianism, On Liberty, and Considerations on Representative Government*, ed. H.B. Acton (1972), 208–18.

work of more modern writers.[62] A connection between the developmental view of participation and the dignitarian justification for adjudicative due process can be perceived. Both ideas focus upon the importance of process rights to the individual as an individual. The dignitarian theme approaches the matter in 'defensive' terms: to judge me without hearing my case, or telling me of my alleged wrong, is to treat me as less than a complete human being. The developmental theme picks up the same idea and infuses it with more positive content: by allowing me to participate in public life, in addition to the skeletal right to vote, you will enable me to fulfil my own potential, and will facilitate my full membership of the community.

e. The Two Visions of Pluralism and the Limits of Participation

The development of participatory process is not a panacea which will solve all the ills, real and imagined, which beset the exercise of public power in society. Difficult and taxing questions will need to be confronted if the law is to be expanded in this direction. Some of these problems have already been considered in the previous chapter, including the dysfunctional consequences which are said to attend the grant of participatory rights. Reference should be made to that discussion, since the generic nature of the problems there canvassed are relevant to any system which seeks to develop participatory rights.[63] They cannot be ignored in the United Kingdom. The object of this section is, however, to focus upon the way in which the choice between the two differing visions of pluralism outlined earlier constrains and shapes the development of participatory rights. This can be perceived in three distinctive, albeit related, ways.

First, both pluralist models place direct or indirect constraints upon the types of groups which can engage in participatory discourse with the central government. If certain groups within society wish to wield power in a manner regarded as antithetical to the organizing principle of the centre, their power will be curbed. The most obvious manifestation of this is the abolition of certain types of local authorities, and the placing of constraints upon the

[62] See the discussion of, e.g., Bachrach, Pateman, Macpherson, and Bottomore, above, ch.3 sec. 2c,d. See also Lucas, *Principles of Politics*, pp. 268–9.

[63] See above, ch. 4 sec. 7b.

remainder, which has characterized Conservative policy in the 1980s.[64] Society may be pluralist, but groups which are seen as differing too radically from the philosophy propounded by the centre will be restrained, or even abolished. It should not, however, be assumed that this is a facet only of the more modern market-oriented pluralism. The earlier UK pluralists can be subjected to the same analysis, the difference residing in the types of group power which they would have to dominate in order for the policies of the centre to be fulfilled. The proximate connection perceived by the early UK pluralists between economic and political liberty, and the necessity for governmental intervention to secure the requisite economic foundations for democracy, led to constraints being placed upon a particularly potent form of group power, private property.[65] This could necessitate 'abolition' of the group power in certain areas, as in the context of nationalization; or it could produce constraints upon the way in which such power is used, as exemplified by the control over private property regimes necessary to effectuate ideas such as a right to work. Neither species of pluralism adheres to the unfettered idea that public policy emerges simply as a result of intergroup competition. Both require domination by the centre of power groups which threaten the prescriptive role for the state which the particular model erects.[66]

Secondly, a natural corollary of this theme is that, even where groups are not perceived as so threatening as to require direct control, the extent to which their views will actually shape or modify central policy will itself be constrained by the compatibility of those views with the fundamental policy dictates of the centre. The duty of a public body to give adequate consideration to the views of those who participate in the policy-making process will be considered immediately hereafter. However, neither of the pluralist models in the United Kingdom support the conclusions that any such duty of adequate consideration can be taken to include the *necessity* of modifying fundamental doctrinal positions on which the policy itself is premised. Both models assume that the realizable debating ground for policy alternatives will be bounded by the doctrinal

[64] See, e.g., M. Loughlin, M. D. Gelfand, and K. Young (eds.), *Half a Century of Municipal Decline, 1935–1985* (1985); M. Loughlin, *Local Government in the Modern State* (1986).

[65] e.g., the treatment of property rights by Laski; see below, ch.6 sec. 3.

[66] Whether constraints placed upon local democracy are 'worse' than those placed upon private property is itself dependent upon a background political theory.

assumptions of the model itself. This is just as true for the early pluralists as it is for their more market-oriented successors.

Thirdly, which of these models we choose to pursue will have significant implications for the specific area within which we espouse participation. The connection may be expressed as follows. Participation is one type of device which we have at our disposal for rendering public power accountable. There are many others, including financial constraints, internal bureaucratic control, judicial review, and political checks. Clearly questions can arise as to how well these different devices fit together in any particular area, and which of them should assume prominence. The 'package' of controls which we devise will be crucial, in part because certain of these tools may not sit easily together, in part because we may wish to know which should be regarded as of prime importance. The answer which we give will depend essentially upon the purpose which we believe regulation within a particular area serves. If, for example, we believe that the prime object of social welfare administration is bureaucratic rationality,[67] meaning the most efficient mechanism for distinguishing true and false claims to welfare benefit, then we would concentrate upon matters such as internal agency controls, training of personnel, hierarchical checks within the organization, etc. Process rights would not be of central importance, and could hinder the realization of the basic aim. If, by way of contrast, we conceive that the principal objective of welfare administration is the settlement of 'entitlements' in a manner analogous to the settling of traditional common-law rights, then our perspective may well be very different. Process rights and the ordinary courts would assume much greater prominence.

The connection between this reasoning and the two differing views of pluralism becomes clear. Precisely what the background aim of regulation within a particular area is, and which areas should be directly regulated by the government at all, are both issues which are affected by the underlying political vision which one chooses to adopt. The appropriate role of participation within any single area can only be adequately determined when answers to these questions have been provided. Privatization is, for example, espoused partly

[67] The example is drawn from J. L. Mashaw, *Bureaucratic Justice* (1983). The point is, however, generalizable to other areas; see P. P. Craig, 'Discretionary Power in Modern Administration', in M. Bullinger (ed.), *Verwaltungsermessen im modernen Staat* (1986), 79–111.

because the market is felt to be more efficient in managing industries. Even a privatized industry may, of course, require regulation,[68] but the role of participation within such a regulatory framework will be seen as part of the general underlying aim of ensuring efficiency through the market. This will in itself shape who is entitled to be represented and the importance of participation when compared with other devices to ensure efficiency, such as management training, aggressive marketing, and financial oversight by the regulatory agency. Participatory rights will, when given, be accorded to 'consumers' of the activity and will be justified in these market terms. The objective of giving participatory rights was, for the early pluralists, broader. It was to enable the individual to participate in the process of government, and to foster the full development of the individual in society.

f. Process, Substance, and Hard Look

The preceding discussion, and that in a previous chapter,[69] both serve to highlight the substantive value judgements which permeate avowedly procedural norms. The difficulty of preserving a division between the two is further exemplified by experience with the hard-look doctrine in the United States. Consideration of the hard-look doctrine is important both because of its relationship with the protection of participatory values, and also because it has been suggested that the doctrine could be usefully imported into the United Kingdom.

The hard-look doctrine developed in the United States as a *via media* between judicial deference to agency discretion and more intensive judicial review.[70] The object of the doctrine is to ensure that the agency has taken a hard look at the relevant evidence and the policy alternatives, and has made a reasoned exercise of its discretion within a particular case.[71] Adequate consideration must be given to the evidence submitted by interest groups, with the objective of preventing the views of any one particular group from

[68] See, e.g., T. Prosser, *Nationalised Industries and Public Control* (1986); Vickers and Yarrow, *Privatization*. See, more generally, S. G. Breyer, *Regulation and its Reform* (1982).

[69] See above, ch. 4 sec. 3b.

[70] See, generally, Breyer and Stewart, *Administrative Law and Regulatory Policy*, pp. 341–73.

[71] For related changes in the law of standing and process rights, see Craig, *Administrative Law*. pp. 25–7.

dominating or capturing the agency which is making the decision. The approach is, therefore, one which 'emphasizes process'.[72] The agency must justify its choice, and make a reasoned decision on the basis of all the relevant considerations. This approach is contrasted with one in which the court undertakes substantive review, under the guise of the arbitrary and capricious test, and rules out certain agency alternatives as irrational or unreasonable.

This distinction may be sustainable in theory; in practice the line between the two approaches can become difficult to draw. The very decision as to whether a consideration should be deemed to be relevant, and the weight which should be accorded to the views of differing protagonists, are both matters in which a court can, under the guise of protecting the decision-making process, play a significant role in defining the range of permitted substantive outcomes.[73] The same point may be made with reference to the judicial insistence that the effects of various policy alternatives be adequately canvassed.

These difficulties are reflected in the varying meanings which have been ascribed to the differing standards of review, and to the problematic nature of classifying cases as ones concerned with 'hard look', or the 'arbitrary and capricious' standard of review. A brief example will illustrate this conundrum. The *Baltimore Gas* case[74] is considered by Breyer and Stewart[75] as an example of the narrow meaning ascribed to the arbitrary and capricious standard of review. The claimant has to establish that the agency decision is devoid of a rational basis, and the court confines itself to determining that the agency took the relevant considerations into account and made some rational connection between them. The *State Farm* case[76] is, by way of contrast, discussed within the hard-look doctrine.[77] The court found that the agency failed to present an adequate basis and explanation for rescinding a regulation concerned with passive restraints in motor vehicles. The foundation for review was, however, once again the arbitrary and capricious test. However, in

[72] Ibid. 341.

[73] Ibid. 372–3. See also S. G. Breyer, 'Vermont Yankee and the Courts' Role in the Nuclear Energy Controversy', 91 *Harv. L. Rev.* 1833 (1978).

[74] *Baltimore Gas and Electric Co.* v. *Natural Resources Defense Council* 462 U.S. 87 (1983).

[75] *Administrative Law and Regulatory Policy*, pp. 336–41.

[76] *Motor Vehicle Manufacturers Assn.* v. *State Farm Mutual Automobile Ins. Co.* 463 U.S. 29, 42–3 (1983).

[77] Breyer and Stewart, *Administrative Law and Regulatory Policy*, pp. 354–62.

this instance the court gave a broader reading to that phrase. The court accepted that it should not substitute its judgement for that of the agency. It could, however, intervene if any of the following defects were present: if the agency relied on factors which Congress had not intended it to consider; failed to consider an important aspect of the problem; offered an explanation which ran counter to the evidence before the agency; or was so implausible that it could not be sustained.[78]

Commentators within the United Kingdom will no doubt perceive the doctrinal analogy with the fluid *Wednesbury* principle.[79] The broad sense of unreasonableness allows the court to intervene if the authority fails to take account of relevant considerations, takes irrelevant considerations into account, acts for improper purposes or *malafide*. The more specific narrow sense of unreasonableness allows judicial intervention if, even in the absence of the above defects, the decision which is reached is so unreasonable that no reasonable public body could have come to that decision. It may well be questioned whether the second limb of the test is actually required; it is arguable that all such cases could be viewed as instances of relevancy, or propriety of purpose, within the first limb of the test. More relevant for present purposes is the fact that the same doctrine can be imbued with significantly different meanings depending upon the opinion of the reviewing court. This is evident from the shifting interpretation accorded to the arbitrary and capricious test in the United States. In the United Kingdom it is manifest in, for example, the divergent meanings ascribed to the second limb of the *Wednesbury* principle. Courts have used this as the basis for intervention in circumstances which fall far short of the extreme situations envisaged by the original formulation of that principle.[80]

Harden and Lewis have argued strongly for the development of a hard-look doctrine within the United Kingdom[81] They consider the difficulties and defects of other attempts to ensure the rational consideration of policy alternatives within government.[82] The hard-

[78] Breyer and Stewart (ibid. 368) admit that the two cases are difficult to reconcile. See now the less intensive attitude to review in *Chevron, U.S.A., Inc.* v. *Natural Resources Defense Council, Inc.*, 467 U.S. 837, 842–3 (1984). For contrasting views on *Chevron*, compare R. Pierce, '*Chevron* and its Aftermath: Judicial Review of Agency Interpretation of Statutory Provisions', 41 *Vand. L. Rev.* 301 (1988), with Aman, 'Administrative Law in a Global Era' and Farina, 'Statutory Interpretation'.

[79] *Associated Provincial Picture Houses Ltd.* v. *Wednesbury Corporation* [1948] 1 K.B. 223.

[80] See Craig, *Administrative Law*, pp. 281–7, 292–6.

[81] Harden and Lewis, *The Noble Lie*.

[82] Ibid., ch. 5.

look doctrine is espoused as a corrective, albeit partial, for these difficulties, arguing that such a development would reinforce the accountability of governmental decision-making. The objective would be, as in the United States, to ensure that policy alternatives are adequately considered, that reasons are proffered for the chosen agency decision, and that differing interests can present their views to the relevant agency, and have those views adequately considered.

There is force in this suggestion. Two comments on this analysis are, however, warranted. First, there is the question as to whether we possess the doctrinal techniques to achieve this result. It is clear that, as the authors themselves recognize, we would have to develop a more general duty to give reasons for administrative decision-making, with the correlative obligation to develop a record of the proceedings. Greater concern for participatory rights would also, as argued above, have to be shown, in order that the range of interests legitimately concerned with agency decision-making could present their views.

The contrast which Harden and Lewis draw between our present legal techniques and those which would be needed to develop the hard-look doctrine is, however, strained in one important sense. They contrast the limited nature of review within the *Wednesbury* principle, allowing the court to intervene if the decision is so unreasonable that no reasonable body could reach it, with the more extensive scrutiny required under a hard-look approach.[83] This narrow sense of unreasonableness has, however, been interpreted liberally, and applied in situations falling short of extreme arbitrariness. More important is the fact that the narrow sense of unreasonableness is, as we have seen above, but part of the *Wednesbury* test. Our courts have intervened on many occasions, using relevancy or purpose as their tool.[84] Their reasoning has not been dissimilar to that of some US cases which are considered within the ambit of the hard-look doctrine.[85] To conclude that the UK use of the *Wednesbury* test has amounted to a 'kid-glove' approach to policy analysis[86] is, therefore, misconceived.

Secondly, the suggestion that, by focusing upon the hard-look

[83] Ibid., e.g. pp. 205, 252, 272.

[84] Craig, *Administrative Law*, pp. 354–8.

[85] Cf., e.g., the reasoning process in *Secretary of State for Education and Science* v. *Tameside Metropolitan Borough Council* [1977] A.C. 1014, with that in the *State Farm* case, above, n. 76.

[86] Harden and Lewis, *The Noble Lie*, p. 272.

doctrine, issues concerning the merits can be avoided is dubious.[87] Deciding whether a particular consideration is relevant, whether a particular object is within the allowable range, whether an adequate hearing has been accorded to interested parties, and whether the reasons ultimately given for the decision are adequate, are all factors which can encroach directly or indirectly upon the merits. The court may not be stipulating a particular substantive conclusion. It may, however, be explicitly or implicitly ruling out certain options by the way in which it addresses and answers the preceding issues. Judicial conceptions of rights, and the balance between such rights and other social goals, will continue to play a role.

There is indeed a connection between this issue, and the first point adumbrated above. Much of the controversy concerning leading cases has arisen precisely because the UK courts have not adopted a purely 'kid-glove' approach to review. They have employed the *Wednesbury* tests of substantive unreasonableness, and relevancy, to engage in more extensive review.[88] The overt recognition of a hard-look doctrine within the United Kingdom would not remove this problem. If a particular interest group challenges an agency decision, claiming that the rights of property owners were not adequately considered, that the interests of the environment were improperly excluded, or that insufficient attention was paid to the plight of welfare recipients, the court will perforce have to examine the agency decision-making to determine the veracity of such claims. Such judicial scrutiny will inexorably entail some vision concerning the nature of such interests within the overall constitutional structure, the relevance of such interests within this particular statutory scheme, and their relationship with other statutory goals.

The very decision to make increased provision for consultation rights, coupled with the desire for a reasoned consideration of policy alternatives by the administrator, will, therefore, lead the courts into making decisions which can constrict the ambit of substantive choices at the disposal of the agency. Fostering effective consultation rights will entail, *inter alia*, judicial scrutiny to ensure that the views

[87] Harden and Lewis, *The Noble Lie*, e.g. pp. 205–6, 234, 263.

[88] See, e.g., Craig, *Administrative Law*, pp. 281–7, 292–6; J. P. W. B. McAuslan, 'Administrative Law, Collective Consumption and Judicial Policy' (1983) 46 *M.L.R.* 1; J. L. Jowell and A.Lester, 'Beyond *Wednesbury*: Substantive Principles of Administrative Law' [1987] *P.L.* 368.

of differing interests were adequately considered; fostering the rational consideration of policy alternatives will necessitate a judicial view as to which options the agency should have explored and whether it did so. Both of these judicial enquiries will take place, and can only take place, against the backdrop of the enabling legislation. They both require an interpretive view from the court as to the goals and purposes which that enabling legislation established.

g. Reinforcing the Legislative Process?

The discussion thus far has concentrated upon the ways in which greater participation in public decision-making might be fostered, and has linked this with themes of pluralist democracy. There is, however, a different aspect of pluralism which requires our attention. This is the tendency of the executive and groups to make policy which bypasses Parliament. Certain interest groups are consulted by the executive, and a policy emerges which may never be cloaked with a legislative mantle at all but will remain in the form of a bargain or understanding. This will be one example of what Daintith has termed the exercise of dominium power.[89] Governments can seek to attain their goals, either through the command of law,—which he terms imperium,—or through the use of government wealth, providing benefits for those who comply with governmental objectives,—which he terms dominium. Imperium may well have both limitations and disadvantages. It may be impracticable, involve the passage of lengthy, complex legislation, and be uncertain in its impact.[90] Dominium can have positive attractions. Where statutory intervention is required, dominium legislation, with its focus upon criteria for expenditure, tends to leave a broad measure of discretion to the implementing authority. Dominium power can also be used in other ways, such as bargaining and informal agreement. This can facilitate short-term experimentation with policy choices and obviate the need for legislative authorization.

The extent to which these developments generate both constitutional

[89] T. C. Daintith, 'The Executive Power Today: Bargaining and Economic Control', in J. L. Jowell and D. Oliver (eds.), *The Changing Constitution* (2nd edn., 1989), ch. 8. See also T. C. Daintith, 'Regulation by Contract: The New Prerogative' (1979) *C.L.P.* 41, and 'Legal Analysis of Economic Policy' (1982) 9 *Jnl. Law and Soc.* 191; Ganz, *Quasi-Legislation*.

[90] Daintith, 'The Executive Power Today', pp. 199–201.

and administrative law problems is in part a reflection of the inherent contestability of the constitutional domain. For Daintith the implementation of governmental policy through dominium does not necessarily imply any breach of existing constitutional law or convention. Moreover, he argues that government would not use this technique unless it was felt to be the optimum method of attaining policy objectives; that those who bargain with the government are often under no constraint; and that ordinary MPs can call the government to account and ensure the modification of the method of policy implementation if they are dissatisfied with the operation of the dominium technique.[91] Daintith does admit that constitutional problems can emerge as the result of the use of dominium, in particular the fact that third parties might be affected as a result of an agreement in which they had no part, or in areas where one private individual had no real choice as to whether to enter such an agreement.[92]

A more cautious approach to the exercise of dominium power might, however, be warranted. Whether the exercise of such power does or does not infringe our existing constitutional law or convention, bears testimony to the skeletal nature of our current constitutional principles and to the fact that many issues remain untested. This is forcibly demonstrated by the contrasting constraints to which the two techniques are presently subject. In general, government cannot use imperium power which alters the existing legal rights of subjects without resort to legislation. Control upon the exercise of dominium power tends to be less tightly drawn. Thus, while the passage of dominium legislation does require parliamentary approval, there is little advance control over the way in which the sums mentioned in the general financial legislation are expended.[93] Where dominium power is exercised independently of legislation, through bargain, agreement, or informal compromise, the contrast is even more marked. Conceptually the government is

[91] Daintith, 'The Executive Power Today', pp. 207–8.

[92] Ibid. 208–18. See also G. Ganz, *Government and Industry* (1977); J. L. Jowell, 'Bargaining in Development Control' (1977) *J.P.L.* 414 and 'Limits of Law in Urban Planning' (1977) *C.L.P.* 63; R. B. Ferguson and A. C. Page, 'Pay Restraint: The Legal Constraints' (1978) 128 *N.L.J.* 515.

[93] See, e.g., A. Robinson, 'The House of Commons and Public Expenditure', in S. A. Walkland and M. Ryle (eds.), *The Commons Today* (1981), ch. 7; M. Ryle, 'Supply and Other Financial Procedures', in S. Walkland (ed.), *The House of Commons in the Twentieth Century* (1979), 329–426; M. Elliott, 'The Control of Public Expenditure', in J. L. Jowell and D. Oliver (eds.), *The Changing Constitution* (2nd edn., 1989), ch. 7.

regarded as having, in addition to its special powers, the legal capacity of an ordinary person, and this provides the justification for the exercise of such bargaining or contractual power.

The very starkness of the above contrast only serves to emphasize the limited nature of our constitutional principles. The distinction between form and substance which underpins the division is manifest. Commands affect individual rights and require legislative authorization. The use of governmental 'wealth' or 'property' is placed within a different conceptual category, and is subject to less stringent controls, even though the same end may be achieved by a different route.[94] The analogies with Reich's analysis in the United States are self-evident,[95] even if one may question the efficacy of his proposed solution. To say that our existing constitutional law has not been infringed should not lead us to assume that any sophisticated constitutional construct has thereby been satisfied.

What *ought* to inform our constitutional law in this area is more contentious. The difficulty of reconciling constitutional principle and effective government is particularly acute. The fact that the executive may well regard the use of dominium power as the optimum way of achieving its policy should, however, be viewed with caution. There is little doubt that the executive, given the choice, might often adopt methods of policy implementation which could prove to be constitutionally objectionable. This might be the case in the context of imperium as well as dominium. A radical increase in the usage of the guillotine procedure would provide a clear example. Furthermore, few would be over-optimistic about the possibility of the legislature being able effectively to curtail methods of policy implementation of which it disapproves. There is little reason to believe that the obstacles to legislative scrutiny would be any the less within this area. If anything, one might suspect that the problems would be exacerbated by the very informal, sometimes covert nature of the executive's exercise of dominium power.

One might, of course, adopt the view that little can be achieved in this area without a more fundamental rethinking of the entire parliamentary process. There is considerable force in this view, and

[94] See, e.g., the relative absence of constitutional enquiry surrounding the sale of state assets pursuant to the privatization process; Craig, *Administrative Law*, pp. 164–6; T.Prosser, *The Privatization of Public Enterprises in France and Great Britain; The State, Constitutions and Public Policy* (EUI Working Paper No. 88/364; 1988), 37–9.

[95] C. Reich, 'The New Property', 73 *Yale L.J.* 733 (1964).

it is a point to which we shall return. This should not, however, blind us to the fact that the courts have recently begun to look at the exercise of executive power in more substantive terms, shorn of some of the formal labels which have dictated judicial responses in the past. Developments concerning the prerogative provide the prime example of this.[96] It is debatable whether one should regard the exercise of dominium power, particularly that which has no legislative base, as a species of the prerogative or as a separate common-law power.[97] Whichever view is taken, the prospect of some form of judicial oversight should be equally plausible. Having begun to dismantle unwarranted formal barriers between statutory and prerogative power, it would be absurd to erect new divisions between prerogative and common-law power.

Providing a conceptual pedestal for judicial intervention is, however, the easier part of the analysis; the direction which such intervention should assume is more difficult. Should the judicial emphasis be upon process rights for third parties, and indeed for those more directly involved in such bargaining? Would it be possible to impose conditions of openness and publicity upon the exercise of certain dominium powers? These are possible courses of action. They would, however, do little to redress the problem with which we are immediately concerned, which is the bypassing of the normal legislative process. If we wish to address this issue we must do so directly. Thus, the judiciary might condition and limit the use of dominium power by insisting that the executive obtain legislative authorization if it wishes to employ certain policies, even where these entail the distribution of government wealth rather than traditional methods of altering rights.

This approach is less novel than might at first sight seem apparent. Judicial constraints upon the manner in which policy is enacted appear at various points within our constitutional history. The judicial control of the prerogative, through which the courts regard themselves as competent arbiters of the limits, and, to an increasing extent, of the manner of exercise of such power, provides but one important example of this phenomenon.[98] In asserting such jurisdiction the courts are, in effect, placing limitations upon the way in which the executive can achieve its desired goals. If the

96 *Council of Civil Service Unions* v. *Minister for the Civil Service* [1985] A.C. 374.

97 Daintith, 'Regulation by Contract', p. 41.

98 e.g. *Case of Monopolies* (1602) 11 Co. Rep. 84b; *Case of Proclamations* (1611) 12 Co.

object does not fall within one of the traditional spheres of the prerogative, the executive will require legislative authorisation to attain its preferred ends.

This in itself raises interesting questions concerning the relationship of dominium power, the prerogative, and the common law. If the exercise of dominium power is to be regarded as part of the prerogative, then it should be subject to the same judicial oversight as other aspects of prerogative power. If, by way of contrast, the extra parliamentary use of dominium is regarded as being based upon a common-law power to contract, it would be odd to regard this power as being unfettered. An awkward and illogical dualism would prevail were we to accept such a conclusion. The judiciary would be constraining the mode of state action by their assertion of judicial competence to determine the limits and manner of exercise of prerogative power. It would be inconsistent to argue that the courts should remain quiescent, if the executive action were to be characterized as an exercise of a common-law power to contract. This would be particularly odd in the light of the rationale for the recent extension of judicial supervision over the prerogative. Part of the reason for this extension is that it may be fortuitous whether the executive exercises discretionary power through the prerogative or pursuant to statute. The choice between prerogative and common-law power may be equally adventitious. We should pause before accepting that substantive differences should follow from such chance categorization.

Precedent does, therefore, exist on which the courts can build. They could thereby reinforce parliamentary power by such a process-related constitutional constraint. The limitations and difficulties of such a venture should, however, be fully borne in mind. There would be conceptual difficulties in defining the type of governmental action which was felt to require parliamentary authorisation. The ability of the executive to proceed by contract is obviously necessary and legitimate in many areas. Reinforcement of the parliamentary process would necessitate deciding that a certain policy choice was sufficiently legislative in nature to demand that it be subjected to scrutiny by Westminster. The courts would,

Rep. 74; *Att.-Gen.* v. *De Keyser's Royal Hotel Ltd.* [1920] A.C. 508; *Chandler* v. *D.P.P.* [1964] A.C. 763; *British Broadcasting Corporation* v. *Johns* [1965] Ch. 32; *Civil Service* case, above n. 96. The courts have reinforced the legislative process through their control over parliamentary privilege; see *Stockdale* v. *Hansard* (1839) 9 A. & E. 1.

therefore, to adapt Tribe's language, be making substantive choices as to how the government can legitimately affect people in society.[99] Moreover, there is the argument advanced by Ganz[100] that the implementation of policy choices by non-statutory means may reflect a preference for a 'voluntary approach' to the regulation of societal activity. Non-statutory codes and the like may be chosen because they are felt to be a more flexible and consensual mode of 'legislating' as compared with statutes *stricto sensu*.

These conceptual problems would be overlaid with those of a more pragmatic nature. Would the whole enterprise be worth the candle? Would the executive's domination of the legislature not mean that parliamentary approval was but a foregone conclusion and an empty gesture? Do we not, therefore, have to rethink the entire parliamentary process? This may well be so. The absence of effective parliamentary scrutiny or control over the executive is a well-documented facet of our political system. This point must, however, be kept separate. Even if actual parliamentary control over legislation devised by the executive were to be radically improved, this would not, in itself, alter the propensity of the executive to bypass the established legislative process and implement policy through informal bargains with interest groups. Some more radical restructuring of our political process would be necessary to prevent such an occurrence. In the absence of any such overhaul, we cannot avoid giving some answer to the central question posed above. Do we wish to reinforce the established legislative process by restricting the way in which the executive and groups implement policy choices, given the difficult substantive decisions which would thereby be entailed?

3. PLURALISM, RIGHTS, AND PUBLIC LAW

While it may be evident from the preceding argument that substantive value judgements will necessarily be entailed in both agency decision-making and judicial review thereof, the nature of such judgements requires closer examination. More specifically, the role and place of rights, within both administrative and constitu-

99 'The Puzzling Persistence of Process-Based Constitutional Theories'.

100 Ganz, *Quasi-Legislation* See, however, Craig, *Administrative Law*, pp. 192–3, for ambiguity in the meaning of the term consensual.

tional adjudication, must be considered. No exhaustive analysis of these issues can, however, be undertaken. Any discussion of the nature of rights entails complex philosophical questions which have generated an extensive literature. This topic will be returned to, and considered in more detail, within the following chapter. The present objective is a more modest one. It is to provide some schematic guidance as to the *ways* in which rights may be of relevance to constitutional and administrative law. The use of the plural in the previous sentence should be emphasized. An understanding of the nature of rights may be of relevance in different ways, depending upon the nature of the precise question which is being posed. Delineation of these distinctive, albeit connected, questions is important. The relationship between a pluralist conception of democracy, and the type of rights which should subsist therein, will be one such question. It is, however, necessary to address some other issues first.

a. The Nature and Application of Rights

At the most basic level, public lawyers require an awareness as to the meaning of rights quite simply because agencies and courts who are applying statutes which fall broadly within public law may have to determine whether a right has indeed been accorded by the particular statute in question. This may seem a trite proposition. It is none the less both important, and more complex than may seem initially apparent. It is important because, whether one reads the wording of a statute as granting a right, or as according the decision-maker a discretion, can have significant consequences for the way in which the agency or court approaches its task. Not all of administrative law is comprised of discretionary power. Parliament may well accord a right to certain benefits upon certain conditions. The ability to recognize the existence of a right is, therefore, of seminal importance when considering the appropriate roles of both agency and court. This task is more complex than may be initially apparent for a number of reasons.

First, the wording of the statute may be unclear as to whether a right is in fact accorded or not.[101] It may be framed expressly in

[101] D. J. Galligan, *Discretionary Powers: A Legal Study of Official Discretion* (1986), 192–4; D. N. MacCormick, 'Rights in Legislation', in P. M. S. Hacker and J. Raz (eds.), *Law, Morality and Society* (1977), 191.

terms of rights or the language of the statute may in effect grant a right even though it does not explicitly use this word. Rights may well be present even if the decision-maker is granted formal authority in discretionary terms. Galligan captures this point well. He acknowledges that an official might regard a grant of discretion, in the absence of clear directions to the contrary, as entailing 'considerations of public policy wider than and possibly in conflict with individual interests, and therefore with any notions of rights'.[102] This interpretation is, however, not the only plausible one.

Some powers might require a continual concern with notions of public interest; others, however, might seem to be concerned primarily with the interests of individuals, and to leave little room for countervailing public policy concerns. Here the notion of right reappears; our reflective official might conclude that in some cases the object of discretion is to confer rights on individuals; accordingly, the only matters to be taken into account are those directed to working out the scope and content of the rights. He might reach this conclusion by recognizing that important interests are at stake, that the legislative purpose demonstrates a sufficient concern that those interests be protected, and that there are, therefore, grounds for duties on the official to provide the protection.[103]

Secondly, any decision as to whether an unclear statute does accord rights or not may depend, not only upon a vision of the legislative purpose, but also on some more basic understanding of what is meant by a right. Philosophers have traditionally adopted two views as to the meaning and explanation of rights. The 'will theory', promulgated most powerfully by Hart,[104] asserts that an individual's possession of a right depends upon the legal or moral recognition of his will, in the sense of his choice, as being 'preeminent over that of others in relation to a given subject matter and within a given relationship'.[105] The 'interest theory', advanced currently by writers such as MacCormick and Raz, argues that the essential element of a right is the legal or moral protection of one person's interests 'against some other person or the world at large, by the imposition on the latter of duties, disabilities, or liabilities in

[102] Galligan, *Discretionary Powers*, p. 193.

[103] Ibid. 194.

[104] e.g. H. L. A. Hart, 'Are There Any Natural Rights?', in J. Waldron (ed.), *Theories of Rights* (1984), ch. 3; H. L. A. Hart, 'Bentham on Legal Rights', in A. W. B. Simpson (ed.), *Oxford Essays in Jurisprudence* (2nd ser.; 1973), ch. 7.

[105] MacCormick, 'Rights in Legislation', p. 192.

respect of the party favoured'.[106] The arguments between the rival theorists become, not surprisingly, complex. The interest theory does, however, appear to be the more convincing. While the ability to choose and to waive a right will often be a part of that concept, it does not appear helpful to render this a necessary element of the constituent definition of the term right.[107]

Under the interest theory, certain features are of central importance to rules which confer rights.[108] They are concerned with 'goods' in the sense of 'advantages', 'benefits', or 'interests' to the recipient. They relate to the enjoyment of such goods by individuals separately, rather than as members of a collectivity 'enjoying a diffuse common benefit in which all participate in indistinguishable and unassignable shares'. While the applicable rule will often deal with classes of individual, the benefit is secured to each and every individual severally upon satisfaction of the relevant conditions. Finally, the benefits are secured to individuals in that the law furnishes normative protection in their enjoyment of them. This protection may take any (or all) of the particular forms identified by Hohfeld.

The rights which are recognized under the interest theory can, as MacCormick states, be analysed from three perspectives.[109] There are institutive provisions which establish the conditions necessary to vest such a right in individuals; consequential provisions which establish the range of normative protections available to holders of the right; and divestitive provisions which furnish the conditions in which the right is lost or transferred.

The point made by Galligan can now be linked with the insights provided by the interest theory. The possibility of a 'rights-based' perspective on administrative law is not simply a position which public lawyers can choose to adopt or not to adopt as one of the possible range of options at the disposal of agencies or courts. It must be integral in the following way. Given that statutes are unclear, and given that rights might be at stake even in instances

[106] Ibid. See, generally, D. N. MacCormick, 'Children's Rights: A Test-Case for Theories of Right', in D. N. MacCormick, *Legal Right and Social Democracy* (1982), ch. 8; T. Campbell, *The Left and Rights: A Conceptual Analysis of the Idea of Socialist Rights* (1983), ch. 5; J. Raz, 'Legal Rights' (1984), 4 *O.J.L.S.* 1 and *The Morality of Freedom* (1986), ch. 7.

[107] MacCormick, 'Rights in Legislation', pp. 207–8.

[108] Ibid. 204–5.

[109] Ibid. 205–7.

where the statute does not formally speak in such terms, both the agency and the court will have to form some view as to whether the statute should be interpreted as granting rights to an individual or group. The institutive and consequential provisions which are attendant upon such a right may be unclear. In so far as this is so, both agencies and courts will have to determine their content and incidence.

b. The Content of Rights

The interest theory of rights considered above may well, therefore, help us to determine whether an existing piece of legislation does in fact confer rights or not. The limitations of the theory should, however, be borne in mind. The interest theory provides, as Raz states, a definition of rights *simpliciter*.[110] It does not, in and of itself, provide an answer to the question of whether a particular interest should be accorded the status of a right. Assertions of rights become intermediate conclusions in arguments from ultimate values to duties. People may well agree that a person should have a right to make promises, or a right to freedom of speech, but may disagree on the interest on which it is based. The language of rights facilitates discourse by operating as a mediatory stage, so that 'not every time a practical question arises does one refer to ultimate values for an answer'.[111] The fact that there is agreement on the existence of a right to make promises becomes a reason in itself from which further conclusions may be drawn, obviating the need for an enquiry into ultimate values on each and every occasion when such a topic is raised.

It is the addition of an adjective to the word right which begins to tell us more about the nature of the rights which an observer believes that we have or ought to have, irrespective of whether they are actually granted by current legislation.[112] Thus phrases such as Kantian rights or economic rights tell us something about the relation of rights to a more general system of political thought, or something directly about the content of the rights in question.

It is readily apparent that the reasons for holding that a particular interest is indeed worthy of forming the basis of a right will be

[110] *The Morality of Freedom*, p. 167.
[111] Ibid. 181.
[112] Ibid. 167–8.

contestable. While the right may be an intermediate conclusion, the existence of the right will perforce be founded upon certain prior arguments which contain the reasons for ascribing the requisite importance to that interest. As Raz states:

> An interest is sufficient to base a right on if and only if there is a sound argument of which the conclusion is that a certain right exists and among its non-redundant premisses is a statement of some interest of the right-holder, the other premisses supplying grounds for attributing to it the required importance, or for holding it to be relevant to a particular person or class of persons so that they rather than others are obligated to the right-holder.[113]

The grounds which justify the interest being of the requisite importance will vary, depending upon, *inter alia*, the nature of the interest in question, and the political and moral theory held by a particular observer. It would be untenable to maintain that the type of democracy will always play a decisive role as a ground for justifying the importance of the interest at stake. It would, however, be equally mistaken to assume that it is a factor which can be disregarded in this enquiry. This can be illustrated by considering briefly the rationale for the right to free speech.

The grounds which have been given for asserting that freedom of speech should be accorded the status of a right have varied.[114] One thesis, traditionally associated with Mill, bases the right upon the value that free discussion has for the discovery of truth. Another thesis regards the major value of free speech as a device to secure individual self-development and fulfilment. A further view regards the justification of this right as flowing from citizen participation within a democracy; citizens should be enabled to understand political issues in order that they can participate effectively in the operation of a democratic society. None of the preceding views is free from difficulty. These have been admirably canvassed elsewhere, and it is not my intention to repeat such arguments here.[115] Nor is it my intention simply to conclude that democratic arguments sometimes play a role in providing the grounds for attributing an interest the required importance for it to be a right. What is of particular relevance to the present enquiry is the way in which the argument from democracy, which despite its shortcomings is

[113] Ibid. 181; see also pp. 182–3.

[114] F. Schauer, *Free Speech: A Philosophical Enquiry* (1980); E. Barendt, *Freedom of Speech* (1985).

[115] By Schauer, *Free Speech*, and Barendt, *Freedom of Speech*.

accorded real weight by commentators,[116] will change its complexion depending upon a more detailed depiction of the type of democracy which is being postulated.

Adherents of the Schumpeterian version of democracy[117] might accept that freedom of speech should be accorded the status of a right for the general background reason that it enables individuals to understand political issues and thereby to participate effectively in the operation of a democratic society. The scope and incidence of the right will, however, be directly affected by the way in which this general background reason is itself shaped by the Schumpeterian vision. This is, as we have seen, a 'top down' view of democracy. Present and potential elected representatives competed for the vote of the people. Political leaders devised the package to be offered to the electorate. The people chose, but the government, once chosen, then governed. Political action between elections was not the business of the ordinary people. Freedom of speech in the inter-electoral period as a method of criticizing the incumbent power groups would not be accorded a high priority. Nor would the related ideas of freedom of association and participation readily be interpreted so as to allow any extensive rights to individuals to participate in, and help shape, such governmental policies.[118]

Supporters of a republican conception of democracy[119] might also accept a right to freedom of speech, and support this for the general background reason that it enables individuals to understand political issues and to participate effectively in the operation of a democratic society. The scope and incidence of this right would, however, be interpreted differently, precisely because the general background reason would be fashioned by a republican vision. An understanding of political issues would be regarded as but part of a broader picture. The general objective would be for the individual to partake fully in public life, and to be 'self-governing' within the polity. Rights to speech and to participation in the governmental process would be seen as connected. They would not be exhausted

[116] e.g. Barendt, *Freedom of Speech*, pp. 22–3.

[117] For more detailed discussion of this view of democracy and its interrelationship with pluralist thought, see above, ch. 3 sec. 2c.

[118] Élite theorists and behaviouralists have drawn just such conclusions, and have based these implicitly or explicitly upon the Schumpeterian model of democracy; see above, ch. 3 sec.2c.

[119] See below, chs. 10 and 11, for a discussion of republicanism and participatory democracy.

by the act of choosing the government. They would continue to be of integral importance in the processes of governmental decision-making which ensued thereafter. Freedom of speech, coupled with the necessity for elected representatives and officials at whatever level to take account of such views, would be regarded as essential to this conception of democracy.[120]

Consideration of the individual, developmental aspect of republicanism leads to a related point. The more specifically one reflects upon the particular type of democracy which is being postulated, the more it serves to call into question the divisibility of the types of background reasons given to justify a right to freedom of speech. In particular it serves to blur the distinction between the argument from self-fulfilment, and that from democracy itself. The idea underlying the former, that people 'will not be able to develop intellectually and spiritually, unless they are free to formulate their beliefs and political attitudes through public discussion',[121] may well be related to a more fundamental concept of human dignity. It is, however, questionable whether adherents of republicanism would regard this as a distinctive argument from that relating to democracy itself. Republicanism and/or participatory democracy encapsulate in themselves a particular vision of self-fulfilment. It is indeed difficult to envision how such a concept could be given any detailed meaning without an explicit or implicit presupposition about the nature of the society in which such self-fulfilment is to occur.[122] Attempts to provide content to this idea in the absence of any such vision of society lead inexorably to questions as to why speech should be more conducive to a person's fulfilment than, for example, housing.[123]

The existence of the interrelationship considered above should not come as a surprise. Raz has in fact argued that fundamental moral rights are often found to be 'an element in the protection of collective goods, or their value is found to depend on the existence of certain collective goods'.[124] Thus he argues that certain aspects of freedom

[120] The precise way in which these ideas would be implemented might, however, differ as between different republican theories; see below, ch. 10.

[121] Barendt, *Freedom of Speech*, p. 14.

[122] Even J. S. Mill's argument for free speech based upon truth requires a particular democratic setting for its realization; Campbell, *The Left and Rights*, pp. 156–7.

[123] Barendt, *Freedom of Speech*, p. 15.

[124] Raz, *The Morality of Freedom*, p. 254. Collective goods are inherent public goods.

of speech are valued as protecting the collective good of an open and democratic society.[125]

It seems clear, therefore, that arguments from democracy can provide one type of ground for attributing the requisite importance to an interest to warrant it being accorded the status of a right; that the particular conception of democracy which is espoused can significantly alter the nature and incidence of that right; and that it may, on closer analysis, overlap with other such grounds which are advanced.

Differing conceptions of democracy may also affect the content of the rights which should feature more generally within a given society. This can be exemplified by contrasting the distinctive pluralist models outlined earlier, and considering the rights which are regarded as central to the realization of the particular democratic visions. The tension which exists between the pluralist aspects of the enterprise, and the more unitary, centralizing thrust of both models, will become evident upon closer examination. One can begin by reflecting on Laski's conception of rights within a pluralist state.

Laski's conception of pluralism altered over time, as has already been seen. In his later work he continued to stress the existence of groups which limit the power of government. He also emphasized the fact that the state was in a powerful position in relation to other associations, being able to use its power to aid those with whom it had an identity of interest. The state was to be rendered accountable through a range of procedural and substantive constraints. An important substantive component was the recognition of rights which the citizen had against the state.

The individual possessed certain inherent rights as a member of society; such rights were necessary for the realization of oneself as a moral being.[126] This did not entail the separateness of each person's existence. Each individual was 'suffused' with social implications; the rights provided the mechanism by which we could act so as to add to the richness of our social heritage.[127] Laski's enumeration of

Public goods are those goods the benefit of which in a particular society is not subject to voluntary control by anyone other than each potential beneficiary controlling his share of the benefits, ibid. 198–9. See also J. Finnis, *Natural Law and Natural Rights* (1980), 218.

[125] Raz, *The Morality of Freedom*, pp. 253–4.
[126] Laski, *A Grammar of Politics*, pp. 39–40.
[127] Ibid. 40, 91, 94.

rights was not limited to those which were presently accorded by statute or the common law, but was focused upon what rights a citizen ought to have.

Particular rights were justified because they were indicative of what an individual must possess in order to contribute to the common stock of welfare. These rights were both economic and civil. There was a right to work, although not in any particular occupation. To be his 'best self' a man must work, and the state should provide an insurance system in the event of unemployment. A right to an adequate wage, and a right to some form of worker participation in industry, were regarded as necessary correlatives.[128] A right to a certain minimum education was essential in order that the individual could make considered judgements concerning the public good. There were rights related more directly to political power, such as the rights to vote, to stand for election, and to be chosen for political office. These rights were founded upon economic justifications as well as the civil libertarian character of democracy. The legislation which emerged would reflect the beliefs of those who framed it. Freedom of speech, association, and access to an impartial judiciary were also to be secured.[129] Property rights were to be strictly circumscribed.[130] Power within the state should be decentralized, and there should be adequate consultation with groups who were affected by government policy.[131] A number of comments upon this conception of rights are warranted.

First, it might be argued that the relevance of Laski's work for the role of public law within a pluralist democracy is diminished simply because of his explicitly left-wing sympathy. While nothing compels the observer to adopt the same position, this objection is none the less misconceived. Any interpretation of pluralism will necessarily entail judgement concerning the meaning of such a political system, the faults in its operation, and the methods of remedying those faults. The early US pluralists made such value judgements in their very depiction of the political system as one which tended towards equilibrium resulting from group exchange, and in their assertion that there was no conception of the public interest separate from that of the groups which composed society. UK pluralism has little of these self-correcting features. It is not surprising, therefore, that some UK pluralists should have seen fit to address taxing

[128] Ibid. 104, 107, 112–13.
[129] Ibid. 116, 118–30, 162–3.
[130] Ibid. 130, ch. 5.
[131] Ibid. 74–5, 133.

substantive issues concerning group rights and economic freedoms as well as traditional civil liberties.[132] Nor is it surprising that other writers on both sides of the Atlantic, while acknowledging the imbalances within pluralism, should have declined to intervene. They do not accept that there are the grounds for attributing sufficient importance to the relevant economic interests in order for them to be accorded the status of a right, and/or regard the ensuing conflict with more traditional property rights as unacceptable.[133]

Secondly, one may question whether Laski's conception of rights makes sense within its own terms. There are two aspects to this enquiry which should be distinguished. On the one hand, it could be asked whether the language of, for example, 'welfare rights' made sense in the light of the previous discussion as to the meaning of the term right. Can such interests be accommodated within the language of rights without doing violence to that concept? There seems little difficulty in according such interests in welfare the status of a right. The consequences of depicting the interest in these terms would depend upon the precise admixture of Hohfeldian claim-rights, privileges, duties, and powers, etc., which were attached to it.[134] This topic will be explored in greater detail within the following chapter.

On the other hand, one may question whether Laski's conception of rights is internally consistent and workable. While the pluralist aspect of Laski's project diminished in his later work, he does not, for example, appear to appreciate fully the latent tension between this and the socialist aspects of his enterprise. This can be exemplified by considering the right to work. A positive right to work may well be inconsistent with a market or capitalist system in which production and employment are determined by market forces, rather than directed by a central authority.[135] While capitalist states can try to encourage activity which will create employment, they cannot actually direct production as a whole without destroying the market system. Moreover, a positive right to work may require a degree of central control which is in tension with the decentralizing impetus of pluralism. As Campbell states, the immediately enforceable duties attendant upon a right to work could

[132] See also A. D. Lindsay, *The Essentials of Democracy* (1929), 49, 78–80; E.Barker, *Reflections on Government*, pp. 107–9, 111–17, 168–205, 418.

[133] e.g. R. Nozick, *Anarchy, State and Utopia* (1974); R. A. Epstein, *Takings: Private Property and the Power of Eminent Domain* (1985).

[134] e.g. C. Wellman, *Welfare Rights* (1982); A. Gewirth, *Human Rights* (1982).

[135] Campbell, *The Left and Rights*, pp. 173, 184.

initially be laid on officials entrusted with the oversight of the community's capacity to create employment. He acknowledges that interpretation of a right to work would be problematic in a less centralized state within which responsibility for meeting needs is diffused throughout society.[136]

The tension which exists between the pluralist and centralizing aspects of the second model is perhaps even more marked, and is exemplified by the conception of rights which this model embraces.

The pluralist, decentralizing aspect of the market-oriented 'new-right' vision is composed of two key elements. On the one hand, there is, as we have seen above, the recognition that public power is wielded by a plethora of interest groups which are not part of government in a formal sense. Competition between such groups for influence over the content of policy characterizes the political process.[137] On the other hand, there is the belief that central control over many economic and social matters is both unnecessary and unjust. It is unnecessary because the market is conceived as a better allocative mechanism than government itself. This 'empirical' argument has a number of different elements, but the constant theme is that government intervention does not work, that any alternative to the market is flawed, and that governmental regulatory failure is more prevalent than market regulatory failure.[138] Moreover, if competition between pressure groups does indeed characterize the policy-making process, then this adds further fuel to the argument that the ordinary market may be a better regulator of this competitive process. Political choice becomes a species of market choice best undertaken by the market itself. This is said to represent the ultimate in pluralistic decentralization, and to be far less prone to the forms of rent-seeking behaviour which are said to characterize much legislative intervention. The argument that governmental intervention is unnecessary is complemented by the contention that it is also unjust. The strongest version of this thesis is that advanced by Nozick.[139] He argues that individuals in the state of nature possess rights which cannot be violated. One

[136] Ibid. 180, 182. It should, however, be noted that Laski perceived limits as to how such rights could be enforced; *A Grammer of Politics*, p. 137.

[137] See above, ch. 5 sec. 4.

[138] See, e.g., F. A. Hayek, *The Road to Serfdom* (1944), and *The Constitution of Liberty* (1960); M. Friedman and R. Friedman, *Free to Choose* (1980); S. Brittan, *The Role and Limits of Government* (1983). This theme is also espoused by right-wing think-tanks such as the Adam Smith Institute and the Centre for Policy Studies.

[139] *Anarchy, State and Utopia*.

important such right is the right to property. A minimal state which serves to protect the lives and property of its citizens can be justified. However, any use of state power beyond this minimum is coercion. Redistributive policies are unjustified, because the justice of any particular set of property rights depends upon the manner in which these holdings have been acquired, and not on whether they conform to any particular distributive pattern. Markets based upon 'voluntary' exchange are not coercive; only human agencies, such as government, which interfere with the process are guilty of this sin.

The rights which this democratic vision espouses reflect this reasoning. Deregulation is advocated, not only because government intervention is felt to be flawed, but also because the result fits so well with the conception of rights inherent in this political model. It is through deregulation that areas are returned to the market-place. Consumer choice is to reign as far as possible. This is designed, not only with the hope that the area will operate more efficiently, but also because it is premised upon the idea of voluntary exchange based upon individual choice. Such exchanges are legitimate under Nozick's thesis. They do not infringe pre-existing property rights, and do not therefore constitute coercion. Small wonder then that the constant theme to be found in, for example, the Adam Smith Institute's Omega project[140] is the idea of accountability, defined principally in terms of market-based efficiency. Responsiveness to those who are affected by the scheme, whether it be education or health, is central. They are to have the maximum feasible individual choice, thereby mirroring as proximately as possible the idea of voluntary exchange.

The decentralizing and pluralist aspects of the new-right vision are, however, qualified by certain unitary, centralizing tendencies which are present within this model. Three such tendencies can be identified.

The first has been touched upon already.[141] This is the necessity for central domination over power groupings within the state which are perceived as placing constraints upon the realization of the market vision. As Gamble states, the 'price of forcing the market to

[140] *The Omega File* (Adam Smith Institute, 1985). The individual reports cover a wide range of areas, including health, social security, education, communications, local government and planning, and employment.

[141] See above, ch. 6 sec. 2e.

be free is a strong state',[142] and the Conservative government has been forced to adopt more authoritarian measures in order to introduce greater freedom into the economy. Consultation with other power groupings within the state will be conducted against a very specific type of agenda, the fundamentals of which are open to little substantive negotiation.

Secondly, the decentralizing impetus of the market is itself limited in two related ways. On the one hand, notwithstanding philosophical theory concerning the appropriate role for the minimalist state, the 'logical' conclusions of such a theory are not pursued to their natural end. Free markets in pornography, child birth, and a host of other matters are not countenanced. The central government continues to reserve such issues for its own determination, and, in such matters as homosexuality, to impose a strong central vision upon society. On the other hand, even where areas are devolved to the market-place, they are often devolved against a statutory framework, which places limits upon the type of voluntary exchange which can then be reached between the individual consumer and the provider of the service in question. The provision of, for example, higher education may well assume a more contractual appearance, but the nature of the contract thus made is itself strongly influenced by the central government's conception of the role and purpose of such education. Statutory regulation may also be needed to police the market regime, in order, at the least, to maintain formal equality between economic agents and, more controversially, to suppress private forms of coercion or discrimination.[143]

The third centralizing facet of the new-right vision is the most problematic, and can only be touched upon here. It concerns the relationship between the market-oriented vision adumbrated above, and the more overtly authoritarian conservatism most explicitly advocated by Scruton.[144] Accountability, efficiency, and individual choice are the talismanic slogans of the market-based new right. Authority, allegiance, tradition, and national security are the concepts which underpin the arguments of writers such as Scruton and Cowling.[145] The minimal state is rejected, as is the idea that the

[142] A. Gamble, 'The Political Economy of Freedom', in R. Levitas (ed.), *The Ideology of the New Right* (1986), 51.

[143] A. Gamble, *The Free Economy and the Strong State* (1988), 33.

[144] R. Scruton, *The Meaning of Conservatism* (2nd edn., 1984).

[145] M. Cowling (ed.), *Conservative Essays* (1978).

central government should not seek to impose a particular conception of the 'good' upon society. The very division between state and society is abandoned, as the centralized organs of the state intrude into any area of social life which is vital to 'the strength of the social bond'. It would be mistaken to assume that the Conservative policy embraces the entirety of such an authoritarian vision, but equally misplaced to believe that it forms no part of such thought. New-right thinking may well be an uneasy alliance between the market-oriented vision and its more overtly authoritarian neighbour.[146]

While the content of the rights which we ought to have is, therefore, a difficult question, it is one which must be addressed by both constitutional and administrative lawyers. Critical analysis of existing rights or presumptions necessarily presupposes some vision of a desired alternative. More detailed reflection on the actual and desired type of democracy will be one type of factor which can provide the ground for attributing an interest the requisite importance for it to be accorded the status of a right. Other factors will also be of importance, including the meaning to be given to concepts such as dignity, truth, and justice. The preceding discussion serves, however, to highlight the interrelated nature of these issues. Some concepts such as that of dignity will alter their complexion depending upon the type of democracy within which an individual lives. More importantly, it can be argued that any detailed depiction of democracy will itself embody a particular conception of justice. The discussion in this and the previous chapter indicates the fluid nature of phrases such as pluralist democracy. It is only by probing more deeply into the descriptive and prescriptive connotations given to such a term that one can reveal the divergent philosophies which rest beneath such a label. And the more deeply one probes, the more one realizes that these interpretations diverge precisely because the content ascribed to ideas such as justice and rights differ. The relationship between a detailed conception of democracy and the rights which should subsist therein will therefore be a reciprocal one. As Finnis states:

There is, I think, no alternative but to hold in one's mind's eye some pattern, or range of patterns, of human character, conduct and interaction

[146] R. Levitas, 'Competition and Compliance: The Utopias of the New Right', in R. Levitas (ed.), *The Ideology of the New Right* (1986), ch. 3. See also A. Belsey, 'The New Right, Social Order and Civil Liberties', in ibid., ch. 6.

in community, and then to choose such specification of rights as tends to favour that pattern, or range of patterns. In other words, one needs some conception of human good, of individual flourishing in a form (or range of forms) of communal life that fosters rather than hinders such flourishing.[147]

[147] *Natural Law and Natural Rights*, pp. 219–20.

7
CONSTITUTIONAL REFORM AND DEMOCRACY: UK

1. INTRODUCTION

Constitutional reform is now advocated by many within the political and legal arena. It is a topic of considerable importance which cannot be ignored. Four central aspects of this debate will be discussed within this chapter, all of which should be considered in the light of, and will be related to, the discussion in the two preceding chapters. First, the eclectic reasons which have been advanced for such reform will be reviewed.[1] These have been dealt with in the literature, and the review will therefore be relatively brief. More attention will be focused upon a second issue, which is connected with, but distinctive from, the first. This concerns the nature of the rights which would be protected were we to adopt a Bill of Rights, and the interpretative problems involved in any adjudication thereon. The third topic to be considered concerns the impact of our membership of the EC on constitutional reform within the United Kingdom. The chapter will conclude with a discussion of the prospects for devolution or independence for Scotland and Wales, and will examine the way in which this could shape any revised constitutional ordering within the United Kingdom.

2. THE RATIONALE FOR CONSTITUTIONAL CHANGE

A range of arguments have been advanced by those who advocate the adoption of a Bill of Rights. These arguments are not always clearly delineated. They can, however, be broadly distinguished into two categories.

[1] Sir Leslie Scarman, *English Law—The New Dimension* (1974); P. Wallington and J. McBride, *Civil Liberties and a Bill of Rights* (1976); J. Jaconelli, *Enacting a Bill of Rights* (1980); C. Campbell (ed.), *Do we Need a Bill of Rights?* (1980); A. Lester, 'Fundamental Rights: The United Kingdom Isolated' [1984] *P.L.* 46; M. Zander, *A Bill of Rights?* (3rd edn., 1985); Lord McCluskey, *Law, Justice and Democracy* (1987); R. Holme and M. Elliott (eds.), *1688–1988: Time for a New Constitution* (1988).

On the one hand, there are what may be termed rights-based arguments. A variety of these are evident and include the following. (i) A Bill of Rights is required in order to ensure that the rights of minorities are not trampled by the power of a democratically elected majority. (ii) There is concern that government legislation has shown scant respect for certain civil liberties which appertain to both majority and minority groups within society. The traditional techniques of the common law, whereby civil liberties have a largely residual character, are felt to be an inadequate bulwark against statutory restrictions on these liberties. The limitations of these traditional techniques become even more marked when there is a government in power with an ambitious, far-reaching legislative programme which can dramatically alter the constitutional ordering which prevailed hitherto. (iii) The reasons adumbrated above are principally of a domestic character. They have been reinforced by arguments drawn from the position in other countries. Thus it has been argued that the United Kingdom should adopt a Bill of Rights precisely because we are one of the very few nations which does not presently possess one. A related contention is that this would be a 'natural' step flowing from our existing commitment to the European Convention on Human Rights. The adoption of a Bill of Rights, or the incorporation of the European Convention into domestic law, would provide a more expeditious and efficacious method of protecting human rights.

On the other hand, there are arguments for constitutional reform which are of a broader institutional nature. These take us beyond the boundaries of a Bill of Rights *per se*, and encompass more extensive constitutional change. A number of such arguments can be distinguished. (i) The most 'formal' of these flows from the suggestion for devolution with a consequential measure of autonomy for different parts of the United Kingdom. It is generally accepted that any such step would necessitate some species of written constitution which would delineate the respective powers of the 'centre' and the 'regions'. It would also require some form of constitutional court or commission which could adjudicate upon disputes as to territorial and subject-matter competence between them. (ii) Other arguments which are directed to more extensive constitutional reform focus upon the way in which the traditional devices for securing legitimacy and accountability have been undermined by changes in the balance of power within government itself. A number of these themes have been dealt with in the preceding analysis.[2] They include the increasing power of the executive over the legislature, the growth of fringe organizations and interpenetration of the spheres of public and private power. The problems generated by these developments are felt to be exacerbated by an 'ending of consensus' as to how society should be ordered. This itself has both a substantive and procedural dimension. Agreement in broad terms as to the type of substantive policies which should be followed has been shaken by the radical policies pursued by the Conservative government and its market-oriented strategy. The tensions thereby produced have led to important alterations in the procedures and techniques through which the government relates to other parts of the political system, such as local authorities.[3]

Two comments on the reasons given for constitutional change are warranted at this juncture. First, in so far as this reasoning is based upon the *relative* propensity of the Conservative administration to infringe civil liberties and/or to disturb the allocation of power between differing tiers of government, it is not supported by rigorous empirical evidence. The nature of this comment should be made quite clear. It may well be possible to point to particular instances of such governmental action. What is largely absent is any detailed historical enquiry which demonstrates that this administration has a record which is worse in relative terms than that of many of its predecessors. Moreover, the depiction of what is alleged to constitute such transgressions is often unattended by any thoroughgoing normative analysis as to why certain action should be regarded as such a breach at all.

The second point is related to the first. The mere fact that constitutional conventions can be said to have altered does not *per se* indicate that the 'new position' is constitutionally objectionable. This may seem a trite proposition, but it is one which is often overlooked in the literature: the 'fact' of constitutional change and the 'fact' of constitutional impropriety are too often assumed to follow one from another. This is obviously not so. Unwritten constitutions, and indeed those which are written, are often dependent upon conventions which alter over time, and are

[2] See above, chs. 5 and 6. See also the concerns voiced by Charter 88.

[3] e.g. M. Loughlin, *Local Government in the Modern State* (1986). See also above, ch. 6 sec. 2e.

intended to do so. Whether these conventions have been 'waived' or simply 'changed' can only be determined by a normative assessment of the new position.[4]

The importance of this proposition can be simply demonstrated. It has been stated, as a straightforward proposition, that the abolition of an elected tier of government (the GLC and the metropolitan authorities) was evidence of a departure from the sanctity of conventions.[5] The abolition of these authorities may well have been regrettable, and the argument that it was in breach of a convention may be plausible; it does, however, require far more rigour to establish such a contention. One would have to argue either that the then present substantive distribution of elected power at the local level represented a constitutional convention; or that it could only be altered by certain procedures which were not adhered to. Neither of these arguments is particularly easy to sustain. It would then have to be contended that the newly emerging division of power between central and local government was constitutionally improper, rather than simply a shift towards a 'new' convention. Again such an argument might be made, but it cannot be assumed. Radical governments, by their very nature, often alter the constitutional fabric which existed hitherto. Whether the new manner of ordering is constitutionally improper requires a normative analysis, not just simple assertion.

3. THE NATURE OF CONSTITUTIONAL REFORM: RIGHTS, LEGITIMACY, AND ACCOUNTABILITY

The technical difficulties of, for example, enacting a Bill of Rights have been fully considered elsewhere and it is not my intention to rehearse them here.[6] The objective of this section is different. It is to provide a more general discussion of the nature of constitutional reform in the United Kingdom and the problems associated therewith.

A constitution and a Bill of Rights are intended, *inter alia*, to provide a 'corset' which constrains the way in which power can be exercised. They impose three differing types of restraint. First, they

[4] Assuming that the earlier position was normatively acceptable.

[5] R. Holme, 'Introduction', in Holme and Elliott (eds.), *1688–1988*, p. 3.

[6] e.g. Jaconelli, *Enacting a Bill of Rights*.

protect certain substantive rights. These rights might be exercised by citizens against the state, or some emanation thereof, and they might be used in actions between citizens. In addition the substantive rights protected by the constitution might delineate the respective spheres of authority of differing branches of government, whether of central and local authority, or central and regional authority. The objective of such substantive rights will be to prevent, for example, certain state action which is in contravention of the protected rights, and this will normally be policed by a court with power to invalidate legislation.

Secondly, a constitutional document will normally stipulate certain procedural rights. The government or some other body will be allowed to pursue particular goals provided that due process requirements are met. The circumstances in which such process rights are demanded, and the precise content which is given to this concept, may well be debated, but some notion of procedural constitutional rights is to be found in most systems. Once again, action which contravenes such procedural rights will normally be declared invalid by a constitutional court.

Thirdly, a constitutional settlement will seek to ensure that the exercise of public power within society is legitimate and accountable. The government will, for example, be allowed to pursue particular policy choices, but only upon the condition that it can be said to be accountable for the choices thus made. It is clear that the idea of procedural constitutional rights adumbrated above may play a necessary part in ensuring this legitimacy and accountability. It is, however, also clear that in the modern state such rights will not usually be a sufficient condition for attaining this end. They will normally have to be complemented by a range of other devices, which may not be enshrined in a constitution at all. They may operate doctrinally through either constitutional or administrative law, and might include the following ideas: participation in policy formation, reasoned decision-making, and accounting controls which assess the value for money achieved when devising and implementing a particular scheme.[7]

The recognition that constitutional constraints can assume the three forms articulated above is neither controversial, nor profound.

[7] The argument is not that it would be logically impossible to incorporate any such ideas within the constitution itself. Rather that it would be unusual for a constitution to embrace all such ideas.

It does, however, serve as an appropriate foundation for two more particular propositions. On the one hand, when we think of constitutional reform we must recognize that whether or not certain rights are to be included in any constitutional document, *and* the content to be ascribed to them, will depend, *inter alia*, upon the particular background political theory through which they are viewed. On the other hand, it must also be accepted that the three species of constitutional constraint interrelate in the following sense. The very meaning to be given to concepts such as legitimacy and accountability will be affected by the meaning ascribed to the substantive and procedural rights, and will be coloured by the political theory which underlies the existence and content of such rights. The remainder of this section will be devoted to the development of these two themes.

a. The Content of Constitutional Rights

The literature concerning the possible incorporation of a Bill of Rights into the United Kingdom has touched upon the interpretative problems which would have to be faced by the judiciary.[8] The focus of the discussion has, however, been directed towards the extent to which such a task would in general politicize the judiciary, and the extent to which our judges might prefer certain types of interest at the expense of others.[9] These are of course important issues, but they will not be directly pursued here. Attention will rather be directed to the unavoidable interpretative difficulties which will have to be encountered, even by the judge striving to do his utmost to arrive at the 'proper' interpretation of the constitutional document.

It is clear that the difficulties of this interpretative process will not be resolved by falling back upon two particular notions, the original intent of the framers, or the 'literal' meaning of the constitutional document. The former has been shown to be unsustainable, in both empirical and philosophical terms.[10] The latter is equally problematic, even if we were to adopt a document such as the European Convention on Human Rights rather than draft such a document for ourselves afresh. A brief example will suffice to make this point.

[8] See, e.g., Zander, *A Bill of Rights?*, and McCluskey, *Law, Justice and Democracy*.

[9] See, e.g., J. A. G. Griffith, *The Politics of the Judiciary* (3rd edn., 1977).

[10] See above, ch. 4 n. 47.

Article 10 of the European Convention protects the right to freedom of expression. Article 14 states that the rights in the Convention shall be secured without discrimination on any ground, including sex, race, birth, status, or property. If the two articles are read together, it might well be argued that the interpretation of the former should take cognisance of the 'worth of' the right to its recipients, and not just the bare existence of the right; that this interpretation is warranted or even demanded by Article 14; and that this justifies either the expenditure of state money to enable disadvantaged groups to advance their views, and/or constraints upon expenditure by the wealthy during political campaigns. Contrary arguments could of course be advanced concerning the interrelationship of the two provisions. It is, however, abundantly clear that an attempt to distil the 'literal' interpretation of these provisions is doomed to failure. Resolution of the issue one way or another will require, *inter alia*, some conception of the relationship between rights and the worth of rights[11] and a view as to how that relationship should operate within the facts of a particular case. Our diligent judge who is striving to arrive at the proper interpretation of the constitutional document will therefore have to probe further and undertake a more complex task than any connoted by literal construction.

The difficulties which this entails then become evident, and they are apparent at two stages of his analysis. On the one hand, the judge will have to decide which of the two background visions of pluralist democracy articulated above provides the best basis through which to interpret the constitutional provisions.[12] The earlier analysis revealed that both of these visions of pluralist democracy were but part of broader, distinctive political theories which embraced differing notions of rights and distributive justice.[13] The judge will implicitly or explicitly have to choose between these very different conceptions in order to answer many of the more particular questions which come before him; or he may advance a conception which differs from both and which is felt to be preferable to them.

On the other hand, even when the judge has reached this initial decision he will then have to face complex questions concerning the

[11] For a full discussion of this issue, see below, ch. 8 sec. 3a(ii).

[12] R. Dworkin, *Law's Empire* (1986), and *Taking Rights Seriously* (1977).

[13] See above, ch. 6 sec. 3.

more precise ramifications of such a theory for any case which comes before him. This can be demonstrated as follows. Let us imagine that a judge, after considered reflection, believes that a just society will include some conception of welfare rights. He might reach this conclusion for a variety of reasons. He might be convinced by the species of pluralist democracy which is articulated by Laski and others of a similar persuasion. His conclusion might be founded upon a reading of Rawls, and the belief that one can extract therefrom the justification for welfare rights. Or he might well base his reasoning upon the thesis advanced by Gewirth. Our judge also believes that this conclusion is compatible with the constitutional document which he is interpreting. Particular provisions of this document, such as those dealing with equality and non-discrimination, could accommodate such a conclusion.

It is, however, one thing to believe that a conception of welfare rights is philosophically sound or meaningful, and quite another to draw out the more particular constitutional consequences which follow therefrom. Whether a conception of welfare rights can in fact be elicited from Rawls's thesis, and whether such rights would be constitutionally protected within that thesis, will be considered in detail in the chapter which follows.[14] The above point can also be illustrated by focusing upon the work of Gewirth.

Gewirth's aim is to provide both a philosophical justification for human rights, and an enumeration of the content of those rights.[15] The philosophical foundation is complex and cannot be examined here. Its essence is, however, that human rights are necessary goods which human beings must have in order 'to be able to act either at all, or with general chances of success in fulfilling the purposes' for which they act.[16] All human beings are equally entitled to have these necessary conditions in order to fulfil the needs of human agency. The objects of rights are, at the most general level, freedom and well-being, and these are said to provide the necessary procedural and substantive conditions of acting.

Particular rights are then perceived as components of well-being and freedom. Well-being is held to comprise three kinds of goods: basic, non-substractive, and additive.[17] Basic goods are the essential

[14] See below, ch. 8 sec. 3b.

[15] A. Gewirth, *Reason and Morality* (1978), and *Human Rights* (1982).

[16] Gewirth, *Human Rights*, p. 4.

[17] Ibid. 55–9.

preconditions of action, such as life, physical integrity, and mental equilibrium. Thus a person's basic rights are violated when he is killed, starved, or physically incapacitated; and when, for example, a person is starving and another could, at no basic cost to himself, give food and knowingly fails to do so. Non-subtractive goods are 'the abilities and conditions required for maintaining undiminished one's level of purpose fulfilment and one's capabilities for particular actions'. The rights associated with these goods are violated when a person is, *inter alia*, lied to, cheated, or where promises are broken; and where he is subjected to degrading conditions of physical labour or housing when resources are available for improvement. Additive goods are the 'abilities and conditions required for increasing one's level of purpose fulfilment and one's capabilities for particular actions.' Such rights are violated, for example, where a person is denied education to the limits of his capacities, or when he is discriminated against on grounds of race, religion, or nationality.

There are also more particular rights which flow from the right to freedom. These consist of rights which are necessary to ensure that a person controls his actions and his participation in transactions by 'his own unforced choice or consent'. The more traditional civil liberties such as speech, assembly, voting etc. are derived in this way.[18]

The recognition that certain rights exist, and that they entail corollative duties for others,[19] does not, however, of itself determine the *type* of legal duties which are thereby imposed, nor does it determine the precise *level* at which these duties operate. More specifically it does not tell us whether the rights should be protected at the constitutional level or in some other way. This is evident from Gewirth's own analysis. The human rights depicted above have consequences for social rules and institutions. 'These are morally right, and persons acting in accordance with them fulfil their moral duties, when the rules and institutions express or serve to protect or foster the equal freedom and well-being of the persons subject to them.'[20]

The precise nature of these consequences, in terms of both the type of legal protection and the level at which it will operate, must, however, be delineated. Gewirth suggests the following.[21] The criminal law will operate to protect certain basic rights from attack

[18] Gewirth, *Human Rights*, pp. 62–3.
[19] Ibid. 2.
[20] Ibid. 60.
[21] Ibid. 59–64.

by others, including the rights to life, physical integrity, etc., and will also set standards as to how this protection is to operate (fair trials, habeas corpus, etc.). The social rules consisting in the criminal law serve a static-instrumental function, by protecting well-being in at least the minimum sense necessary to ensure that basic rights are not infringed.

Social rules also possess what is termed a dynamic-instrumental character. They are designed to enhance the well-being of persons pursuant to the supportive state, which provides protections of basic and other rights where these cannot be obtained through an individual's own efforts. There is a recognition that persons are dispositionally unequal in their ability to attain their rights, and one object of social rules is to remove this inequality.[22] In general it is social and economic rights which are protected by the supportive state. These include the provision of food and housing for those who cannot obtain them by their own efforts, and the removal of 'dangerous or degrading conditions of work and housing'. It also includes the existence of public goods which will 'increase the opportunities for productive employment'.

A third species of legal enforcement of human rights flows from the necessary—procedural justification for social rules. This follows from the freedom aspect of Gewirth's thesis: social rules are morally right so far as people have freely consented to them. The traditional civil liberties are justified on this basis.

It can be seen that the recognition of welfare rights does not itself determine the type and level of protection accorded to them. In Gewirth's thesis personal security rights are protected by the criminal law, social and economic rights by the supportive state, and political and civil liberties by the 'Constitution with its method of consent'.[23] Our reflective judge may therefore decide that, even though it is meaningful to talk of welfare rights which the state should protect, and even though the Constitution could be read so as to embrace them, he should decline to take this step. He may decide instead that the legal duties which flow from these rights impose an obligation upon the supportive state to protect such social and economic rights, but that such rights are not themselves to be

[22] 'Thus, where the static phase (the criminal law) tries to restore an occurrent antecedent status quo of mutual nonharm, the dynamic phase tries to move toward a new situation in which a previously nonexistent dispositional equality is attained or more closely approximated' (ibid. 62).

[23] Ibid. 63.

regarded as constitutional rights. An individual could not therefore seek to mount a constitutional challenge against, for example, legislation, on the basis that such rights were infringed with the consequence that the legislation should be declared invalid.[24]

A reasoning process of the type adumbrated above will necessarily be entailed in any attempt to interpret a putative constitutional document which enshrines human rights, whether it is one which is incorporated from outside, or one which we develop for ourselves afresh. It is these complex interpretative problems which will prove as taxing and controversial as any which flow from the alleged bias as to the interests which a less reflective and conscientious judge may choose to protect.

b. Legitimacy, Accountability, and Constitutional Reform

Public lawyers in the United Kingdom who have expressed concern with constitutional reform have not on the whole devoted much space to a consideration of constitutional rights. They have written of the need to increase the legitimacy and accountability of government, without detailed reference to the nature of such rights. This is too narrow a focus, and one which risks distortion. It was argued above that the very meaning to be given to concepts such as legitimacy and accountability will be affected by the meaning ascribed to such substantive and procedural rights, and will be coloured by the political theory which underlies the existence and interpretation of them. The nature of this connection must now be explored.

The very existence of the connection is manifest in the unitary view of the constitution espoused by Dicey.[25] On this view all significant public power resided with Parliament, which possessed a legislative monopoly. The legislature controlled the executive and was itself controlled by the electorate. Legislation was legitimate, since it was the result of a democratic process of choice in which the wishes of the people were accurately and faithfully transferred into statute by the legislature which constrained the executive. Constitutionally enshrined rights were not required, since this unitary conception of democracy was also perceived to be largely self-correcting: because the legislature was controlled by the electorate,

[24] Cf. the similar conclusion reached by Rawls; see below, ch.8 sec. 2c, 3b.
[25] See above, ch. 2.

and in turn constrained the executive, Parliament would not enact legislation which contravened individual rights.

The connection is also evident in other conceptions of the constitution. Bentham's view, that talk of natural rights was 'nonsense upon stilts', was heavily influenced by the way in which such rights could impede the attainment of the utilitarian calculus which was to guide government in its decision-making.[26] Bentham was, however, keenly aware of the need to render the exercise of public power both legitimate and accountable, and to this end he developed a complex set of institutional, political, and external checks.[27] Not surprisingly the particular conception of legitimacy and accountability which underlies these varying devices is itself utilitarian.

The nature of this connection exemplified in the two preceding paragraphs must, however, be explored further. No attempt will be made to survey generally the complex literature on the meaning of legitimacy.[28] Certain themes within that literature are, however, particularly relevant for the present discussion. The distinction drawn between the ability of an order to generate belief in its legitimacy, and the truth or falsity of the beliefs themselves, is particularly important in the present context. Thus Habermas has criticized the Weberian conception of legitimacy for being based upon the presence of belief that the existing order is legitimate, rather than focusing upon the issue of whether such beliefs are well grounded or whether they in fact rest upon mystification, false ideology, etc. For Habermas, 'every effective belief in legitimacy is assumed to have an immanent relation to truth . . . that can be tested and criticized'.[29] If belief in legitimacy is conceived without this relation to truth, then it becomes of 'psychological significance' only.

The importance of this point is readily apparent. On the Habermas view, one of the tasks of critical theory is 'to clarify and vindicate rational standards against which beliefs in legitimacy (or

[26] See J. Waldron, *Nonsense upon Stilts: Bentham, Burke, Marx and the Rights of Man* (1987).

[27] P. P. Craig, 'Bentham, Public Law and Democracy' [1989] *P.L.* 407.

[28] See, e.g., J. Habermas, *Legitimation Crisis*, trans. T. McCarthy (1976); C. Offe, *Contradictions of the Welfare State*, ed. J. Keane (1984); W. E. Connolly (ed.), *Legitimacy and the State* (1984); J. H. Goldthorpe (ed.), *Order and Conflict in Contemporary Capitalism* (1984).

[29] Habermas, *Legitimation Crisis*, p. 97.

illegitimacy) can be tested and to conceptualize a modern form of life which deserves and receives the reflective allegiance of its members'.[30] This requires a criterion.

how would members of a social system, at a given stage in the development of productive forces, have collectively and bindingly interpreted their needs (and which norms would they have accepted as justified) if they could and would have decided on the organization of social intercourse through discursive will-formation, with adequate knowledge of the limiting conditions and functional imperatives of the society?[31]

Now the particular answers which are forthcoming from such a discussion may well be contestable, in much the same way that the particular outcome of the reasoning which occurs in the Rawlsian original position can be contentious.[32]

The significance of this for the use of the term legitimacy within public law is now apparent. The particular meanings attributed to that term will be reflective of the more general norms which one believes would be forthcoming from the discourse described above; and what those norms are will themselves be dependent upon some view as to which interests should be regarded as rights, and some view as to distributive justice within society. Viewed in this way, the concept of legitimacy can have both a substantive and a procedural dimension within public law.

Two examples of the substantive aspect of legitimacy can be proffered. The first of these can be drawn from the discussion of welfare rights considered above. As has been seen, one might attempt to justify such rights by reliance upon differing schools of thought. The above discussion also revealed why one might be unwilling to protect such rights directly within the Constitution, with the consequence that an individual could not argue that legislation which contravened such rights would be invalidated by a supreme court. The existence of such rights does, however, impose an obligation on the 'supportive state' to advance the interests in question.[33] Now of course it might be debatable which policies best served this end. Notwithstanding this sphere of 'applicational

[30] W. E. Connolly, 'Legitimacy and Modernity', in Connolly (ed.), *Legitimacy and the State*, p. 12.

[31] Habermas, *Legitimation Crisis*, p. 113.

[32] See below, ch. 8 sec. 2.

[33] Cf. the obligation on the legislature to advance the interests protected by the second principle of justice within Rawls's theory; see below, ch. 8 secs. 2, 3b.

uncertainty', it is meaningful to speak of the operations of the state as being legitimate or illegitimate to the extent to which they do or do not protect such interests. Or to put the same point in a different way, any statement concerning such interests which maintains that governmental action is illegitimate presupposes that such interests should be protected by the state, and that it is deficient in not doing so.[34]

The importance of being clear about the connection between legitimacy and the underlying political theory which provides the foundations for the conception of rights and distributive justice advanced within a particular society can be demonstrated by a second example. It has been argued that the courts should recognize certain substantive principles, such as proportionality and legal certainty, and use them to control discretionary action by administrators.[35] Some of the difficulties that can be encountered with such an approach have been canvassed elsewhere.[36] One particular problem is of relevance here. The application of substantive principles will require the proper articulation of a background political theory which will serve to explain why a particular principle is said to produce or demand a particular result in a given case.

To say that a certain principle is a substantive principle at all presupposes some articulation of what that substance actually is. To respond in terms of *concepts* such as proportionality does not solve the problem precisely because differing *conceptions* of this idea could produce radically differing results. Those with distinctive political philosophies may accept a general concept of proportionality, but their particular conception thereof could differ considerably. For example, assuming for the sake of argument that some notion of proportionality might be said to underlie discrimination cases,[37] the content that should be given to this notion will differ depending on whether the commentator is a utilitarian, a Rawlsian liberal or a modern communitarian. Similar difficulties arise from attempts to

[34] The point being argued in this paragraph is generalizable to any assertion that state action with respect to certain interests is illegitimate.

[35] J. L. Jowell and A. Lester, 'Beyond *Wednesbury*: Substantive Principles of Administrative Law' [1987] *P.L.* 368, and 'Proportionality: Neither Novel nor Dangerous', in J. L. Jowell and D. Oliver (eds.), *New Directions in Judicial Review* (1988), 51–72.

[36] P. P. Craig, *Administrative Law* (2nd edn., 1989), 297–300.

[37] As argued by Jowell and Lester, 'Beyond *Wednesbury*' and 'Proportionality'.

apply such ideas to particular decided cases. Whether, for example, the provision of subsidized bus fares[38] should be viewed as disproportionately favouring user interests versus ratepayer interests is a question which would be approached very differently by an advocate of early UK pluralism and an adherent of the more market-based pluralism which has characterized recent governmental policy. To argue therefore that substantive principles are required in order to render the exercise of discretionary power legitimate will necessarily entail investigation of the background political theory which gives real content to the particular conception of, for example, proportionality which is adopted.

Legitimacy, as stated above, also has a procedural dimension which is of relevance to public law; this too will be reflective of the underlying political theory which informs that society. The analysis of participation rights adumbrated above exemplifies this connection.[39]

It was argued therein that the extent of such rights presently accorded is itself reflective of the model of unitary, self-correcting majoritarian democracy articulated by Dicey.[40] If all public power were truly concentrated in and exercised through Parliament; and if the wishes of the electorate really were accurately represented by a legislature which controlled the executive, then the exercise of public power might be said to be both legitimate and accountable. There was little need or room within this model for the existence of participatory rights in addition to that guaranteed by the vote. Between elections one participated vicariously through one's MP, which was 'fine' precisely because electoral wishes were, on this model, faithfully implemented by the powerful legislature which restrained the executive.

The ways in which the early pluralists upset this vision have been related above.[41] The twin realizations that Parliament did not wield a monopoly of public power, and that it did not control the executive, but vice versa, undermined the previous harmony. It raised a plethora of questions as to how the exercise of public power, both within government and by other institutions, could be legitimated. An increase in participatory rights was one such theme.

38 *Bromley London Borough Council* v. *Greater London Council* [1983] 1 A.C. 768.

39 See above, ch. 6 sec. 2e.

40 See above, ch. 2 secs. 3, 5. See also Craig, *Administrative Law*, ch. 1.

41 See above, ch. 5 sec. 2.

The arguments for such a development were considered above, and there is no intention to repeat them.[42]

One aspect of this argument must, however, be stressed. The particular conception of participation which is espoused, in terms of both its incidence and its objective, will be reflective of the broader political theory of which it is but one part. The incidence and objective of securing increased participatory rights differ considerably as between the two variants of pluralism discussed above.[43] Danger resides in not perceiving the full extent of this connection, and in proposing uses of participatory rights which implicitly reflect the value of such rights within a different political theory from that which, for example, the government of the day espouses.

The political theory advocated by the incumbent government can of course be challenged directly; and its conception of participatory rights and their legitimating role can be vigorously scrutinized. Thus one can, for example, attack a market-based pluralist democracy and the vision of participatory rights adopted therein. For any such challenge to be meaningful it must address directly, *inter alia*, the normative foundations of such a theory.[44] What is not possible is to suggest that a certain conception of participatory rights associated with a *different* conception of democracy can somehow be 'attached to' such a market-based regime. It is manifestly clear that Conservative policy is not based upon any communitarian philosophy of the type to be considered below.[45] Any suggestion that central aspects of this policy, such as the regulation of privatized industry, should be legitimated by a conception of participatory rights which flows from a communitarian thesis would simply be rejected by those who do not espouse any such thesis.[46]

4. CONSTITUTIONAL REFORM: THE IMPACT OF THE EC

Any discussion of constitutional reform or change within the United Kingdom would obviously be deficient if it did not take account of our membership of the European Community (EC). The ensuing

[42] See above, ch. 6 secs. 2c, d.
[43] See above, ch. 6 sec. 2e.
[44] See above, ch. 1.
[45] See below, chs. 10, 11.
[46] Cf. T. Prosser, *Nationalised Industries and Public Control* (1986).

analysis will consider two central aspects of the 'European dimension'. There will, firstly, be a discussion of the impact of membership of the EC upon the traditional constitutional doctrine of parliamentary sovereignty. It will be followed by a broader discussion of democracy and decision-making within the EC itself. This latter question is of considerable importance and has received relatively scant attention from public lawyers within the United Kingdom.

a. The EC and Legal Sovereignty

Space precludes any exhaustive analysis of this doctrinal issue; a complete exegesis upon this topic could well occupy a 'chapter' in itself. A schematic discussion of the impact of EC membership on the traditional doctrine of parliamentary sovereignty will, however, serve to convey the present writer's view. The argument will, for the sake of clarity, be presented in a series of discrete, albeit connected, stages.

(i) Dicey's view of parliamentary sovereignty possessed, as has already been seen,[47] a dual dimension: Parliament could make or unmake laws on any subject whatsoever, and no other institution could override or set aside the legislation which had been thus made. This conception of sovereignty could be regarded in either of the following ways. It might be argued that this view was a 'logical' product of the idea of sovereignty itself; that it was logically inconsistent to regard a body as a sovereign body, and yet say that it was subject to constraints as to subject-matter or form. Whether this form of argumentation is sustainable or not cannot be explored here. It is moreover clear that Dicey did not principally base his conclusions concerning sovereignty on this species of reasoning. The structure of his argument was, as seen above,[48] a blend of the empirical and the normative. The empirical aspect of the analysis consisted of an examination of past constitutional practice in order to determine whether there were any other institutional rivals who had successfully limited Parliament's power. This was complemented by the normative aspect of the reasoning in which Dicey sought to legitimate this unlimited power by demonstrating that it was

[47] See above, ch. 2 sec. 2. For reference to literature on sovereignty, see above, ch. 2 n. 1.

[48] See above, ch. 2 sec. 2.

consonant with the democratic ordering of the state. The flaws in this aspect of the argument have been considered in detail above.[49]

(ii) An important point follows from the preceding analysis. The idea of unlimited parliamentary power cannot be regarded, on Dicey's own species of reasoning, as immutable. It is not a static, unchangeable concept but one which is dynamic and capable of transformation. This transformation could be effected by the empirical evidence altering, in the sense that some other institution does begin to assert control over the subject-matter or form of parliamentary legislation. The change in the traditional idea could also come about because of a reassessment of the normative foundations on which Dicey constructed his own analysis. The realization that these foundations were flawed, even at the time when Dicey himself wrote, and that they have been further undermined since then, may well cause some other institution, such as the courts, to consider whether they should be exercising control over parliamentary power.

(iii) The argument adumbrated in the previous paragraph can be reinforced in the following manner. Let us accept for the sake of argument that the Diceyan view of sovereignty still holds sway, and that it constitutes the main part of the ultimate legal principle or rule of recognition in the United Kingdom.[50] Hart has demonstrated that talk of the validity of the rule of recognition is inappropriate. Such a rule is 'simply accepted as appropriate for use',[51] as the criterion by which the validity of other rules within the system is judged. The distinctive nature of the rule of recognition is captured in the following passage.

> The assertion that it exists can only be an external statement of fact. For whereas a subordinate rule of a system may be valid and in that sense 'exist' even if it is generally disregarded, the rule of recognition exists only as a complex, but normally concordant, practice of the courts, officials, and private persons in identifying the law by reference to certain criteria. Its existence is a matter of fact.[52]

The insight into the nature of the rule of recognition serves to reinforce the argument in part (ii) above. Given that the content of

[49] See above, ch. 2 secs. 4b, c.
[50] H. L. A. Hart, *The Concept of Law* (1961), 102–7.
[51] Ibid. 105–6.
[52] Ibid. 107.

the rule of recognition is based upon factual acceptance by those who operate the system, and that it only exists if this is present, then it follows also that the content of this rule could alter if the practice of those who operate the system itself changes.

The dynamic nature of the rule of recognition is exemplified by reflecting upon our history. It is manifestly clear that the Diceyan formulation only ever begins to make sense after the constitutional struggles of the seventeenth century. Prior to then the content of the rule of recognition would have been very different. Moreover, notwithstanding Dicey's own empirical survey, the position of Parliament in the eighteenth century was very different from that which it had become one hundred years later. Dicey's formulation concerning parliamentary power is only really plausible from approximately the 1830s onwards. His vision of parliamentary power, in which the Commons wielded real control over the executive, was moreover to prove ephemeral.[53] It is, therefore, perfectly possible for the rule of recognition to alter and for constraints to exist upon what was previously taken to be untrammelled parliamentary power.[54] Whether it has in fact altered can only be determined by considering the practice of those who operate the system, in particular the courts and Parliament itself.

(iv) The present evidence concerning the EC and its impact on sovereignty is not entirely clear.[55] The European Communities Act 1972, section 2(4), provides that 'any enactment passed or to be passed, other than one contained in this part of the Act, shall be construed and have effect subject to the foregoing provisions of this section . . .'. There is little difficulty in construing section 2(4) such as to give priority to EC law in relation to any UK legislation passed prior to 1972. Parliament can, under Diceyan orthodoxy, state that all previous legislation is subject to the terms of a more recent statute.

More difficulty is caused when there is a clash between statutes passed after 1972 and EC law, particularly when the statute is more

[53] See above, ch. 2 sec. 4c.

[54] It is inherent in this analysis that, even if constraints are imposed upon parliamentary authority, and these constraints are accepted by those who operate the system, this position could itself alter at some future date. It would be possible for new types of constraints to be added, for the nature of the constraints to be modified, or for the constraints to be 'abolished' by later participants in the system.

[55] See T. C. Hartley, *The Foundations of European Community Law* (2nd edn., 1988), 236–45.

recent in time than the particular EC rule. On traditional Diceyan reasoning, any inconsistency should be resolved in favour of the statute. EC law would be regarded as part of UK law, which would be altered or changed according to the latest expression of parliamentary intent. The fact that section 2(4) seems to accord priority to EC law even in relation to clashes with UK statutes not yet passed would, on traditional theory, not make any difference. Under the Diceyan view Parliament cannot limit its own powers for the future, and therefore section 2(4) would be ineffective if it was intended to deprive Parliament of the ability to enact statutes which would override EC law.

At least two options are then open to the courts. On the one hand, they could take the step of modifying Diceyan orthodoxy, and state expressly that Parliament, while still within the EC, must abide by EC law and accord priority to such law over any UK statute inconsistent therewith. This would be a step towards modifying the rule of recognition, the effectiveness of which would depend, *inter alia*, upon Parliament's response.

On the other hand, the courts could, less dramatically, treat section 2(4) as a rule of interpretation to the effect that Parliament is presumed not to intend statutes to override EC law. On this view inconsistencies between UK statutes and EC law would be resolved in favour of the latter, unless 'Parliament clearly and expressly states in a future Act that it is to override Community law'.[56] This appears to be the view taken by at least some judges, although the extent to which the courts are willing to read statutes so as to conform to EC law has differed from case to case.[57] The longer that we remain within the Community the more likely it is that the courts will adopt this rule of construction, which serves to preserve the formal veneer of Diceyan orthodoxy while undermining its substance.

b. *The EC, Political Sovereignty, and Democracy*

To rest content with the conclusions articulated above concerning the impact of the EC upon traditional constitutional concepts which we have employed in the United Kingdom would, however, be to

[56] Ibid. 243.

[57] Compare *Macarthys Ltd.* v. *Smith* [1979] 3 All E.R. 325, 329, and *Litster* v. *Forth Dry Dock & Engineering Co. Ltd.* [1989] 55 C.M.L.R. 194, with *Duke* v. *G.E.C. Reliance* [1988] 1 All E.R. 629.

adopt too narrow a focus. It leaves untouched an aspect of the EC which is in reality of greater importance. The point may be presented as follows.

While we remain in the EC increasing areas of economic, social, and legal regulation will be dominated or determined by the organs of the EC. Our concerns over constitutional reform in the United Kingdom must, therefore, also embrace the EC in so far as the latter effectively legislates over an expanding sphere of our lives. To talk of democracy, rights, legitimacy, and accountability in the United Kingdom without alluding to similar issues within the EC is to wear blinkers which artificially narrow the scope of the enquiry. This is all the more important because some commentators who express concern over these issues within the United Kingdom appear not to comprehend the reality and scale of such problems within the EC. It is readily apparent that consideration of these issues could, like that of sovereignty undertaken in the previous section, become protracted. Exigencies of space require that such discussion be kept within bounds. The nature of the problem can, however, be conveyed within these limits.

The general nature of the concern can be expressed as follows. Any discussion of decision-making within the EC must distinguish between two distinctive issues: the substantive desirability of the legislation which is thereby enacted, and the democratic legitimacy of the enactment process. This is a trite proposition, which is only stated in this stark form because the two matters are often elided or confused. Whether one believes, for example, that closer monetary union is desirable or not on economic grounds, the consequences of any such union and the accountability of the central financial institutions which would thereby be created must be clearly evaluated.

The reason for emphasizing this dichotomy can be expressed shortly. Decision-making within the EC is imbued with less democratic legitimacy, as this phrase is normally understood, than in any other nation state which is governed by some species of democratic ordering. This proposition must obviously be sustained, and the ensuing discussion will be divided temporally between the position as it existed prior to 1986, and the effect of the reforms promulgated in that year.

The EC Treaty created three principal decision-making organs: the Council, the Commission, and the Assembly or European

Parliament.[58] The Council is comprised of delegates of member states, who will be of ministerial rank. The Commission consists of individuals who are appointed by the member states but who do not, and are not intended, to represent the interests of their state.[59] They are instructed to pursue the general interests of the EC itself. The European Parliament is composed of representatives elected from the member states. Until 1976 the members were in fact chosen by their national legislatures and it was only at that date that the representatives were directly elected.

The nub of the problem prior to 1986 was as follows. Power to legislate was concentrated in the Commission and the Council, with the 'legislature', the Parliament, being accorded limited power of any real significance. The Parliament was given the right to be consulted on proposed legislation in many instances, but neither the Council nor the Commission was bound to follow the Parliament's opinion. The power possessed by the Parliament flowed rather from its role in the budgetary procedures.[60]

Notwithstanding the democratic foundation of the Parliament, the EC Treaty accorded the major powers to the unelected institutions, the Council and the Commission. The precise details of the legislative process cannot be examined here.[61] One of the principal characteristics of this process in the years prior to 1986 was the tension which existed between the Council and the Commission, and the consequential effects on decision-making in the EC.

The Council composed as it is of representatives of member states, is the forum in which each state will seek to protect its own vital interests. A gradual but perceptible split became evident between Council and Commission as to the nature of the EC. The Council increasingly perceived the Community in 'intergovernmental' terms. The EC Treaty was regarded as the same as any other international treaty in which the consenting states should continue to hold the reins of power. Progress in attaining the Community's aims should proceed only if all could agree on the nature and pace of this progress. If they could not, then further discussion should ensue; no state interests should be readily sacrificed to attain the greater Community good. The Commission's view was very different, and

58 For more detailed discussion, see Hartley, *Foundations*, ch. 1.
59 Merger Treaty, Art. 10(2).
60 On which see Hartley, *Foundations*, pp. 39–45.
61 See ibid., ch. 1.

may be described as 'federal' in its orientation. It saw the economic community as but one step towards closer social and political union, and as a mechanism for moving towards a more federal Europe. To this end it endeavoured to press policies through the legislative process as rapidly as possible, and to utilize the fact that the EC Treaty demanded only qualified majorities from the Council in many subject-matter areas after the first two stages of the establishment of the Common Market. The significant range of powers accorded to the Commission by the Treaty, of a legislative, executive, judicial, and administrative nature, appeared to place it in a good position to effectuate its conception of the EC.

The political reality was to prove otherwise, as the balance of power tilted to favour the Council. The story of how this was achieved cannot be fully described here. Suffice it to say that the 1960s and 1970s witnessed a number of institutional developments outside the strict letter of the Treaty, through which the member states ensured that their interests would not be sacrificed against their will. The Luxembourg Accords instituted a *de facto* requirement of unanimity in voting within the Council which gave a negative power to member states to veto developments affecting their 'vital interests' of which they did not approve.[62] The invention of the management-committee procedure enabled the member states to exert more positive control over the detail of legislation which the Commission was devising than had been envisaged by the Treaty.[63] This positive control over detail was augmented by the development of *ad hoc* meetings of heads of state, which were to become known as meetings of the European Council. This institution served to ensure that the overall direction of Community policy, as well as the detail thereof, should be subject to a degree and form of member-state control which had not been hitherto envisaged.

The position prior to 1986 was therefore not encouraging in terms either of the substantive attainment of the Community's objectives, or the institutional legitimacy by which successful legislation had

[62] The Accords developed as a result of a crisis in the Community in 1965 in which the French boycotted the Council. One of the principal reasons for this boycott was that 1966 was to have been the beginning of qualified majority voting and the French objected to this development.

[63] See C. Bertram, 'Decision-Making in the E.E.C.: The Management Committee Procedure' (1967–8) 5 *C.M.L. Rev.* 246; P. Schindler, 'The Problems of Decision-Making by Way of the Management Committee Procedure in the European Economic Community' (1971) 8 *C.M.L. Rev.* 184.

been promulgated. The EC was not as advanced towards its economic objectives as it ought to have been; and the manner by which the legislation had been passed lacked any real democratic legitimacy. These facts were not lost upon a plethora of bodies which investigated the malaise within the EC, all of which, to some extent, pointed the incriminating finger at the recalcitrance and selfishness of those within the Council.[64]

The Single European Act 1986 has undoubtedly had an impact upon the problems identified above.[65] In substantive terms it has established 1992 as the deadline for the completion of the internal market in the EC, and has imbued discussion of a number of issues from workers' rights to monetary union with a vigour which they had not possessed before. In institutional terms it appears that the Council's veto will be less readily utilized than in the past.[66] The SEA has also increased the *de jure* power of the European Parliament, the object of the reforms being to accord the Parliament more power in some of the areas where it has to be consulted.[67]

Notwithstanding the passage of the SEA, it would be over-sanguine to suggest that the problems of securing democratic legitimacy within the EC have been solved. The European Parliament still does not possess anything like real legislative power or capacity, and its ability to control the other non-elected institutions is still limited. What is of greater concern is the fact that the ramifications of according the Parliament such increased powers could have more far-reaching consequences than are normally envisaged. A few words of explanation on this theme are warranted. Three particular problems can be identified.

First, the relationship between a truly empowered Parliament and the Council and Commission is not self-evident. It has been suggested that, if such a Parliament were to develop, then the Commission would be transformed into a government responsible to the Parliament, with the Council becoming a 'senate' representing national interests.[68] It is, however, difficult to envisage the continued justification for the present membership or power of the

[64] See, e.g., Report on European Institutions (Three Wise Men's Report) (1979). See also L. Tsoukalis (ed.), *The European Community; Past, Present and Future* (1983).

[65] A. Arnull, 'The Single European Act' (1986) 11 *E.L.R.* 358; A. Campbell, 'The Single European Act and the Implications' (1986) 35 *I.C.L.Q.* 932.

[66] Hartley, *Foundations*, pp. 18–20.

[67] Ibid. 32–5.

[68] Ibid. 45–6.

Commission under these altered circumstances. If the Parliament were to have its powers increased in the above manner, it would be odd to regard a Commission appointed from national, unelected representatives as the government, even if it were responsible to the Parliament. The Parliament will, in a manner explained more fully below, have a spectrum of differing political views, and it would be natural to expect that the majority therein, howsoever determined, should be reflected in the 'government'. The coexistence of a truly empowered legislature, directly elected, with a government formed from non-elected, nationally appointed individuals appears to be neither rational, workable, nor legitimate.

Secondly, if the Parliament's powers were increased in the above manner, the tensions which could exist between its aims and those of the Commission and the Council would be problematic. The fact that the Commission and the Council wield a preponderance of power has concentrated attention upon the tension between the 'federal' perspective of the former and the 'intergovernmental' stance of the latter. If the Parliament were to become a 'real legislature', this tension could be rendered more rather than less complex. The attitude or approach of such a Parliament would itself be questionable. Although the European MPs are elected from national constituencies, they do not sit in national but political groupings. This, combined with past experience of the Parliament's behaviour, would lead one to doubt that it would approach issues on purely nationalistic lines.[69]

To conclude that the Parliament will adopt a federal perspective which is identical or similar to that of the Commission is, however, over-simplistic. The Parliament is composed of different political parties which reflect a spectrum of opinion from left to right with varying intermediate shades of belief. A federal social democratic perspective on a particular issue will not necessarily be the same as a federal conservative or socialist approach. What constitutes the public interest is no more self-evident at the European level than it is within particular nation states. The answer may depend upon the political persuasion of a particular political grouping, and is

[69] This 'conclusion' may be falsified by the Parliament gaining real power. It could be argued that the current approach of the Parliament, whereby national groupings are not the norm, is reflective of the fact that the Parliament does not possess real power; that, if it did obtain such power, the pressures on MEPs to represent their own constituencies would become much stronger.

increasingly likely to do so as the EC tackles topics of a social and political nature. One of the principal themes of this book is that the meaning of democracy, and the consequences for rights, distributive justice, and accountability which ensue therefrom, is not self-evident. The more precise meaning with which such terms are to be imbued can only be ascertained by more specific delineation of the type of democratic ordering which is envisaged. This is equally true for the EC as it is for any nation state. To accord the Parliament more power may well be a necessary condition for attaining democratic legitimacy within the EC. The shape and content of, *inter alia*, European public law will, however, necessarily depend upon the specific type of democratic ordering which emerges. This serves to reinforce the first point adumbrated above. It is difficult to imagine how precisely an empowered Parliament which possesses, for example, a current socialist majority would interact with a 'governmental Commission' which was non-elected and not necessarily reflective of the same political ideals.

The third problem which is presented by the existence of an empowered Parliament is distinctive from those previously discussed. It is, however, no less serious, and is the problem of governmental 'overload'. The difficulties of a government coping with a wide range of issues, and the consequential difficulties of preserving some species of parliamentary accountability, even within individual nation states, are well known. The ability of an empowered European Parliament to achieve this, with a government howsoever formed, may well be doubted. It is at the very least a cause for concern. This concern is heightened as the Community increases both in size and in the range of issues over which it exerts authority. The difficulties of devising, administering, and monitoring complex legislation which is to be applied within member states which possess differing social, cultural, and legal traditions should not be underestimated. The value of securing greater democratic legitimacy within Europe by increasing the powers of the Parliament may well be undermined if any such institution is unable to assert more than limited scrutiny of the legislation which is enacted.

c. *The EC: Conclusion*

We are members of the EC and are likely to remain so. The implications of such membership for constitutional reform cannot be ignored. One may well believe that such membership is a 'good thing' in terms of the substantive policies which the EC has pursued. It is, however, difficult to regard the institutional process by which such legislation is enacted as satisfactory or legitimate in democratic terms. Public lawyers in the United Kingdom must, therefore, be willing to include the EC within any realistic discussion of constitutional ordering. Not to do so would mean that an increasing amount of legislation which affects our lives would be regarded as outside the realm of 'relevant constitutional discourse'. If the EC is to move closer to some species of federal Europe, then it must meet the challenge of institutional reform. The existence of such a powerful polity in which real authority is vested in non-elective organs is not acceptable. Whether such a polity could survive if power were truly vested in the elective organs remains to be seen.

5. CONSTITUTIONAL REFORM: THE IMPACT OF NATIONALISM

Recent attempts to secure some degree of devolution of power to Scotland and Wales have failed.[70] Notwithstanding this failure, any discussion of constitutional reform which did not take this issue into account would be ignoring an important aspect of our constitutional order. The topic is one which may well become of current political importance again should demands for greater self-government re-emerge, and should this occur at a juncture when the dominant political parties see the necessity or electoral benefit of supporting such a development. Moreover, quite apart from the relative likelihood of any such development, the inherent importance of the issue warrants its treatment within any meaningful discussion of constitutional reform.

a. The Movement for Reform

The reasons which motivate those who desire a greater degree of autonomy for Scotland and Wales are complex both in and of

[70] See, generally, D. N. MacCormick (ed.), *The Scottish Debate* (1970); H. Calvert (ed.), *Devolution* (1975); E. Craven (ed.), *Regional Devolution and Social Policy* (1975); J. Cornford (ed.), *The Failure of the State* (1975); A. H. Birch, *Political Integration and Disintegration in the British Isles* (1977); J. Mercer, *Scotland: The Devolution of Power* (1978); V. Bogdanor, *Devolution* (1979); H. Drucker and G. Brown, *The Politics of Nationalism and Devolution* (1980).

themselves, and because the degree of autonomy which is advocated itself varies. Some desire a limited measure of devolution, others seek a more federal structure within the United Kingdom, while yet others advocate complete independence. The argument is made more complicated because the same meaning is not always ascribed to distinctive terminology. In the discussion which follows there will be an attempt to distinguish the differing reasons which have been advanced for reform, linking where necessary the type of reason being advanced with the species of autonomy which is being advocated.

i. The nationalist argument It is appropriate to begin with arguments which are directed principally at securing independence, not necessarily because such arguments have the maximum support, but rather because, if effectuated, they would bring about the greatest measure of change to the status quo.

The case for independence could, as Neil MacCormick has remarked, be argued upon 'a very pure nationalist principle', this being that 'because Scotland is a nation she ought to be a separate state'.[71] The only issue left for rational discussion would then be as to whether Scotland was or was not a nation. A distinctive form of argument is what MacCormick has described as utilitarian nationalism: independence may be proposed as the best means to secure the well-being of the Scottish people. The essence of this argument has been put as follows.

It is that Scottish society is at present a sick society because it lacks a democratic political centre, specifically responsible to the Scottish electorate for tackling Scottish problems and determining Scottish priorities. Parliamentary democracy does not involve the electorate directly in solving problems, but it does enable them to participate in settling the broad priorities, and to accept them willingly by virtue of their own responsibility for them. In a modern state it is evident that the radical social and technological changes which have been accelerating over the past fifty years must be to a large extent regulated and implemented by government; a modern state is necessarily an interventionist state. But this produces in a community such as Scotland a sense that these changes (whether good or bad) are outside the control of its members, which inhibits constructive discussion or willing implementation of change. Whatsoever one dislikes

[71] D. N. MacCormick, 'Independence and Constitutional Change', in D. N. MacCormick (ed.), *The Scottish Debate*, p. 52.

can be pilloried as an alien intrusion. The cure for this sickness is to create an independent centre of political life in Scotland to take control of Scottish Affairs.[72]

A utilitarian form of argumentation is, as MacCormick himself acknowledges,[73] open to two kinds of qualification or attack. On the one hand, the content of the argument adumbrated above could also be used to support some lesser form of autonomy, such as devolution or federalism. On the other hand, the utilitarian form of analysis presupposes that the disadvantages of independence (or indeed devolution) would have to be weighed against the advantages secured through its attainment.

The nationalist argument is not, however, wholly dependent upon the type of analysis presented above. It can be supported in other, albeit related, ways. Two may be briefly mentioned here, the one historical, the other more theoretical.

The historical perspective does not have to rest wholly or even principally upon, for example, the circumstances surrounding the Acts of Union 1707. A broader historical survey can be of assistance in helping us to understand that the modern version of the unitary nation state is a relatively new phenomenon. It was not until the second half of the nineteenth century that Bismarck united Germany, and Cavour and Garibaldi created Italy. Some of the other countries in Eastern Europe only attained their shape after the Second World War, and often exhibit tensions between diverse national groupings which have been thrust, more or less willingly, together in some species of federation. The strains within such groupings are becoming more evident as they break from the grip of Soviet hegemony. A desire for national identity is a powerful force, but it would be mistaken to believe that present geographical boundaries are either the best expression of that identity, or that they are set in stone. The fact that Scotland and England combined to form a Union in 1707 should not in itself lead one to conclude that this best expresses the sentiments of the two peoples in the present day.

A more theoretical argument can be based upon the pluralist foundations considered above, more particularly the earlier species of pluralism which evolved in the late nineteenth and early twentieth centuries.[74] If one accepts even part of that thesis concerning the

72 D. N. MacCormick, 'Independence and Constitutional Change', pp. 52–3.

73 Ibid. 54–5.

74 See above ch. 5 sec. 2.

benefits to be attained from the dispersal of power and the diverse bodies to which individuals do have a sense of attachment, it is difficult to argue that Scotland and Wales should not be included as prime candidates for such dispersion of power, at least as far as some form of devolution is concerned.

ii. The economic and administrative arguments In addition to arguments which have focused principally upon nationalism in one form or another, there are a range of other arguments which are of a more economic and administrative nature. It may be helpful to distinguish varying forms of this latter type of argument, while accepting that some overlap between them is inevitable. Four aspects of this general theme can be distinguished.

First, there is the government-overload thesis. Modern governments have undertaken an increasingly wide range of regulatory functions, in areas such as social welfare, planning, regional policy, health and safety, and the like. The difficulties of administering such policies in a state which insists upon centralized administration from London increases as the complexity of the sphere of governmental responsibility broadens. Various devices, such as contracting out certain functions, and hiving off others to fringe organizations, are introduced in order to combat the problem of administrative overload. Such 'solutions', however, bring fresh problems in their wake, including the difficulty of securing the accountability of those institutions to whom such tasks have been given. Speaking of this increased complexity of modern government, Iain MacCormick has said, 'We are accused of being behind the times; we are told that it is old-fashioned to think in terms of national sovereignties. Yet it is precisely because our present system of government does not and cannot meet up to the demands of modern conditions that we seek independence.'[75]

It, is of course, true that one of the administrative developments which has been devised, in part, to cope with administrative complexity has been to 'devolve' certain issues to the Secretary of State for Scotland.[76] This has not, however, cured the problem, but displaced it. As Bogdanor states,

[75] I. S. M. MacCormick, 'The Case for Independence', in D. N. MacCormick (ed.), *The Scottish Debate*, p. 96.

[76] For a discussion of the Scottish system, see J. G. Kellas, *The Scottish Political System* (3rd edn., 1984). For Wales, see A. B. Philip, *The Welsh Question: Nationalism in Welsh Politics, 1945–1970* (1975).

the wide range of responsibilities enjoyed by the Secretary of State, covering matters for which nine U.K. departments are responsible leads to the overloading of the executive in Scotland, and makes it difficult to ensure that sufficient attention is being given to each area of policy. To take one example, education which in England is the responsibility of five ministers is, in Scotland, the responsibility of the Secretary of State and a parliamentary under-secretary who also has to deal with social work, sport and the arts.[77]

This problem is exacerbated by the fact that the pressures upon the Secretary of State mean that he can spend relatively little time actually in Scotland. When Parliament is in session he is unable to spend more than half of the week there, and 'he has to include in this period his constituency business and meetings with Scottish Office officials as well as the numerous pressure groups who demand an audience with him'.[78]

Secondly, there is the sense that the problems of, for example, Scotland and Wales are treated very much as peripheral and tangential to the concerns occupying those at Westminster. The population of both Scotland and Wales is small compared to that of England. As a consequence, the 'hard facts of democracy demand that governments' chief preoccupations must be with the deep south where the majority of the population live, and where a maximum number of votes is to be garnered'.[79] Legislation is primarily devised with such areas in mind, with too little thought for its impact in other areas where the conditions may be significantly different. The real decisions of principle will be made by the central government and the Secretary of State for Scotland will transform such policies into action with little discretion or room for manœuvre.[80]

The sense of being upon the periphery was heightened by the economic problems which beset the United Kingdom in the latter part of the 1960s. The existence of, for example, the Secretary of State for Scotland has served as a focal point which has helped to ensure that Scottish interests were not ignored in the policy-making process. Such success was premised implicitly upon a buoyant economy in the United Kingdom as a whole, in order that any Scottish gains would not be seen as being made at the expense of

77 Bogdanor, *Devolution*, p. 84.

78 Ibid. 83.

79 I. S. M. MacCormick, 'The Case for Independence', p. 98.

80 Ibid. 97. See also Bogdanor, *Devolution*, pp. 87–8.

other parts of the UK. However, this 'consensus was breached by the economic difficulties of the late 1960's, since when many Scots have come to believe that economic policy-making is shaped too greatly by England's requirements, and that Scotland's problems receive insufficient attention'.[81]

The third important factor of an economic and administrative nature is the United Kingdom's membership of the EC. This has had a twofold impact upon the movement for reform within the UK. On the one hand, it has heightened the sense that Scottish (and Welsh) concerns are peripheral to mainstream political decision-making. As more issues fell within the authority of the Commission and the Council, so it was felt that Scotland would be even more remote from the locus of real power. There would be no separate representation of their interests and there was a concern that Scottish affairs would become simply one tangential issue of European regional policy.

On the other hand, membership of the EC increased the benefits to be gained from some measure of independence and reduced the disadvantages which might ensue therefrom. Independence would mean separate representation in the Council, Commission, and Parliament, with all the connected mechanisms for lobbying on behalf of Scottish interests. Moreover, while England still remained within the EC, there would be no danger of Scottish industry being ruined by the imposition of English tariffs, since these are illegal within the EC. Thus members of 'fairly small societies like Scotland can now gain many of the advantages of belonging to a large market for the exchange of goods and services without the sacrifice of local autonomy that has previously been a necessary concomitant'.[82]

The final aspect of the economic and administrative arguments is principally of relevance to those who advocate outright independence. It concerns the macroeconomic prospects for an independent Scotland. The economic issues involved in this debate are too complex and contentious to summarize here.[83]

[81] Bogdanor, *Devolution*, pp. 88–9.

[82] Birch, *Political Integration*, p. 173.

[83] See, e.g., D. Simpson, 'Independence: The Economic Issues', in D. N. MacCormick (ed.), *The Scottish Debate*, chs. 9, 11b, and K. J. W. Alexander, 'The Economic Case against Independence', in ibid., chs. 10, 11a. The nature of this aspect of the debate will, moreover, be affected by developments within the EC itself, such as those relating to capital movements and monetary union.

b. Constitutional Consequences of Reform

The failure of legislation designed to accord greater powers to Scotland and Wales has been related in detail elsewhere, as have the political manœuvres which were such an integral part of that failure.[84] The discussion within this section will, therefore, concentrate upon the issues of principle which will necessarily be involved in any future movements for reform; failures of the past will be alluded to only in so far as these enlighten the problems which any future reform movements will encounter.

It is readily apparent that the consequences of any change in our constitutional structure will be dependent upon the nature of that change. Three principal modifications of that structure are possible.

The least extreme is that of *devolution*. This consists of the transfer to a subordinate elected body, normally on a geographical basis, of functions at present exercised by Parliament.[85] A key feature of devolution is that the newly created bodies are subordinate to the Parliament at Westminster, which retains its sovereignty. In constitutional theory the subordinate elected bodies would possess powers delegated to them by the Westminster Parliament. The latter could add to, or derogate from, the authority of the subordinate bodies, and could abolish them if it wished to do so. The Westminster Parliament could also choose which types of powers to devolve. These could be of a legislative nature, or could be of a more limited executive kind, wherein the subordinate body would have the power to make decisions within a legal framework established by the Westminster Parliament.

The impact of any scheme for devolution depends crucially upon the ambit of powers which are devolved, the method of determining whether a particular issue is within that sphere, the financing of the newly created body, and the representation of the relevant geographical area within the Westminster legislature. These issues will be considered briefly in turn.

The Westminster Parliament can, as stated above, choose which matters to devolve and can add to or subtract from that list. For

[84] See Report of Royal Commission on the Constitution (Kilbrandon), Cmnd. 5460 (1973); T. C. Daintith, 'Kilbrandon: The Ship that Launched a Thousand Faces?' (1974) 37 *M.L.R.* 544; Bogdanor, *Devolution*, chs. 6, 7; Drucker and Brown, *The Politics of Nationalism*, chs. 5–9; Birch, *Political Integration*, chs. 9, 10.

[85] Bogdanor, *Devolution*, p. 2.

example, under the Scotland Act 1978[86] devolved matters fell within the following areas: health, social welfare, education, housing, local government and finance, planning, pollution, transport, agricultural land, certain civil and criminal law matters, and tourism. An issue was not, however, within the legislative competence of the Scottish Assembly if it extended to any part of the United Kingdom other than Scotland, if it imposed or abolished a tax, or if its effect would be to amend the Scotland Act.

The existence of limits to the legislative competence of the Scottish Assembly presupposed that an institution or person would adjudicate on those limits where necessary. Normally bills passed by the Scottish Assembly were to become law when approved by Order in Council. Where, however, the Secretary of State believed that a bill was *ultra vires* the powers of the Assembly, he could refer the matter to the Privy Council (pre-assent judicial scrutiny). If the Privy Council found that the bill was *ultra vires*, then the Secretary of State could not submit it for approval by Order in Council. Provisions also existed for judicial scrutiny post-assent, and to enable the *ultra vires* doctrine to be applied to the acts of the Scottish executive. The powers of the Scottish Assembly were subject, not only to scrutiny by the courts, but also to control by the Westminster Parliament. Thus, if, for example, the Secretary of State believed that a bill enacted by the Assembly might affect a reserved matter, and that its enactment would not be in the public interest, he could lay the bill before Parliament. A reserved matter was an issue which concerned Scotland but was not within the competence of the Scottish Assembly. When the bill was laid before Parliament, it could be defeated by a negative resolution passed within twenty-eight days.

The success of any scheme for devolution depends, *inter alia*, upon the financial provisions which are attendant thereon. Clearly the subordinate legislature must have power to spend money More contentious is the question whether it should be enabled to raise revenue by direct or indirect taxation. This question has given rise to considerable controversy, as the debates over Irish Home Rule[87] and devolution to Scotland and Wales exemplify. If the new

[86] The Act was repealed because of a provision that 40% of those entitled to vote in a referendum had to support the legislation. In the event a majority of those voting did support devolution, but the number was less than that required by the legislation.

[87] Bogdanor, *Devolution*, ch. 2.

legislature is dependent solely upon block grants to be allocated by the Westminster Parliament, then this would almost certainly limit the freedom of the former institution, because expenditure upon devolved areas would be carefully scrutinized by central government departments. It does not appear to be impossible to resolve such financial issues, as experience in other countries indicates.[88] Finance is, however, 'the spinal cord of devolution',[89] and the degree of real autonomy possessed by the devolved administration will be determined by the provisions dealing with this topic.

The existence of a new subordinate legislature raises the question as to representation at Westminster. This produces problems of principle and also of practical politics. There is no reason for the areas to which power has been devolved to be represented at Westminster at all in so far as that Parliament enacts legislation which relates solely to the domestic affairs of the remainder of the United Kingdom. Such areas should not, however, be under-represented in voting on other legislation which affects the whole of the UK. The difficulty of resolving this conundrum is exacerbated by the structure of practical politics at Westminster. The central government could well be dependent upon the votes of MPs from areas which possess devolved administrations. If these votes were excluded on certain topics, the very existence of the 'governing party' could be called into question. This problem would be alleviated should devolution also take place within England itself, in the form of provincial governments, but there appears to be little prospect of this occurring.

The discussion thus far has concentrated upon devolution. A more radical modification of the existing constitutional structure would be *federalism*. This involves the division of supreme power between Parliament and newly created provincial bodies. The respective scope of power possessed by each branch of government would be defined by a written constitution, and interpreted by the judiciary, as in the United States. The Westminster Parliament would no longer be supreme, and provisions would have to exist whereby any modification of the constitutional document could only be made with the consent of the various Parliaments. Any serious federal proposal would require a plethora of problems to be resolved, including, for example, the division of authority between

[88] Bogdanor, *Devolution*, pp. 194–206.
[89] Ibid. 194.

the respective branches of government. How successful any such scheme would be in the United Kingdom is difficult to determine. Any form of federalism within England is extremely unlikely. A federal solution for the UK as a whole would, therefore, mean that a significant imbalance in power, population, and wealth would exist as between the constituent parts. This would not auger well for the success of such reforms.

Complete *independence* for Scotland and Wales would obviously be the most extreme alteration to the status quo. There appears to be relatively little support for such a measure within Wales, or at present within Scotland, although voters' preferences have altered quite rapidly, particularly within Scotland. Moreover, membership of the EC has, as seen above, modified the terms of this debate. Industry could not be barred from access to English markets, individuals seeking employment could not be discriminated against on grounds of nationality, and firms could not be prevented from becoming established within England merely because they were of Scottish origin. The interests of, for example, Scotland might also be better protected by having her own seat on the Council, and in the Commission, and her own members of the European Parliament. Time will tell whether these considerations lead to a revival of separatist sentiment.

6. CONCLUSION

The unitary conception of the state represented by the Diceyan thesis is inaccurate in descriptive terms, and its prescriptive foundations are questionable. The task of replacing it by constitutional constructs which accord better with reality, and which may be more desirable in prescriptive terms, is perhaps the major role for public lawyers in the United Kingdom. Shortcuts are, however, not possible. One must be prepared to reveal the conception of democracy which underlies specific proposals, and be ready to defend the broader political theory of which it is but one part. Only then can one talk sensibly of the content of particular constitutional rights, and only then can terms such as legitimacy be given meaningful content.

Any such discussion must also include the 'territorial dimension', whether this relates to the present reality of our membership of the

EC, or to the future possibility of dispersion of power within the United Kingdom. The democratic implications of both such developments must be properly assessed, and in this sense there is a link between the two. At the EC level, we should not be content with the relatively narrow issue concerning the impact of the Community upon our notions of sovereignty. We must also be aware of the problems of democratic legitimacy which subsist within the EC, for which we have some responsibility while we remain therein. Empowering the European Parliament may be a necessary step in resolving this problem, but the more specific *type* of democratic ordering which emerges will then have to be determined. A more democratic Europe may choose in principle any of the particular conceptions of democracy considered within this book.[90] The same theme is apparent in the discussion of dispersion of power within the United Kingdom. Constitutional modifications of this type may be defended on the ground, *inter alia*, that such changes render the system more democratic. One may, for the sake of argument, accept this and yet appreciate at the same time that the particular conception of democracy to be pursued within this new constitutional order must still be resolved.

[90] Or, of course, some other species thereof.

8
LIBERALISM: THE RIGHT, THE GOOD, AND THE SCOPE OF PUBLIC LAW (I)

1. INTRODUCTION

Liberalism is not, in and of itself, a theory of democracy, and therefore one may wonder at its inclusion within this book. The answer is readily forthcoming, and has both a conceptual and a practical aspect. In conceptual terms, we have already seen that theories of democracy when pressed reveal themselves to be but part of a broader political theory, which entail a vision of rights and distributive justice. This point was made at the outset of the discussion.[1] It has also been exemplified in the discussion within the previous chapters, where we began with, for example, a pluralist conception of democracy and discovered that, when pressed, such a conception led in different directions depending upon the broader political theory of which it was but one part.[2] Liberalism reflects this interconnection from the opposite direction. The political theory of liberalism, including the role of rights and the meaning of distributive justice, is initially established; the consequences for democracy then unfold.[3]

In more practical terms, a consideration of liberalism is vital precisely because it has been the doctrine against which much of the legal literature from both left and right has rebelled. Public lawyers have, for example, challenged liberal doctrine for the inconsistency and indeterminacy of its prescriptions,[4] while others have sought to

[1] See above, ch. 1 sec. 1b.

[2] See above, chs. 3, 4, 5, 6.

[3] No assumption is being made that liberalism is consonant only with a democratic form of society.

[4] See, e.g., M. V. Tushnet, 'Darkness on the Edge of Town: The Contributions of John Hart Ely to Constitutional Theory', 89 *Yale L.J.* 1037 (1980), and 'Following the Rules Laid Down: A Critique of Interpretivism and Neutral Principles', 96 *Harv. L. Rev.* 781 (1983); G. E. Frug, 'The Ideology of Bureaucracy in American Law', 97 *Harv. L. Rev.* 1276 (1984), and 'Why Neutrality?', 92 *Yale L.J.* 1591 (1983). See also the discussion of public-choice theorists, above ch. 4 sec. 1.

come to its defence, and to answer the charges laid against it.[5] Whether one believes that the doctrines of liberalism are right or wrong may well be a question on which people can differ. Understanding what liberalism actually means is, however, a precondition for any such assessment.

In determining the meaning of liberalism there is, however, an initial problem, which is the diversity of interpretation surrounding this concept. Now one approach might be to proceed by abstracting from these differing interpretations a number of general ideas which could be called 'liberal', and then to assess the legal implications which flow from them. This could be complemented by a critical evaluation of the merits of liberalism as depicted in this way. This approach, although not without attraction, will not be employed here.[6] Such abstraction runs the risk of distorting the more particular conceptions of liberalism which abound.[7] It is, moreover, extremely difficult to work out the public-law implications of liberalism if the discussion is left at this abstract level. A different approach will, therefore, be adopted. No attempt will be made to canvass the plethora of meanings associated with liberalism. Attention will rather be focused upon a dominant brand of liberalism which has prominence within the present literature, which captures a central core of liberal belief, and which has been the focus of attack by those opposed to liberalism. The liberal vision of Rawls will be considered in some detail, with reference being made to the related but distinct version of the same type of thesis advanced by Dworkin. It is only by detailed enquiry of a particular liberal vision that one can assess the implications of such a vision for public law. The more abstract arguments which have been levelled against liberalism will be fully considered; the cogency of such arguments can, however, be more accurately evaluated once one has a detailed understanding of what one central liberal conception entails.

The analysis within this and the next chapter will be structured in the following manner. First, we shall examine the Rawlsian conception of liberalism in order to understand the enumeration of rights therein. Secondly, the implications which this has for the role of public law will be considered. The latter enquiry will itself be

[5] e.g. R. B. Stewart, 'Regulation in a Liberal State: The Role of Non-Commodity Values', 92 *Yale L.J.* 1537 (1983).

[6] For two interesting works in this vein, see R. M. Unger, *Knowledge and Politics* (1975); B. Barber, *Strong Democracy: Participatory Politics for a New Age* (1984).

[7] See also J. Rawls, 'The Idea of an Overlapping Consensus' (1987) 7 *O.J.L.S.* 1, 5–6.

subdivided into two parts for reasons which will become clearer in the course of the analysis. There will be a discussion of the role of public law within 'ideal theory'; this will be followed by consideration of its role in 'non-ideal theory'. Rawls's theory has, of course, been subjected to detailed philosophical scrutiny by many writers, who have pointed to difficulties within his thesis. These criticisms will be included within the analysis where relevant. Thirdly, some of the broader criticisms which have been levelled at liberalism will be considered within the chapter which follows. The cogency of such criticisms will be assessed in the light of what has been learned of liberalism from the more specific enquiry.

2. RAWLS'S THEORY OF JUSTICE

The theory of justice espoused by Rawls is well known,[8] but it may be helpful to set out some of its central features here, more particularly because certain aspects of the theory have undergone change in Rawls's more recent work.

a. The Priority of the Right over the Good

Sandel captures the core idea of liberalism in the following extract.

> 'Deontological liberalism' is above all a theory about justice, and in particular about the primacy of justice among moral and political ideals. Its core thesis can be stated as follows: society, being composed of a plurality of persons, each with his own aims, interests, and conceptions of the good, is best arranged when it is governed by principles that do not *themselves* presuppose any particular conception of the good; what justifies these regulative principles above all is not that they maximize the social welfare or otherwise promote the good, but rather that they conform to the concept of *right*, a moral category given prior to the good and independent of it.'[9]

[8] The main references to Rawls's work will be taken from J. Rawls, *A Theory of Justice* (Oxford, 1973) (hereafter cited as *TJ*); 'Fairness to Goodness' (1975) 84 *Philosophical Review*, 536; 'Kantian Constructivism in Moral Theory' (1980) 77 *Journal of Philosophy*, 515; 'Justice as Fairness: Political not Metaphysical' (1985) 14 *Phil. & Pub. Affairs*, 223; 'The Basic Liberties and their Priority', in S. M. McMurrin (ed.), *Liberty, Equality and Law* (1987), 1–87 (hereafter cited as Basic Liberties); 'The Idea of an Overlapping Consensus'; 'The Priority of Right and Ideas of the Good' (1988) 17 *Phil. & Pub Affairs*, 251; 'The Domain of the Political and Overlapping Consensus', 64 *N.Y.U.L. Rev.* 233 (1989).

[9] M. J. Sandel, *Liberalism and the Limits of Justice* (1982), 1; italics in the original. See also Rawls, 'Justice as Fairness' and 'The Idea of an Overlapping Consensus'; R. Dworkin, *A Matter of Principle* (1985), chs. 8–10.

The essence of this fundamental idea requires further explanation since it forms the foundation for this central conception of liberal philosophy. This explanation is best furnished by contrasting liberalism with teleological theories such as utilitarianism and perfectionism.

The liberal assumes as a basic premiss that people in society hold divergent conceptions of the 'good', meaning that individuals have a variety of conflicting conceptions of the value and purpose of human life. Society is in this sense 'pluralistic'[10] (although the conclusion drawn from the usage of this term is very different from that surveyed in the earlier chapters.)[11] State power should not be used to support one particular conception of the good at the expense of another, simply upon the grounds that the particular conception of the good is preferred for some reason. The state must, therefore, be neutral with respect to different conceptions of the good. Toleration of divergent values between individuals, and toleration by the state of these diverse goals, assume centrality.[12]

The liberal contrasts the preceding analysis with that of teleological theories, such as utilitarianism and perfectionism. In a teleological theory the good is specified independently of the right.[13] The nature of the good varies as between differing teleological theories. Perfectionism regards the realization of human excellence in the various forms of culture as the good to be advanced; hedonism defines the good in terms of pleasure; classical utilitarianism specifies the good as securing the 'greatest net balance of satisfaction summed over all the individuals belonging to it'.[14] The power of the state can be and should be used to advance whichever of these conceptions of the good is espoused.

This is objectionable to the liberal for a number of reasons. The very choice of a particular conception of the good which is then to govern the entirety of societal relations is regarded as highly controversial. The choice once made is then capable of overriding particular conceptions of the good held by individuals, and of allowing those individuals to be 'sacrificed' to the pursuance of the general good, should the latter so demand.[15]

[10] e.g. Rawls, 'The Idea of an Overlapping Consensus', pp. 4–5.

[11] See above, chs. 3, 4.

[12] Rawls, 'The Idea of an Overlapping Consensus'; 'Justice as Fairness'.

[13] *TJ* 25, 30, 325–32. Cf. W. Kymlicka, *Liberalism, Community, and Culture* (1989), ch. 2.

[14] *TJ* 22, 25, 26. There are, of course, different forms of utilitarianism; D. Lyons, *The Forms and Limits of Utilitarianism* (1965).

[15] e.g. Rawls, 'The Idea of an Overlapping Consensus', pp. 4–6.

b. The Determination of the Right: Method

Society must, however, be regulated. How is this to be achieved without presupposing some conception of the good? How are we to judge whether the distribution of goods in society is fair, and what criteria are to guide the legislators in their task? In short, what exactly does it mean to say that there is a concept of the right which is prior to the good and independent of it, which then provides the justification for the regulative principles upon which society operates? What Rawls provides is an account of how principles of justice might emerge which constitute the 'right'. Three ideas are central to this scheme: the thin theory of the good, the original position, and the veil of ignorance.

Rawls clearly wishes to arrive at principles of justice which avoid both of the following pitfalls. On the one hand, they should not be open to the charge that they are too abstract or transcendental. On the other hand, it is equally important not to allow the choice of such principles to be influenced by contingent and arbitrary differences in the positions of individuals. If a person knows that she is wealthy, or likes opera, the principles of justice chosen by such a person could well be affected by such knowledge. The thin theory of the good, and the original position together with the veil of ignorance, are the responses to these problems respectively.

The thin theory of the good furnishes the motivational assumptions of those in the original position. It is prior to the concept of the right which has yet to be established.[16] This theory of the good has to be 'thin' in order not to jeopardize the priority of the right over the good. It is, therefore, restricted to the 'bare essentials',[17] and its object is to establish the premisses concerning primary goods which are necessary in order to proceed to the principles of justice. The thin theory of the good states that individuals, in order to advance whatever are their aims, require more rather than less primary goods.[18] Primary goods are: the basic liberties; freedom of movement and free choice of occupation against a background of diverse opportunities; powers and prerogatives of offices and positions of responsibility; income and wealth; and the social bases of self-respect.[19]

[16] *TJ*; Rawls, 'Basic Liberties', pp. 21–2.

[17] *TJ* 396.

[18] *TJ* 142–3, 397.

[19] Rawls, 'Basic Liberties', pp. 22–3; J. Rawls, 'Social Unity and Primary Goods', in A. Sen and B. Williams (eds.), *Utilitarianism and Beyond* (1982), ch. 8.

The veil of ignorance and the original position serve to prevent individuals from deciding upon principles of justice too heavily influenced by their own contingent circumstance. Thus Rawls posits a hypothetical original position in which an agreement is made, the content of which contains the principles of justice.[20] The principles of justice emerge because they represent the best way for each person to secure their ends, given the limits placed upon their knowledge and beliefs.[21] The objective is therefore to establish a fair procedure, 'so that any principles agreed to will be just'.[22] 'Pure procedural justice'[23] is to be the basis of the theory, but in order for this to operate the agreement reached in the original position must be concluded under the veil of ignorance. Thus no one knows of his place in society, class, or social status; nor does any person know about his wealth, intelligence, or talent; nor is any individual cognizant of his conception of the good; and there is no knowledge of the particular level of civilization and welfare which has been attained.[24] Certain information is, however, available, including an understanding of political affairs, the general ideas of economic theory and psychology, and any other general information helpful to the parties in deciding upon the principles of justice.[25] Subject to the preceding constraints upon information, the parties in the original position are to proceed as 'rationally autonomous representatives.'[26] They are not guided by any prior principles of right or justice (for none yet exist); and reason only by what they believe is for the 'determinate good of the persons they represent'.[27] What then are the principles of justice which would emerge from the original position? It is to this question that we must now turn.

c. The Determination of the Right: Content

In analysing the content of the principles of justice which emerge from the original position it may be helpful to proceed in two stages,

[20] *TJ* 21, 120. For difficulties with the concept of the original position, see R. Dworkin, 'The Original Position', in N. Daniels (ed.), *Reading Rawls* (1975), ch. 2.

[21] *TJ* 118–19.

[22] Ibid. 136.

[23] Pure procedural justice operates when there is no independent criterion for the right result: 'instead there is a correct or fair procedure such that the outcome is likewise correct or fair, whatever it is, provided that the procedure has been properly followed' (*TJ* 86).

[24] *TJ* 137.

[25] Ibid. 138.

[26] Rawls, 'Basic Liberties', pp. 20–1.

[27] Ibid. 21.

by setting out what those principles are, and then analysing why they have been chosen.

Two principles are derived from the original position, and constitute the special conception of justice.

> 1. Each person has an equal right to a fully adequate scheme of equal basic liberties which is compatible with a similar scheme of liberties for all.
>
> 2. Social and economic inequalities are to satisfy two conditions. First, they must be attached to offices and positions open to all under conditions of fair equality of opportunity; and second, they must be to the greatest benefit of the least advantaged members of society.[28]

These basic principles of justice are supplemented by two priority rules.[29] The first priority rule (the priority of liberty) states that the principles of justice are to be ranked in lexical order. A lexical ordering is one in which the first principle in any particular ordering has to be satisfied before moving on to the second, the second before moving on to the third, and so on.[30] Applied to the principles of justice this means that liberty can be restricted only for the sake of liberty. This can occur either where a less extensive liberty strengthens the total system of liberty shared by all; or where a less than equal liberty is acceptable to those with the lesser liberty. Liberty cannot, subject to what will be said below, be restricted by the second principle of justice; it cannot be 'traded' for an increase in wealth or other monetary benefit. The second priority rule (the priority of justice over efficiency and welfare) states that the second principle of justice is lexically prior to the principle of efficiency and to that of maximizing the sum of advantages; and that fair opportunity is prior to the difference principle. Thus an inequality of opportunity must enhance the opportunities of those with the lesser opportunities; and an excessive rate of saving must on balance mitigate the burden of those bearing this hardship.

What reasoning by 'rationally autonomous individuals' produces these principles, ranked in this order? The answer to this question is both complex and contentious, and it occupies a considerable portion of Rawls's book. Some bare outline of the argument can,

[28] This formulation is taken from Rawls, 'Basic Liberties', p.5, modifying *TJ* 302–3.

[29] *TJ* 302–3.

[30] Ibid. 43.

however, be provided. Difficulties with the analysis will be presented at various appropriate stages of the subsequent discussion.

The parties within the original position know that they cannot have all that they want; the very existence of other people prevents this.[31] Nor can they win special advantages for their 'type' of person, because this is precluded by the veil of ignorance. The rational starting-point is, therefore, to accept an equal division of everything, including equal liberty, and equal income and wealth.[32] However, this does not have to be acknowledged as the final choice. Certain inequalities might operate to make everyone better off and they would be accepted in the original position. This reasoning produces what Rawls terms the general conception of justice, as opposed to the special conception adumbrated above. The general conception states that all primary goods (liberty and opportunity, income and wealth, and self-respect) are to be distributed equally unless an unequal distribution of any or all of these goods is to the advantage of the least favoured.[33]

How then do we move from the general conception to the special conception with its lexical ordering of the two principles of justice? Rawls's opinion on this matter has shifted. The original reasoning was that, once the parties assumed that their basic liberties could be effectively exercised, they would not exchange a lesser liberty for an improvement in their economic welfare.[34] With the improvement of the conditions of life, the marginal significance for our good of further social and economic advantage diminishes relative to the interests in liberty, 'which become stronger as the conditions for the exercise of equal freedoms are more fully realized'.[35] This argument was criticized by Hart,[36] who contended that there was no basis for asserting that those *in the original position* would necessarily prefer a society in which trade-offs between liberty and other primary goods were prohibited. This assertion rested upon an implicit ideal vision of the person who prized political activity as one of the principal things of value in life, and who would not tolerate any diminution in such liberty merely for the sake of extra wealth. Rawls has accepted part of this criticism, and has proffered a modified argument as to

[31] Rawls, *TJ* 118–19.
[32] Ibid. 150–1.
[33] Ibid. 302–3.
[34] Ibid. 151–2, 542.
[35] Ibid. 542.
[36] H. L. A. Hart, 'Rawls on Liberty and its Priority', in Daniels (ed.), *Reading Rawls*, pp. 250–2.

why priority should be accorded to liberty. This priority is now said to flow from a certain conception of the citizen as a free and equal person. The argument is complex, but the central core of the thesis can be presented through linking a number of propositions in the following manner.

(i) Rawls posits a certain conception of the person together with a certain ideal of social co-operation.[37] Fair terms of social co-operation are those terms upon which, as equal persons, 'we are willing to co-operate in good faith with all members of society over a complete life'.[38] The concept of the person which Rawls espouses has three features. Citizens are regarded as having the capacity for a sense of right and justice, and the capacity for a conception of the good. These two facets of moral personality are said to follow from the capacity which citizens have for social co-operation.[39] The third feature which individuals have is that they possess differing determinate conceptions of the good, which should be respected provided that they do not transgress the limits of the chosen principles of justice.[40]

(ii) These underlying ideas provide the backdrop to the discussion which then takes place in the original position, with the appropriate assumptions concerning the thin theory of the good, and the veil of ignorance. The ideal of social co-operation and the conception of the person are used to indicate how the basic liberties with their priority belong to the fair terms of social co-operation. However, as Rawls admits, the reasons for the basic liberties themselves, and for their priority, will differ as between the liberties, even given the underlying ideas in (i) above.[41] He then proceeds to exemplify the type of connection between these background ideas and the particular liberties in specific areas, in order to demonstrate the reasons for that liberty and for its priority.

(iii) Liberty of conscience is, for example, defended by pointing out the links between it and two of the features of the person adumbrated above: the presence of a determinate conception of the good, and the capacity for a conception of the good.[42] While

[37] Rawls, 'Basic Liberties', p. 13; see the genesis of these ideas in *TJ* 505, 561.

[38] Rawls, 'Basic Liberties', p. 17.

[39] Ibid. 15–16.

[40] Ibid. 14, 17–18.

[41] Ibid. 18, 23–4.

[42] Rawls also employs arguments which are derived from the capacity for a sense of justice; ibid. 29–39.

individuals do have particular determinate conceptions of the good, the veil of ignorance prevents them from knowing what they are in the original position. None the less the very fact of such determinate conceptions will lead those in the original position to choose equal liberty of conscience. Why? Because they will not be able to know whether their view is a minority or majority view. They cannot, therefore, take the chance of according minority beliefs a lesser liberty, because this would not be to take the determinate religious or moral convictions of people seriously. Such conceptions of the good are 'non-negotiable', and cannot be sacrificed to the second principle of justice.[43]

The preceding argument is complemented by arguments flowing from the capacity for a conception of the good. This capacity encapsulates the idea that we can form, revise, and rationally pursue a determinate conception of the good; liberty of conscience, and thus the liberty to make mistakes, can be regarded as a necessary part of the social conditions for the exercise of this power.[44]

Whether this reasoning fully answers the point raised by Hart, and how generalizable it is, will be considered in more detail later.[45] We must now move on to consider a further crucial part of the argument which must be sustained if the lexical ordering of the two principles of justice is to withstand scrutiny.

(iv) Rawls readily admits that, even if one accepts what I have depicted as steps (i)–(iii), there is still a further obstacle to be faced before the priority of liberty can be affirmed. This is the objection that the basic liberties and their priority may prove unacceptable unless individuals possess the material means through which to advance their aims.[46] In *A Theory of Justice* Rawls had drawn a distinction between liberty and the worth of liberty. The inability to take advantage of one's rights because of lack of wealth went only to the worth of liberty, 'the value to individuals of the rights that the first principle defines'. A lesser worth of liberty was not, however, held to infringe the equality of liberty, and the lexical priority of the first principle over the second was not affected. Such inequalities were to be remedied only through the difference principle *within* the second principle of justice.[47] This thesis was challenged by Daniels,

43 Rawls, 'Basic Liberties', pp. 25–6. See also *TJ* 206–7.

44 Rawls, 'Basic Liberties', pp. 16, 27–8.

45 See below, ch. 8 sec. 3a (ii).

46 Rawls, 'Basic Liberties', pp. 39–40.

47 *TJ* 204–5; 'Basic Liberties', pp. 40–1.

who argued persuasively that the same types of consideration which would lead those in the original position to stipulate for equal liberty would also lead them to argue for the equal worth of liberty,[48] *and* that the application of the difference principle would not, in any event, necessarily maximize the worth of liberty to those least advantaged in society.[49]

Some response to this critique is vital since the priority of the two principles of justice depends upon a division between liberties (protected by the first principle), and other primary goods (protected by the second). Rawls's response is as follows. The first principle is now held to incorporate a concept of 'fair value' for political liberties.[50] The *worth of political liberties* must be roughly equal to all citizens, irrespective of their social and economic position, in the sense that everyone has 'a fair opportunity to hold public office and to influence the outcome of political decisions'.[51] Those in the original position are taken to understand that the political liberties will be treated in this way when they assign priority to liberty. The idea of fair value for political liberties is incorporated into the first principle because 'it is essential in order to establish just legislation and also to make sure that the fair political process specified by the constitution is open to everyone on a basis of rough equality'.[52] The same idea of fair value is rejected for other liberties because it would be irrational, superfluous, or socially divisive.[53] The cogency of this response by Rawls will be considered in more detail later.

(v) An important thread which runs through the entirety of Rawls's analysis is that the two principles of justice would be chosen in preference to principles derived from utilitarianism or some form of perfectionism.[54] Space precludes any assessment of this reasoning.

d. The Relationship between the Right and the Good

Let us for the present accept the principal tenets of Rawls's thesis. Before proceeding to consider the legal implications of this brand of

[48] N. Daniels, 'Equal Liberty and Unequal Worth of Liberty', in Daniels (ed.), *Reading Rawls*, ch. 11, pp. 263, 268–9.

[49] Ibid. 270–1.

[50] 'Basic Liberties', pp. 41–2. See also *TJ* 224–8, 233–4, 277–9, where the issue of fair value of political liberties is discussed, but not as directly as in the later work.

[51] 'Basic Liberties', p. 42.

[52] Ibid. 45.

[53] Ibid. 44.

[54] e.g. *TJ* 122–4, 161–75, 183–92.

liberalism, we must, however, clarify the relationship between the right and the good a little further. We have already seen that one of the foundations of liberal philosophy is that people have differing determinate conceptions of the good, and that state power should not be used to support one such conception at the expense of another. We have also seen, however, that the right, in the sense of the two principles of justice, is prior to the good. This priority serves to constrain the range of conceptions of the good which can be pursued within society. Citizens cannot pursue literally *any* conception of the good, but only such conceptions which are consonant with the principles of justice which have been chosen.[55] It should be remembered that Rawls is primarily considering justice within an ideal society, in which the principles of justice will be strictly complied with by those therein. The constraint imposed by the right upon differing conceptions of the good can be demonstrated in three ways.

First, the principles of justice are principles which apply to the basic institutions of society. Having been chosen, they then continue to govern the range of choices open to those institutions in the following manner. Rawls posits a four-stage sequence,[56] the first stage of which is the choice of the principles themselves. This is followed by a constitutional convention which will devise a constitution with the object of effectuating the chosen principles. The constitution should enshrine the liberties contained in the first principle of justice.[57] Rawls believes, however, that the second of these principles is unsuited to being enshrined within the constitution, because opinions upon the effect of economic policy differ markedly, and therefore it may often be unclear whether the difference principle is being violated.[58] The constitutional convention is itself followed by legislation, and the legislature does have an obligation to pursue policy which not only safeguards the equal liberties, but also advances the interests of the least advantaged in accord with the difference principle.[59] The final stage concerns administration, adjudication, and the following of rules generally by citizens.

Rawls's four-stage sequence serves, therefore, to restrict the pursuit of differing conceptions of the good. The ideal legislature can

[55] e.g. *TJ* 446–7.
[56] Ibid. 195–201.
[57] Ibid. 197, 199.
[58] *TJ* 199; 'Basic Liberties', pp. 51–2, 54.
[59] *TJ* 199.

only promulgate legislation which is compatible with the two principles of justice.[60] This can impose significant constraints upon legislative action. As Hart has stated, many laws restrict liberties relating to speech, the use of private property, or freedom of movement, not on the grounds that liberty is being restricted for the sake of liberty, but rather because liberty is being restricted to protect against 'harm or loss of amenities or other elements of real utility'.[61] Now it may well be possible to express the justification of, for example, environmental laws in terms of restricting liberty for the sake of liberty. The justification for almost any legislation could be formally expressed in this way, but the plausibility of such explanation quickly becomes strained.[62] The concept of the right as enshrined in the two principles of justice therefore places limitations on the type of legislation which a liberal state can enact. The implications which this can have for legal discourse will be considered more fully below.

Secondly, the right also constrains the good as manifested in the behaviour and choices of individuals. We have seen in the preceding analysis that the principles of justice are those which apply to institutions in the sense of the basic structure of society. These are complemented by principles of natural duty and obligation which apply to individuals.[63] They are regarded as an integral part of the concept of right, and would be chosen by individuals in the original position. There are various natural duties, the most important of which is to 'support and further' just institutions, meaning that we should comply with just institutions, and that we should assist in the establishment of just arrangements which do not exist.[64] This particular natural duty flows from the very existence of a just society, and is not dependent upon voluntary acts by an individual. Obligations, by way of contrast, are dependent upon the voluntary acceptance of a benefit under a just scheme.[65] A person elected to an office would, therefore, be under such an obligation.

The addition of natural duties and obligations to the concept of the right which would be chosen in the original position limits an individual's particular conception of the good in the following manner. While an individual may have specific ideas as to what

[60] Ibid. 198, 357, 563–6.
[61] Hart, 'Rawls on Liberty', p. 245.
[62] Ibid. 245–7.
[63] *TJ* 108–17, 333–50.
[64] Ibid. 333–5.
[65] Ibid. 342–3.

constitutes the value of life for him, he cannot support parties or policies which would be contrary to the two principles of justice. A person may privately believe that those with superior intellect should have special privileges, and that the pursuit of a scholarly life is the highest good attainable. The concept of natural duty entails, however, that the rational citizen should vote for the party which best conforms to the principles of justice, and this would preclude supporting a party committed to granting those with superior intellect unequal liberty, or excessive wealth.[66]

The third and final way in which the right limits the good is rather different from the two which have been outlined above. It cannot, however, be ignored because Rawls devoted much of Part Three of *A Theory of Justice* to this issue. It relates to the way in which justice and goodness can become congruent within a well-ordered society.[67] Once again, only the bare outlines of a complex argument can be presented.

Rawls has already explained to us the derivation and the content of justice. He then proceeds to explore in detail what is entailed by the idea of goodness. This is captured by the idea of rationality: our good is determined 'by a plan of life that we would adopt with full deliberative rationality if the future were accurately foreseen and adequately realized in the imagination'.[68] Now conceptions of the good can of course differ, subject to the constraints on the content of these plans derived from the principles of justice. However, justice is said to generate its own support, in the sense that the moral development of the individual will proceed in such a way that a person will voluntarily or naturally acquire a sense of justice which will govern the development of his own conception of the good.[69] A person's rational plan of life (the good) will support and affirm the sense of justice (the right). Particular conceptions of goodness can still differ, but all such choices are 'framed within definite limits'[70] provided by the right. An individual will not, on the whole, attempt to devise a rational plan of life which will be in contravention of the principles of justice. In a well-ordered society a person would not generally plan his life so as to obtain power over others which is beyond that allowed by the principles of justice. In the words of Rawls:

66 *TJ* 334–5.

67 Ibid. 395, 513–14, 563–7.

68 Ibid. 421.

69 Ibid. 456, 462–91.

70 Ibid. 563; see also pp. 513, 528, 567.

Thus in drawing up our plan of life we do not start *de novo*; we are not required to choose from countless possibilities without given structure or fixed contours. So while there is no algorithm for settling upon our good, no first person procedure of choice, the priority of right and justice securely constrains these deliberations so that they become more manageable.[71]

3. PUBLIC LAW WITHIN IDEAL THEORY

The vision of justice depicted by Rawls is, as we have seen, primarily concerned with ideal theory. The principles of justice are worked out for a society which is 'well ordered', and are acknowledged and applied by both institutions and individuals within that society. The implications which this has for public law within such a society must be considered before any assessment can be made of Rawlsian liberalism within a society which is not ideal in this sense. The nature of these implications will differ as between the first and second principles of justice, which will be considered separately.

a. Equal Liberties

Four main problems arise from the application of the first principle of justice. First, how are conflicts between liberties to be resolved? Secondly, what are the implications to be drawn from the fair value of political liberties? Thirdly, how far does the first principle impose limits on the type of legislation which the ideal legislature can pass? Finally, what role is there for judicial review within such a system?

i. Conflicts between liberties The original formulation of the first principle of justice was framed so as to secure to each person the 'most extensive total system' of liberties which was compatible with a similar system of liberty for all. Rawls has, however, amended this formulation by substituting the phrase 'fully adequate scheme' for 'most extensive total system', hence the wording of the first principle provided above.[72] The alteration was a response by Rawls to criticism from Hart, the latter arguing that the original version of the first principle gave little idea of how conflicts between liberties

[71] Ibid. 563–4.
[72] See above, ch. 8 sec. 2c.

were to be resolved.[73] The reasoning behind Rawls's revised version is as follows.

The real *purpose* behind the grant of liberties is not, in any simple quantitative sense, to maximize anything. These liberties are granted rather to guarantee equally to all citizens 'the social conditions essential for the adequate development' of the citizens' moral powers.[74] Now we have already seen that Rawls has a particular conception of the person, and uses this conception to justify the priority of liberty. The same idea is utilized to resolve conflicts between liberties. Liberties guarantee the adequate development of the citizens' moral powers in the sense of advancing the capacity for a sense of justice, and advancing the capacity for a sense of the good. Thus the equal political liberties and freedom of thought are integral to the capacity for a sense of justice; they secure the 'free and informed application' of the principles of justice.[75] Liberty of conscience and freedom of association help to secure the capacity for a sense of the good; they enable the individual to exercise deliberative rationality and to pursue a conception of the good over his whole life.

This explanation of the purpose behind granting liberties also provides the criterion for assessing *conflicts* between them. Rawls introduces the notion of 'significance'.[76] A liberty is more or less significant depending upon whether it is more or less essentially involved in, or is a more or less necessary institutional means to protect, the full and informed exercise of the preceding moral powers of the individual. Significance is said to serve as the qualitative criterion[77] to resolve such conflicts which can take two forms. On the one hand, a particular liberty can simply conflict with a different liberty; the relative weight to be accorded to the two liberties will be judged by the idea of significance. On the other hand, particular liberties must also be self-limiting.[78] Given that any basic liberty must be the same for all, the grant of a particular liberty to me, for example the right to unimpeded access to public places in pursuance of a right of political speech, would necessitate giving this right to all. The consequences of according such a right to everyone might,

[73] Hart, 'Rawls on Liberty', pp. 239–44.
[74] Rawls, 'Basic Liberties', p. 47.
[75] Ibid. 49.
[76] Ibid. 50.
[77] Ibid. 56 n. 28.
[78] Ibid. 56–7.

however, be so divisive as to reduce the effective scope of freedom of speech. Citizens in the original position would, therefore, accept a more limited and regulated right of political speech, and this would be in accord with the idea of significance given above. It is readily apparent that using this criterion in detailed situations may be contentious. The idea does, however, serve as a standard through which conflicts between liberties can be resolved, and Rawls exemplifies in some detail how the technique can operate.[79] There may, however, be a more fundamental problem with this technique flowing from the conception of the person on which it is based. This will be explored below.[80]

ii. Political liberties and fair value We have already seen why it was essential to Rawls's argument for the lexical priority of the two principles of justice to provide some answer to the argument that those in the original position would choose the equal worth of liberty as readily as they would choose equal liberty itself. If this criticism could not be deflected, then the priority of liberty over other primary goods could not be sustained in its original form. Rawls's response was to accept that political liberties should have their fair value secured within the first principle of justice, but that the same idea should not be extended to the other liberties. This distinction is not said to reflect a belief that the political liberties are the pre-eminent good for individuals; this would be inconsistent with liberalism's neutrality between competing conceptions of the good. The guarantee of fair value finds its place in the first principle, because 'it is essential in order to establish just legislation', and to ensure that the fair political process is open to all on a basis of rough equality. What does this entail?[81]

Certain formal consequences follow. The political liberties will be enshrined within the constitution, including it seems a guarantee of the fair value of those liberties.[82] Legislation should be in accord with the idea of justice, and this would include the dictate of fair value for political liberties. Individuals have a natural duty to support just institutions and this will include a duty to protect the

[79] Ibid. 55–79.
[80] See below, ch. 8 sec. 3a (iii), ch. 9 sec. 3.
[81] Rawls, 'Basic Liberties', p. 45. See also *TJ* 224–5, 227.
[82] Rawls, 'Basic Liberties', pp. 52, 53.

fair value of these liberties, and an office-holder would also be under an obligation to do so. This much follows from the preceding general analysis of justice.

The practical consequences are more difficult to determine. Rawls tells us that political parties should be independent of large concentrations of private economic and social power, and he would support legislation which imposes limits upon campaign contributions and the like.[83] Money must be made available to facilitate free public discussion, and tax revenue should be used to allow parties to be free from private economic interests.[84]

This analysis appears to be problematic in the following way. The discussion of fair value for political liberties is undertaken in the context of ideal theory. This is clear from Rawls's argument both within his original work and in his later writing.[85] Notwithstanding the fact that he is talking of ideal theory, he presents us with two arguments which require fair value for political liberties. One is an instrumental argument: in the absence of fair value, just laws will not be made; those who have greater means will exercise a larger influence over legislation and the pleadings of privileged groups will receive 'excessive attention'.[86] The other argument is dignitarian: when equal political liberty has secured its fair value, it will have a 'profound effect' on the moral quality of civic life.[87]

Let us accept, therefore, that fair value is necessary in order to establish just legislation, and to prevent bias in favour of privileged interests, even within ideal theory. However, if this is the rationale for incorporating fair value within the first principle of justice, it may require far more extensive measures to ensure that this rationale is effectuated than Rawls would appear to countenance. Freeing parties from dependence upon private social and economic interests is not to be achieved simply by the provision of public funding for political parties, nor by limiting campaign contributions. The ability to exert a larger influence over the development of legislation can assume a plethora of more indirect forms, which are related to the general distribution of all primary goods within society. Rawls is, therefore, caught in a dilemma. On the one hand,

[83] Rawls, 'Basic Liberties', 42–3. See also *TJ* 225–6.
[84] Rawls, 'Basic Liberties', pp. 75–8; *TJ* 226.
[85] See *TJ* 221–7; 'Basic Liberties', pp. 41–2, 45.
[86] Rawls, 'Basic Liberties', p. 45; *TJ* 225–6.
[87] Rawls, 'Basic Liberties', p. 45; *TJ* 233.

his very basis for incorporating fair value into the first principle of justice stems from economic and social inequalities which can produce unjust legislation favouring particular classes. On the other hand, the 'remedy' of fair value cannot be defined too widely without indirectly undermining the general division between liberty and other primary goods and thereby upsetting the lexical ordering of the two principles.

iii. The limits of legislation In ideal theory the legislators can pass laws only if they satisfy the two principles of justice and any limits established within the constitution. This criterion can be indeterminate in the sense that it is not always clear precisely which 'of several constitutions, or economic and social arrangements',[88] would be adopted in order to effectuate the principles of justice. Provided, however, that the choice of constitution, and the laws enacted therein, are within the allowed or permitted range, they would satisfy the principles of justice. Thus people may differ over the most appropriate economic arrangements which would effectuate the difference principle and benefit the least advantaged. There may not be only one agreed economic approach which the legislature can pursue. This is relatively uncontroversial. The limits of legislative action do, however, become more problematic.

It is clear that liberty can only be restricted for the sake of liberty. We have already touched upon a problem raised by Hart in this context: much legislation in modern society restricts liberties, not for the sake of other liberties, but for the protection 'from harm or loss of amenities or other elements of real utility'.[89] The ideal legislature cannot enact such legislation; it would not be within the permitted range, and would violate the first principle of justice.

Rawls does not respond to this problem directly. Three arguments which are apposite do, however, emerge from his later work. First, he distinguishes between the restriction and regulation of basic liberties.[90] The priority of liberty is not infringed when liberty is regulated, for example by rules of order in a debate. Secondly, he also accepts that the basic liberties are self-limiting.[91] The consequence of granting a liberty to me is to grant it equally to everyone, and this may have

[88] *TJ* 201; see also pp. 198–9.
[89] Hart, 'Rawls on Liberty', p. 245.
[90] 'Basic Liberties', pp. 9–11.
[91] Ibid. 56–7.

results which are 'socially unworkable or divisive'. This would be the case, for example, with unimpeded access to public places pursuant to a liberty of free speech. Given these consequences, those in the original position would not press the particular liberty to this extent because to do so would reduce its effective scope. Environmental legislation might, for example, be justified by using this reasoning. The right to the exclusive use of property could be 'self-limited' so as to exclude the possibility that this liberty entailed my ability to use such property in ways which would destroy the environment. The general application of a particular liberty would mean that all people were entitled to do so; this would be socially divisive and unworkable and would therefore not be agreed to in the original position. The final way in which Rawls might respond to Hart's objection is to allow such environmental legislation by arguing that it can be justified because some other liberty would be affected by the unrestricted exercise of, for example, your proprietary liberty.

All three of these arguments only meet the original objection at the risk of undermining the priority of the first principle of justice, with its correlative prohibition on trade-offs between liberties and other primary goods. The argument from self-limitation operates to confine the range of a liberty within the first principle of justice by pointing out how the generalization of that liberty should serve to restrict its effective scope. This limitation is achieved by a trade-off between the unimpeded exercise of that liberty, and the disadvantageous consequences which can ensue therefrom to *other* interests, including 'the destruction of forms of social life or amenities which otherwise would have been available to the individual';[92] self-limitation is justified because of the 'unworkable and socially divisive consequences' of not doing so. A trade-off between liberty and other primary goods takes place *within* the first principle, and hence weakens the claim that liberty can only be restricted for the sake of liberty. Nor can this objection be met by arguing that self-limitation only operates to secure the 'central range' of that liberty.[93] This does not deny the existence of the trade-off. Moreover, the precise ambit of the central range may be unclear and contentious to those in the original position, and depend upon differences in temperament.[94]

92 Hart, 'Rawls on Liberty', p. 247.

93 Rawls, 'Basic Liberties', pp. 9–10, 56–7.

94 As Hart states ('Rawls on Liberty', p. 246):

Some persons, given their general temperament, might reasonably prefer to be

The argument that, for example, environmental legislation can be justified by pointing to other liberties which are being affected by the unrestricted exercise of a person's proprietary liberty fares little better. Such reasoning may well be implausible or strained.[95] More importantly this technique carries an analogous danger to that of self-limitation presented above. The first principle is designed to prevent trade-offs between liberties and other primary goods. This will be undermined in substance if any piece of legislation is formally vindicated by 'hunting' for some other liberty which might conceivably be said to be affected by the liberty now being restricted by the statute. If the real object of such legislation is some general social good which necessitates the restriction of liberty, nothing but masquerade is to be attained by pretending that the sanctity of the first principle is still pure and that the liberty has been restricted only for the sake of liberty. What the ideal liberal legislature can actually legislate about, therefore, continues to be problematic.

iv. The role of judicial review The potential role of judicial review within ideal theory is far from clear. Those who frame a constitution for a well-ordered society would certainly establish a judiciary to adjudicate upon disputes arising from legislation. What is far less clear, as Michelman notes,[96] is whether or not such a constitution would accord the power of constitutional review to the judiciary to enable them to enforce constitutional rights against the will of the legislative branch. The principles of justice apply to institutions, and the concepts of natural duty and obligation apply to individuals. Legislators should enact laws which are consistent with both the constitution and the two principles of justice, and in this sense the ideal legislature would appear to render judicial review superfluous. The idea that such review would be unnecessary is further strengthened by the congruence between justice as fairness and goodness as rationality that is expected to emerge in an ideal

free to libel others or to invade their privacy, or to make use of their own property in whatever style they like, and might gladly take the risk of being exposed to these practices on the part of others and to the consequences of such practices for themselves and the general social and physical environment. Other persons would not pay this price for unrestricted liberty in these matters, since, given their temperament, they would value the protections offered by the restrictions higher than the unrestricted liberty.

[95] Ibid. 245.

[96] F. I. Michelman, 'In Pursuit of Constitutional Welfare Rights: One View of Rawls' Theory of Justice', 121 *U. Pa. L. Rev.* 962, 993 (1973).

society.[97] Notwithstanding this reasoning, constitutional review might be justified in the following manner.

The representative citizens who have formulated the two principles of justice now draft a constitution. They will have to decide, *inter alia*, how far the procedure of majority rule should be restricted by the mechanisms of constitutionalism.[98] Such devices can 'limit the scope of majority rule, the kinds of matters on which the majority has final authority, and the speed with which the aims of the majority are put into effect.'[99] Such citizens recognize that the actual political process is one of imperfect procedural justice, meaning that, while there is an independent criterion for the correct outcome, there is no certainty that this result will always be attained.[100] The correct outcome is that the constitution (and the laws made thereunder) should be in accord with the principles of justice, but there is no certainty that this will always be achieved.[101] Any devices which limit majority rule will, therefore, have to be justified upon the basis that legislation which is in accord with justice will be more likely to result if such constitutional limits are present. A decision to introduce such limits would then be justified within the first principle of justice: a less extensive freedom of political participation (flowing from the constitutional constraints on majority rule) would be outweighed by the greater security given to the other liberties. Liberty can be restricted for the sake of liberty. A Bill of Rights with judicial review could be justified in principle on this basis.[102]

The application of such review could none the less be problematic. This can be exemplified by considering its potential role in the three areas considered above: conflicts between liberties, the fair value of political liberties, and the limits on allowable legislative action.

Rawls may well be correct in stating that it is easier to discern a breach of the first, than of the second, principle of justice, but the problems of adjudicating upon a conflict of liberties should not be underestimated. The criterion for resolving such conflicts is, as we have seen, the idea of the significance of liberty, this itself being based upon the concept of the person which Rawls espouses. It is

[97] See above, ch. 8 sec. 2d.

[98] *TJ* 228, 356–62.

[99] Ibid. 228.

[100] Ibid. 85–6.

[101] Ibid. 229.

[102] See also Rawls, 'Basic Liberties', p. 54.

clear that the detailed application of this idea may well be contentious. The relevant question at present is why the courts' view on this matter should be preferred to that of the *ideal* legislature, staffed by representatives imbued with a desire to achieve justice? The answer would presumably be along the following lines. Given that the political process *is* characterized as one of imperfect procedural justice, different people, while agreeing upon the desired goal of prescribing just laws, might disagree as to how best to achieve this in a particular area. The majority view, although honestly held, could, for example, accord too little opportunity for minority groups to express their beliefs when freedom of speech clashes with some other liberty; judicial review, and the opinion of the court on how this conflict should be resolved, would be justified, because legislation which is in accord with justice would be more likely to result if such constitutional limits were present.

The role of judicial review in protecting the fair value of political liberties is problematic for rather different reasons. Rawls's assumptions about legislative behaviour can be viewed from a general and a special perspective, and it is not clear how well they fit together. The general assumption of legislative behaviour in ideal theory is that legislators have an obligation to act in accord with justice, that their own rational conception of the good will incline them in this direction, and that the legislature as an institution will try to make laws which advance the agreed outcome of justice.[103] The special assumption concerning legislative behaviour in ideal theory enters the picture in the discussion of the fair value of political liberties. The most important reason for according fair value to political liberties is in order to ensure that unjust legislation biased towards particular dominant interests does not emerge.[104] Unless fair value is secured the legislators will bend before such concentrations of power. This is the reason why those *in the original position* who are devising the principles of justice will ensure that the priority of liberty is treated in this way.[105] The special assumption concerning legislative behaviour is therefore *causally prior* to the general assumption. It is only when fair value has been secured that we can expect our legislators to behave on the general assumption outlined above.

[103] *TJ* 198–201, 343–4, 356–62.
[104] Rawls, 'Basic Liberties', p. 45; *TJ* 225.
[105] Rawls, 'Basic Liberties', p. 42.

This clearly has significant implications for judicial review, because, *until* fair value has been secured, we cannot be sure that the legislature and the representatives therein will act to advance justice as posited by the general assumption. It follows that we cannot leave it to the legislature to decide whether fair value is presently satisfied or not. The majority may believe that a statute which, for example, limits campaign contributions suffices to ensure fair value. This view may, however, simply reflect the existence of power groupings which support the majority, who wish to do the minimum possible to undermine their own privileged position. There would have to be a court which would assess claims from a minority that the campaign contributions statute had an abundance of loopholes. Such a court would, moreover, have to be willing to operate in a more positive fashion. It would have to judge whether to order that public monies be provided for the assistance of political parties on the grounds that this was integral to fair value, and was being refused by the current majority.

The role of the court in assessing the boundaries of permitted legislative action is more questionable. It is fundamental to ideal theory that the legislators act in accordance with both the constitution and the two principles of justice on which the constitution itself is based. One of the central features of this arrangement, perhaps the central feature, is the priority of the first principle over the second, and the prohibition on trade-offs between liberties and other primary goods. The courts might, therefore, be expected to police the boundaries of allowable legislative action, and to strike down legislation which is based upon such prohibited trade-offs. This view is strengthened by the fact that Rawls believes that the first principle of justice would be enshrined within the constitution, but that the second would not.[106] Constitutional review could, therefore, exist to protect the rights listed in the constitution, and to prevent their limitation by 'policy'-based arguments derived from, for example, the general welfare.

This conclusion is, however, only sustainable if one incorporates a modified version of the argument used in the context of conflicts between liberties. It is important to remember that we are operating within ideal theory, and we may also presume that the 'general assumption' concerning legislative behaviour holds. This means that the legislature as an institution wishes to act in accord with

[106] 'Basic Liberties', pp. 51, 53; *TJ* 198–9.

justice, that the legislators therein have an obligation to do so, and that their own conceptions of the good incline them in this direction. They do not wish to pass legislation which would contravene the lexical priority of the principles of justice. Given these assumptions, the question would be whether the court was in a better position to determine whether a liberty had been sacrificed for some other primary good than the legislature itself. The very determination of whether liberty is being sacrificed in this way can, as we have seen, be difficult. A modification of the argument stemming from imperfect procedural justice would, therefore, be required in order to complete the justification for constitutional review. Applied in this context the reasoning would be as follows. Given that the political process is one of imperfect procedural justice, different people, while agreeing upon the desired goal of prescribing just laws, might disagree as to how best to achieve this in a particular area. Their chosen statute might not always succeed, in the sense that it might not always be in accord with justice; the majority might honestly believe that they are only limiting liberty for the sake of liberty, but in reality the main effect of the proposed law would be, for example, to restrict speech rights for the sake of the general welfare in a way which falls particularly onerously on minorities; constitutional review should, therefore, exist, because the detached view of the courts concerning the allowable limits to legislative action is more likely to be accurate. There is a greater likelihood that its opinion will be successful in determining whether a particular statute really is in accord with the constitution and the two principles of justice. Some such reasoning must be accepted if judicial review is to have a role within this area.

b. Fair Equality of Opportunity and the Difference Principle

Four main areas require discussion if we are to understand the role of public law within ideal theory as it applies to the second principle of justice. First, the conceptual basis of fair equality of opportunity and the difference principle must be explored, if we are to evaluate the potential legal consequences which flow from these ideas. Secondly, the institutional foundation of the second principle of justice will be analysed. Thirdly, the legal implications flowing from the second principle of justice will be examined. Finally, the role of the courts in this area will be considered.

i. The conceptual basis of the second principle We have already seen the way in which a certain conception of the person is of central importance to the priority of the first principle of justice, and to the resolution of conflicts between liberties. A particular conception of the person also provides the conceptual basis for the second principle of justice, and it is important to understand this before proceeding further.

Rawls acknowledges that the second principle could be interpreted in diverse ways. One interpretation is termed natural liberty. This states that 'a basic structure satisfying the principle of efficiency and in which positions are open to those able and willing to strive for them will lead to a just distribution'.[107] This interpretation is rejected because it allows distributive shares to be determined by factors 'so arbitrary from a moral point of view'.[108] These factors are social position and natural talents. An individual does not deserve any advantages which flow from such factors, and it is, therefore, unsatisfactory to base a distributive system upon such chance contingencies.

A second interpretation, which Rawls terms liberal equality, is also rejected. This conception of equality takes the distribution of natural talents as given, and then seeks to ensure that those who have the same level of talents 'should have the same prospects of success regardless of their initial place in the social system'.[109] Liberal equality is, therefore, different from a system of natural liberty, because under the former system there is an attempt to counter the effect of social position upon the ability to develop one's natural talents. Rawls none the less rejects this interpretation, because there 'is no more reason to permit the distribution of income and wealth to be settled by the distribution of natural assets than by historical and social fortune'.[110]

Rawls's preferred interpretation is termed democratic equality. On this view natural talent and social fortune are both regarded as morally arbitrary. The natural distribution of talent and wealth is neither just nor unjust *per se*. What is unjust is 'the way that institutions deal with these facts'.[111] Given that 'no one deserves his place in the distribution of native endowments, any more than one deserves one's initial starting place in society',[112] the object of the

[107] *TJ* 66.
[108] Ibid. 72.
[109] Ibid. 73.
[110] Ibid. 74.
[111] Ibid. 102.
[112] Ibid. 104.

difference principle is to treat such natural talents as a 'common asset and to share in the benefits of this distribution whatever it turns out to be'.[113] Thus those who do have the good fortune to have considerable natural talent are only allowed to benefit thereby if the position of the least advantaged is improved.[114]

The objective of interpreting fair equality of opportunity in this way, and combining it with the difference principle, is to allow the idea of pure procedural justice to operate within the second principle of justice. This conception of procedural justice obtains when there is no independent criterion for the right result, but rather a fair procedure such that the outcome is correct, whatever it is, provided that the appropriate procedure has been properly followed.[115] However, this form of procedural justice can only operate if the basic structure of society, including a just arrangement of social and economic institutions, exists.[116] An integral part of such a just structure is not to allow distribution to be based upon morally arbitrary criteria. Once such a just framework has been established, pure procedural justice can operate. It is no longer necessary to engage in complex and endless calculations about the particular benefits held by particular individuals.[117]

The connection between the conception of the person employed by Rawls to underpin the priority of liberty, and that used as a foundation for the second principle, will be explored more fully below.[118] For the present it is important to note that the latter aspect has provoked particular controversy. The individual and his attributes are regarded as separate. This is the consequence of treating both natural talents and social position as morally arbitrary and undeserved. It is this assumption which is said to justify treating such natural talents as common assets which others can share.

ii. The institutional basis of the second principle The conception of the person adumbrated above provides the conceptual foundation for the second principle. The social system must, however, be justly organized before this principle can operate as one of pure procedural justice. A brief outline of this institutional structure can be given.

A constitution exists which protects the liberties considered in the preceding sections and the legislature aims to enact just legislation.

[113] Ibid. 101.
[114] Ibid. 101–2; see also p. 75.
[115] Ibid. 86.
[116] Ibid. 87.
[117] Ibid. 87–8.
[118] See ch. 9 sec. 3.

Fair equality of opportunity demands that the government attempts to ensure equal chances for those similarly endowed, either by subsidizing private schools or by a public school system. Equality of economic opportunity is advanced by policing the conduct of firms and through competition policy designed to break down barriers to entry and the like. The government provides a social minimum, either by family allowances, unemployment benefits, etc., or by a graded income supplement.

Four branches of government perform different roles in attaining this overall plan.[119] These do not correspond to established divisions within government, and each branch may consist of more than one agency. Thus the 'allocation branch' regulates market power and ensures that the market system works efficiently, and the 'stabilization branch' helps to maintain reasonably full employment. The social minimum is the responsibility of the 'transfer branch', and the 'distribution branch' is to preserve an approximate justice in distributive shares through taxation and adjustments in property rights. The possible legal implications of the work performed by these branches of government will now be considered.

iii. The legal implications of the second principle The legal implications which flow from the second principle of justice can best be addressed by considering the work of the differing branches of government set out above. The extent to which the law will play a role will differ depending upon the functions to be performed by these differing branches.

Thus it seems relatively clear that the operation of the allocation branch will require agencies concerned with competition policy/antitrust in order to prevent the formation of unreasonable market power and barriers to entry. The courts would presumably play an adjudicative role in this area, either by way of original jurisdiction or through the exercise of a supervisory role over the operation of more specialized agencies which have been given the initial responsibility for enforcing such policy.

The distribution branch has, as we have seen, the task of preserving justice in distributive shares by means of taxation and adjustments in property rights. Inheritance rights are to be limited in order that inequalities of wealth do not exceed a certain limit and thereby jeopardize the fair value of political liberties and fair

[119] *TJ* 276–7.

equality of opportunity. The law and the ordinary courts would be the most obvious arbiters should any dispute arise in this context.

The legal implictions which flow from the work of the transfer branch are more debatable, and it is unclear how far welfare rights would be generated. The transfer branch is to ensure that each person receives a 'social minimum'. This claim could be satisfied by the legislative creation of welfare rights concerning minimum levels of service to meet needs such as subsistence and health, but it would also be satisfied by general monetary transfer schemes such as a negative income tax.[120] Michelman's conclusion is that it is difficult to derive welfare rights from the difference principle itself, because, although that principle would imply a right to the disadvantaged, it would appear to be a less justiciable income right, rather than a more justiciable set of welfare rights.[121] He is, however, more optimistic about deriving such rights from the idea of fair equality of opportunity. Rawls considers that the opportunity principle implies equal educational opportunity for those similarly endowed and motivated. However, as Michelman points out, it is difficult to see how educational opportunities could effectuate the fair equality idea without attention being given to subsistence or health.[122] This argument for the existence of welfare rights is then complemented by the general role which self-respect plays in Rawls's thesis. As Michelman notes, self-respect is, in one sense, the pre-eminent social good, and the fundamental objective of both principles of justice. If welfare rights can be shown to be integral to self-respect in any sense additional to those in which the two principles of justice imply such rights, then 'justice as fairness implies them in this additional sense as well'.[123]

iv. The role of judicial review The role of the courts in applying the second principle of justice has already been touched on in the preceding section. There is little doubt that the courts would have a part to play as a forum for determining the application of rules on antitrust or on the use of property implied by the limits placed on the ability to bequeath such goods. The potential role of the courts as an organ of constitutional review which can strike down

[120] Ibid. 275; Michelman, 'In Pursuit of Constitutional Welfare Rights', p. 976.
[121] Michelman, 'In Pursuit of Constitutional Welfare Rights', pp. 966, 976.
[122] Ibid. 989. See also *TJ* 275.
[123] Michelman, 'In Pursuit of Constitutional Welfare Rights', p. 990.

legislative action is, however, as problematic in this context as it is in the context of the first principle of justice. Two examples will illustrate the nature of these problems.

First, let us assume that welfare rights can be derived from the principles of justice. The justification for constitutional review to protect such rights, with the attendant invalidation of legislation which violates them, is still fraught with difficulty.[124] The root of the problem is the same as that encountered in our previous discussion of judicial review. In ideal theory we assume a legislature which aims to pass just legislation, and legislators who have an obligation to do so, and whose own sense of the good inclines them in this direction. Given these assumptions, and given the fact that precisely which social and economic policies will best effectuate the second principle will be controversial, why should the opinion of the reviewing court be preferred to that of the legislature?[125] The very difficulty of determining which social and economic policies best advance the second principle inclined Rawls to the view that this principle should not be enshrined in the constitution at all, but should serve rather as a guide to the legislature when passing statutes.[126] Any justification for such constitutional review would therefore once again have to be found by utilizing the argument from imperfect procedural justice, suitably modified, to this context. There is little doubt that such an argument could be formally set up, but how convincing it would be in substance is less clear.

Secondly, the interrelationship between the first and the second principles of justice means, however, that the possibility of constitutional review cannot be excluded in this area. The problem can be presented as follows. The priority of liberty can only be restricted for the sake of liberty; trade-offs between liberty and other primary goods are precluded. The difficulty which this produces concerning the subject-matter which the legislature can legislate about has been discussed above. This same difficulty can arise from the legislative application of the second principle. The legislature within ideal theory will pass laws designed to effectuate fair equality of opportunity and the difference principle. In doing so it cannot sacrifice or trade-off liberties embraced within the first principle against other primary goods. However, it may be contentious

[124] Michelman, 'In Pursuit of Constitutional Welfare Rights', pp. 993–7.
[125] Ibid. 995–6.
[126] *TJ* 199; 'Basic Liberties', p. 53.

whether a particular legislative policy designed to effectuate the second principle does infringe an individual right.

A clear example of this conundrum can be found in the discussion concerning the legitimacy of affirmative action programmes as they affect entrants to, for example, universities. Such a policy might be defended upon the basis that it is an aspect of ensuring fair equality of eductional opportunity within the second principle, or upon more general social utilitarian grounds that increasing the presence of minorities in professions for which university education is a prerequisite will reduce the degree to which a society is racially conscious. However, such a policy could not be sustained, irrespective of the beneficial effects on social welfare, if individual rights were violated. It therefore becomes of crucial importance to determine whether such a violation has occurred. The arguments of those who deny that any such infringement has taken place are complex, and cannot be fully considered here.[127] The foundation of such claims appears, however, to rest ultimately upon the conception of the person adumbrated above.[128] It is integral to this conception that attributes of natural talent and advantages secured from social position are morally arbitrary. The possession of such attributes is not 'deserved', and undeserved inequalities call for redress.[129] Thus having the attribute of intelligence does not mean that one 'deserves' to be admitted to university because this ability is just a matter of good fortune; and no one is entitled to claim that universities reward any particular kinds of qualifications.[130] There is no antecedent right to be judged by a particular criterion. Individual rights are not therefore infringed, and the affirmative action policy can proceed.

Whether one agrees with this reasoning or not is incidental for the purposes of the present argument. What the debate shows is that the question whether a trade-off has taken place between individual rights and other primary goods can arise in important contexts pursuant to legislative (or other) action designed to effectuate the second principle, and that the answer will often depend upon a fundamental hypothesis as to the nature of the person.

The implications that this type of problem has for constitutional review must still be reasoned through. We are operating within ideal

[127] See, e.g., R.Dworkin, *Taking Rights Seriously* (1977), ch. 9.

[128] Sandel, *Liberalism and the Limits of Justice*, pp. 135–47.

[129] *TJ* 100, 103.

[130] Sandel, *Liberalism and the Limits of Justice*, p. 137, from which this discussion in the text has drawn heavily.

theory. Whether constitutional review should exist in this context must depend once again on a further stage of reasoning derived from the idea of imperfect procedural justice which characterizes the political process. Such reasoning would be analogous to that deployed in the context of the boundaries of permitted legislative action set out above, to which reference should be made.[131] Unless some such reasoning is sustainable, the courts should not be the arbiters of the type of problems being addressed here.

4. PUBLIC LAW WITHIN NON-IDEAL THEORY

The discussion thus far has been concerned with ideal theory, and the public law implications which should follow from such a model. The meaning of non-ideal theory, and the role of public law within this model must now be considered. The greater part of Rawls's book is devoted to the ideal model, and relatively little is said about non-ideal theory. It is however apparent that the realization of the ideal theory may be impeded in various ways, or to put the same point in a different way, society may be non-ideal for differing reasons.

a. *The Degree of Economic Development*

It will be remembered that Rawls's two principles of justice, and their lexical ordering, represent a special conception of justice. This is developed from a more general conception, which states that all social primary goods, including liberty and opportunity, income and wealth, and the bases of self-respect, are to be distributed equally unless an unequal distribution of any or all of these goods is to the advantage of the least favoured.[132] The general conception may well obtain in non-ideal theory, and thus trade-offs between liberties and other primary goods would be allowed. The essential reason for this is that, until 'the basic wants of individuals can be fulfilled, the relative urgency of their interest in liberty cannot be firmly decided in advance'.[133] A fairly primitive stage of economic development may well therefore render the model non-ideal in the sense that the

[131] See ch. 8 sec. 3a(iv).
[132] *TJ* 303.
[133] Ibid. 543.

full lexical ordering of the two principles of justice cannot be established. If a society is at this stage, then a denial of equal liberties can be accepted 'if it is necessary to enhance the quality of civilization so that in due course the equal freedoms can be enjoyed by all'.[134] Certain political liberties and the rights of fair equality of opportunity may be forgone when the longer-term benefits suffice to turn a 'less fortunate society into one where equal liberties can be enjoyed'.[135]

Rawls's original argument, which sought to explain the emergence of the two principles of justice, and the priority of liberties, was based upon the hypothesis that, once a reasonable standard of economic well-being was established, individuals would not exchange a lesser liberty for a further improvement in their economic status. It followed that the lexical ordering of the two principles of justice was 'the long run tendency of the general conception pursued under reasonably favourable conditions'.[136] Rawls has, as we have seen, now significantly modified his explanation for the priority of liberty. This shift in position does not, however, affect the point which is in issue here. A society may be non-ideal because the stage of its economic development renders the effective establishment of liberties impossible. In such circumstances trade-offs between primary goods and some liberties may be possible.

b. Departures from Justice

Injustice can arise in one of two ways.[137] On the one hand, legislation or administration may depart in a particular instance from standards that are basically just. On the other hand, the administration of the state may indeed conform to society's conception of justice, but this very conception may itself be unreasonable, having been imposed by the dominant class. The dividing-line between the two may well become blurred. The position of the citizen confronted with such situations would appear to be as follows.

First, the fact that a particular law is unjust does not remove the individual's duty of compliance with such a law, at least where the general society is in a situation of near justice.[138] The reason resides in the concept of imperfect procedural justice, which is characterized

[134] Ibid. 542.
[135] Ibid. 247.
[136] Ibid. 542.
[137] Ibid. 352.
[138] Ibid. 353–4.

by the existence of an independent criterion which will determine the correct outcome, but where there is no absolutely certain way of attaining this end. Majorities will sometimes make mistakes, even if they are zealously attempting to implement the principles of justice. The natural duty incumbent upon each citizen to uphold just institutions therefore binds them to comply with unjust laws, or not to oppose them by illegal means, 'provided that they do not exceed certain limits of injustice'.[139]

Secondly, the preceding duty of compliance is problematic in situations which approximate more closely to the second instance of injustice adumbrated above, as in the case of groups which are permanent minorities, who have suffered from injustice for many years. The duty to comply with unjust laws is required 'only to the extent necessary to share equitably in the inevitable imperfections of a constitutional system'.[140]

Thirdly, the citizen who is a victim of an unjust law may well express his grievance through an act of civil disobedience. For Rawls (and for Dworkin), such action is taken by those who may well accept the fundamental foundations of the society and acknowledge its legitimacy.[141] Civil disobedience is a mode of addressing the community's sense of justice; the individual seeks to persuade the community that its very idea of justice is being transgressed in this instance. Such action assumes the form of a 'public, non-violent conscientious yet political act contrary to law',[142] the object of which is to bring about a change in government policy. An individual should only have recourse to such disobedience on matters of real importance, where the infringements of the principles of justice are substantial and readily apparent, as exemplified by the denial of the vote to certain sections of society, or the repression of particular religious groups.[143] Potential infractions of the difference principle should not, by way of contrast, furnish the basis for civil disobedience, since there are widely divergent economic theories as to how this principle can best be effectuated.[144] For Rawls the constitutional theory of civil disobedience is based upon a conception of justice.

[139] *TJ* 355.
[140] Ibid.
[141] *TJ* 363. Dworkin, *A Matter of Principle*, p. 105.
[142] *TJ* 364.
[143] Ibid. 364.
[144] Ibid. 372–3. See also Dworkin, *A Matter of Principle*, p. 112.

By engaging in civil disobedience one intends, then, to address the sense of justice of the majority and to serve fair notice that in one's sincere and considered opinion the conditions of free co-operation are being violated. We are appealing to others to reconsider, to put themselves in our position, and to recognize that they cannot expect us to acquiesce indefinitely in the terms they impose upon us.[145]

c. The Role of the Courts

Two related, but distinctive, questions must be addressed concerning the role of the courts in non-ideal theory, one of which is specific, the other more general. The more specific question concerns the judicial response to cases of civil disobedience. The more general issue relates to the role of constitutional review in situations where enacted law does not conform to that which would emerge under ideal theory.

i. Civil disobedience and the law Rawls devotes little space to this specific question. He does, however, remark that the courts should take account of the civilly disobedient nature of the individual's act, and of the fact that it appears justifiable by the principles underlying the constitution; in such cases the legal sanction should be 'suspended or reduced'.[146]

Similar themes are developed by Dworkin, who, in effect, pursues two lines of thought.[147] On the one hand, a court might decide that what appeared to be a violation of the law was in fact sanctioned by the constitution itself. On the other hand, the fact that the conduct impugned was of a civilly disobedient character could be a legitimate factor to take into account when deciding upon the exercise of prosecutorial discretion, and in determining the appropriate severity of punishment.

ii. Constitutional review and non-ideal theory The role of the courts and of constitutional review within non-ideal theory raises complex issues which relate to both principles of justice. These are best addressed separately.

The liberties protected by the first principle are enshrined in the constitution itself. However, as we have already seen, this does not

[145] *TJ* 382.
[146] Ibid. 387.
[147] *A Matter of Principle*, pp. 113–17. See also *Taking Rights Seriously*, ch. 8.

automatically entail the existence of constitutional review within *ideal theory*.[148] Three main problems can occur within the first principle: clashes between liberties, ensuring the fair value of political liberty, and determining the limits of allowable legislative action in order to ensure that trade-offs between the first and second principle do not occur. In none of these areas is constitutional review necessarily warranted, although arguments for its existence can be conjectured in all such areas, particularly the second.

The potential role of such review within *non-ideal theory* requires separate treatment precisely because the assumptions of the reasoning from ideal theory may now have been removed. The primary assumption of *ideal theory* was that the legislature would attempt to effectuate the principles of justice, and that the members thereof would be under an obligation to do so. How far this assumption still holds depends upon the nature of the deviation from the ideal. It was noted earlier that a society could depart from the ideal in two ways: a particular piece of legislation could be said to depart from a system that was basically just; or legislation might conform to a society's conception of justice, but that conception might itself be unreasonable, having been imposed by a dominant class.

The potential role for the judiciary may differ depending upon which type of deviation is in issue. If the alleged departure from the ideal is of the former kind, then a role for the judiciary will still entail many of the same problems considered above.[149] Thus if an individual alleges that a clash between two liberties has been improperly resolved by the legislature, the legitimacy of any constitutional review will turn upon the arguments addressed earlier. Given that the legislative process is characterized as one of imperfect procedural justice, it would have to be argued that the opinion of the court as to how this clash should be resolved was justified because just legislation was more likely to result if such constitutional limits were present.

The potential for constitutional review is, however, likely to be greater where the alleged departure from the ideal is of the latter kind. Rawls tells us that in such instances the course of action to be followed depends largely upon how reasonable the accepted doctrine is, and 'what means are available to change it'.[150] If society is

[148] See above, ch. 8 sec. 3a(iv).
[149] See above, ch. 8 sec. 3a(iv).
[150] *TJ* 352–3.

regulated by principles which favour narrow class interests, one may have to oppose 'the prevailing conception and the institutions it justifies in such ways as promise some success'. This could well include constitutional review, particularly given that the crucial assumption underlying ideal theory (that the legislature is attempting to effectuate the principles of justice) no longer holds. At the very least it would strengthen the argument that the court should exercise review to ensure the fair value of political liberty, and to monitor the limits of allowable legislative action. Without such oversight the prominent class interest represented in the legislature could, for example, attempt to limit certain liberties in order further to augment the value of other primary goods which they possess.

The potential role for constitutional review within non-ideal theory so far as it affects the second principle of justice is more difficult. The previous discussion of ideal theory revealed the problems of deriving justiciable welfare rights from Rawls's second principle, and the related but distinct problem of whether constitutional review to protect any such rights should be recognized.[151] The question which is now apposite is the extent to which a stronger claim for any such welfare rights might be made when society departs from the ideal? We have already seen that departure from the lexical priority of the two principles is permitted in circumstances where the society is still at a relatively low level of economic development. The potential role of welfare rights where it is society's sense of justice which is underdeveloped, rather than its economic capacity, is more uncertain.

Michelman is ambivalent on this issue.[152] On the one hand, he is doubtful whether review to vindicate welfare rights which are not strictly associated with basic liberties would be countenanced even in non-ideal theory. To engage in such review would contradict the priority of liberty. Provided that the basic liberties and their effective enjoyment have been given to all, 'justice as fairness might well insist that all other claims gain recognition in the participatory forum'. On the other hand, welfare rights can promote self-respect, even where basic needs have been fulfilled, and self-respect is an ultimate goal underlying both principles of justice. Thus 'in order to secure the enforcement of certain rights, all looking ultimately to self-respect, the framers might be prepared to sacrifice some of their

[151] See above, ch. 8 secs. 3b(iii), (iv).

[152] Michelman, 'In Pursuit of Constitutional Welfare Rights', pp. 1000–2.

rights of equal political liberty by authorizing politically aloof courts to override the popular legislative will'.[153]

A different argument for the existence of welfare rights within non-ideal theory might assume the following form. First, it is important to remember that the division of liberties and other primary goods are related, in both the general and the special conception of justice. The general conception of justice posits an equal distribution of all primary goods unless an unequal distribution of any or all of these goods is to the advantage of the least favoured. The special conception sees the introduction of the two principles of justice with the lexical priority operating between them. It is clear, even under the special conception of justice, that the two principles are integrally related. They 'hang together' in the sense that those in the original position choose them as a package. We have already seen the difficulties of justifying the priority of the first principle over the second, and there is no need to rehearse them again here.[154] A related aspect of this argument is, however, of relevance. Even if one accepts Rawls's arguments for the priority of liberty over other primary goods, those in the original position will only agree to the 'package' if protection is afforded to these other primary goods. The representative individual in the original position does not know his economic status, and will therefore want the safeguards provided by the second principle.

Secondly, we have already seen that the first principle is enshrined in the constitution, while the second serves to guide the action of the legislature. Let us assume that there has been an alleged departure from justice, in one of the two senses posited above. We are, therefore, in the realms of non-ideal theory, in which, for example, a dominant class exercises considerable control over the legislative process and enacts legislation which contravenes the second principle. This may of course be difficult to prove, but let us presume that the underdeveloped sense of justice is at least arguably manifesting itself in this fashion. The following reasoning would seem plausible in such a situation. The constitution itself only protects the first principle of justice, while the second principle is to guide legislative action. However, the underlying theory which informs the constitution and the legislative process is the special conception of justice within which the two principles are integrally

153 Michelman, 'In Pursuit of Constitutional Welfare Rights', pp. 1001.

154 See above, ch. 8 sec. 2c.

related in the above fashion. It would be contrary to this underlying theory to allow those who have a 'defective' sense of justice to contravene the second principle. They cannot be allowed to pursue economic policies which do not benefit the least advantaged. Constitutional review might then be seen as a corrective, albeit partial, to this malaise. Welfare rights could be viewed as a mechanism, more justiciable than minimum income rights, for ensuring that this 'deep theory' of the constitution was properly effectuated. This argument could be further buttressed by drawing upon the discussion of the fair value of political liberties. We have already seen that Rawls admits the necessity of safeguarding the worth of political liberties.[155] To protect such liberties effectively could, however, well require more controls than he appears willing to accept. Realistic provision to ensure the worth of political liberty may itself require some welfare rights. These would be necessary in order that the political liberties themselves could be exercised, *and* in order to break the grip upon the legislature exercised by a dominant grouping which is the very cause of the defective sense of justice.

[155] See above, ch. 8 sec. 3a (ii).

9
LIBERALISM: THE RIGHT, THE GOOD, AND THE SCOPE OF PUBLIC LAW (II)

1. INTRODUCTION

Liberalism has come under considerable fire in recent years. The attacks differ in degree, and the content of such critical appraisal varies from writer to writer.[1] This chapter does not aim to furnish any complete guide to all such critiques, whether derived from philosophy or anthropology. Limits of personal competence as well as space preclude any such undertaking. The objective is more modest. It is to focus upon the principal criticisms of liberalism, and to evaluate their relevance to, and usage by, public lawyers.

An important starting-point is to realize that the challenge to liberalism is in fact a series of distinctive, albeit related, attacks. These must be distinguished and separately evaluated. Lawyers are fond of firing general broadsides at liberalism; painting, or perhaps caricaturing, with a broad brush is prevalent. More detailed scrutiny is, however, required in order to assess the veracity of these arguments. The preceding analysis of Rawls's theory will be drawn upon during the course of the discussion which follows.

2. THE RADICAL CRITIQUE: INDETERMINACY AND INCONSISTENCY

A prominent criticism of liberalism may be termed the 'radical critique'. Attention is focused upon the inconsistency and indeterminacy of legal result which is said to follow from tensions within

[1] See generally, e.g., R. M. Unger, *Knowledge and Politics* (1975); M. J. Sandel, *Liberalism and the Limits of Justice* (1982); R. Bernstein, *Beyond Objectivism and Relativism: Science, Hermeneutics, and Praxis* (1983); M. J. Sandel (ed.), *Liberalism and its Critics* (1984); B. Barber, *Strong Democracy: Participatory Politics for a New Age* (1984); A. MacIntyre, *After Virtue* (2nd edn., 1984), and *Whose Justice? Which Rationality?* (1988); R. N. Bellah, R. Madsen, W. M. Sullivan, A. Swidler, and S. M. Tipton, *Habits of the Heart* (1985).

liberal theory itself. Those who adopt this approach may well also dislike the substantive content of the legal rules which are said to flow from liberal doctrine. The indeterminacy and inconsistency of outcome is, however, viewed as an argument in its own right to be levelled against liberal theory. This type of criticism will be addressed from a somewhat different perspective in a later chapter.[2] Attention must, however, be focused upon it here, since it occupies an important place in the general critique of liberalism. It is hoped, therefore, that readers will tolerate some overlap in the two discussions. The work of Tushnet and Frug exemplifies this type of critique of constitutional and administrative law respectively.

Thus Tushnet argues that constitutional theory has been characterized by an effort to reconcile three central propositions about law and society: the justification principle, the restraint principle, and the principle of value-free adjudication.[3] The first principle asserts that occasions exist when judicial review is justified to displace legislative decisions; the second affirms that judges must however accept restrictions on their behaviour; the third states that objective values are not available as criteria for ordering social institutions, in the sense that there is no consensus on such values, irrespective of whether it is possible to discover philosophically valid principles of justice. No constitutional theory satisfactorily reconciles these principles, and the resulting incoherence is said to be reflective of tensions internal to liberalism itself.[4] The first two principles are said to be responses to what Unger has termed the principle of arbitrary desire, whereby every person is driven to satisfy desires for which no criteria of evaluation exist.[5] These principles reflect the need to avoid 'the tyranny that can result when someone motivated by arbitrary desire occupies a position of power'.[6] Thus judicial review exists to prevent majority tyranny, and judicial constraint is needed to preclude judicial tyranny. Liberalism does not, however, provide a means to obtain this result. The rule of law may seem to be

[2] See below, ch. 11 secs. 4a, b.

[3] M. V. Tushnet, 'Darkness on the Edge of Town: The Contributions of John Hart Ely to Constitutional Theory', 89 *Yale L.J.* 1037, 1038 (1980).

[4] Ibid. 1057. See also M. V. Tushnet, *Red, White and Blue: A Critical Analysis of Constitutional Law* (1988).

[5] *Knowledge and Politics* (1973), pp. 42–6; for Unger's more general argument concerning the incompatibility of reason and desire, see pp. 49–55.

[6] Tushnet, 'Darkness on the Edge of Town', p. 1061.

a candidate. However, either it is defined in formal, neutral terms and remains empty; or it is given substantive content which subjects it to a particular political view which contradicts the principle of value-free adjudication.

Frug's attack is equally strident.[7] He argues that all attempts to justify bureaucratic power turn upon a particular combination of subjective and objective factors, the precise mixture of which cannot be justified. All such attempts have undertaken two tasks. On the one hand, they have attempted to show that such power is constricted by some form of objectivity, some species of shared values. On the other hand, they have tried to demonstrate that bureaucracy does not stifle self-expression, that it does not negate the subjective values of individuality. Each of these terms is in reality a 'dangerous supplement' to the other, which constantly threatens to encroach on the other's preserve. They cannot be separated, and any such separation, or mixture of the two, simply reflects the preferences of a particular commentator. For example those who seek to legitimize public bureaucracies through the idea of interest representation have to ensure that all relevant subjective interests are included in the decision-making process, since otherwise it would be illegitimate, while at the same time coping with the problem of objectivity, in the sense of ensuring that the results of the interest-group representation do not exceed the boundaries laid down by the legislature.[8]

The tensions within liberalism which generate this problem are indeed recognized by Rawls to exist even in a well-ordered society.[9] This, together with the philosophical centrality of the division between subject and object in liberal thought, will be evaluated more fully in the ensuing discussion.[10]

The strength of this type of criticism of liberalism can, however, only be evaluated if we have some more fully developed idea of the structure of a political theory. When these structural features are revealed, the force of the preceding criticism diminishes.

One can begin by drawing upon the important distinction drawn by Dworkin between constitutive and derivative political positions.[11]

[7] G. E. Frug, 'The Ideology of Bureaucracy in American Law', 97 *Harv. L. Rev.* 1276 (1984).

[8] Ibid. 1301.

[9] J. Rawls, *A Theory of Justice* (Oxford, 1973,) 228–30, 240–1, 497–8 (hereafter cited as *TJ*).

[10] See below, ch. 9 secs. 3, 4.

[11] R. Dworkin, *A Matter of Principle* (1985), 185, 408 n. 1.

A constitutive position is a political position valued for its own sake such 'that any failure fully to secure that position, or any decline in the degree to which it is secured, is *pro tanto* a loss in the overall political arrangement'. A particular theory may be comprised of a number of constitutive positions, none of which is absolute; such positions may well clash *inter se*. A derivative position is then a strategy for achieving the constitutive goals. Thus a theory might hold free enterprise to be valued, not in itself, but as a mechanism for attaining a constitutive position of efficiency. Two important points follow from this dichotomy, one of which is obvious, the other less so but ultimately more important.

On the one hand, disagreement as to the best way to effectuate the constitutive goals will be endemic in *any* political theory. The strategies, or derivative positions, which can best attain the central objectives of utilitarianism, republicanism, or liberalism will always be a matter of contention and debate. A constitutive position which comprises the core of a political theory will not inexorably dictate one particular derivative strategy by which it can be achieved, although it might well rule out certain options. In this sense the type of indeterminacy which Tushnet and Frug describe can be expected. Moreover, similar contention would surround the concrete strategies for effectuating constitutive goals, even if some species of, for example, participatory democracy were to be substituted for liberal theory.[12]

On the other hand, the precise derivative strategies which actually emerge or are advocated will in fact reflect competing tensions or dispositions within the constitutive objectives. This requires explanation. We have already seen that there may be a number of constitutive positions which comprise a political theory, and that these will have to be balanced when determining more concrete derivative strategies. What is less immediately apparent is that *each* such abstract constitutive position may itself be the product of certain competing dispositions, and that the more particular rules which emerge will depend upon the blending of these dispositions.

Thus Barber identifies three dispositions which operate within liberalism, the anarchist, the realist, and the minimalist.[13] The anarchist disposition views the person as an autonomous being living in a condition of natural freedom. This very freedom

[12] See below, ch. 11 secs. 4c, d for a more detailed demonstration of this.
[13] *Strong Democracy*, pp. 6–20.

possessed by all runs the danger of being self-destructive. The realist disposition posits the creation of the sovereign to forestall any such 'battle' between individuals. This, however, serves to substitute one threat to liberty for another. The dangers of intemperate state power must be checked. This tension between the anarchist and realist dispositions within liberalism brings forth the third disposition, that of minimalism. The risks of excessive state power are constrained by according only a limited role to the state, by allowing individuals to pursue their own conception of the good, and through checks and balances, including those of a judicial nature, which help to protect important rights. Rawls, while not employing these labels, makes the same type of point.[14] Thus he accepts that, *even* in a well-ordered society, coercive powers of government may be necessary to ensure the stability of social co-operation. Men may lack full confidence in each other, and may be unsure that each is doing 'his part'. The existence of 'effective penal machinery serves as men's security to one other', and Rawls explicitly terms this as the Hobbesian thesis.[15] However, to accord such power to the state runs the risk that sanctions 'will wrongly interfere' with a person's freedom. Limitations upon state power must, therefore, be devised, including, for example, the rule of law which serves to ensure that the law is regularly and impartially administered.

There are doubtless some who would disagree with the precise labels given by Barber. It is, however, the idea which is expressed in the preceding paragraph which is of importance in evaluating the formal critique of liberalism. *Any* political theory will have constitutive positions, and *any* such theory will have competing dispositions in the preceding sense, which operate to shape the more concrete strategies which emerge. Decisions concerning the derivative strategies will implicitly or explicitly reflect the balancing of those dispositions. The very decision whether to employ judicial review and other devices of constitutionalism within Rawlsian ideal theory, and the extent of such controls, exemplifies this interplay between the dispositions within one particular area.[16] Even where a particular political theory possesses, or may be said to possess, only one constitutive position, there may still be disagreement as to the best derivative strategies to attain the desired end.

[14] *TJ* 238–40, 240–1, 497–8.
[15] Ibid. 240.
[16] See above, ch. 8 sec. 3a (iv).

This critique of liberalism must, therefore, be based upon one of two assumptions. One presupposition might be that a different political theory would not suffer from *competing* dispositions in the same way as liberalism. This argument will not withstand examination. A different political theory such as republicanism, or some form of participatory democracy, possesses its own constitutive positions, and is permeated by its own dispositions. Decisions as to more particular derivative strategies will be affected by the precise blending of the dispositions which inhere within such a theory. The nature of this balancing or blending process will be contentious, and no less complex than that which arises within liberalism itself. A more detailed examination which demonstrates this will be undertaken in the following chapters.[17]

The other presupposition underlying this critique might be that the particular dispositions which operate within liberalism are 'flawed' in certain ways, and that these defects would not be present within some alternative theory. Now this may or may not be correct. It is, however, clear that this is an attack upon the *substance* or *content* of liberal doctrine, and must be assessed in those terms. It is no longer a critique based upon the inconsistency or indeterminacy of legal result for which liberal theory is said to be responsible. Whether the substantive challenge to liberalism is sustainable is itself a complex issue which must be properly evaluated.

The present critique *does* none the less have value. Using the language of the preceding analysis, it helps us to see the breadth of derivative strategies which are at our disposal when constitutive principles are translated into more concrete legal terms. The very process of deconstructing traditional legal doctrine and exhibiting the tensions within it is instructive and beneficial.[18] Liberalism is not, however, 'responsible' for this in the sense that other political theories would render our choice less complex. Any political theory will have constitutive positions; any such theory will have competing dispositions which shape that theory. The precise balancing of these dispositions will mould the choices we make concerning derivative strategies, including particular legal doctrines.

[17] See below, ch. 10 sec. 5, ch. 11 secs. 4c, d.
[18] See below, ch. 11 sec. 2.

3. THE LIMITS OF LEGISLATIVE ACTION: LIBERALISM'S CONCEPTION OF THE PERSON

The analysis of Rawls's theory of justice revealed, *inter alia*, two related themes, both of which shaped the limits of legitimate legislative activity: trade-offs between the first and the second principle of justice were prohibited; legislative activity designed to redistribute economic wealth was allowed, indeed mandated by, the second principle, provided that the first principle was not thereby infringed. The earlier discussion also indicated that a particular conception of the person underlay this conclusion.[19] This enquiry must now be pursued. The conception of the person which underpins the second principle of justice will be examined initially, since the argument is more readily apparent at this level of Rawls's theory. This will be followed by an examination of the first principle of justice, and it will be argued that similar problems beset the analysis at this stage. Reference will also be made to other prominent liberal theories to indicate the analogous difficulties which exist therein.

a. *The Concept of the Person and the Second Principle of Justice*

The earlier discussion of the second principle of justice revealed the reasons why Rawls chose to adopt the interpretation which he terms democratic equality. The other possible interpretations were rejected because they were said to be dependent upon criteria which were morally arbitrary.[20] Each stage in this reasoning process exhibits what Sandel has termed 'the dispossession of the person'.

> With each transition, a substantive self, thick with particular traits, is progressively shorn of characteristics once taken to be essential to its identity; as more of its features are seen to be arbitrarily given, they are relegated from presumed constituents to mere attributes of the self.[21]

Thus, following Sandel,[22] the progression towards democratic

[19] See above, ch. 8 sec. 2c.

[20] See above, ch. 8 sec. 3 b(i).

[21] *Liberalism and the Limits of Justice*, p. 93. Rawls does not believe that liberal theory is tied to this conception of the person ('Justice as Fairness: Political not Metaphysical' (1985) 14 *Phil. & Pub. Affairs*, 223, 239 n. 21), but provides no detailed critique of Sandel's analysis. For a perceptive critique of the more extreme aspects of Sandel's thesis, see W. Kymlicka, *Liberalism, Community, and Culture* (1989), 52–61.

[22] *Liberalism and the Limits of Justice*, pp. 93–4.

equality can be seen in the following terms: (i) Aristocratic/caste society: the self is 'thickly constituted', in the sense that life prospects are tied to the hierarchy in which one is born. (ii) Natural liberty: removes the fixed status of birth, but otherwise allows the individual to compete 'freely' in the market. The self is, however, still thickly constituted in the sense that differences of social positions and natural talent are taken as given. Legislative action to redress the effect of such factors is not countenanced. (iii) Liberal equality: removes differences based upon social position since they are regarded as morally arbitrary. Legislative correctives are allowed for such inequalities, and the self becomes 'thinner'. Inequalities which flow from differences in natural talent are, however, accepted. (iv) Democratic equality: seeks also to remove inequalities which flow from differences in natural talent, since 'no one deserves his place in the distribution of native endowments any more than one deserves one's initial starting-place in society'.[23] Legislative action to redistribute 'wealth' in accord with the difference principle now has its conceptual foundation. The self becomes thinner still as a person's character, values, and convictions become relegated to the contingent, 'as features of my condition rather than as constituents of my person'.[24] As Bell has stated, the person has disappeared, only attributes remain.[25]

The idea that the individual does not 'deserve' the benefits which flow from his natural talents, and the related but distinctive corollary that such benefits are to be regarded as 'common assets' which can be redistributed by the state, have been the subject of philosophical debate.[26] The present objective is not to repeat this doctrinal controversy, but to indicate the strains placed upon liberal theory which follow from accepting this 'thin' theory of the self. An example will be offered which demonstrates the difficulties which such a theory poses for the legitimate boundaries of legislative action in the realm of distributive justice.

Even a theory such as democratic equality which regards the initial distribution of natural talents as morally arbitrary and therefore subject to legislative redress encounters difficulties in

[23] *TJ* 104.

[24] Sandel, *Liberalism and the Limits of Justice*, p. 94.

[25] D. Bell, *The Coming of Post-Industrial Society* (1973), 419. Cf. W. Kymlicka, *Liberalism, Community, and Culture* (1989), 70 n. 3 who denies that this produces a disembodied conception of the person. The force of this rejoinder turns upon the meaning to be ascribed to the phrase 'constituents of the self'.

[26] A good summary and analysis is to be found in Sandel, *Liberalism and the Limits of Justice*, pp. 96–107; for a different view of liberalism, see J. Gray, *Liberalism* (1986).

determining more precisely which aspects of natural endowment should be treated as arbitrary in this sense. Dworkin's work exemplifies this conundrum.[27] He argues that, if people *did have* equal talent, then the fact that they choose to live their life in different ways, with the consequence that some accumulate more wealth than others, is no reason for economic redistribution. 'Equality of resources' must be judged over a whole life. Thus if X and Y have equal talent and the same resources, but X chooses to work singlemindedly, while Y values leisure time more highly, Y cannot later complain that he has less material goods than X.[28] However, people do not have equal talents, and Dworkin, like Rawls, believes that differences in natural talent or 'native capacities' are undeserved. Talents or endowments are conceived by Dworkin as something separate from ambition. This poses a difficult problem for the state. Distribution of resources *must be* 'ambition sensitive', in the sense of reflecting the types of choices made by X and Y above. These choices stand. Distribution of resources *must* , however, be 'endowment sensitive'; inequalities which arise from differing talents must be redressed.[29] The Dworkinian conception of the self is therefore also thin, but motivation or ambition are regarded as constituent elements of the person in a way in which talent or endowment are not. The latter are contingent and fortuitous attributes which a person happens to possess, and are morally arbitrary.

The dichotomy is, however, difficult to sustain. It appears to be based upon the involuntary or voluntary nature of the respective qualities. Thus native capacities (or endowments) differ between people 'through no choice of their own'; people are 'differently favoured by chance' in these respects. Ambition, by way of contrast, is said to be the product of 'choices' which are made as to how one should live one's life.[30] There are considerable problems with this rationale. On the one hand, ambition is not a psychological fact which exists in a vacuum. It is surely related in a complex way with a host of other variables, including social situation, position, and talent.[31] If these are to be regarded as contingent attributes which

[27] R. Dworkin, 'What is Equality? Part 2. Equality of Resources' (1981) 10 *Phil. & Pub. Affairs*, 283.

[28] Ibid. 304, 310.

[29] Ibid. 306–8, 311–12; *A Matter of Principle*, pp. 206–7.

[30] Dworkin, 'Equality of Resources', pp. 310–11; *A Matter of Principle*, p. 207.

[31] See, e.g., C. R. Sunstein, 'Legal Interference with Private Preferences', 53 *U. Chi. L. Rev.* 1129 (1986).

are not deserved, which are morally arbitrary, with the consequence that differential incomes arising therefrom should be redressed, why should ambition be placed in a 'separate category'? On the other hand, to treat the *types* of ambitions which differing individuals have as reflective of choices which they have made is itself questionable. Whether I am ambitious *in a way favoured by the market economy* appears to be as much a product of psychological chance as is the fact that I have been endowed with financial acumen or a gift for the violin. Why, therefore, is ambition a constituent aspect of the person, whereby the individual can retain the rewards thereof, rather than a contingent attribute which that person happens to possess by chance?

b. The Concept of the Person and the First Principle of Justice

Thus far we have concentrated on the way in which the liberal conception of the person shapes the second principle of justice, and the limits of legislative action concerned with distributive justice which are allowed thereunder. We must now consider the equally important, but less explored issue, concerning the way in which the liberal concept of the self moulds the first principle of justice, and serves to prohibit any legislative action which amounts to a trade-off between the first and second principles of justice. The central issue is, therefore, how a concept of the person serves to justify the shift from the general conception of justice—in which all primary goods are equally distributed, unless an unequal distribution of *any* of these goods is to the advantage of the least favoured—to the special conception of justice with the priority of liberty.

The earlier discussion revealed the shift which is apparent in Rawls's more recent work.[32] The original justification for the priority of liberty was that, once the parties had assumed that their basic liberties could be effectively exercised, they would not exchange a lesser liberty for an improvement in economic welfare; with the improvement in the conditions of life, the marginal significance of any further social and economic advantage diminished relative to the interests in liberty.[33] Criticism of this argument by Hart has led Rawls to found the priority of liberty explicitly upon a certain conception of the person. Individuals have a capacity for

[32] See above, ch. 8 sec. 2c.
[33] *TJ* 151–2, 542.

justice and for a conception of the good (both of which flow from the capacity for social co-operation). Individuals also have differing determinate conceptions of the good, which should be respected provided that they do not transgress the limits of the chosen principles of justice. These features of the person are then used to justify the liberties *and* their priority in the manner described above.[34]

The concept of the person which emerges from this analysis is disembodied or dispossessed, albeit in a sense different from that examined earlier. The individuals who have these conceptions of the good and of justice are in the original position, and do not, therefore, know their own particular talents or endowments. This is indeed the objective of the veil of ignorance from behind which they make their decisions as to the principles of justice. It is, however, one thing to depict the individual in this fashion; quite another to conclude that this construct fulfils the role ascribed to it, which is to provide a convincing argument for the liberties *and* their priority. Whether the project is successful can only be determined by examining the reasoning more closely.

Having defined the two aspects of moral personality possessed by the individual in the original position, Rawls then reasons from these capacities. *Assumptions* are made as to which primary goods will best effectuate the capacity in question. The capacity for a conception of the good is defined as the capacity 'to form, to revise and rationally to pursue a determinate conception of the good'.[35] Liberty of conscience and 'therefore' the liberty to fall into error is treated as a social condition necessary for the development and exercise of this power, and this is regarded as a reason for affirming the existence of this liberty and its priority.[36] The capacity for a sense of justice precedes the actual choice of particular principles of justice. This capacity signifies that the principles of justice which are selected will lead to the development by individuals of a corresponding sense of justice.[37] It is then argued that the two principles of justice with their lexical priority form the most stable conception of

[34] See above, ch. 8 sec. 2c.

[35] J. Rawls, 'The Basic Liberties and their Priority', in S. M. McMurrin (ed.), *Liberty, Equality and Law* (1987), 16, 27.

[36] Ibid. 27.

[37] Ibid. 30: 'It means only that whatever principles the parties select from the alternatives available, the persons the parties represent will be able to develop, as citizens in society, the corresponding sense of justice to the degree to which the parties' deliberations, informed by common-sense, knowledge and the theory of human nature, show to be possible and practicable'.

justice, and that they best safeguard self-respect.[38] The assumptions drawn from the two capacities are reinforced by more familiar arguments concerning an individual's determinate, but as yet unknown, particular conception of the good. Thus liberty of conscience is required because individuals would not take the risk that they might belong to a minority sect once the veil of ignorance is lifted. Such beliefs are 'non-negotiable' and cannot be abandoned under the second principle of justice.[39]

It is by no means certain that the response by Rawls really does overcome the initial objection raised by Hart, who contended that there was no basis for asserting that those in the original position would necessarily prefer a society in which trade-offs between liberty and other primary goods were prohibited. This assertion rested on an implicit vision of the person who prized political activity as among the chief goods in life, and who would not tolerate any such diminution for the sake of extra wealth.[40] The Rawlsian response which is framed in terms of an individual's determinate conception of the good challenges this by simply stating that citizens would regard religious or moral convictions as non-negotiable. He does, however, admit that *if* someone were to maintain that there is some rate of exchange between differing human interests, there would be an impasse.[41] The answer which Rawls draws from the capacity for a conception of the good appears to be equally problematic, and not necessarily generalizable from liberty of conscience to other liberties. *Some* within the original position might believe that a certain level of material well-being (above the Rawlsian minimum) was 'among the social conditions necessary for the development and exercise' of a power to 'revise and rationally to pursue a determinate conception of the good'. They may well believe that such primary goods are more important than certain traditional liberties in exercising this capacity. They might still be willing, as Hart suggests,[42] 'to surrender certain political rights . . . if there were good reasons for believing that this would bring a great advance in material prosperity', which would facilitate the exercise of their capacity for a conception of the good. *Others* within the original position might

[38] Ibid. 30–4.

[39] Ibid. 25–6.

[40] H. L. A. Hart, 'Rawls on Liberty and its Priority', in N. Daniels (ed.), *Reading Rawls* (1975), 250–2.

[41] Rawls, 'Basic Liberties', p. 26.

[42] Hart, 'Rawls on Liberty', p. 250.

agree with Rawls that political liberties are indeed more important for the exercise of this capacity, and agree also that the fair value thereof should be protected in order to prevent biased legislation emerging. They may, however, believe that the fair value of political liberties cannot be treated in isolation, since the ability of certain groups to exercise a disproportionate influence over the development of legislation can only be remedied by considering the general distribution of all primary goods within society. Economic and social inequalities are the cause of the problem, which can only be effectively redressed by measures which include hitherto prohibited trade-offs between the principles of justice.[43]

c. *Problems and Tensions*

Rawlsian liberalism has to justify *both* the shift from the general to the special conception of justice, *and also* the redistribution of assets which are allowed thereunder. The concept of the person provides, as we have seen, the central tool for achieving these objectives. It is used to justify both the lexical priority of the first principle over the second, and the redistribution of wealth which occurs within the latter. There are three problems with the conception of the person which emerges.

The first is that the boundaries to this concept of the self are problematic. A fundamental tenet of liberalism is that individuals have a plurality of differing conceptions of the good, and that these should be respected, subject to the constraints of justice. A corollary, or perhaps premiss, is that the individuals which comprise society possess diverse talents or endowments which, together with differing social situation, family background, etc., shape the particular conceptions of the good which citizens possess. They do not, however, deserve any of these attributes, and thus, while society should respect the pursuit of their differing conceptions of the good, it should not feel any compunction in treating the rewards which flow therefrom as 'common assets' which can be redistributed by the state. The thin theory of the self emerges, originally brought into play to justify the interpretation of the second principle. It is the boundaries of this conception of the self which produce the tensions within the theory. These are evident in both principles of justice,

[43] See above, ch. 4 sec. 4.

and the justification for these boundaries is contentious, given the premisses underlying the thin theory of the self.

On the one hand, this 'thinness' is bounded by distinctions drawn between ambition and endowment which shape the appropriate sphere of legislative action designed to attain distributive justice. Ambition is regarded as a constitutive part of 'me', and not simply an attribute which I contingently happen to possess. Choices which I make as to how to live my life, the type of ambition which I possess, are to be accepted by the state. They are not to provide the rationale for redistributive policies, in the manner which is advocated for inequalities flowing from 'undeserved' differences in talent.

On the other hand, the thinness of the self is bounded within the first principle of justice by the very process of asserting and justifying the priority of liberties. Under the *general* conception of justice, all primary goods are to be distributed equally unless an unequal distribution of *any* or *all* such goods is to the advantage of the least favoured; trade-offs between liberties and other primary goods are tolerated.[44] The reasoning process used to justify the priority of liberty prohibits such trade-offs and in doing so sets boundaries to the thin concept of the self. *Traditional* liberties *are* regarded as constituent parts of me. They are no longer seen as contingent attributes which I happen fortuitously to have. A person is born with the following traits. He has a gift for football, and is a computer expert; he also has certain moral beliefs and an interest in political participation. The first two such traits are treated as endowments which this individual contingently possesses, but which he does not morally deserve. Society can, therefore, share in the rewards which flow from the exercise of such talents by redistributing these gains, and, moreover, society can devise policies which affect the attractiveness or even viability of these pursuits if that is necessary to attain the objectives of the difference principle. The third and fourth traits are regarded as constituents of that person. The moral beliefs which comprise part of the determinate conception of the good are regarded as non-negotiable, they are a constitutive part of him, and neither these nor the desire for political participation can be overridden by arguments of general economic need, etc. They can only be restricted for the sake of other liberties.

44 *TJ* 303.

Now of course it may be argued that this is the very objective of denominating certain interests as rights, and according priority to them. The aim is to provide a sphere of autonomy which cannot be overridden by trade-offs with other primary goods. This 'aim' must, however, be substantiated. The liberal tries to show both that those in the original position would indeed accord priority to liberty *and* that these liberties would be traditional civil liberties rather than rights of a more economic or social nature. This is not a self-evident proposition, as witnessed by the complex arguments which Rawls advances to substantiate just such a conclusion. The difficulties with such reasoning have been considered above.

The second difficulty with the liberal concept of the self flows from the first, and relates to the legitimate sphere of legislative activity, an issue which has been touched upon already in the previous analysis.[45] Liberal theories of the type espoused by Rawls and Dworkin are rights-based, in the sense of prohibiting trade-offs between individual rights and some wider social interest. However, as Sandel notes, 'both rely on a theory of the subject that has the paradoxical effect of confirming the ultimate frailty, perhaps even incoherence, of the individual whose rights they seek to secure'.[46] It is the thinness of the self depicted above which produces this conclusion. Nothing which lies between rights and ambition is truly mine. None of my traits which lie between these parameters is deserved. The legitimacy of legislative action then turns upon fine questions of characterization, and the individual awaits the outcome with some trepidation. Affirmative action programmes can be supported because they do not transgress the individual rights of those who would otherwise have gained entry to university. There is said to be no conflict between rights and a desirable social goal. No one chooses his level of intelligence or deserves the particular intellectual capacities which he possesses; nor can anyone demand that universities reward particular kinds of qualifications. Given that individual rights are said not to be infringed, social policy can be decided on appropriate utilitarian considerations; society would benefit by having a broader representation of ethnic groups within its professions.[47] This conclusion does not however follow automatically, *even if* one accepts the thin theory of the self which liberalism espouses.

[45] See above, ch. 8 sec. 3a (iii).
[46] Sandel, *Liberalism and the Limits of Justice*, p. 138.
[47] See above, ch. 8 sec. 3b (iii).

The arbitrariness of an individual's assets argues only against the proposition that the individual owns them or has a privileged claim to their benefits, not in favour of the proposition that some particular society owns them or has a privileged claim with respect to them. And unless this second proposition can be established, there would seem to be no grounds for favouring a utilitarian dispensation of such assets and endowments rather than just letting them lie where they fall.[48]

The third problem with the liberal concept of the self flows from the second, as the second followed from the first. As the preceding quotation makes apparent, the liberal may well have to espouse some theory of community which provides the foundation for treating the undeserved talents of individuals as common assets which can be used for the benefit of society. It is, however, not clear that the liberal assumption of the self allows this to be achieved. Identifying the rationale for the difficulty is important.

The problem does *not* stem from a supposed liberal attachment to a conception of the self which sees individuals in atomistic terms, as 'egoists' who are incapable of any feelings of a communal or associative nature. Liberalism is not attached to such a conception of the person. The citizens who comprise liberal society have differing conceptions of the good, and these may well be of an associate, communal, or altruistic nature. These citizens do not have to embrace primarily individualistic values, 'if this means ways of life that lead individuals to pursue their own way and to have no concern for the interest of others'.[49] Moreover, the priority of the right over the good, and the content of the principles of justice which comprise the former, are inconsistent with any such simplistic view of the liberal self. Rawlsian citizens accept the two principles of justice integral to which is the thin theory of the self. This provides the medium through which endowments are treated as common assets which can be used for the benefit of the community. Thus, even if a particular individual's conception of the good does happen to embrace certain individualistic values in the above sense, he will still have a natural duty to foster just institutions, and laws made thereunder. This will entail some redistribution of the benefits which this individual happens to have secured for himself through the medium of the difference principle.[50]

[48] Sandel, *Liberalism and the Limits of Justice*, p. 141.

[49] e.g. J. Rawls, 'Fairness to Goodness' (1975) 84 *Philosophical Review*, 536, 550.

[50] See above, ch. 8 sec. 2c, d.

The difficulty resides rather in the particular sense of community which liberalism does espouse. Rawls, for example, rejects the idea that communal ties should be regarded as social arrangements designed solely to advance the private aims of each individual. Institutions should not be seen as devoid of value in themselves; social arrangements should not be viewed in such a way that the activity of engaging therein is perceived as a burden.[51]

Community is perceived as valuable in its own terms.[52] A sense of community enables the individual to participate in the collective resources of others. Each individual will, through exigency of time and contingency of natural talent, develop only certain skills. Community provides the means whereby these diverse skills can be enjoyed by others. The talents which particular individuals develop will often be complementary, and can therefore only be fully realized through social organization.

The criticism of this liberal sense of community is that it is too limited. The essence of this critique is that for the liberal a sense of community can never be more than an attribute of a well-ordered society, in the same way that a person's endowments and values are merely attributes and not constituents of the self. The liberal account of community is said to be individualistic in the sense that an idea of community is one possible aim of an antecedently given individual which must compete with other possible objectives; it cannot be a constituent of a person's identity as such.[53] This vision is contrasted with a stronger view, which Sandel terms the constitutive conception of community.

> On this strong view, to say that the members of a society are bound by a sense of community is not simply to say that a great many of them profess communitarian sentiments and pursue communitarian aims, but rather that they conceive their identity—the subject and not just the object of their feelings and aspirations—as defined to some extent by the community of which they are a part. For them, community describes not just what they *have* as fellow citizens but also what they *are*, not a relationship they choose (as in a voluntary association) but an attachment they discover, not merely an attribute but a constituent of their identity.[54]

[51] *TJ* 521.

[52] *TJ* 520–30; Rawls, 'Basic Liberties', pp. 34–9.

[53] Sandel, *Liberalism and the Limits of Justice*, p. 64. For critical evaluation, see L. Green, *The Authority of the State* (1988), ch. 7.

[54] Sandel, *Liberalism and the Limits of Justice*, p. 150; italics in the original.

It is this limited sense of liberal community which is said to be an inadequate foundation for the social claim to treat the 'undeserved talents' of individuals as common assets.[55] It is the wish to embrace the stronger, constitutive sense of community which underlies some of the recent writing on republicanism and participatory democracy.

Whether this particular aspect of the critique is warranted is debatable for two related reasons. On the one hand, one might argue that society can redistribute the assets which individuals fortuitously happen to possess, even within the conception of community as espoused by Rawls. It could, for example, be contended that society has a privileged claim on the rewards flowing from these assets precisely because such rewards were only realizable at all within a societal ordering. Such an argument would appear to be perfectly plausible within the conception of community utilized by Rawls.

On the other hand, the very meaning of a strong, constitutive sense of community which is proffered by Sandel is itself problematic. The extent to which any such idea of community leaves the individual encumbered by socially given ends is uncertain. Gutmann captures this point well.

> By interpreting Rawls's conception of community as describing 'just a feeling', for example, Sandel invites us to interpret Aristotle's as describing a fully constituted identity. The same mode of interpretation that permits Sandel to criticize Rawls for betraying 'incompatible commitments' by uneasily combining into one theory 'intersubjective and individualistic images' would permit us to criticize Sandel for suggesting that community is 'a mode of self-understanding *partly* constitutive' of our identity.[56]

4. THE LIMITS OF LEGISLATIVE ACTION: LIBERALISM AND NEUTRALITY

A criticism of liberalism which is related to that considered above seeks to undermine liberalism's claim to neutrality. The cogency of this criticism must be assessed with care for two reasons. Firstly, the common thread which permeates these challenges is that the types of action regarded as legitimate for the liberal state, and the legislature therein, are not in fact neutral between competing

[55] Ibid. 152–4. See also C. Taylor, 'Hegel: History and Politics', in M. J. Sandel (ed.), *Liberalism and its Critics* (1984), ch. 9.

[56] A. Gutmann, 'Communitarian Critics of Liberalism' (1985) 14 *Phil. & Pub. Affairs*, 308, 317; italics in the original. See also Kymlicka, *Liberalism*, pp. 52–61; Green, *The Authority of the State*, pp. 209–15.

conceptions of the good. The precise form which this argument assumes does, however, differ markedly , and such arguments must be separately evaluated. Secondly, care is warranted in order that the nature of liberalism's claim to neutrality is not misrepresented.

a. *'Rival Justices, Competing Rationalities'*

One of the most general attacks upon liberalism's neutrality comes from MacIntyre. He argues that divergent conceptions of justice are themselves based upon differences in the meaning of rationality. The very object of rational argument was a product of the Enlightenment, which sought to displace authority and tradition by the power of reason. Rational justification was the 'appeal to principles undeniable by any rational person', abstracted from contingent historical and social circumstance.[57] This ideal proved, however, impossible to attain; a plethora of competing principles emerged, each group of which were said to be founded upon rational argument.[58] MacIntyre argues for an alternative approach, one in which the process of rational enquiry is inseparable from the social and intellectual tradition in which it is embodied; a conception 'according to which the standards of rational justification themselves emerge from and are part of a history in which they are vindicated by the way in which they transcend the limitations and provide remedies for the defects of their predecessors within the history of the same tradition'.[59]

He contends that liberalism does not in reality embody a rationality which is independent of tradition, but that it embraces a particular tradition of its own which is not neutral between differing perceptions of the good.[60] The essence of the argument is as follows.[61] First, the expression of individual preference is essential to liberalism. Individuals hold differing conceptions of the good, differing wants, and the state should not endorse certain of these at the expense of others. Within the public realm an individual can pursue such preferences subject to the constraints of justice. Any single individual may well have a variety of conceptions of the good within

[57] MacIntyre, *Whose Justice?*, pp. 1–2.

[58] Ibid. 6: 'One kind of answer was given by the authors of the Encyclopédie, a second by Rousseau, a third by Bentham, a fourth by Kant, a fifth by the Scottish Philosophers of Common Sense and their French and American disciples.'

[59] Ibid. 7.

[60] Ibid. 335, 343, 345.

[61] Ibid. 335–46.

the different 'compartmentalized' spheres (political, family, economic) which comprise his life. The claims of any one such sphere to resources are determined by the 'summary of individual preferences and by bargaining' in ways analogous to market choice.

Secondly, the very process of recognizing expressions of desire as themselves reasons for action, as premisses for practical reasoning, was novel.

In Aristotelian practical reasoning it is the individual *qua* citizen who reasons; in Thomistic practical reasoning it is the individual *qua* enquirer into his or her good and the good of his or her community; in Humean practical reasoning it is the individual *qua* propertied or unpropertied participant in a society of a particular kind of mutuality and reciprocity; but in the practical reasoning of liberal modernity it is the individual *qua* individual who reasons.[62]

Thirdly, the function of the liberal rules of justice is determined by liberalism's conception of rationality. This function has both a negative and a positive aspect. In negative terms, they are not said to be concerned with enshrining one particular conception of human good, 'since no overall theory of the human good is to be regarded as justified'.[63] In positive terms, such rules operate as constraints upon the bargaining process through which individuals express their preferences.[64] A justification must be given to each individual *qua* individual for weighing his preferences in a particular way, and justification must also be furnished for differential treatment between persons. Prima facie equality is therefore required in the goods which it is presumed are valued by all: 'freedom to express and to implement preferences and a share in the means required to make that implementation effective'.[65] The debate between liberal theorists then turns upon the more particular meaning to be accorded to these ideas.

Thus for MacIntyre the starting-points of liberal theorizing are never neutral, they are always liberal starting-points.

Liberalism thus provides a distinctive conception of a just order which is closely integrated with the conception of practical reasoning required by public transactions conducted within the terms set by the liberal polity. The principles which inform such practical reasoning and the theory and practice of justice within such a polity are not neutral with respect to rival and conflicting

[62] Ibid. 339.

[63] Ibid. 343.

[64] Ibid. 337, 344.

[65] Ibid. 344.

theories of the human good. Where they are in force they impose a particular conception of the good life, of practical reasoning, and of justice upon those who willingly or unwillingly accept the liberal procedures and the liberal terms of debate. The overriding good of liberalism is no more and no less than the continued sustenance of the liberal social and political order.[66]

Two comments on the preceding analysis are warranted. First, many modern liberal theorists would accept, and indeed acknowledge, that liberalism rests within a particular historical tradition. Rawls, for example, has stressed the social and historical conditions which frame the search for justice within a modern democratic state. He sees such conditions as having their origin in the Wars of Religion which followed the Reformation, and 'the subsequent development of the principle of toleration, and in the growth of constitutional government and the institutions of large industrial market economies'.[67] It is these conditions which Rawls regards as profoundly affecting workable conceptions of justice; and it is such historical circumstances which provide the foundation for the idea that any such modern conception of justice must tolerate rival and incommensurable conceptions of the good.[68] What may well serve to distinguish the modern liberal from his critics is not that the former reasons from a position which is free of historical, social, and economic circumstance. Disagreement resides rather in the conclusions which should be drawn from those conditions, and in the relative mutability of the conditions themselves, as evidenced by the calls from more radical theorists for rethinking patterns of hierarchy which underpin established modes of thought.[69]

Secondly, it is not clear that liberals claim neutrality in the sense which MacIntyre ascribes to them. It is to this topic that we must now turn.

b. Two Conceptions of Neutrality: 1. Foundational Neutrality

i. The nature of the problem The extent to which liberalism is and can be neutral as between differing conceptions of the good has given rise to

[66] MacIntyre, *Whose Justice?*, pp. 344–5.

[67] Rawls, 'Justice as Fairness', pp. 223, 225; J. Rawls, 'The Idea of An Overlapping Consensus' (1987) 7 *O.J.L.S.* 1, 4. See also, Kymlicka, *Liberalism*, pp. 63–70.

[68] Cf. MacIntyre, *Whose Justice?*, p. 356, who does acknowledge that some liberals base their theory on a particular tradition.

[69] See below, ch. 11.

a debate of considerable complexity. This is unsurprising, given the central importance of this issue in liberal thought. The controversy is of particular concern to public lawyers because actual constitutional cases may implicitly or explicitly turn upon the judiciary's perception of the appropriate limits of government action; as MacIntyre has stated, it is the lawyers who are the clergy of liberalism.[70] In the ensuing analysis a distinction will be drawn between two different senses of neutrality.

'Foundational neutrality' may be depicted in the following way. We have already seen that the social and historical conditions in which Rawls's theory of justice is to subsist must allow for 'a diversity of doctrines and the plurality of conflicting, and indeed incommensurable, conceptions of the good' which are affirmed by members of existing democratic societies. The objective of the original position with the veil of ignorance is to generate neutral principles in the following sense. The principles should not be based upon any particular, determinate conception of the good which some individuals may happen to possess. No such conception should be allowed to be the 'single, general and comprehensive conception',[71] which could only be maintained by the oppressive use of state power. Rawls then employs the conception of the person described above, together with the list of primary goods, to determine the principles of justice which would emerge. The foundational neutrality of this enterprise has been attacked.

It has been argued that such neutrality is flawed because the primary goods themselves are not 'equally valuable in pursuit of all conceptions of the good'.[72] While Rawls can assert that the device of the original position, etc., precludes the pursuit of any particular conception of the good, Nagel counters by contending that such neutrality is flawed because the list of primary goods favours certain *general* conceptions of the good more than others. Thus he argues that the primary goods will be less useful in 'implementing views that hold a good life to be readily achievable only in certain well-defined types of social structure', or 'only given certain types of economic relations among men'.[73] The general conception of the good which underlies the original position is said not to be neutral

[70] *Whose Justice?*, p. 344.

[71] Rawls, 'The Idea of an Overlapping Consensus', p. 4.

[72] T. Nagel, 'Rawls on Justice', in Daniels (ed.), *Reading Rawls*, pp. 1, 8–10. For a response by Rawls, see 'The Priority of Right and Ideas of the Good' (1988) 17 *Phil. & Pub. Affairs*, 251, 265–8.

[73] Nagel, 'Rawls on Justice', p. 9.

but to reflect 'a liberal individualistic conception according to which the best that can be wished for someone is the unimpeded pursuit of his own path, provided that it does not interfere with the rights of others'.[74] These views are echoed by Raz, who states that some conceptions of the good will be harder to satisfy than others; that non-individualistic conceptions of the good will be amongst these, because such conceptions require the co-operation of others, which may well have to be bought.[75] MacIntyre's critique, that the *overriding* good of liberalism is no more and no less than the continued sustenance of the liberal social order, is similar in tenor.[76]

ii. An individualistic bias? The precise nature and meaning[77] of the individualistic bias which is said to form or underly the general conception of the good espoused by Rawls is not entirely clear. *In part* it appears to be based upon the motivational assumptions of mutual disinterest and absence of envy which inform Rawls's approach; these are said to have the effect of 'discounting the claims of conceptions of the good that depend heavily on the relation between one's position and that of others'.[78] However, such assumptions are not necessarily tied to an individualist ethic. Indeed counter-assumptions might appear more at home in such a philosophy. A society in which 'atomistic individuals' envy the possessions of others, and attempt to improve themselves at their expense, is just the type of society which is often taken as the epitome of possessive market individualism.

In part, the neutrality is said to be flawed because the primary goods are not equally valuable in pursuit of all conceptions of the good. The phrase 'equally valuable' is ambiguous, and could bear one of two meanings.

On the one hand, it could be interpreted to mean[79] that a market mechanism will determine the value of primary goods required to pursue conceptions of the good; that some conceptions of the good will require primary goods of greater value for their realization; that

[74] Nagel, 'Rawls on Justice', p. 10.
[75] Raz, *The Morality of Freedom*, pp. 119–20.
[76] See above, ch. 9 sec. 4a.
[77] As is evident from the ensuing discussion, it is not entirely clear what precise meaning the critics attribute to the term 'individualistic'. Varying hypotheses are therefore assumed in the textual discussion.
[78] Nagel, 'Rawls on Justice', p. 9.
[79] Raz, *The Morality of Freedom*, pp. 119–20.

Rawlsian theory discriminates against expensive tastes which are harder to satisfy;[80] and that non-individualistic conceptions are likely to be amongst these. This is debatable. It will depend entirely upon the precise type of individualistic or non-individualistic conception of the good which a person seeks to satisfy. There is no reason to expect the latter to be generally more expensive than the former. The fact that these require a person to convince others of his position or buy them out does not provide the answer, since the expenditure of primary goods to achieve this will depend upon how highly those primary goods are valued in this context. There is, moreover, no necessary reason why the pursuit of a conception of the good in a non-individualistic manner should exceed the cost of such a pursuit in an individualistic manner. Arthur's conception of the good is to save an endangered species. He can pursue this by himself, but believes that a national association will have more impact. The organization of such an association will entail costs to Arthur, in terms of convincing others, buying them, etc. The costs borne by Arthur to attain the desired good may still be less when pursued through this co-operative strategy than if he had advanced the same end by himself. He will benefit from, for example, the expertise of others committed to the same conception of the good who possess information which Arther does not himself have.[81]

There is a further difficulty with this first sense of 'less valuable'. Assertions that Rawlsian theory is permeated by an individualistic bias often carry the implication that this is a bias *towards* an individualist market economy, and *against* some other form of social ordering. In so far as the argument being analysed does have cogency, it would run against this implication, or have to be seriously qualified. *If* the value of primary goods required to further non-individualistic conceptions of the good *is* likely to be more expensive, then this would discriminate *against* the establishment of a merger, trade association, consumer pressure group, competitive sport franchise, or many of the other quintessential hallmarks of market capitalism. It might be argued that these are all in fact examples of individualistic conceptions of the good. This is

[80] Rawls would not accept that his theory does necessarily have this effect; see 'Social Unity and Primary Goods', in A. Sen and B. Williams (eds.), *Utilitarianism and Beyond* (1982), 159, 168–9.

[81] See the discussion of public-choice theory, (above, ch. 3 sec. 2b) for a general analysis of the relative advantages of individual and co-operative action.

questionable in itself. Such characterization would restrict the idea of non-individualistic conceptions of the good to the pursuit of aims which require co-operative effort of some kind but where these co-operative ventures are not a 'central part' of the market mechanism.[82]

On the other hand, the argument that the primary goods are not equally valuable in pursuit of all conceptions of the good, but import an individualistic bias, could bear a different meaning. It could mean that the primary goods are less useful, not in the 'quantitative' sense considered above (namely, that some conceptions of the good will require primary goods of greater value for their realization), but in a more 'qualitative' sense, in that they are less amenable to furthering certain types of conceptions of the good. This appears to be the thrust of the examples which Nagel provides, when he states that the primary goods are less useful 'in implementing views that hold a good life to be readily achievable only in certain well defined types of social structure, or only in a society that works concertedly for the realization of certain higher human capacities and the suppression of baser ones, or only given certain types of economic relations among men'.[83]

The cogency of this critique depends upon two related assumptions: that the primary goods do preclude or impede the attainment of such conceptions of the good, *and* that this reveals the individualistic bias which is said to underpin the whole enterprise. It is not, however, clear that this argument can be sustained. This can be demonstrated by focusing upon Nagel's second example. Peter may embrace a conception of the good which requires society to foster the higher human capacities and believes that intellectual endeavour is prime amongst these. It *is* true that the Rawlsian analysis precludes those in the original position from furthering a particular, determinate conception of the good which should be elevated above all others. That is its central objective, achieved by the veil of ignorance. However, nothing in the list of primary goods affects the example one way or another, *and* it is difficult to see why the result reveals any individualistic bias. The idea appears to be that some conceptions of the good require a particular social setting for their

[82] The coherence of this meaning of non-individualistic may well be questioned. In any event, why would the cost of primary goods necessarily be high in these areas, whatever precisely they are?

[83] Nagel, 'Rawls on Justice', p. 9.

attainment, some particular form of interrelationship with others, that this is what is meant by non-individualistic conceptions of the good, and that these are more difficult to attain. However most, perhaps all, conceptions of the good require or assume some such social setting.[84] David's particular conception of the good rests on a belief that society should further an acquisitive culture which allows those who earn large sums to retain a large proportion thereof with minimal social responsibility. His conception of the good clearly assumes a particular manner of interrelating with others. Are we therefore to characterize his conception of the good as non-individualist? The difficulty of attaining the particular conceptions of the good held by Peter and David does not follow from any inherent bias in the primary goods towards individualistic conceptions of the good. It stems from the crucial assumption that those in the original position cannot further their own particular conceptions of the good, whether they be individualist or non-individualist in nature.

iii. Neutrality, primary goods, and the concept of the person There is, however, a crucial sense in which the foundations of liberalism may not be neutral, which is different from the argument considered above.

The principles of justice which are to be devised are set within a particular social and historical tradition, as we have seen above. The object is to devise a workable conception of justice given these conditions. The by now familiar fabric of the original position and the veil of ignorance are brought into play. It is, however, the conception of the person with the two powers of moral personality (the capacity for a sense of justice and the capacity for a conception of the good), together with the list of primary goods which provide the foundation for the reasoning which produces the principles of justice.

The 'link' between these is important. The list of primary goods is not decided primarily by 'asking what general means are essential for achieving the final ends which a comprehensive empirical or historical survey might show that people usually or normally have in common'.[85] There might be few such ends, and these might not

[84] Sally's conception of the good may be to live an hermetic or reclusive existence of inner contemplation; this too would require a particular type of social structure or relationship with others in order to enable her to do this.

[85] Rawls, 'Social Unity and Primary Goods', p. 166; 'Basic Liberties', pp. 21–2.

serve the purposes of a conception of justice. The determination of primary goods does involve some general knowledge of the requirements of social life, but it does so 'only in the light of a conception of the person given in advance'.[86] It is this conception of the person with the two moral powers which is used, together with considerations relating to a person's determinate but as yet unknown conception of the good, to decide why such primary goods are required, *and* for deciding upon the priority of liberty over other primary goods.[87]

Rawls admits that this picture of the original position and the conception of the person therein is not morally neutral.[88] This does not, of course, entail any necessary bias towards a particular conception of the good. However, if there is a flaw in the foundational neutrality, it is to be found in the way in which the reasoning process based upon the conception of the person is said to produce the conclusion which justifies liberties and their priority over other primary goods. It is this rather than any supposed bias in the primary goods themselves which could undermine or weaken the claim to neutrality.

The nature of this reasoning process has already been considered above.[89] The conclusion which is drawn therefrom is that the traditional civil liberties would be accorded priority over other primary goods because of their importance in effectuating the capacity for a conception of the good, and the capacity for a sense of justice, and for the protection which they afford to an individual's determinate, albeit as yet unknown, conception of the good. This reasoning is, as we have seen, controversial, and it is unclear whether the argument which is directed towards particular civil liberties can be generalized.[90]

Two questions follow from this reasoning. First, how far does it indicate some general conception of the good which underlies the enterprise? The effect of this reasoning process is to make the determination of the principles of justice turn on an underlying general conception of the good which is individualistic in the following sense. The primary goods are not regarded as equal in

[86] Rawls, 'Social Unity and Primary Goods', p. 167; 'Basic Liberties', p. 22.

[87] Rawls, 'Social Unity and Primary Goods', pp. 165–6; 'Basic Liberties', pp. 24–46. See also above, ch. 8 sec. 2c.

[88] 'Basic Liberties', p. 20 n. 20; 'The Priority of Right', pp. 251–3, 265–8.

[89] See ch. 8 sec. 2c.

[90] See ch. 8 secs 2c, d.

value in the pursuit of any conception of the good by anyone; they are not conceived to be equally important in fulfilling the two capacities of the self, or in protecting particular conceptions of the good which are as yet unknown. Traditional individual liberties are viewed as more important than other primary goods in serving these ends, hence their priority. This priority prohibits trade-offs between liberties and these other goods. Liberties are, in this sense, taken off the political agenda.[91] They form a constitutive part of the identity of each individual which can only be restricted for the sake of other liberties. Trade-offs between any of the primary goods which were tolerated under the general conception of justice are now barred, and particular conceptions of the good can only be advanced if they are within the frame allowed by the lexical priority of the principles of justice.

The second question is whether this undermines the foundational neutrality of the theory? If we take political neutrality to mean giving all persons 'an equal ability to pursue in their lives and promote in their societies any ideal of the good of their choosing',[92] this need not be infringed by the arguments considered above, since those in the original position would agree that their conceptions of the good should be framed in the above manner. The parties in the original position act as rationally autonomous representatives who agree to those principles which they believe are best for those they represent, as seen from these persons' conceptions of the good and their capacity to revise such conceptions.[93] Those in the original position would, therefore, only choose conceptions of the good which were consonant with the general reasoning considered above. They are the representative individuals who have decided that the primary goods should not be accorded equal value, and who have determined that liberties should have priority.

This reconciliation is clearly only formal. Neutrality is not infringed by the general underlying conception of the good set out above, because all rational representatives have accepted and reasoned on these assumptions. It is, however, the correctness of this reasoning and the assumptions drawn from it which is the very question in issue. It is in this deeper sense that foundational neutrality is circumscribed. Particular conceptions of the good are framed by the general individualistic conception adumbrated above.

[91] Rawls, 'The Idea of an Overlapping Consensus', pp. 13–14.
[92] Raz, *The Morality of Freedom*, p. 115.
[93] Rawls, 'Basic Liberties', p. 19; 'The Priority of Right', pp. 260–3.

Some such circumscription of neutrality is, however, inevitable, even though it does not have to assume the form described above. The primary goods do not 'speak' for themselves. Those in the original position have to reason *from* these, and they now do so in the light of the capacities of the person. Any such reasoning is bound to embody some background general conception of the good, which will frame the more particular choices made by individuals. In this most basic sense there is no neutrality to be had, a proposition from which neither Rawls nor Dworkin[94] would probably dissent. The background conception of the good is, however, only general, and within its boundaries the theory still strives for neutrality concerning more particular conceptions thereof. How far such neutrality is attainable, and how far it should be sought, will be considered within the ensuing section.

c. Two Conceptions of Neutrality: 2. Internal Neutrality

The debate concerning 'foundational neutrality' must be distinguished from a related, but distinctive, controversy concerning what may be termed 'internal neutrality.' The latter term will be given the following connotation. How far should the state be neutral as between competing conceptions of the good once the principles of justice have been chosen; how far should it be neutral *within* the system which has been established through the reasoning of those in the original position? The answer to this question entails issues of considerable complexity. It may, however, help in understanding the nature of this debate to be clear about the nature of the contested ground.

i. The uncontested ground Some discussions and criticisms of 'liberal neutrality' assume that liberals somehow refuse to pass any judgement on differing conceptions of the good once the principles of justice have been chosen. This is quite wrong and the mistake is an important one. The reason is as follows.

The principles of justice, once chosen, frame the pursuit of more particular conceptions of the good.[95] The legislature should only promulgate legislation which is compatible with the two principles of justice, and individuals have a natural duty to support just institutions. While an individual may have specific ideas as to what

[94] See, e.g., Dworkin, *A Matter of Principle*, ch. 9.

[95] See above, ch. 8 sec. 2d.

constitutes the value of life for him, he should not support parties or policies which would be contrary to the two principles of justice. Particular conceptions of goodness may differ, but all such choices are 'framed within definite limits' provided by the concept of the right as enshrined in the principles of justice.[96]

The liberal is therefore not neutral *nor* does he pretend to be, as between the attainment of differing conceptions of the good *within* a society governed by the principles of justice. Pursuit of conceptions of the good which infringe either of the two principles of justice will not be countenanced, and may be constitutionally prohibited through the courts.[97]

This point, obvious once stated, is of considerable importance for public lawyers. Many of the controversial issues which arise in public law *are* provided with answers[98] by liberals precisely because they *do* come within the area adumbrated in the previous paragraph. Liberals do not refuse to give answers to these issues on the supposed ground that to do so would offend neutrality. Quite the contrary. Answers are provided, and enforced, where conceptions of the good impinge upon the principles of justice. Thus particular conceptions of the good espoused by the current legislative majority will not be upheld if they infringe the liberties enshrined in the constitution. Liberals are not, therefore, neutral about free speech, discrimination, association, the protection of disadvantaged groups, and the like, nor about many other issues which comprise the core of public law. If legislative behaviour infringes the principles of distributive justice, it too will be condemned. As Rawls states:

> The principles of right, and so of justice, put limits on which satisfactions have value; they impose restrictions on what are reasonable conceptions of one's good. In drawing up plans and in deciding on aspirations men are to take these constraints into account. Hence in justice as fairness one does not take men's propensities and inclinations as given, whatever they are, and then seek the best way to fulfil them. Rather, their desires and aspirations are restricted from the outset by the principles of justice which specify the boundaries that men's systems of ends must respect. We can express this by saying that in justice as fairness the concept of right is prior to that of the good.[99]

96 e.g. *TJ* 513, 528, 563, 567.

97 See above, ch. 8 sec. 3.

98 Which does not, of course, imply that these answers will be uncontroversial. See above, ch. 8 secs. 3a (i), (ii).

99 *TJ* 31.

ii. The contested ground The nature of the contested ground can be presented as follows. It has been argued that the deontological liberalism of Rawls and Dworkin does not allow a government sufficient latitude for action. The state should be allowed to intervene *not only* in defence of the principles of justice, *but also* in order to promote what is valuable and good in life. This view of 'perfectionist liberalism' has been espoused in the recent important work of Raz.[100] '"Perfectionism"' is merely a term used to indicate that there is no fundamental principled inhibition on governments acting for any valid moral reason, though there are many strategic inhibitions on doing so in certain classes of cases.'[101]

The nature of the arguments for and against perfectionist liberalism cannot be fully examined here. They involve complex philosophical issues which are beyond the scope of the present work. A brief glance at the main themes in this debate is, however, instructive in understanding the nature of the controversy concerning neutrality and its implications for public law. The outline of the argument for perfectionist liberalism can be presented in four stages.

First, 'it does not make sense to say of a state of affairs that it is good but that fact is no reason whatsoever to do anything about it'.[102] Thus, prima facie at least, the fact that an act is good is a reason to do it.

Secondly, the types of issue which deontological liberals are willing to pronounce upon, and those which they are not, in fact stem from a common moral root. This undermines the claim that it is acceptable to pronounce only upon those moral issues which are contained within the principles of justice, but not to pass judgement on moral issues which arise independently thereof.[103]

Thirdly, governments should act for reasons which should guide their subjects and apply to them. Governments should not, however, always aim to enhance the good. They should do so only where their action can effectively attain the end in view; and they should not intervene where it is more important that 'the matter is best left to their subjects to decide for themselves than that they should get the right results'.[104]

Finally, subject to the preceding caveats, the government ought to

[100] *The Morality of Freedom.*

[101] J. Raz, 'Facing Up: A Reply', 62 *S. Cal.L. Rev* 1153, 1230 (1989).

[102] Ibid.; Raz, *The Morality of Freedom*, pp. 134–7.

[103] Raz, *The Morality of Freedom*, pp. 110–3, 136–7, 140, 193–216.

[104] Ibid. 140–2; and 'Facing Up', p. 1231.

pursue policies which seek to advance the good within society. This can be attained while accepting 'moral pluralism', namely the idea that there are 'many valuable forms of life which are incompatible with each other'.[105] Moreover, Raz argues that there is no more reason to believe that the government is likely to be wrong about the nature of the good life than about the types of moral consideration which people agree should influence political action, such as freedom of speech, etc.[106]

These are powerful arguments. They are also controversial.[107] These controversies cannot, as stated above, be explored here. Two brief comments may, however, be ventured, both of which serve to diminish, albeit not obliterate, the division between the two species of liberalism.

On the one hand, certain policies which the perfectionist liberal regards as legitimate governmental action in pursuit of morally valid ideals may also be espoused by deontological liberals who may perceive such action as a legitimate application of the principles of justice themselves. For example, Raz argues that governmental rules which prohibit commercial transactions involving babies is one area in which the state should intervene to uphold an ideal which is morally valid.[108] A deontological liberal of the Rawlsian mould might, however, reach the same conclusion by arguing that such transactions should be prohibited because they infringe the personal liberty and dignity of the child.[109]

On the other hand, the 'gap' between the two approaches may be narrowed in so far as the perfectionist liberal himself bases his intervention on support of sound moral ideals *and* on grounds of distributive justice. Raz has responded to criticism of his suggestion that resort should be had to taxation, etc., to support sound moral ideals by arguing that this critique assumed that the tax was not justified for redistributive reasons. He urges that this misrepresents

[105] Raz, *The Morality of Freedom*, pp. 161, 369–429.

[106] Ibid. 160.

[107] e.g. J. Waldron, 'Autonomy and Perfectionism in Raz's *Morality of Freedom*', 62 *S. Cal. L. Rev.* 1098 (1989). See also the reply by Raz, 'Facing Up', pp. 1225–35. See also T. Morawetz, 'Persons without History: Liberal Theory and Human Experience', 66 *Boston U.L.Rev.* 1013 (1986); Rawls, 'The Priority of Right', pp. 262–9; Kymlicka, *Liberalism*, ch. 2.

[108] 'Facing Up', p. 1231.

[109] Another, more difficult, example might be respect for the Arts. The perfectionist liberal may wish to expend money to this end. Could the deontological liberal do so? See Dworkin, *A Matter of Principle*, ch. 11.

the thrust of his analysis, and that the 'protection and promotion of autonomy provides the basic grounds which determine issues of justice and distribution'.[110] However, in so far as expenditure is warranted for the attainment of distributive justice, it would clearly also be sanctioned, indeed demanded by, Rawls and Dworkin.

5. CONCLUSION

Two general points may be made by way of conclusion.

First, the preceding analysis reveals the complexity and contestability of the general critiques which have been levelled at liberalism. It is only by paying close attention to the distinctive nature of these critiques that one can assess their force.

Secondly, those who advance such criticism can themselves be challenged in the following manner. The normative foundations of liberalism may be contestable in certain respects. The fact that one can reveal strains and tensions within liberal theory is, however, in a paradoxical way, the result of the sophistication of the analysis itself. Those who challenge liberalism, and its depiction of rights and distributive justice, must therefore advance a distinctive view of societal ordering; they must reveal the *detailed* normative foundation of their political vision, and the implications which follow therefrom for public law. The earlier discussions revealed the weaknesses in the normative argumentation of interest-group pluralism.[111] Subsequent discussion will indicate the distinctive difficulties which are present for those who espouse some form of communitarianism or participatory democracy.[112]

110 'Facing Up', p. 1233.
111 See above, ch. 4.
112 See above, chs, 10, 11.

10

REPUBLICANISM, CIVIC VIRTUE, AND PARTICIPATORY DEMOCRACY

1. INTRODUCTION

Critics of interest-group pluralism[1] and of liberalism[2] differ concerning the shape and content of any alternative vision of society. A prominent theme which is the focus of current debate is that a more participatory, communal form of democracy would be preferable. The language in which this is expressed differs. Some writers talk directly in terms of participatory democracy. Others draw upon the language of republicanism to depict a society in which participation, civic virtue, and the public good are central themes. The precise content which falls within either label is itself variable, as writers struggle to depict how such a participatory society would 'look' and 'operate' in the modern world. The present chapter and that which follows will examine the general concept of participatory democracy/republicanism, and its relationship to public law.

The present chapter will focus upon republicanism and the structure of the argument will be as follows. First, there will be an historical enquiry as to the meaning and direction which has characterized this theory. This discussion will include an analysis of the strains which beset republicanism because of the changing social and economic conditions resulting from an emergent capitalist society. Secondly, the discussion will address the role of republicanism in the debates concerning US independence and the drafting of the Constitution.

The third stage of the enquiry will examine the usage of

[1] See above, ch. 3 sec. 2d. The materials in n. 2 are also relevant.

[2] e.g. R. M. Unger, *Knowledge and Politics* (1975); M. J. Sandel, *Liberalism and the Limits of Justice* (1982); R. Bernstein, *Beyond Objectivism and Relativism: Science, Hermeneutics, and Praxis* (1983); A. MacIntyre, *After Virtue* (2nd edn. 1984); M. J. Sandel (ed.), *Liberalism and its Critics* (1984); B. Barber, *Strong Democracy: Participatory Politics for a New Age* (1984); R. N. Bellah, R. Madsen, W.M. Sullivan, A. Swidler, and S. M. Tipton, *Habits of the Heart* (1985). Further references to relevant material will be provided in the course of the chapter.

republicanism by modern public lawyers who have sought to modify classical republican theory and to apply it to constitutional and administrative law. The doctrinal implications of this modified republicanism will be considered.

The final parts of this chapter will critically examine the modern republican revival. The analysis will be directed towards two connected aspects of this revival. On the one hand, the normative foundations of modified republicanism will be considered. It will be argued that these are crucially ambiguous at certain vital points, and that these ambiguities have important implications for the legal results which are said to ensue from the theory. On the other hand, attention will be directed towards the institutional, social, and economic conditions which are necessary in order for republicanism to thrive. It will be argued that the historical evidence indicates the difficulties of fostering republicanism in a capitalist society which tolerates extreme disparities of wealth. Current writers who advocate a republican revival place their emphasis upon the power of judicial doctrine to reorder society. This court-centred emphasis will result in only minor changes to societal ordering. If something more is required then there would have to be more radical institutional, social, and economic transformation. A modified republicanism may contain the seeds of such radical change. These are, however, unlikely to bear fruit without the more general changes adumbrated above.

2. REPUBLICANISM: HISTORICAL FOUNDATIONS

a. Self-Government, Political Association and Civic Virtue

Republicanism, as a species of political thought, has a considerable historical lineage. Certain aspects of the doctrine are controversial, but its fundamental tenets may be depicted as follows.

Pocock has explained the roots of modern republicanism in the following manner.[3] Towards the end of the medieval period there was a belief that only the universal, the timeless, was truly rational.

[3] J. G. A. Pocock, *The Machiavellian Moment: Florentine Political Thought and the Atlantic Republican Tradition* (1975), chs. 1, 2: J. G. A. Pocock, 'Civic Humanism and its Role in Anglo-American Thought', in J. G. A. Pocock, *Politics, Language and Time* (1971), 80–1.

This generated a correlative problem of how to understand the particular, or the transitory. The humanists of fifteenth-century Florence sought to find universality within the framework of the Aristotelian polis. Speaking of the humanists, Pocock states:

The need to make the particular intelligible had given rise to the idea of conversation, the idea that the universal was immanent in participation in the web of life and language, and so the highest values, even those of non-political contemplation, had come to be seen as attainable only through conversation and social association. But it must follow that association was itself a high and necessary good, a prerequisite for obtaining the universal, and the entire Athenian and Aristotelian tradition was emphatic that the highest form of human association was political, the community of distribution, decision and action which Aristotle had seen in the polis.[4]

The Athenian model not only fostered political association. It also furnished the requisite link with universality.

There did exist in the Athenian political tradition means of asserting that the republic was a partnership of all men aimed at the realization of all values. If it was this it was a universal entity; but this assertion rested on the theory that it could achieve a distribution of authority such that every citizen's moral nature would be fulfilled. Without such a distribution the republic would be neither universal, just, nor stable, and its citizens could not rely on the support of a cosmic order in the way that a King and his subjects could, since the polity did not claim to mirror the cosmic order as a monarchy did. The theory of the polis and its constitutional structure thus became crucial to the humanist enterprise.[5]

Certain key elements within this constitutional structure become readily apparent.[6] Citizenship and political association assume central importance. Citizen participation within the political process was the highest form of active life, and the object was the pursuit of the public good which must take precedence over the good of a particular individual. It was crucial that political power should not be distributed unevenly. A particular group should not be enabled to equate its particular good with the good of all. This would entail a loss of virtue for all those within society. The universal good could only be pursued if the citizens possessed sufficient equality to remain autonomous. Corruption would occur should one part become too powerful, and the republic would then enter a further degenerative

[4] *The Machiavellian Moment*, p. 64.
[5] Ibid. 66. See also 'Civic Humanism', in *Politics, Language and Time*, p. 86.
[6] Pocock, 'Civic Humanism', in *Politics, Language and Time*, pp. 86–7.

stage of the Polybian cycle.[7] Trade and economic diversification were suspect precisely because of their destructive corrupting potential.[8] Societies founded upon such diversity provided ever-increasing opportunity for individuals to foster their own private satisfactions at the expense of the universal good. The tensions which this posed for a theory of republicanism are a recurring theme which will be considered in more detail at a later stage.

The passage of republican, participatory theory from Renaissance Italy to England, and thence to the United States, is a complex one.[9] The ideology of civic participation and of citizenship was not readily compatible with conceptions of monarchy and monarchical order. Normative notions of a mixed government could not be reconciled with the Tudor theory of descending authority.[10] A *necessary* step in the emergence of republican thought within England was, therefore, the reluctant acceptance by the monarchy of the very existence of mixed and balanced government. The inception of this radical shift of views was occasioned, not surprisingly, by dramatic social upheaval.[11] Advisers to Charles I persuaded him to issue a document in which it was asserted that the government of England was vested in three estates, the King, the Lords, and the commons, *and* that the health of the system was dependent upon maintaining a balance among these branches. Government was not conceived of as a direct product of divinely held authority, of which the monarch was the living embodiment.[12] This departure from the concept of descending authority has been described as a 'disastrous tactical error in royalist polemic',[13] which none the less became rapidly accepted by those who wished to limit royal power.

While the grudging acceptance of a mixed and balanced government was a necessary step towards embracing republican rhetoric, it was not *sufficient*. The English had only adopted the language of balance and republic because their traditional constitutional order of monarchy and custom had been so severely shaken.[14] A resort to classical republicanism was but one way of resolving this

[7] Pocock, 'Civic Humanism', in *Politics, Language and Time*, p. 88.

[8] Ibid. 89–90.

[9] See Pocock, *The Machiavellian Moment*, ch. 10, for an examination of this complex transition.

[10] Ibid. 355. [11] Ibid. 361. [12] Ibid. 362.

[13] Ibid. 361. For a detailed discussion of this development, see C. C. Weston, *English Constitutional Theory and the House of Lords* (1965).

[14] Pocock, *The Machiavellian Moment*, p. 365.

dilemma, but it was not the only conceptual tool which was used.[15] It was James Harrington who was fully to develop the humanist strains which had been partially revealed by the collapse of the established order.

Harrington's 'utopian' thesis has both a negative and a positive side.[16] In negative terms, Harrington rejects the Hobbesian imagery with its foundation of acquisitive, warring man who can be pacified only by submission to the all-powerful sovereign.[17] He also set out to demonstrate that no return to the traditional or ancient constitution was plausible or desirable, arguing that the distribution of authority therein had always rendered such constitutional constructs unstable.[18]

The positive side of Harringtonian thought drew upon Machiavelli, and the ideal of the balanced republic: the object of the republic was pursuit of the common good which was always to be preferred to the good pursued by particular sectors of society.[19] Personal autonomy in the sense of self-government was of crucial importance to classical republicanism, and also to the Harringtonian version thereof. The basis of this autonomy was of particular concern to Harrington. Thus he regarded the possession of freehold property as an integral base for the citizen's autonomous participation in politics.[20] The object of freehold property was to prevent the individual from being placed in a relation of dependence upon others. Such dependence would inevitably lead to the triumph of particular interests over the general good. It is for this reason that Harrington regards defects in the distribution of property as the principal cause of corruption. Citizens would cease to act virtuously, not simply because of some form of moral corruption, but because proprietary distribution which veered away from the equal freehold would reduce some to the status of vassals, and elevate others to the status of lord.[21] Military and proprietary independence were both of seminal

[15] Ibid. 366, 370–1.

[16] J. Harrington, 'The Commonwealth of Oceana', in *The Political Works of James Harrington*, ed. J. G. A. Pocock (1977).

[17] Ibid. 161–6, 184–5. There were, however, some points on which the disagreement between Hobbes and Harrington was less marked; see Pocock, *The Machiavellian Moment*, pp. 397–8.

[18] Pocock, *The Machiavellian Moment*, pp. 385, 389, 404.

[19] Harrington, 'The Commonwealth of Oceana', pp. 161–2, 171–2; Pocock, 'Civic Humanism', in *Politics, Language and Time*, pp. 90–1.

[20] Harrington, 'The Commonwealth of Oceana', pp. 164–5, 180–2.

[21] Ibid. 231–41. See Pocock, *The Machiavellian Moment*, pp. 387–8.

importance. To be a vassal meant that one's sword belonged to the lord. Freehold ensured that the sword was one's own, at the disposal of the commonwealth. The function of property became 'the liberation of arms, and consequently of the personality, for free public action and civic virtue'.[22]

The form of government within the Harringtonian republic is participatory and mixed, drawing upon classical ideas of government constituted of the one, the few, and the many.[23] It is participatory in the sense that there are numerous levels within the community as a whole in which citizens can express and exercise choice. Individuals are chosen to serve both by election and by lot, and the latter medium emphasizes the idea that the individual thus chosen is less a representative in any normal sense but rather a citizen who is taking his turn at community participation and service.[24] It is mixed in the sense that, within the central government, the senate proposes, the people resolve, and the magistracy execute. Republican theory was designed to achieve the harmonious balance between the one, the few, and the many. Differences of natural talent existed among the people, such that within any decision-making process a minority of leaders would normally emerge. These would be leaders in the sense that they possessed talents required for the analysis of policy choices, agenda-setting, and the like. It would, however, be unwise to allow such leaders to make the dispositive choice as to which particular policy should be pursued. This could lead to the triumph of the particular good over that of the general good, by providing a temptation to the leaders to equate their own vision of the good with the needs of the commonwealth as a whole. To forestall this eventuality was the rationale for structuring the government in the way adumbrated above: the few propose, the people, as represented in the assembly, choose.

[22] Pocock, *The Machiavellian Moment*, p. 386. It should be noted that a different view of Harrington's conception of property has been advanced. This reading of his work asserts that Harrington in fact conceived of the relationships between men as market relationships, a consequence of the emerging capitalist emphasis upon entrepreneurial activity; see C. B. Macpherson, *The Political Theory of Possessive Individualism: Hobbes to Locke* (1962), ch. 6. For a response by Pocock, see *The Machiavellian Moment*, pp. 390–1. More detailed treatment can be found in Pocock, 'Machiavelli, Harrington, and English Political Ideologies in the Eighteenth Century', in Pocock, *Politics, Language and Time*, pp. 110–14, and in 'Authority and Property: The Question of Liberal Origins', in J. G. A. Pocock, *Virtue, Commerce and History* (1985), ch.3.

[23] Harrington, 'The Commonwealth of Oceana', pp. 172–4, 210–89.

[24] Pocock, *The Machiavellian Moment*, p. 393.

The political theory of Harrington provides the crucial link in the transfer of republican thought from England to the US colonies, where it exercised considerable influence on the revolutionaries and upon the framers of the Constitution. Republicanism has more recently been expressed to be the organizing principle of US constitutional and administrative law. However, before considering these developments it is necessary to review the tensions within Italian and English republicanism. This is not merely for historical interest. These tensions affected the US perception of republican ideology. They are also of crucial importance in assessing the viability and meaning of republicanism as an organizing ideology for modern society.

b. Republicanism: Virtue under Stress

The problems of attaining and maintaining a republican polity appear repeatedly within both Italian and English political thought. The state of society as it actually was, had been, and might become, was an endemic theme within this literature. Both Guicciardini[25] and Machiavelli[26] spend considerable effort in analysing faction, its corrupting influence, and the best method of forestalling it. Nor is it self-evident that the ideal of civic virtue and the suppression of private interest was ever fully obtained, or at least not for any length of time. Recent study of the much-praised Venetian republic leaves considerable doubt as to how far the patriciate were in fact virtuous, and how far their action was guided by baser motive.[27] It is, however, in post-restoration England that the tensions within the republican ideal become most marked. The conflict within this period is particularly interesting, because it demonstrates the difficulty of accommodating republican ideals in a society which is becoming increasingly reliant upon trade, commerce, and public finance. Political debate was republican in character, and the language of corruption and virtue was much used. The problem was how this should be applied to a society which was ceasing to be wholly agrarian. This debate was carried on between the neo-Harringtonians,[28] who were principally members of the 'country'

[25] Ibid. 126–7, 132–3, 135–6.

[26] Ibid. 208–10.

[27] D. E. Queller, *The Venetian Patriciate: Reality versus Myth* (1986).

[28] For the principal differences between Harrington and neo-Harringtonians, see Pocock, 'Machiavelli, Harrington and English Political Ideologies', in *Politics, Language and Time*, pp. 135–6.

party, and their protagonists, who were chiefly those of the 'court' party.

The central theme within the country ideology in the late seventeenth and early eighteenth centuries was that society was composed of court and country.[29] The court was the administration, while Parliament was comprised of both court and country members. The country party was composed of men of property, and it was this property which was the fount of liberty. England should be ruled by a balanced government, within which the role of Parliament was to supervise the executive. This equilibrium, and the function of Parliament within it, was, however, endangered by executive power exercised in a variety of forms.[30] The executive seduced members by offering them positions or pensions, and by persuading them to endorse measures such as standing armies or the National Debt, which activities were beyond Parliament's power to control. Such seduction led inexorably to corruption, to a loss of independence, and hence to the end of liberty.[31]

The very existence of virtue and a commitment to the public good in an age which was increasingly concerned with trade and credit became the subject of intense debate, a discourse in which the details of the argument can blur partisan division.[32] The neo-Harringtonians feared the emerging capitalist society for a variety of reasons which overlapped, but which can be distinguished. One strain of thought emphasized the lack of independence, and hence of virtue, which characterized the type of individual generated by the emergent commercial society. They were potentially corrupt. The stockholder who earned income on funds lent to the government and the bureaucrat were both examples of such suspect categories. As Pocock states: 'The social crime of these individuals was that their being was definable in terms of their dependent relationship to government, whereas that of the citizen—the only truly virtuous and indeed human being—was defined in terms of his independence of the government in which he participated'.[33]

Another line of argument stressed the corrupting effect of all

[29] Pocock, *The Machiavellian Moment*, chs. 12, 13, esp. pp. 446–8; Pocock, 'Machiavelli, Harrington and English Political Ideologies', in *Politics, Language and Time*, pp. 124–5.

[30] Pocock, *The Machiavellian Moment*, pp. 406–7.

[31] Ibid. 408.

[32] Ibid. 447–9.

[33] 'Civic Humanism', in *Politics, Language and Time*, p. 93.

commercial exchange. The individual should ' desire nothing more than freedom, nothing more than the public good to which he dedicated himself'.[34] The reality of commercial exchange placed this ideal in jeopardy. Inherent within such bargains was the possibility of exchanging individual autonomy for some other satisfaction. Citizenship was founded upon a proprietary base which could not be traded without a consequential loss of independence.

A third, and less metaphysical, aspect of commercial society which caused concern was its tendency to concentrate attention upon the particular, and away from the universal good.[35] Commerce generated power relationships between particular interests within the commonwealth. It was an important cause of luxury, with all the opprobrious overtones which this word possessed for eighteenth-century thought. The trader was asked to be frugal in order to minimize the corrupting effects of his very existence. A concern for the particular, as opposed to the universal, was augmented by the specialization and division of function which is characteristic of emergent capitalist society.[36]

The final strain which the nascent capitalist society placed upon republican virtue was the way in which it weakened, and placed in jeopardy, the empirical foundations for citizenship. Although Harrington's own conception of citizenship may not, in a strict sense, have been founded upon a particular conception of the economic order, it was, as we have seen, premised upon freehold property. The distribution of this property was crucial to the stability of the commonwealth, and corruption would ensue if the distribution became too unequal. One of *the* defining traits of the commonwealth was a society in which the 'whole people be landlords' and in which the land be divided so that no man or group 'overbalance' the remainder.[37] If, by way of contrast, the nobility own half and the people half, then there is no remedy 'but the one must eat out the other'; where a prince owns half the dominion and the people the other half then the government becomes a 'very shambles'. The phrase, an 'empire of men, and not of laws', defines a society in which law is indeed present but where this law reflects the private interests of particular groups rather than the general

[34] Pocock, *The Machiavellian Moment*, p. 431.
[35] Ibid. 444–5.
[36] Ibid. 501–2.
[37] Harrington, 'The Commonwealth of Oceana', pp. 163–4.

the general good.[38] Such laws were the inevitable byproduct of inequality in a commonwealth. This created parties which were in 'perpetual variance', the one party endeavouring to preserve their eminence, and the other to obtain equality.[39] It was for this reason that Harrington placed so much importance upon his agrarian law, the object of which was to secure considerable equality in the division of the freehold land. Possible objections to this system were set up and dismissed.[40]

The neo-Harringtonians may not have been egalitarian in the modern sense of that term, but they were none the less alive to the problems which the emergence of trade presented for the Harringtonian conception of citizenship and virtue. Harrington's agrarian law had been designed to equalize the material conditions of civic virtue. The very object was to secure the independence and authority required of the citizen. The dilemma posed for the neo-Harringtonians was the growing realization that 'land could not be freed from its dependence on trade, or trade from its dependence on credit'. To conceive of the equivalent to an agrarian law for a speculative society was unknown and perhaps unthinkable at that time.[41] Moral autonomy founded upon freehold property could not be maintained within the emergent economic order, and corruption through the satisfaction of private wants which were distinctive from the universal good was seen as endemic in the speculative economy.

The objections and fears of the country party did not go unanswered. The responses of the court party were less prominent and less organized than the arguments of their adversaries which we have just considered. They are, however, of particular significance to an understanding of republican thought. The transformation of virtue which we will witness is of importance for an appreciation of US republican ideology and ultimately for the success of the republican ideal as an organizing force for modern public law.

Divergent strains of argument are evident in the literature of the court party. One theme espoused by, for example, Defoe was the

[38] Harrington, 'The Commonwealth of Oceana', p. 161.

[39] Ibid. 180.

[40] The arguments were elaborately staged and were sophisticated. They are still worthy of attention. Ibid. 231–41.

[41] Pocock, *The Machiavellian Moment*, p. 485. As Pocock states, p. 486: 'What may be termed the ideology of the Country was founded on a presumption of real property and an ethos of the civic life, in which the ego knew . . . itself in its relation to a . . . common good, organized as a polity, but was perpetually threatened by corruption operating through private appetites and false consciousness.'

interconnected nature of land, trade, and credit.[42] Land could not thrive without trade; trade could not exist without money; money required credit. Another depicted credit as something positive, virtuous in its own right. Thus, although there were continuous references to the instability and apparent irrationality of credit which drew upon Machiavellian language of disorder or *fortuna*,[43] there was an increasing tendency to depict it as virtuous. If society was healthy, so too would be credit.[44] If credit thrived, real wealth would be created which would benefit society. A third aspect of the court argument is to be found in the emerging thesis which equated private interest with the public good. Modern economics was yet to evolve, but the early eighteenth century produced the work of Mandeville,[45] with his innovative equation of private vice and public interest.

A final and important part of the response to the fears of the country party is present in the works of those, such as Hume, who provided a positive defence for commerce, the arts, and the species of government in which the executive exerted influence over the legislature.[46] Hume believed that commerce and learning had been essential to the emancipation of the people from vassalage. He attacked those who believed that primitive society, or some remote ancestors, were the true exemplars of virtue. Sparta was regarded, not as an ideal to be recaptured, but as evidence that men could not be ordered so as to pursue the public good without tyrannical enforcement of equality and austerity. Commerce was a necessary catalyst in the development of meaningful civilization. If there were no incentives for industry, man would naturally lapse into indolence or dissipation. This defence of commerce gained further force in the late eighteenth century from the writings of Adam Smith and the Scottish School, who depicted social development as proceeding naturally through the four stages of hunting, pasturage, agriculture, and commerce.

The general significance of the shift in thinking of those who adhered broadly to a court ideology is captured by Pocock. Credit

[42] Ibid. 449. This was a fact being increasingly realized by the adherents of the country party.

[43] Ibid. 452–4.

[44] Ibid. 456.

[45] B. Mandeville, *The Fable of the Bees*, ed. J. P. Harth (1970).

[46] Hume's essays on commerce and the arts can be found, together with other related work, in *David Hume: Writings on Economics*, ed. E. Rotwein (1970).

was accepted as a measure of economic value, and passion and interest were regarded as the criteria of human behaviour.

In the place of virtue it stressed the ego's pursuit of satisfaction . . . and was beginning to explore theories of how the diversities of passionate and self-interested action might be manipulated and co-ordinated, or might magically or mechanically co-ordinate themselves, into promoting a common good no longer intimately connected with the inner moral life of the individual. Since it did not regard virtue as politically paradigmatic, it did not regard government as founded upon principles of virtue which needed to be regularly reasserted; it readily accepted that men were factious and interested beings and, instead of regarding these characteristics as fatal if unchecked to virtue and government, proposed to have them policed by a strong central executive, which did not itself need to be disciplined by the principles of virtue, but might without suffering harm appeal to the passions and interests of men. It saw personal morality as private rather than public . . .[47]

The tension between country and court throws into sharp relief the dilemma confronting republicanism. How could republican ideals of citizenship, civic virtue, and the public good be pursued in the changing world which witnessed the emergence of a capitalist economy? This dilemma is one which plagued not only England. It is also evident in US republicanism, to which we should now turn.

3. REPUBLICANISM AND THE US CONSTITUTION

a. Independence

The once prevalent image of the American Revolution, and the Constitution which it generated, as being fundamentally liberal and Lockean[48] in nature has undergone considerable revision within the last twenty years. Recent study,[49] though not uncontested,[50] has

[47] Pocock, *The Machiavellian Moment*, p. 487.

[48] See, e.g., L. B. Hartz, *The Liberal Tradition in America: An Interpretation of American Political Thought since the Revolution* (1955).

[49] C. Robbins, *The Eighteenth-Century Commonwealthman: Studies in the Transmission, Development and Circumstance of English Liberal Thought from the Restoration of Charles II until the War with the Thirteen Colonies* (1959); B. Bailyn, *The Ideological Origins of the American Revolution* (1967) and *The Origins of American Politics* (1970); G. S. Wood, *The Creation of the American Republic, 1776–1787* (1969). For a review of literature on republicanism, see R. E. Shalhope, 'Republicanism and Early American Historiography', 39 *Wm. & Mary Q.* 334 (1982).

[50] See, e.g., I. Kramnick, 'Republican Revisionism Revisited', 87 *Am. Hist. Rev.* 629

emphasized the strongly republican sentiments and ideology which permeated US thought within the period leading up to independence. The language employed in revolutionary literature was replete with reference to corruption, vice, and virtue. The heroes were those of the country party; the villains were those of the court.

The mid-eighteenth century was a neo-classical period within US society. Towns were given classical names, and the architecture strove to replicate the symmetry of the masters of antiquity. The sacrifice of the individual interest to the public good formed the 'essence of republicanism' and the 'idealistic goal of the Revolution'.[51] Americans perceived themselves as engaged in a historic venture, what one writer has termed a 'final attempt'[52] to attain a Commonwealth in which pursuit of the common good would be the only objective of government. Europe was considered to be corrupt precisely because of the prevalence of the particular over the general good, and because narrow oligarchical interests dominated the political arena. A fear that this corruption would, in a literal sense, infect the emergent US polity provided an increasing impetus towards separation from the Crown. Underlying the republican emphasis upon service of the general good was the assumption that the people were a homogeneous body with common interests.

Since everyone in the community was linked organically to everyone else, what was good for the whole community was ultimately good for all the parts. The people were in fact a single organic piece . . . with a unitary concern that was the only legitimate objective of governmental policy. This common interest was not, as we might today think of it, simply the sum of consensus of the particular interests that made up the community. It was rather an entity in itself, prior to and distinct from the various private interests of groups and individuals.[53]

A corollary of this conception was that party and faction were dangerous and would naturally espouse causes divergent from those of the general good.[54] The representatives of the people would speak for the public good. Little tension was perceived between pursuit of the public good and individual liberty, principally because the most

(1982); J. P. Diggins, *The Lost Soul of American Politics: Virtue, Self-Interest and the Foundations of Liberalism* (1984). See also M. J. Horwitz, 'Republicanism and Liberalism in American Constitutional Thought', 29 *Wm. & Mary L. Rev.* 57 (1987–8).

[51] Wood, *The Creation of the American Republic*, p. 53. [52] Ibid. 54. [53] Ibid. 58.

[54] R. Hofstadter, *The Idea of a Party System: The Rise of Legitimate Opposition in the United States, 1780–1840* (1970), ch. 1.

important liberty was political liberty, the public rights of the collective people against the interests of their rulers. If government were invested in the people,[55] it could not be despotic. Abuse of such power would lead to anarchy but not tyranny. The classical republican stress upon the need for civic virtue as a precondition for the attainment of the republican ideal was prevalent within discourse in the late eighteenth century. If the public good was to prevail, then the people must be public spirited. The Mandevillian idea that the public good could be attained through the pursuit of private vice was rejected by the great majority. Excessive and selfish pursuit of private interest would spell disaster for the public good.[56]

The 'material' basis of American republicanism was, however, permeated by a latent tension. We have already seen how important the roughly egalitarian freehold proprietary law was to Harringtonian political theory.[57] The concept of equality in colonial republicanism was ambivalent, stressing on the one hand equality of opportunity which could generate social differences, and on the other equality of condition which would deny these very social differences. Americans in 1776 did not in general conceive of any process of social levelling. Pre-eminence would continue to exist as a result of difference in capacity or virtue. Subordination which resulted from artificial preferment, such as that exercised by the Crown, would be eradicated. None the less a causal nexus between equality of opportunity and equality of condition was perceived.

> It was widely believed that equality of opportunity would necessarily result in a rough equality of station, that as long as the social channels of ascent and descent were kept open it would be impossible for any artificial aristocrats or overgrown rich men to maintain themselves for long. With social movement founded only on merit, no distinctions could have time to harden.[58]

The questionable assumptions behind this reasoning were to plague US republicanism within the next century. Yet the very spectre of increased social inequality could also be used as a spur to revolution. Thus Paine could argue that independence must be sought, because to delay would be to risk disaster. The United States was still principally agrarian. Corruption flowing from

[55] Wood, *The Creation of the American Republic*, pp. 61, 63.

[56] Ibid. 69.

[57] See above, ch. 10 sec. 2b.

[58] Wood, *The Creation of the American Republic*, p. 72; see also p. 73, where Wood describes the latent tensions within this ideal.

increased commerce would generate increased wealth and social divisiveness. The republican ideal would be lost forever. Fear that republicanism was in danger was exacerbated by the recognition among Americans themselves that their society was not free from the corrupting influences which pervaded the Old World. The presence of luxury and vice was acknowledged. This served however as a spur to revolution. Only by severing ties with Britain could the United States not be further infected by these ills.[59] Revolution became the antidote to further moral decay, a theme espoused with increasing vigour by the clergy. The establishment of a republican form of government was conceived as a way of injecting republican values in the people, and of stemming any further tendency towards corruption and decay.[60]

The decade which followed independence proved, however, to be disappointing. The colonial yoke had been shed, and yet republicanism was perceived to be under threat from new sources. It became difficult to distinguish between a laudable desire to excel in order to promote the public good, and the opprobrious object of aggrandizing power in order to promote particularistic interests. Parties emerged in order to pursue factional objectives, and were regarded much like a disease which would kill the nascent republican polity if it was not 'cramped in embrio'.[61] A multiplicity of laws emerged from the new state legislatures. This legislative product was viewed with suspicion. Many statutes were thought to be ill-conceived and the result of factional pressure. The republican experiment was believed to be endangered, and this fear was heightened by increasing evidence of private greed assuming prominence over the pursuit of the public good. Constitutional reform within the state legislatures did little to assuage the growing disillusionment with US political behaviour.[62] It was the problems with state government as well as the weaknesses of the Articles of Confederation which were to play a major role in the movement towards a strengthened federal government.[63]

b. The Constitution

How far republican ideals permeated the thinking of the framers of the Constitution is a topic on which there has been much disagreement. Opinions differ markedly on the main themes which

[59] Ibid. 107–8, 110.
[60] Ibid. 116–7, 123.
[61] Ibid. 403.
[62] Ibid. 415–16.
[63] Ibid. 467.

can be said to characterize the thought of both Federalists and Anti-Federalists.

One reading of the constitutional debates depicts the arguments of the Federalists, and particularly those of Madison, in pluralistic rather than republican terms.[64] Madison believed that it was axiomatic that an individual or group would tyrannize others unless restrained in some manner.[65] The Madisonian strategy was to forestall the occurrence of this danger. To ensure the existence of a non-tyrannical republic the accumulation of all powers—legislative, judicial and executive—within the same hands was to be avoided. It was this which was to provide the basis from which many of the checks and balances which are characteristic of the US Constitution have developed. Separation of governmental power was not the only condition for a non-tyrannical republic. The other was to prevent factions from acting adversely to the rights of other citizens or to the aggregate interests of the community. Minority factions could be outvoted. The possibility of a majority faction presented greater difficulty. The response was to broaden the franchise. A majority faction was less likely to exist, and less likely to act as a unity, the more extended and diverse were the interests of the electorate. In an enlarged republic a majority would lack stability, thereby reducing the threat to minority interests. The pluralist reading of Madisonian thought therefore stresses balance and the separation of power, the avoidance of powerful faction, and competition between interests.

This interpretation has been challenged by those who argue that Federalist thought cannot be reduced to a species of interest-group pluralism, and that it more accurately represented a modified form of republicanism. It is necessary to understand the nature of the debate in order to comprehend this interpretation of the Constitution. The Federalists were responding in part to the arguments of the Anti-Federalists.[66] The latter believed that government should be devoted to pursuit of the public good, and that decentralization was necessary to ensure that the people could participate in the governmental process. It was only where society was sufficiently decentralized that sufficient homogeneity of interest would exist to

[64] R. A. Dahl, *A Preface to Democratic Theory* (1956), ch. 1.

[65] Many of these arguments are to be found in *Federalist*, No. 10; see C. Rossiter (ed.), *The Federalist Papers* (1961).

[66] H. Storing (ed.), *The Complete Anti-Federalist* (1981); H. Storing, *What The Anti-Federalists Were For* (1981); R. Ketcham (ed.), *The Anti-Federalist Papers and the Constitutional Convention Debates* (1986).

allow the predominance of the public good over heterogeneous factional interest; only localized government could prevent the citizen from being distanced from the state. The Anti-Federalists accepted the need for representation rather than direct citizen participation, but feared that a remote national government would entail loss of control over the representatives.

The response of the Federalists[67] was, it is argued,[68] not to abandon republican principle, but to modify it. Corruption—and the consequential emergence of faction—was inherent in the nature of man. It was also likely to be most dangerous within the *small* republic, where a powerful group could more easily attain political control. Hence the emphasis placed upon the large republic, and the conflict between diverse groups which would prevent the ascendancy of any particular group for any length of time. This reading of Madisonian thought therefore stresses the role of groups as preventing the dominance of a particular faction. The essential aim of government is still to enhance the public good, and the pluralist idea that the result of interest-group competition *is* the public good is said to be absent from Madisonian and Federalist thought.[69] A large republic would also be less likely to produce representatives who were too closely tied to local interests, and would thereby increase the chance that the representatives would act for the public good.[70] The structural provisions of the Constitution, and the separation of powers, are said to be designed to achieve the same end. Checks and balances at the federal level were intended to be a restraint against factional tyranny 'in the event that national officials failed to fulfil their responsibilities' of legislating for the public good.[71] In the words of Sunstein:

> In important respects, the departure from traditional republicanism could not have been greater. Madison willingly abandoned the classical republican understanding that citizens generally should participate directly in the process of government. Far from being a threat to freedom, a large republic would help to guarantee it. At the same time, Madison's understanding was

[67] This is not intended to imply that there was a uniform, fixed view among all the Federalists. They differed on important matters: Wood, *The Creation of the American Republic*; G. Stourzh, *Alexander Hamilton and the Idea of Republican Government* (1970).

[68] C. R. Sunstein, 'Interest Groups in American Public Law', 38 *Stan. L. Rev.* 29 (1985); 'Constitutionalism After the New Deal', 101 *Harv. L. Rev.* 421, 430–7 (1987).

[69] Wood, *The Creation of the American Republic*, p. 505.

[70] Ibid. 505–6, 508–10.

[71] Sunstein, 'Interest Groups', p. 44.

sharply distinct from that of the modern pluralists. He hoped that national representatives operating above the fray, would be able to disentangle themselves from local pressures and deliberate on and bring about something like an objective public good. Those representatives would have the virtue associated with classical republican citizens.[72]

4. REPUBLICANISM AND MODERN US PUBLIC LAW

Lawyers who have recently evinced an interest in republican political theory have not been motivated by purely historical interest. They have sought to draw upon this historical tradition to determine the direction which modern public law should pursue. The objective has been both normative and descriptive. In normative terms it has been argued that a modified republicanism furnishes a theory which is preferable to that of interest-group pluralism. In descriptive terms it has been argued that legal doctrines should be interpreted in such a way as to effectuate the aims of republicanism. Sunstein and Michelman have been two of the principal advocates of this approach.

Sunstein, while admitting that there are a variety of approaches which could be described as republican,[73] argues that the normative aspect of republicanism entails an attachment to four central commitments: deliberation, political equality, universalism, and citizenship. *Deliberation* connotes the idea that political actors do not come to the political process with interests 'that operate as exogenous variables'. The purpose of politics is not to aggregate private preferences, but rather to 'achieve a measure of critical distance from prevailing desires and practices, subjecting these desires and practices to scrutiny and review'.[74] Deliberation has not only a procedural but also a substantive connotation. Constraints are placed upon both the inputs to the dialogue and the outcomes which are to be tolerated. The requirement of deliberation thus embodies 'substantive limitations that in some settings lead to uniquely correct outcomes'.[75]

[72] 'Interest Groups', p. 42. See also G. Wills, *Explaining America: The Federalist* (1981); D. F. Epstein, *The Political Theory of the Federalist* (1984). Cf. R.W. Krouse, 'Classical Images of Democracy in America: Madison and Tocqueville', in G. Duncan (ed.), *Democratic Theory and Practice*, ch. 5.

[73] C. R. Sunstein, 'Beyond the Republican Revival', 97 *Yale L.J.* 1539, 1547–8, 1564–71 (1988).

[74] Ibid. 1548–9.

[75] Ibid. 1550–1; see also p. 1550 n. 54.

Political equality in republican terms requires that all individuals and groups have access to the political process. Thus measures designed to reduce the influence of wealth on the political process, or to furnish access to the media, are applauded.[76] Sunstein is, however, ambivalent about the precise interrelationship of political and economic equality.

Universalism entails a 'belief' in the possibility of mediating different approaches to politics, or different conceptions of the public good, through discussion or dialogue.[77] This dialogic process is designed to produce substantively correct outcomes 'understood as such through the ultimate criterion of agreement among political equals'. Republicans are not, however, said to believe in some unitary conception of the public good, and it appears to be accepted that individuals will have competing conceptions of the good which cannot be reconciled notwithstanding deliberation *inter se*.[78]

Citizenship requires mechanisms for citizen control of national institutions, and also for 'decentralization, local control and local self-determination'.[79] Participation is valued, not only on instrumental grounds, but also as a vehicle for the inculcation of empathy, virtue, and feelings of community.

The difficulties and ambiguities which beset these normative foundations of modified republicanism will be examined below.[80] Before doing so some idea of the doctrinal implications which are said to follow from an adherence to republican thought can be conveyed.

Thus Sunstein argues that the rationality requirement of the equal-protection and due-process clauses, which is difficult to comprehend for those who regard politics as a process of pure interest-group pluralism, is readily explicable for modified republicanism.[81] The requirement in such cases that there be some independent 'public interest', and not just naked political bargain, exemplifies the republican concern with pursuit of the public good. The requirement that a contract can only be abrogated if a legitimate public value is to be promoted, and the analogous principle of public use which is necessary to justify a taking of property under the eminent domain clause, are said to demonstrate

[76] Ibid. 1552–3, 1576–8.

[77] Ibid. 1554–5.

[78] Ibid. 1555.

[79] Ibid. 1555–6.

[80] See, ch. 10 sec. 5.

[81] 'Interest Groups', p. 49.

the same theme.[82] Legislative deliberations based solely upon private pressure are condemned, and representatives are exhorted to direct their attention to the public good.[83] Sunstein, however, accepts the limitations of his own thesis. Statutes are in fact rarely invalidated, and the court is often willing to hypothesize legitimate ends even in those instances where it is unlikely that the ends in fact accounted for the legislation. He concedes that it would be foolish to suggest that, at any time since the decline of substantive due process, the court has really engaged in a serious effort to police the operation of interest-group politics, but asserts that it would be equally foolish to attempt to explain the present law as a system in which interest-group politics is fully accepted.[84]

Similar themes are said to be identifiable within administrative law. Participation by groups interested in the agency determination fosters citizen involvement in the governmental process, and is designed to prevent any single faction from securing exclusive hearing rights before the decision-making body. The hard-look doctrine furthers this aim by helping to ensure that the resultant agency decision considers the relevant evidence, and does not unduly reflect the concern of a particular private faction rather than the overall general good.[85]

A general normative analysis has also recently been provided by Michelman,[86] who, following Pocock, traces the connection between Harringtonian republicanism, and the ideology which permeated the latter part of eighteenth-century US thought. Michelman argues that Harrington's conception of republicanism was composed of seven main principles: self-government, practical deliberation or dialogue, equality (of ruling and being ruled), antistatism (immediacy), rationally cognizable values (the general good), a role-differentiated constitution in which civic virtue was attained through balanced government and proprietary independence, and action by promulgation of laws.[87] Self-government is seen as the main organizing theme around which the other elements of

[82] 'Interest Groups', p. 50.

[83] Ibid. 52.

[84] Ibid. 53–4, 59.

[85] Ibid. 61, 63, 65. See also C. R. Sunstein, 'Naked Preferences and the Constitution', 84 *Col. L. Rev.* 1689 (1984); C. R. Sunstein, 'Public Values, Private Interests, and the Equal Protection Clause' (1982) *Sup. Ct. Rev.* 127; Sunstein, 'Beyond the Republican Revival', pp. 1576–89; Sunstein, 'Constitutionalism', pp. 463–74.

[86] F. I. Michelman, 'Foreword: Traces of Self-Government', 100 *Harv. L. Rev.* 4 (1986).

[87] Ibid. 47.

Harringtonian discourse revolve. Certain of these elements are conceived of as subjective or volitional aspects of self-government which describe the participatory aspects of republican thought. These are practical deliberation, equality of ruling and being ruled, and antistatism. The remaining components are conceived of as objective elements: the common good, civic virtue, and legality. For Michelman these latter elements are 'all essential to the Harringtonian conception but not fundamental within it';[88] they are components which must be true or possible if self-government is true or possible.

Michelman reviews the passage of post-Harringtonian republican thought from England to the colonies, and accepts that diverse interpretations of the Constitution, from a pluralist to a republican perception of government, still persist.[89] He then endeavours to elaborate upon a republican vision which places self-government at the forefront of constitutional design. This is, as he admits, not an easy task, 'because the document so obviously charters not a participatory democracy but a sovereign authority of governors . . . distinct from the governed'.[90] Sunstein's thesis, that the Constitution was designed to ensure that the representatives would behave with republican virtue, deliberating in pursuit of the public good under the ever-careful gaze of the reviewing court lest they should stray from the appointed task, is sympathetically reviewed. Michelman, however, finds the constitutional vision of self-government more fruitfully embedded in Ackerman's thesis, which allocates civic virtue to each citizen.[91]

Ackerman has argued that the Constitution embodies a dual system of law-making.[92] 'Normal politics' comprise the everyday pluralist-type legislative bargain in which private self-interest is manifest. 'Constitutional politics' occur relatively rarely, and comprise those instances when the people exhibit the public-spirited vision of republican citizens. Such activity is characterized by appeal to the common good, 'ratified by a mobilized mass of American citizens expressing their assent through extraordinary institutional forms'.[93] Judicial review finds its justification in this

[88] Ibid.

[89] Ibid. 48–50.

[90] Ibid. 57.

[91] Ibid. 59–61.

[92] B. Ackerman, 'The Storrs Lectures: Discovering the Constitution', 93 *Yale L.J.* 1013, 1022, 1042 (1984).

[93] Ibid. 1022.

very ideal nature of politics. Congress forms the institutional arena for normal politics which is characterized by private pressure. The politicians who make such bargains are stand-ins for the people. When such representatives respond to special interests in ways which jeopardize the fundamental principles of the Constitution, the judge has the duty to 'expose them for what they are: merely "stand-ins" for the people themselves'.[94] Judicial review therefore operates as a tocsin bell. It warns the mass of citizens that something special is happening in the halls of power, and that their representatives are attempting to legislate in ways 'that few political movements in American history have done with credibility'.[95] This is the function of the court when it declares a statute to be unconstitutional. The court becomes guardian for 'We the People'. It performs a signalling function by indicating to the people that a fundamental constitutional initiative is being entertained by Congress. This, according to Ackerman, is what the court was doing when it initially resisted New Deal ideas in the name of traditional principles. However, the court must not only operate as a signal; it must be an equally astute receptor. 'The People' may well indicate, as they did in the 1930s, that they endorsed the political change of direction which was manifested in New Deal policies. This then becomes an example of constitutional politics in which 'the People' render their vision of the common good apparent and act in a public-spirited rather than factious capacity.[96] When this has become evident, it is for the court to accept this 'structural amendment', and no longer hinder the new path of society. This, says Ackerman, is precisely what occurred in the court's volte-face over New Deal policies.[97] Ackerman ends by exhorting the reader to accept and employ his dualist vision.[98] Changes within the Constitution brought about through structural amendment should be recognized. The old and outdated should be discarded. The transformation of constitutional doctrine by the proclamation of new principles 'in the name of the People' should be acknowledged. All such higher law principles 'enacted by the People' in the last two centuries should be organized into a coherent whole.

94 Ackerman, 'The Storrs Lectures:', p. 1030.

95 Ibid. 1050.

96 Ibid. 1053–4.

97 Ibid. 1055–6; for Ackerman's use of the idea of structural amendment, pp. 1051–7.

98 Ibid. 1071–2.

Michelman expressess ambivalence about Ackerman's thesis. He is sympathetic to the idea that civic virtue resides with each citizen, and with what he perceives to be Ackerman's ultimate aim, the reinvigoration of citizenship.[99] He is, however, sceptical of the idea that 'the People' are truly self-governing in any realistic sense during the moments of constitutional politics.[100] It would, says Michelman, be fantasy, not history, to imagine the People in the 1930s consciously engaged in transforming the meaning of past constitutional events. Moreover, how is one to distinguish between intense public-regarding civic involvement as an example of self-government, and equally passionate participation which is the result of domination and ideological manipulation from above? It is for this reason that he interprets Ackerman as ultimately placing self-government within the judiciary. The court becomes the representation of the People's absent self-government. It is the judiciary which signals the constitutional hazard arising from novel legislation endangering received constitutional principle. It is the judiciary which decides ultimately, in its receptor role, whether the public has evinced sufficient assent to novel governmental strategies to warrant recognizing the transformation of constitutional doctrine. It is the court which will perform the holistic narrative enterprise which Ackerman recommends to us in his conclusion.

The 'migration' of self-government from the people to the court which Michelman perceives in Ackerman's thesis is, however, not a transition which the former deplores.[101] It is rather interpreted as the most practicable manifestation of self-government which is possible in modern society. The citizen of Geneva could conceive of direct democratic self-government, a 'sovereignless process of ruling and being ruled'. The citizen of the United States could not realistically expect national politics to offer the possibility of positive freedom secured through self-government. Separation of ruler from the ruled was integral to US government. It was, therefore, for the court to take on the job of 'modelling' self-government, which citizens found to be practically beyond their own reach.

Michelman utilizes Dworkin's recent work[102] to substantiate this

[99] Michelman, 'Foreword', pp. 59–60, 62.

[100] Ibid. 65 and n. 352. See also F. I. Michelman, 'Law's Republic', 97 *Yale L.J.* 1493, 1520–1 (1988).

[101] Michelman, 'Foreword', pp. 66, 74–5.

[102] R. Dworkin, *Law's Empire* (1986).

picture of the judicial role. Thus the conception of legal integrity, which forms the core of Dworkin's thesis, is said to correspond closely to the idea of personal integrity or self-government. An individual will show such integrity or self-government by acting according to convictions which shape the entire life of the individual rather than acting for capricious reasons. The Dworkinian narrative model of legal interpretation is 'part of an account of political self-government through which socially situated individuals realize moral freedom or personal integrity'.[103] A judge achieves integrity through the narrative method and thereby manifests his own self-government. Citizens can share in this process of self-government in a double sense. They may feel the authors of the decisions made by those who govern them, whether as legislator or as judge.[104] This authorial sense may, however, seem too strained for many. Where this is so, the value of legal integrity becomes representational. The judge represents integrity and hence self-government to the community. Virtual representation reappears in the political arena. The judge 'represents by his own self-government our missing self-government, by his own practical reason our missing dialogue'.[105]

5. THE REPUBLICAN REVIVAL: NORMATIVE ASSESSMENT

a. Deliberation and the Public Good: The Dilemma of the Legislator

The centrality of deliberation to Sunstein's thesis is evident from the preceding discussion; the dilemmas which this poses for the legislator are not so apparent and these will be examined within this section.

For Sunstein the acquisitive self-regarding face of an individual acting in a private capacity is to be transcended or ameliorated by the representative at the public level. The representative is to be virtuous, and is to deliberate in order to determine which preferences can be regarded as distorted through social inequality, status, etc.[106] In this way a conception of the good which is

[103] Michelman, 'Foreword', p. 69.
[104] Ibid. 69.
[105] Ibid. 73; see also the discussion on p. 72.
[106] Sunstein, 'Interest Groups', pp. 81, 84; 'Beyond the Republican Revival', pp. 1548–51.

distinctive from the pure aggregation of private utilities may be obtained. There are two problems with this approach.

First, as Sunstein's own work demonstrates,[107] almost all preferences could be regarded as the result of distorting circumstances. All of our personal utilities could be said to be contingent upon social circumstances of wealth, position, status, and other variables. The individual is socially situated, and therefore one may choose to describe the preferences which emerge as 'distorted' by these circumstances. Yet this very fact serves to reveal the continuing nature of the problem. Our deliberating representative is faced by two options.

The less radical, though still far-reaching, option would be to regard all or most expressions of preference as suspect in the search for the public good. How then should he 'select, evaluate and shape these preferences' rather than merely 'implement' them?[108] And in this selection process is there any guarantee that those preferences which are conditioned by, for example, wealth will be treated as more or less given than those which arise from other circumstances?

The more radical option is to seek to achieve obliquely what the eighteenth- and nineteenth-century theorists did not believe could be achieved at all. Traditional republicanism saw moral autonomy and citizen independence as founded upon proprietary independence. This was the rationale for Harrington's agrarian law, which ensured a rough equality in the disposition of freehold land. The dilemma perceived by the neo-Harringtonians was the way in which commercial society undermined these principles. It was not possible for them to conceive of the equivalent to an agrarian law for a speculative society. Such a law would be necessary to provide the equality required for citizen autonomy within the changed economic order. The radical option for Sunstein's deliberative legislator would be to attempt just that. If all or most preferences are shaped and determined by wealth, position, status, etc., then the 'solution' would be to address the social, contingent causes which produced these differences in utilities. The individual's own preferences, and his or her own conception of the good, are distorted in the above manner. The deliberating representative does not merely implement

[107] C. R. Sunstein, 'Legal Interference with Private Preferences', 53 *U. Chi. L. Rev.* 1129 (1986), and 'Disrupting Voluntary Transactions', in J. W. Chapman and J. R. Pennock (eds.), *Markets and Justice: Nomos 31* (1989), ch. 10.

[108] Sunstein, 'Interest Groups', p. 82.

these preferences, but chooses to remove as far as possible the reason for the distortion. This requires addressing the social and economic inequalities which are the causes thereof, in order that the individual can attain the moral autonomy required for citizen independence, and a 'truer' perception of the public good. Civic virtue and attachment to the common good, which reside initially in the representatives, are used by them to create the conditions of equality in which the ordinary citizen can exercise judgement and determine preference freed from the distorting influence created by disparities in wealth or position.

It may, of course, be that the neo-Harringtonians were wrong, and that such a social position could be achieved. Ideas concerning both capitalism and equality have after all changed considerably in the past two centuries. The change has not, however, been only in one direction. There may now be evidence of greater concern for equality, but there is also a considerably greater attachment to the capitalist order, which is accepted by many as the norm. The plausibility of pursuing the radical option, while remaining within the US capitalist ethos, is highly debatable. The United States now appears a much less likely candidate for a Christian Sparta than ever it did to the Founders. It is difficult, therefore, to believe that the radical option would prove acceptable, more particularly in the light of the transformation of republican thought considered below. If the radical option proves unacceptable, then the content of the public good which subsists independently of private preference will be limited in scope. When statutes do assume the form of private bargains conducted at the public level, then modified republicanism will exert some control over such naked deals. This will, however, only scratch the surface. The effect of such doctrine upon the social and economic disparities which cause such exercises of power will be interstitial.

The second problem is related to, but distinctive from, the first. It is also more serious. The conscientious legislator cannot determine whether he should pursue the less radical, more radical, or indeed any other strategy, precisely because the nature of the public good which is intended to result from this deliberative process is never specifically defined.

Deliberation, as noted above, has both a procedural and a substantive dimension. The former embraces the idea that existing preferences should not be treated as exogenous variables, but should rather be subjected to scrutiny, review, and revision.[109] The latter encapsulates the idea that deliberation imposes constraints on both inputs and outcomes.[110]

If, however, this modified form of republicanism is to guide the deliberating legislator, or the courts, then the underlying political theory which justifies the nature of these constraints must be articulated. It is only by doing so that the deliberating legislator can make any determination as to how to revise or scrutinize existing preferences; and it is only by doing so that the notion of the public good for which the legislator strives can be imbued with any meaning. The importance of this point can be more fully appreciated by considering its impact upon republican notions of rights and distributive justice.

b. *Republican Rights and Distributive Justice: The Position of the Legislator*

This section will be concerned with the content of rights and the notion of distributive justice which subsist within a republican polity. Answers to both of these issues will be necessary if our deliberating legislator is to know the public good which he is seeking to advance.

The conscientious, deliberating legislator is to revise or scrutinize existing preferences, and is to place substantive constraints on the inputs and outcomes of the deliberative process, with the objective of attaining the public good. The political theory which 'directs' this deliberative process, and the role of rights and distributive justice therein, must however be articulated, since it is only by doing so that the legislator can fulfil the tasks assigned to him adumbrated above. There are, however, crucial ambiguities and uncertainties in the depiction of rights and distributive justice by modern exponents of republicanism.

Sunstein argues that republican theories are not hostile to the protection of rights, and specifies certain of the rights which would subsist within a republican polity.[111] Liberty of conscience, expression, and the right to vote are regarded as the 'basic preconditions for republican deliberation'. Property rights have been traditionally perceived as an important guarantee of security and virtue within

[109] Sunstein, 'Beyond the Republican Revival', pp. 1548–9.
[110] Ibid. 1550–1.
[111] Ibid.

republican theory.[112] Sunstein accepts this, with the caveat that republicans should not be hostile to measures designed to redistribute wealth with the objective of equalizing political influence. Two related comments on this picture are warranted.

On the one hand, the justification for these rights draws heavily upon the reasoning of deontological liberals such as Rawls, and indeed Sunstein stresses the interconnection between liberalism and republicanism.[113] The Rawlsian theory, and its application to public law, have been considered in detail above.[114] If, however, republicanism is to be conceived of in this manner, it is difficult to see precisely what contribution it is making to political thought which has not been already expressed in more analytic detail by liberal theorists. The complex reasoning which serves to justify rights within liberalism has already been considered.[115] The sophistication of this analysis exceeds that offered by advocates of modern republicanism, and such liberals also reject any conception of social justice founded upon naked legislative bargain. If our deliberating legislator is really concerned to advance the public good, and to understand the meaning thereof, he would derive more guidance from Rawls directly.

On the other hand, the content of republican conceptions of rights and distributive justice is uncertain at particular crucial junctures. The earlier discussion of liberalism revealed that the conception of distributive justice therein was contentious, as was the relationship between rights and distributive justice. The rationale for the lexical priority of the first principle of justice over the second continues to provoke discussion.[116] This earlier analysis also revealed, however, two issues of relevance for the present discussion. The rights accorded to citizens and the conception of distributive justice are integrally related; they come as a package. That analysis also revealed that the legislators must have *some* conception of distributive justice to guide them, since without it they simply *cannot know* which types of legislation they should enact in order to advance the public good.

It is precisely at this juncture that the modern advocates of republicanism are most uncertain. Thus, while Sunstein expresses

[112] See above, ch. 10 sec. 2a.
[113] 'Beyond the Republican Revival', pp. 1551, 1566–9.
[114] See above, ch. 8.
[115] See above, ch. 8 secs. 2, 3.
[116] See above, ch. 8 sec. 2c.

an attachment to some measure of wealth redistribution in order to equalize political influence,[117] he also admits that the notion that political equality depends upon economic equality is controversial among republican theorists.[118]

This uncertainty produces a considerable 'gap' in the analysis. Our conscientious deliberating legislator, who is seeking to scrutinize existing preferences and to advance the public good, is left without a map at the point he requires one the most. He is without explicit direction on two central issues. He is left unsure as to what distributive justice does mean for modernized republicanism, *and* he is left without guidance as to whether any such advancement of economic equality can be achieved through a limitation of rights. These issues are, as the earlier discussion of liberalism revealed, of seminal importance in determining the obligations of the legislature.

The uncertainty surrounding these issues also produces difficulties of a corresponding nature for related parts of the republican analysis. The substantive constraints upon inputs and outputs which are placed upon the deliberative process[119] will obviously be directly affected by the answer to the preceding questions. Whether, for example, a policy which restricts certain proprietary or political rights, in order to advance a certain conception of economic equality, is acceptable depends upon answers to the two central issues outlined above.

The discussion thus far has focused upon the uncertainty surrounding republican conceptions of rights and distributive justice, and the difficulties which this creates for the legislature. There is, moreover, a further dimension to the problem. The preceding analysis of liberalism and public law revealed that while the state should seek to protect and enhance the principles of justice, it should in other respects be neutral as to conceptions of the good. The justification for, and difficulties of this position, have already been considered. In so far as Sunstein links republicanism with liberalism, it is unclear whether he subscribes to this dichotomy, or whether the liberalism with which he has greater affinity is really the perfectionist form espoused by Raz.

The 'choice' between the two versions of liberalism can, as has been seen, have significant consequences for the legitimate scope of

[117] 'Beyond the Republican Revival', p. 1551.
[118] Ibid. 1552–3.
[119] Sunstein, 'Beyond the Republican Revival', pp. 1550, 1568.

legislative activity. Perfectionist liberalism countenances state action in pursuit of morally valid ideals, in a manner which deontological liberals reject.

The conception of neutrality which Sunstein adopts leaves the answer to this important issue unclear. Thus neutrality is said to be a plausible concept if it is taken to mean 'the consistent application of the correct substantive theory, or even the consistent application of the speaker's own substantive theory'.[120] Whether this would entitle the legislature to pursue perfectionist aims is uncertain. The history of republican thought, and the centrality accorded to the idea of the public good, could lead one to an affirmative response. Clarity on this issue, one way or the other, is, however, of considerable importance if the deliberating legislator is to determine the legitimate boundaries of state action.

c. Republican Rights and Distributive Justice: The Role of the Courts

Those who espouse a modified form of republicanism encounter two problems in articulating a role for the courts.

i. The rationale for a republican interpretation The first problem is the rationale for suggesting that the courts should adopt a republican perspective at all when adjudicating upon issues which come before them. The problem is approached differently by Sunstein and Michelman, but neither approach is free from difficulty.

Sunstein, as we have seen, regards the deliberative legislator as the principal bearer of the republican mantle. The role is buttressed by reference to the republican themes which were present in the debates of the framers of the Constitution, such as Madison. However, as Sunstein recognizes, the reference to republican elements within Madisonian thought cannot itself resolve the issue concerning the basis of constitutional interpretation now, unless one relies on some species of originalism which he rejects.[121] Sunstein's response is, in effect, to urge that the court should base its reasoning upon modified republican principles, both because such ideas do have historical lineage in US constitutional thought, and because it is the better political theory when compared to 'naked pluralist bargain'. However, even if republicanism is regarded as a 'better'

[120] Sunstein, 'Beyond the Republican Revival', p. 1568.
[121] Ibid. 1563.

political theory than 'naked pluralism', it is not self-evident that it should be preferred to the wholesale adoption of the type of deontological liberalism propounded by Rawls.

Michelman's approach is rather different. We are told that the court is to supply the missing self-government of the citizen. This is problematic. Self-government is a malleable conception and nowhere is this more apparent than in the 'transfer' of power from citizen to court. Let us accept for the present that legal integrity in the Dworkinian sense can, as Michelman argues, be roughly equated with personal integrity.[122] Let us assume also that both personal and legal integrity imply self-government.[123] The individual demonstrates integrity by acting according to convictions which shape his whole life rather than by caprice; the judge evinces a similar integrity by insisting, through the narrative technique, upon consistency of principle across the range of the legal standards the community now enforces, including the principles necessary to justify those decisions. The court, we are told, is to mould the active self-government which the citizens find to be pragmatically beyond their reach. This would seem to indicate that the court should use its power to construct rights which are conducive to the republican ethic. Although Michelman does not define in detail the nature of such rights, he does provide some indication of his thoughts. Thus we are told that republicanism is a 'thoroughly and irredeemably process-based and centered theory';[124] and that republican rights should be concerned with 'participation, capacitation and emancipation'.[125]

The problem with this view is that 'technique' and 'result' become elided. One may well agree with the Dworkinian idea of legal narrative and integrity. One may well believe that republican rights would be desirable. The idea that the one, properly used, will generate the other is far from clear. Dworkin himself is, as is well known, a prominent and powerful advocate of liberalism,[126] who appears to believe that the liberal view is supported by the narrative theory

[122] Michelman, 'Foreword', pp. 68–9. Whether this equation can be sustained is itself debatable.

[123] Ibid.

[124] Ibid. 42 n. 223.

[125] Ibid. 43 n. 229; see also p. 41 n. 214. For comment on these ideas, see below, ch. 10 sec. 5c (iii).

[126] R. Dworkin, 'Liberalism', in S. Hampshire (ed.), *Public and Private Morality* (1978), 113–43.

which he expounds.[127] He might accept the language of self-government as descriptive of the process of judicial integrity. The content of the constitutional rights which flow from this narrative process will, however, be different from those proposed by a republican advocate.[128] It is Dworkin and liberalism which have been prominent targets for those who champion some modernized form of republicanism or participatory democracy.[129] It is the latter who play a major role in Michelman's own analysis.[130]

Now it could of course be argued by way of response that the 'technique' does after all fit the desired 'result'. A properly informed Hercules would in fact reach the conclusion that republicanism provided the best fit for all the available materials, and the scheme of principles necessary to justify them. This enterprise is not explicitly undertaken, nor would it be an easy claim to vindicate. Historical evidence that republican themes informed the framers of the Constitution is doubtless present, but the extent to which the Constitution as a whole should be seen as republican, rather than pluralist, Lockean, or liberal, still evokes disagreement.[131] Subsequent social and economic developments in the nineteenth century indicate the changing nature of republican ideology.[132] Judicial decisions, while arguably consonant with Madisonian republicanism, could also be read as modified pluralism. Moreover, much of the literature, legal and non-legal, indicates that liberalism represents the 'dominant element' in the status quo which should be altered for some more communal perspective.[133]

The aim in presenting the foregoing argument is not to uphold liberalism at the expense of republicanism. It is to point out that the conceptual step entailed in moving from citizen self-government, to

[127] Dworkin does not make this explicit, but see *Law's Empire*, pp. 271–3 (a defence of liberalism against the CLS); pp. 354–9 (The Constitution). Although Dworkin expresses reservations about the usefulness of the division between liberal and conservative, pp. 357–9, Hercules, once on the Supreme Court, reasons much like a Dworkinian liberal, see the summary, pp. 397–9; pp. 407–10 ('on law's dreams') reinforces this view, as does the discussion on pp. 276–312 (the common law). See also Dworkin's political philosophy, in particular, 'What is Equality? Part 4. Political Equality', 22 *Univ. of San Francisco L. R.* 1 (1987–8).

[128] See above, chs. 8, 9.

[129] See above, ch. 10 n. 2.

[130] Michelman, 'Foreword', pp. 17–33.

[131] See above, ch. 10 nn. 49-50; see also J. Appleby, *Capitalism and a New Social Order: The Republican Vision of the 1790s* (1984).

[132] See below, ch. 10 sec. 6.

[133] This is the prevalent theme in much of the literature, above ch. 10 n. 2.

the court-modelling self-government in the republican image for the citizen through the use of Dworkinian techniques, is not as easy as it might appear. There is the real danger that the technique could fashion a conception of citizen self-government very different from the republican image.

ii. The content of constitutional rights (1) The second problem faced by advocates of modern republicanism concerns the *content* of the constitutional rights and principles which are to be enforced by the courts.

The twofold nature of this difficulty can be stated at the outset, and is reflective of the previous discussion. The constitutional rights which are relatively certain are in fact borrowed piecemeal from liberalism, which begs the question as to the distinctive nature of republicanism. Other principles of constitutional adjudication, some of which are novel, others of which are not, are uncertain in their application precisely because the specific content of republican rights and distributive justice are themselves ambiguous.

This twofold difficulty can be perceived by focusing upon certain of the examples which Sunstein proffers of republican constitutional adjudication.

Sunstein favours the regulation of campaign finance and disapproves of Supreme Court decisions which have invalidated such regulation.[134] The rationale for such regulation is that it serves to enhance political equality. The argument draws explicitly upon the Rawlsian idea that the fair value of political liberties should be secured through constitutional adjudication.[135] This approach may well be desirable, but the adoption of this reasoning by republicans merits two comments. On the one hand, it serves to highlight the fact that republican conceptions of rights tend to be most certain when they borrow directly from deontological liberalism. On the other hand, the very problems which exist with the distinction between protecting the fair value of political liberties and not protecting the fair value of other liberties are not addressed at all. Nor is there consideration of whether the fair values of political liberties can be effectively protected without recourse to more general concern for the value of other liberties. The nature of these

[134] 'Beyond the Republican Revival', pp. 1576–8.
[135] Ibid. 1577 n. 206.

arguments has been considered above and reference should be made to that discussion.[136]

Rationality review is, as has already been seen,[137] defended as a natural corollary of the deliberative aspect of republican politics. Legislation cannot be naked pluralist bargain, and the Constitution requires 'some showing that a burden was imposed, or a benefit denied, for a reason other than the exercise of political power by the advantaged class'.[138]

The idea of rationality review is, of course, not novel, and one may well agree that legislation should not be regarded as a naked pluralist deal. Republicanism does not, however, furnish any sure guide as to how the courts should employ this review. The requirement of deliberation demands that the legislator scrutinize/revise existing preferences, and that substantive limits should be placed upon inputs and outputs in the legislative process. However, the substantive political theory never tells us enough concerning the nature of republican rights and distributive justice in order, except in the most obvious of cases, to determine *which* preferences should be revised, and *which* limits should be placed on input and outcome. This renders it difficult for a court to determine whether the burden which was imposed on the particular group was rational and for the public good, or whether it was an illegitimate exercise of pure political power for the advantaged class.

The same type of difficulty besets the treatment of disadvantaged groups. Republicanism is said to provide the basis for countering classifications in areas such as race, sex, and poverty. The values which support such classifications are said to be the product of social power, and must therefore be subject to scrutiny and review. Discrimination against such groups is to be tackled through republican beliefs in political equality and deliberation.[139]

The protection of some disadvantaged groups through the equal protection clause is, like the concept of rationality review, an existing feature of constitutional adjudication. The republican approach to the treatment of such groups highlights the uncertainties which persist within their notions of rights and distributive justice. These can be represented as follows.

[136] See above, ch. 8 sec. 3a (ii).
[137] See above, ch. 10 sec. 4.
[138] Sunstein, 'Beyond the Republican Revival', p. 1579.
[139] Ibid. 1580–1.

First, if groups such as the poor are to be protected, it is doubtful whether this can be realistically achieved through concepts such as 'political equality and deliberation', even using those terms with a republican connotation. Nor can such protection be secured if it only operates when the legislature actually 'classifies' the poor in some manner. The poor or an ethnic group may be harmed by the fact that legislation does not address their particular needs, as much as by the fact that it classifies them in an 'unacceptable' manner. The ambiguity in republican theory as to whether, and to what extent, economic equality plays a role in guiding legislators or courts is nowhere more apparent than here.

Secondly, it is not possible to determine what response the *legislators or the courts* should make to this issue without some articulated notion of distributive justice. The earlier discussion of liberalism revealed that the answer to this question was a condition precedent to a plethora of more particular, seminal questions concerning the treatment of disadvantaged groups.[140]

The articulation *and* defence of a particular conception of distributive justice will, for example, underpin any decision as to whether welfare rights should be recognized. It will also affect the decision as to whether any such distributive concerns should generate constitutional welfare rights which could be protected by the courts, or whether they would instead impose an obligation on the legislature *per se*.[141] The relationship between the attainment of the particular conception of distributive justice, and other rights which are recognized, will also be of crucial importance For example, the extent to which the legislature is or is not entitled to restrict other rights in order to advance the distributive objectives can only be answered by considering the relationship between these two aspects of the underlying theory. It is only when modern republican theory provides answers to these questions that any coherent approach to the position of disadvantaged groups can be attained.

iii. The content of constitutional rights (2) The earlier discussion revealed the differences of nuance and approach which subsist within different theories of modern republicanism. The present discussion would, therefore, be incomplete if it did not address the distinctive

140 See above, ch. 8 sec. 3b.
141 See above, ch. 8 secs. 3b (iii), (iv).

reasoning of Michelman concerning the nature of republican constitutional adjudication more closely.

Michelman's more recent work[142] develops his earlier writing.[143] He specifically addresses the tension which exists between traditional republicanism, which presupposed a degree of moral consensus, and a modern, diverse liberal society, in which such consensus is absent.[144] The tension between consensus and plurality is one of the central issues which he seeks to resolve, and in doing so he articulates a role for the courts.

The essence of the argument is as follows. Agreement on the principles and content of laws by citizens is a prerequisite for their acceptability.[145] However no 'ideal speech situation' will suffice to guarantee the requisite validation, given the modern supposition of 'pre-political dissensus'. The existence of this plurality is said to mean that a political process will validate a norm as a law which individuals accept for themselves only if certain conditions are met, namely that: participation in the process results in some shift in understanding on the part of some participants; there are 'prescriptive social and procedural' conditions which prevent any such modification from being coercive or a violation of one's identity; and these conditions actually prevail in the discursive process.[146]

Political plurality is then conceived of in the following sense. The process of dialogue contemplates a 'self whose identity and freedom consist, in part, in its capacity for reflexively critical reconsideration of the ends and commitments that it already has and that make it who it is'.[147] This conception of plurality, and what Michelman terms dialogic constitutionalism, draws explicitly upon the work of communitarian writes such as Sandel.

The idea of *legal plurality* which flows from this is based upon indeterminacy in the following sense. The objective of political dialogue is to encourage and enhance self-reflection and transformation. Legal indeterminacy encourages this by fostering doctrines such as deconstruction, deviation, and immanent critique, which serve to prevent closure and enhance reconsideration of previous 'givens'.[148] The role of the court, and of constitutional adjudication, in fostering self-government emerges forcefully in the following extract.

[142] 'Law's Republic'.
[143] 'Foreword'.
[144] e.g. 'Law's Republic', p. 1526.
[145] Ibid. 1500, 1526.
[146] Ibid. 1526–7.
[147] Ibid. 1528.
[148] Ibid. 1528–9.

The Court helps protect the republican state—that is, the citizens politically engaged—from lapsing into a politics of self-denial. It challenges 'the people's' self-enclosing tendency to assume their own moral completion as they now are and thus to deny to themselves the plurality on which their capacity for transformative self-renewal depends.[149]

Two comments on the preceding analysis, and its implications for more particular constitutional rights, are warranted.

The first concerns the role of the court in establishing the *conditions* for the process of dialogue. This process can only operate where certain 'prescriptive social and procedural conditions' exist which serve to prevent any such modification from being coercive or a violation of one's identity. This stipulation is, as Michelman notes, both crucial and problematic.[150]

The precise nature of these conditions is, however, unclear, as is the exact role of the court in their realization. It may well be that the earlier reference to constitutional rights of 'participation, emancipation and capacitation'[151] is intended to provide the basis for the realization by the court of the prescriptive conditions adumbrated above. If this is so, much then depends upon the more particular content accorded to these terms. These could, of course, be given a radical interpretation which is consonant with historical themes in republican discourse. They could, for example, be utilized as the foundations for the rough equality in ownership which was regarded as a necessary condition for the attainment of civic virtue and self-government. Whether this can be achieved within a modern capitalist order is more debatable as the earlier[152] and subsequent discussion reveal.[153]

The very fact that these prescriptive conditions must be satisfied does, moreover, lead one to doubt the viability of any claim that republicanism can be regarded as a 'thoroughly and irredeemably' process-based theory,[154] or at the least to the realization that this claim can only be accepted if interpreted in a certain manner. Republicanism, as depicted by Michelman, may be seen to revolve around a dialogic *process*. The establishment of the prescriptive conditions which are necessary for the process to operate will,

[149] Ibid. 1532.
[150] Ibid. 1527.
[151] Michelman, 'Foreword', p. 43 n. 229; see above, n. 125.
[152] See above, ch. 10 sec. 2a.
[153] See below. ch. 10 sec. 6.
[154] See above, ch. 10 sec. 4.

however, almost certainly necessitate *substantive* intervention by the court to establish the conditions under which the process can operate.

This very discussion brings us back, albeit in a different way, to the same problem encountered when discussing Sunstein's thesis: the ambiguity and uncertainty in the conceptions which inform the theory, and a correlative uncertainty in the elaboration of particular constitutional rights. The prescriptive social and procedural conditions which must exist in order to prevent the dialogic process from being coercive, invasive, or a violation of one's identity depend upon a *normative* assessment of what terms such as 'coercive' or 'invasive' mean. It is only when this has been provided that specificity can be imbued into constitutional correctives for such coercion, etc., which are to be based on ideas such as emancipation or capacitation.

The second comment upon the Michelman analysis relates to the judicial role in evaluating the *outcomes* of the process of dialogue. Now it might be thought that such control is unnecessary *if* the prescriptive social and procedural conditions for the dialogic process are fulfilled. The norms which emerge thereafter are, by definition, self-given laws which should be regarded as valid.[155] This view would be mistaken for two connected reasons. On the one hand, the fulfilment of these conditions will take time to achieve, and may (always) be imperfect. On the other hand, Michelman accepts that the attainment of those conditions does not necessarily mean that rational and passionate disagreements based upon differences of perspective will necessarily be dissolved.[156]

The situation which confronts us is, therefore, as follows. Citizens may engage in a dialogue within which they are willing to listen to the views of others, and to reconsider their own beliefs in the light of this discursive process. They may, however, continue to have 'rational and passionate' disagreements as to particular conceptions of the good, even if the discursive process causes them to see these convictions in a new light.[157] The majority may wish to translate their beliefs into a social norm, and the court will then have to determine whether the norm is constitutionally acceptable. It will have to decide who can do what, to whom, and in what manner. In adjudicating in this way the court will perforce be making *substantive*

[155] Michelman, 'Law's Republic', pp. 1526–7.
[156] Ibid. 1527.
[157] Ibid.

value judgements concerning the outcomes of the dialogic *process* which are to be regarded as permissible.

Thus the decision in *Bowers* v. *Hardwick*,[158] in which the court upheld a Georgia law which criminalized homosexual sodomy between consenting adults in private, is criticized as a denial of liberty and privacy. The state law, which did not apply to heterosexual partners, is regarded as a denial or impairment of the citizenship and constitutive identity of homosexuals.[159]

The role of the court either in ensuring that the prescriptive conditions for the dialogue are present, or in monitoring the outcomes thereof, may, however, be more complex and controversial in other areas. This can be exemplified by focusing upon property rights.

The centrality of property to republican conceptions of citizenship has been considered above.[160] Proprietary independence was regarded as a constitutive condition for the attainment of the independence required for civic virtue. It may, however, be a matter of contingent social and historical circumstance whether the attainment of this independence is best promoted by emphasizing the possessory or redistributive facet of constitutional property rights. The former carries the standard connotation of keeping what one already has; the latter signifies the positive claim to certain endowments or shares.[161] Legal discourse normally emphasizes the possessory aspect of proprietary rights. However, it may well be that when the Constitution was originally framed the pattern of property-holding, whereby production was envisioned to be based upon small roughly equal holdings, meant that political independence could indeed be secured by protecting the possessory conception of ownership.[162] The emergence of large-scale capitalist modes of production cast doubt on this assumption. Disparities of wealth, and the subjection of individuals to the proprietary power of others, generated the feeling that redistribution would be needed if the requisite conditions for political independence were to be preserved.[163]

[158] 478 U.S. 186 (1986).
[159] Michelman, 'Law's Republic', pp. 1532–7.
[160] See above, ch. 10 sec. 2.
[161] F. I. Michelman, 'Possession vs. Distribution in the Constitutional Idea of Property', 72 *Iowa L. Rev.* 1319 (1987).
[162] Ibid. 1332–3.
[163] Ibid. 1334–7. See also below, ch. 10 sec. 6.

The problem with this shift in focus is, as Michelman states, that it is difficult to formulate substantively defensible distributive norms in the form of abstract, simple, and impersonal legal standards; and it is equally difficult to reconcile distributive and possessory proprietary claims. Judicial intervention on distributive grounds will, if undertaken, produce a reorientation of the judicial role and a significant alteration in the traditionally conceived rule of law.[164]

Difficult though this problem might be, *some* resolution thereof is necessary if republicanism is to constitute a viable basis for public law. Without such resolution it will be impossible to determine, within this area, what, if anything, the court ought to be doing to ensure that the prescriptive social conditions for dialogue are present; and it will be equally difficult to decide what constraints upon outcomes a court ought to be imposing. In order to arrive at any such resolution two distinctive questions must be asked and answered by republicans.

First, *why* do citizens require proprietary shares, and *what* shares do they deserve or need within a modern state based upon republican principles? This question of principle should precede any consideration of institutional competence, namely whether the answer which is forthcoming is capable of generating legal norms enforceable by a court. Liberalism[165] and interest-group pluralism[166] both provide answers, albeit divergent, to this issue of principle, and so must republicans. The two facets ('why' and 'what') of the preceding question are obviously related. The traditional, and indeed modern,[167] response to the 'why' question is that property is a matter of constitutive political concern because it provides the foundations for the independence which the citizen requires to contribute to public life. Whether this rationale for distributive shares is still plausible or realizable within a modern capitalist order will be considered below.[168] Assuming for the present that such a rationale is still plausible, the nature of the distributive shares which such citizens require must be imbued with some greater measure of specificity. These may, for example, take the form of minimum-income requirements, or welfare entitlements.

164 Michelman, 'Possession vs. Distribution' pp. 1321, 1334–6, 1349–50.

165 See above, ch. 8.

166 See above, ch. 4.

167 e.g. Michelman, 'Law's Republic', pp. 1504–5, 1535.

168 See below, ch. 10 sec. 6.

The second question which must be resolved concerns the institutional realization of the desired distributive entitlements. There are two options to be considered: the legislature and the courts. If, for the reasons given above, it is felt that the distributive entitlements are not readily susceptible to being enshrined in legal norms, the articulation of such distributive goals may still generate a *political obligation* for the legislature. This is, for example, the approach adopted by Rawls towards the effectuation of his conception of distributive justice.[169]

One should, moreover, distinguish between two different senses in which such distributive concerns may or may not be susceptible to legal encapsulation. It may be extremely difficult for a court generally to demand the provision of, for example, minimum-income entitlements, with the consequential implications that this would entail for the direction of economic policy. This does not, however, mean that the court should reject as unconstitutional attempts at redistribution which have been made by the legislature.[170]

6. THE REPUBLICAN REVIVAL: INSTITUTIONAL REALIZATION

Consideration of the normative foundations of republican thought is essential if the desirability of a republican revival is to be properly evaluated. The social and economic preconditions for the institutional realization of such a regime are equally important, and will be examined within this section. At its most fundamental this raises the compatibility of republican ideals with a capitalist economic order. The strain placed upon English republicanism by the emergence of commerce, trade, and public finance has already been examined. How to preserve a conception of the public good and civic virtue in this economic milieu formed one of the important focal points for debate. Similar tensions can be observed in the development of US republican thought in the nineteenth century.

[169] See above, ch. 8 sec. 3b.

[170] Cf. *Buckley* v. *Valeo* 424 U.S. 1 (1976); Michelman, 'Possession vs. Distribution', pp. 1340–5; O. Fiss, 'Free Speech and Social Structure', 71 *Iowa L. Rev.* 1405 (1986); L.BeVier, 'Money and Politics: A Perspective on the First Amendment and Campaign Finance Reform', 73 *Cal. L. Rev.* 1045 (1985).

a. Continuity and Change in Republican Thought

Americans had begun the Revolution assuming that the people were a homogeneous entity in society set against the rulers. But such an assumption belied American experience, and it took only a few years of independence to convince the best American minds that distinctions in the society were 'various and unavoidable', so much so that they could not be embodied in the government. Once the people were thought to be composed of various interests in opposition to one another, all sense of graduated organic chain in the social hierarchy became irrelevant, symbolized by the increasing emphasis on the image of a social contract. The people were not an order organically tied together by their unity of interest but rather an agglomeration of hostile individuals coming together for their mutual benefit to construct a society. The Americans transformed the people in the same way that Englishmen a century earlier had transformed the rulers: they broke the connectedness of interest among them and put them at war with one another, just as seventeenth-century Englishmen had separated the interests of rulers and people and put them in opposition to each other.[171]

Thus does Wood conclude his study of the creation of the American republic, thereby echoing his earlier words that the revolution had been a 'final attempt' and a 'desperate attempt'[172] to realize the ideal of a traditional commonwealth dedicated to the pursuit of the public good. It represented an effort to bring under control the 'selfish and individualistic impulses of an emergent capitalist society that could not be justified'.[173] The revolution marked the 'end of classical politics', the termination of a vision of the political order which stressed the timeless, ordered nature of society resting upon the concept of a mixed constitution and balanced social hierarchy.[174] It came, however, increasingly under strain. The consequence was either the retention of the language of republicanism but gradual alteration in its substantive meaning; or the discarding of this language and its replacement by rhetoric more directly expressive of an equation between private interest and public good.[175] The reasons for this transformation were complex. Tensions produced by the changing economic order, and a distinctive, but related, shift in the concept of party, were important causes of the

[171] Wood, *The Creation of the American Republic*, pp. 606–7.
[172] Ibid. 54.
[173] G. S. Wood (ed.), *The Rising Glory of America, 1760–1820* (1971), 5.
[174] Wood, *The Creation of the American Republic*, p. 606.
[175] See above, ch. 10 sec. 2, for not dissimilar developments in the UK.

changing content of republican ideals. These two issues will be examined in turn.

It was axiomatic to the revolutionaries that a republican government required an economic and social order which would foster virtue amongst its citizens.[176] The framers of the Constitution were, as we have already seen, alive to the debates of the country-court parties in England, debates which had been strongly informed by the difficulty of securing commitment to the public good in a society increasingly motivated by the essentially private-regarding interests of the capitalist order. It was fear of being tainted by the corruption which was perceived to infect the machinations of the court faction which had been an important cause of independence itself. The dangers of luxury and avarice which were felt to be attendant upon commerce were a recurring theme. Acceptance of the Constitution prompted debate as to how best the nascent republic could be secured against similar evils. Republicanism had to be defined in concrete terms, and the social and economic conditions for its existence had to be thought through. Two visions became apparent, that of Madison and Jefferson on the one hand, and that of Hamilton on the other.

The Madisonian and Jeffersonian strategy entailed what one writer has termed a development across space.[177] The evils of the old world could best be avoided by concentrating upon agricultural production, which would be facilitated by the availability of considerable unowned land. Westward expansion provided the key. Agricultural surplus would then be traded for the types of manufactured goods which the Americans had declined to make for themselves.[178] American society could thus be maintained at a middle stage of social development and avoid the descent into Polybian decay which had characterized previous republics. The emphasis placed upon freehold land reinforced the classical republican ideal which saw the landowner as the epitome of the independent virtuous citizen who was committed to the public good. The Hamiltonian strategy stood in stark contrast to this ideal. Hamilton, influenced by the ideas of Hume, espoused the alternative vision of development through time.[179] He was sceptical about the

[176] D. R. McCoy, *The Elusive Republic: Political Economy in Jeffersonian America* (1980), 7.

[177] Ibid. 136.

[178] Ibid. 186, 236–7; See also pp. 83–5 for earlier development of similar themes.

[179] Ibid. 136, 146.

viability or desirability of economic agrarianism, and came to accept that commercialization of society was not only inevitable but also salutary. It is little wonder that Hamilton came to be feared as another Walpole, determined to ruin the pure republic at its birth. The debate over economic policy came increasingly to resemble that between country and court, a fact not lost on the participants themselves.

Jefferson came to power in 1800 determined to return to economic principles of true republicanism, and to contain the damage done by Hamilton.[180] Notwithstanding this desire, commerce and manufacturing would not be so easily defeated. The reasons are instructive. On the one hand, belief in the special nature of freehold land as inculcating a particular degree of civic virtue was beginning to be questioned.[181] The speculative nature of many investments in land, rapid transfers thereof, and the relative ease of acquisition with the opening up of the West, all conspired to weaken the dichotomy between freehold and other species of property. The 'monopoly' of virtue exercised by the independent yeoman was shaken. Merchants and other small manufacturers claimed to possess civil attachment in equal degree.[182] On the other hand, commerce continued to exercise influence and to grow, in part because the Madisonian–Jeffersonian model was never as simple as the above description might suggest. Commerce in the form of foreign trade had always been integral to the republican vision. It was such trade which was to absorb the excess agricultural production. Commerce in the form of the manufacture of 'necessaries' had also been accepted. It was more general large-scale industry, and the production of luxury goods, which had been frowned upon. However, even this fear had to be counter-balanced against the vices of idleness and degeneracy.[183]

Political crisis often produces a re-evaluation of social and economic norms. The commercial problems of the 1780s had already led some to modify their views on the role of manufacturing within a republican polity.[184] The war of 1812 and its aftermath

[180] McCoy, *The Elusive Republic*, pp. 152–3, 185–6.

[181] R. Berthoff, 'Independence and Attachment, Virtue and Interest: From Republican Citizen to Free Enterpriser, 1787–1837', in R. L. Bushman, N. Harris, D. Rothman, M. Solomon, and S. Thernstrom (eds.), *Uprooted Americans: Essays to Honor Oscar Handlin* (1979), 110–12.

[182] Ibid. 113–15.

[183] McCoy, *The Elusive Republic*, pp. 112, 113, 116, 150–1, 237, 242, 243.

[184] Ibid. 106, 112–13.

produced a similar reorientation among republican supporters. Entrepreneurial interests had long formed one element within the republican party,[185] and the post-war debate produced a more definite emphasis upon the development of domestic manufactures and an extensive home market for US produce. Some Jeffersonians began to accept the need or inevitability of large-scale manufacturing. This did not represent a 'sudden capitulation to the Hamiltonian vision'.[186] It was rather the subtle adaptation of republican ideals to the exigencies of a changing world. Thus republicans began to comprehend the value of manufacturing as a means of ensuring full employment, and the avoidance of idleness.

This shift in republican thinking, and its accommodation to modernity, should not be overstated. The commitment to an agricultural society and the fear of industry were not shed overnight. Notwithstanding this formal attachment to an increasingly dated ideal, commentators have noted both the gradual alteration in the substantive meaning of republican language, and also its replacement by rhetoric which more directly expresses the equation between private interest and public good. Thus Berthoff notes that the further the classical ideal receded from the dynamic reality of the nineteenth-century economy, the more Americans liked to think of themselves in its terms.[187] Businessmen claimed to be heir to the old yeoman virtues of economy, thrift, and honesty. The equation of private, material success with national prosperity and the public good became ever closer. While the emergent ideas of *laissez-faire* economics could be used overtly to buttress this reasoning, it was preferable to express the same conclusion in the more respectable cloak of republican imagery. Hard work, self-denial, and pursuit of material self-interest could be depicted as the essence of civic virtue, to be contrasted with the spectre of idleness and vice.[188] Free enterprise came to be seen as the 'heart of the republican ethic', and 'entrepreneurial success' as an investment in the general welfare. The force of this change is well captured by Berthoff.

> The anarchy and oligarchy that it produced were more insidious than any in ancient Rome or the England of Walpole, because the engine of change was the republican ideal itself. Long before the United States reached its

[185] Ibid. 188.
[186] Ibid. 238.
[187] 'Independence and Attachment', p. 106.
[188] Ibid. 119–20.

centennial celebrations the 'equally free and independent' citizen of 1776 had been corrupted into what in 1876 was just beginning to be recognised as the modern embodiment of both these classical specters: the entrepreneur set free, by the American dream of virtuous independence, to dominate a society grown so narrowly acquisitive that it could only admire his success.[189]

The tensions produced by the changing economic order were attended, as stated above, by a related but distinctive shift in the concept of party which also served to alter the substance of republican thought.

Party or faction was an opprobrious epithet in eighteenth-century discourse.[190] Factional interests inhibited the overall consensus which would otherwise evolve; they were the mechanism whereby sectional interests would impose their will upon society; they were antithetic to pursuit of civic virtue and the public good. The role which faction played for the framers of the Constitution has already been examined. Selfishness was sown in the nature of man and was made manifest in political life through faction. The Madisonian 'solution' to this problem, and the extent to which this can be interpreted as pluralist or modified republicanism, is, as we have seen, still contentious.

It is, however, the role played by the party in the ensuing years which is apposite here. The framers of the Constitution might well have believed that faction was inexorable, but they did not in general believe it to be desirable. A dominant theme in the first fifty years of the new republic was, therefore, not surprisingly, the attempt to end party conflict. This was to be achieved, not primarily by arriving at an accommodation with the interests of the rival party, but by absorbing as many of the opposition as possible, leaving the remainder as an impotent minority.[191] The quest for unanimity fitted well with traditional republican ideals of consensus, commitment to the public good, and the avoidance of sectional conflict. This search did not require the elimination of all difference of opinion within the party, but only of irreconcilable and impassioned disagreement.

[189] 'Independence and Attachment', p. 120. See also R. Berthoff and J. M. Murrin, 'Feudalism, Communalism and the Yeoman Freeholder', in S. G. Kurtz and J. H. Hutson (eds.), *Essays on the American Revolution* (1973), 282–4. See the similar themes expressed by Wood, in *The Rising Glory of America*, pp. 8–9; McCoy, *The Elusive Republic*, p. 188.

[190] Hofstadter, *The Idea of a Party System*, pp. 12–13, 41.

[191] Ibid. 151, 152.

The ideal of party competition as a positive good changed only later. Van Buren was one of its principal architects. Party, it was argued, could be seen as a means of institutionalizing conflict, and of fostering cohesion between different sections of the populace at the national level.[192] The 'opposition' should be valued as a check in its own right on the exercise of governmental power.[193] The party should be recognized as legitimate, so should the conditions for its existence. Patronage and the caucus began to be seen as something other than the visible manifestation of executive corruption.[194] Republican rhetoric was called in aid. Party competition could 'inform the people, cure apathy, check dishonesty and corruption, and become conducive to the larger social peace'.[195] Reference to republican themes could not conceal the significance of the substantive change in this context, any more than it had served to mask transformation in the economic order considered above.

> the most decisive new departure taken by the Regency politicians lay in their break with the old ideal of national unanimity, or of a consensus transcending party, and in their acceptance of the idea that a sustained opposition has value in its own right. They saw the necessity of giving up the ancient ideal of social harmony that had haunted men from Bolingbroke to Washington and Monroe, and accepted the useful, the constructive contributions of political competition and conflict. To do this meant at last to accept opposition as a permanent fact.[196]

The growing acceptance of political competition and conflict, and the rejection of a transcendent harmony, paved the way for development of the modern party system. It laid the foundations for intra-party competition, in which the diverse interests within each party would jockey for power. It was in accord with the changing perceptions of the economic order, which increasingly envisioned competition between private interests as conducive to the public good.

b. Institutional Realization: Dilemmas and Future Prospects

The principal focus for the institutional realization of modified republicanism which is proposed by Sunstein and Michelman is circumscribed. Both writers place their main emphasis upon the role

192 Ibid. 226.
193 Ibid. 251.
194 Ibid. 225–6.
195 Ibid. 251; see also pp. 252–3.
196 Ibid. 248.

of national representatives and courts to direct society towards a republican polity. This focus may be too narrow for reasons of both an economic and a socio-political nature.

The economic reason for regarding this focus as too narrow follows from the analysis presented above. If, in normative terms, it is felt that a republican conception of distributive justice warrants a certain type of economic equality, and if it is felt that it is not plausible to achieve this through legal norms, then greater attention will have to be focused upon the general structure of economic organization if this goal is to be attained. This view is buttressed by the historical enquiry presented above, which testifies to the difficulty of reconciling republican ideals with an emergent capitalist order. If the basic economic institutions of the existing order are preserved, and emphasis is concentrated on the modification of judicial doctrine, how significant will the revival of republicanism prove to be?[197]

The concentration upon courts and national representatives may also be too narrow for reasons of a socio-political nature. The emphasis placed upon the courts and national representatives serves to divert attention from the possibility of the citizen taking a more direct role in the governmental process, whether at national or local level. The plausibility of a more radical proposal which considered citizen participation within government itself, and the institutional changes that would be needed to accommodate this within modern society, are therefore not pursued in any detail.[198] Moreover, it can be argued that political discourse, including constitutional discourse, takes place in a range of institutions, including nominally 'private' organizations such as the corporation and civic associations; and that judicial doctrine will be influenced by the values generated by such institutions.[199]

The possibility of more radical change cannot, however, simply be espoused in general terms. The direction of any such shift must be subjected to the same scrutiny as that aimed at more moderate proposals. Any suggestion for radical change must be carefully

[197] There is some recognition of this point; see, e.g., Sunstein, 'Interest Groups', pp. 72, 76, 77; and 'Beyond the Republican Revival', pp. 1552–3, 1576–9.

[198] Mention is made of topics such as industrial democracy but the analysis concentrates none the less on the courts and national representatives.

[199] P. Brest, 'Further beyond the Republican Revival: Toward Radical Republicanism', 97 *Yale L.J.* 1623, 1624, 1628 (1988). See also P. Brest, 'Constitutional Citizenship', 34 *Clev. St. L. Rev.* 175 (1986).

evaluated in order to determine its normative validity, the institutional conditions which are necessary for its realization, and the implications which it will have for public law. The following chapter will undertake these tasks in relation to two recent radical proposals. Only then can any realistic assessment be made as to the options which are at our disposal.

11
PARTICIPATORY DEMOCRACY: THE RADICAL VIEW

1. INTRODUCTION

It is readily apparent from the preceding discussion that the stimulating work of Sunstein, Michelman, and Ackerman could result in fairly radical change, but could also have a far more limited impact. The existing institutional structure within society is generally preserved, and civic virtue is either located within the national representatives, under the watchful eye of the court, or resides in the court itself, which supplies the self-government which the citizen cannot pragmatically obtain. Emphasis is placed upon the power of judicial doctrine to reorient society towards a republican polity.[1] Reflection and experience may convince us that a relatively modest change of direction is all that can realistically be attained, and that the radical implications of more recent work would not be plausible. Before one accedes to any such conclusion, one must, however, understand the more radical interpretation of participatory democracy, and evaluate the potential role of public law within such a system.

The argument of this chapter will be structured in the following manner. First, two recent visions of participatory or empowered democracy will be considered, those advanced by Barber and Unger. As has already been seen, the possibility of some form of participatory democracy is a recurring theme amongst the critics of pluralism.[2] The rationale for focusing upon the work of Barber and Unger is that both writers delineate the theoretical and institutional aspects of such a societal ordering in considerable detail. This

[1] Although Sunstein (C. R. Sunstein, 'Interest Groups in American Public Law', 38 *Stan. L. Rev.* 29 (1985)) admits that it is highly unlikely that the courts acting by themselves could bring the political process much closer to the Madisonian conception (p. 68).

[2] e.g. T. B. Bottomore, *Elites and Society* (1964); C. Pateman, *Participation and Democratic Theory* (1970); C. B. Macpherson, *The Life and Times of Liberal Democracy* (1977); P. Bachrach, *The Theory of Democratic Elitism: A Critique* (1967). See above, ch. 3 sec. 2d.

facilitates examination of the normative foundations of the theory, the institutional setting required for its realization, and the role of public law within such a society. It is only by examining such issues that any realistic judgement can be made concerning the desirability and plausibility of such a venture.

Secondly, the enquiry will focus upon the central normative assumptions underlying these theories which are not always self-evident. These will be critically analysed. This second stage of the analysis will also examine the institutional ordering of the society which is required to effectuate these objectives. More specifically it will reveal the tension between decentralization and centralization which is present therein, and will question how far such theories really do sustain their own claim that society should be open to continual transformation.

Thirdly, the role of public law within a participatory democracy will be discussed. This will include a consideration of the extent to which any such role succeeds in avoiding the dilemmas which are said to beset the courts under liberal political theory.

2. TWO VISIONS OF PARTICIPATORY DEMOCRACY

a. *'Strong democracy'*

Strong democracy is a distinctively modern form of participatory democracy. It rests on the idea of a self-governing community of citizens who are united less by homogeneous interests than by civic education and who are made capable of common purpose and mutual action by virtue of their civic attitudes and participatory institutions rather than their altruism or their good nature. Strong democracy is consonant with—indeed it depends upon—the politics of conflict, the sociology of pluralism, and the separation of private and public realms of action. It is not intrinsically inimical to either the size or the technology of modern society and is therefore wedded neither to antiquarian republicanism nor to face-to-face parochialism. Yet it challenges the politics of elites and masses that masquerades as democracy in the West and in doing so offers a relevant alternative to what we have called thin democracy—that is instrumental, representative, liberal democracy in its three dispositions.[3]

[3] B. Barber, *Strong Democracy: Participatory Politics for a New Age* (1984), 117. Barber provides a 'formal' definition of strong democracy as, p. 132: 'politics in the participatory mode where conflict is resolved in the absence of an independent

Thus does Barber begin his articulation of strong democracy. The thesis has both theoretical and institutional aspects which will be considered in turn.

Participation in the form of citizen action is of integral importance to the theory of strong democracy. Citizen action is the objective. It is this very activity which facilitates the creation of community.[4] Participation must involve citizens who are capable of exercising an autonomous choice, albeit one which recognizes that public action must be at least reasonable even if it cannot be stated to be unequivocally correct.[5] The existence of conflict is regarded as a given, but strong democracy seeks to transform such conflict through the medium of citizen participation, public deliberation, and civic education. Transformation is central to the theory, and is contrasted with bargain and adjudication, which are said to be the modes of conflict resolution associated with liberal democracy.[6] The methods and goals of participation include: the articulation of individual interests; persuasion; agenda-setting; exploring mutuality; affiliation and affection; the reformulation of values; and the creation of a citizen body which is capable of public thinking,[7] and able to envisage a 'common future in terms of genuinely common goods'.[8]

The theory is said to be self-contained in the sense that it is independent of any external norm such as natural rights or contractarianism.[9] Transformation plays a role here once again. The legitimacy of action is taken to depend, not upon concepts of abstract right or popular consent *per se*, but on the 'active consent of participating citizens who have imaginatively reconstructed their own values as public norms through the process of identifying and empathizing with the values of others'.[10] In this sense the theory is one of process, wherein individual values are legitimated through being debated, refined, and transformed through the medium of public discourse. Public action does not, therefore, flow deductively from some prior postulate, but is created through the very act of public participation and community deliberation. Concepts such as

ground through a participatory process of ongoing, proximate self-legislation and the creation of a political community capable of transforming dependent, private individuals into free citizens and partial and private interests into public goods.'

[4] Barber, *Strong Democracy*, p. 133.
[5] Ibid. 135.
[6] Ibid. 119, 135.
[7] Ibid. 178.
[8] Ibid. 197.
[9] Ibid. 42–4, 135.
[10] Ibid. 137.

freedom, equality, and justice do not serve as pre-established criteria for decision-making; their very content is the topic of contentious political debate, the answers to which are in a constant state of re-evaluation.[11]

The vision of the person portrayed by strong democracy is said to be very different from that portrayed by liberal democratic theory. The latter is said to depict the person as solitary and adversarial, a creature who enters social relationships out of fear or necessity.[12] Participatory democracy visualizes the person as a social animal who achieves self-realization through society. The individual is dependent on others, a dependency which can only be adequately legitimized through common citizenship.

The nature of the relationship between citizen and state is correspondingly distinctive.[13] Liberal democratic theory posits individuals as autonomous parties who bind themselves through, for example, a prior contract. Citizenship becomes a relationship between citizen and government, while bonds between fellow citizens remain private in character. The relationship between citizen and state becomes one of reciprocal control and accountability. This pact is monitored through representation itself, and by external agents such as the judiciary. For the strong democrat, social behaviour is not something which is built on to an individual's natural separateness. A person is regarded as a social being, who is dependent upon others. The civic bond becomes the legitimator of this natural dependency, and the strict line between government and citizens which characterizes liberal democracy is absent. Individuals become involved in government by participating in the common institutions of self-government.

The preceding theoretical framework for strong democracy is complemented by consideration of its institutional realization. Barber is very much alive to the problems of complementing an 'attractive theory' by 'convincing modern practice'. An institutional framework for strong democracy must, he acknowledges, be realistic, and not utopian.[14] It must not succumb to a romantic atavism, and must be capable of dealing with the problems of scale and technology which are characteristics of modern society. It is for this reason that Barber constructs his institutional frame to complement and be compatible with 'the primary representative

[11] Ibid. 151, 156–7.
[12] Ibid. 213–15.
[13] Ibid. 217–23.
[14] Ibid. 261–2.

institutions of large-scale modern societies'.[15] Strong democracy can only be realized by modifying liberal democracy.

This modification assumes a number of forms.[16] Neighbourhood assemblies should be introduced into all districts. They would provide a forum for local discussion of regional and national issues, for the venting of grievances, and the defence of local interests. Broader forums for consideration of both regional and national issues would also be required, and Barber advocates the use of technology to enhance communication and to combat the problems of scale. A new Civic Communications Co-operative should be established, which would be responsible for the constructive use of telecommunications and technology. The postal provision of political and economic information should be subsidized, in order to foster civic education. Local office-holding should be by lot, and town meetings too large for direct participation should become representative, with the membership thereof also chosen by lot and then rotated. There should be greater use of the referendum at both state and national level. Experimentation with some form of voucher system for education, and perhaps transportation and housing, should be attempted. Universal citizen service, whether in a military or non-military capacity, should be considered, and there should be experiments in industrial democracy.

b. 'Empowered Democracy'

Unger's recent work is major both in size and in the scale of the undertaking.[17] Summarizing the essence of an often complex argument is difficult, but necessary. The objective, at the most general level, is to furnish an explanatory theory of society, and to suggest a programme for social reconstruction. These two themes are best considered separately.

i. The explanatory theory The explanatory theory of societal development and change has both a negative and a positive aspect.

The *negative* aspect is devoted to undermining what Unger

[15] Barber, *Strong Democracy*, p. 262.

[16] Ibid. 261–311.

[17] The work has three parts: R. M. Unger, *Social Theory: Its Situation and its Task* (1987); *False Necessity: Anti-Necessitarian Social Theory in the Service of Radical Democracy* (1987); *Plasticity into Power: Comparative Historical Studies on the Institutional Conditions of Economic and Military Success* (1987).

believes to be the two dominant styles of social explanation: deep-structure theory and positivist social science.[18] Deep-structure theory, of which Marxism is taken as the principal example, is said to possess certain central characteristics. On the one hand, there is an effort to 'distinguish in every historical situation the routines of practical and imaginative conflict from the basic framework, structure or context that shapes these ordinary disputes while resisting their subversive effects'.[19] The framework itself is regarded as an indivisible type of social organization, albeit one which can be repeated at different times in different societies. On the other hand, these frameworks are regarded as the result of 'lawlike tendencies or deep-seated economic, organizational, and psychological constraints'.[20] Deep-structure theory is rejected both because there do not appear to be 'a small number of possible trajectories of social evolution'; and also because the alleged law-like tendencies or determining constraints 'fail to explain the actual identity and sequence of frameworks for social life'.[21] Explanatory failure is concealed only by laws which 'are left so vague that they can be made, retrospectively, to explain anything'.[22]

Positivist social science is said to approach social explanation very differently. It regards social life as an endless series of episodes of interest accommodation and problem-solving. It denies the centrality of the contrast between the shaping context and the shaped routines, with the consequence that our ability 'to see a whole institutional and imaginative ordering of social life as something connected, distinctive and replaceable' is weakened.[23] In reality such a framework does however exist, but is concealed, with the result that the premisses which underlie the framework are not readily made apparent or contested.[24]

The *positive* aspect of Unger's work is the provision of an alternative social theory which avoids the problems which he identifies in deep-structure theory and positivist social science The essence of these complex ideas can be presented as follows.

The individual is continually caught in a dilemma. He cannot in reality act as if everything were up for grabs, but neither is he warranted in regarding any particular context as definitive. Similarly

[18] *Social Theory*, pp. 1–18, 87–113, 130–65; *False Necessity*, ch. 1.

[19] *False Necessity*, p. 14.

[20] Ibid. 15.

[21] Ibid.

[22] Ibid.

[23] Ibid. 16.

[24] Ibid. 16–17.

the individual must live in some form of shared community, and yet all such communities run the risk of subjugating individuals, and subjecting them to unwarranted hierarchy and domination.[25] Unger's central theme is that these tensions can be diminished to the extent that we can invent contexts that 'give us the instruments and opportunities of their own revision and that thereby help us diminish the contrast between context-preserving routine and context-transforming struggle'.[26]

Formative contexts differ in the extent of their immunity to disturbance. Thus, 'hereditary castes, corporately organized estates, and social classes mark the presence of institutional and imaginative frameworks increasingly open to challenge and revision'.[27] The more mutable the formative context, the greater the sense of individual empowerment. The disentrenchment of formative contexts serves to undermine stable social hierarchies, and to empower people by granting them greater individual and collective mastery over the shared terms of their activity.

Particular formative contexts are not regarded as indivisible packages which 'stand or fall as a single piece', nor can they be placed on a 'predetermined list of possible types of social organization'.[28] However, as will become apparent below, a particular formative context is not a 'random juxtaposition of freely recombinable or replaceable elements'.[29] A certain socio-economic regime may be required in order that a particular formative context can be plausible. By seeking the formative context which is least entrenched, which is most susceptible to transformation, the danger of unwarranted hierarchy is diminished, and the possibility of real individual empowerment is enhanced.

ii. Social reconstruction and empowered democracy The programme for social reconstruction which Unger advocates also possesses what may be termed a negative and a positive aspect.

The *negative* aspect of the analysis is designed to demonstrate that the formative contexts which we currently employ are still 'too entrenched'. They protect certain hierarchical divisions within society and serve to perpetuate particular types of domination. The formative context which exists within any society is said to be

[25] *False Necessity*, pp. 32–3.
[26] Ibid. 32.
[27] Ibid. 35.
[28] Ibid. 36–7.
[29] Ibid. 37; see also pp. 95–6, 126.

influenced or framed *inter alia* through the work-organization complex, the private rights complex, and the governmental-organization complex.[30] Unger then proceeds to argue that the interpretation presently accorded to these central themes is unsatisfactory in the sense that that interpretation serves to entrench certain patterns of domination and hierarchy. The nature of this argument can best be appreciated by considering its application in the organization of private rights and of government.

For Unger the current system of private rights is 'pivoted' upon an absolute (or nearly absolute) conception of property rights, meaning the existence of 'nearly absolute claims to divisible portions of social capital'.[31] These are absolute in temporal terms, in the sense that the rights are unbroken by voluntary transfer or inheritance; and they are also near absolute in scope, in the sense that there are very few limits as to the uses to which such property can be put. This idea of property 'presupposes and is presupposed by'[32] a particular doctrine of contract in which the norm is the fully articulated agreement. To allow obligations to arise from trust and reliance would undermine 'consolidated property and the general system of rights modelled upon it'.[33]

The conception of rights adumbrated above is said to perform two complementary functions.[34] On the one hand, it defines a 'pre-political space' which, although theoretically open to legislative control, can in fact only be marginally influenced by the course of electoral politics. On the other hand, it connects a 'particular way of organizing a market, with all its effects of dominion and dependence, to the instruments by which the individual can defend his own sphere of autonomy'.[35] This facet of the formative context thereby entrenches a certain societal ordering by giving 'bosses and investment managers the authority to organize labour in the name of accumulated property', and by setting the 'basic terms on which disinvestment can frustrate reform'.[36]

The existing system of private rights is criticized, not only for the way in which it limits social change, but also because the system is itself beset by paradoxes which undermine it. Thus the contract and property system is said to be unable to govern 'crucial features of the

[30] Ibid. 68–75.
[31] Ibid. 70.
[32] Ibid.
[33] Ibid.
[34] Ibid. 71.
[35] Ibid.
[36] Ibid.; see also pp. 195–6.

practical dealings among people without the help of arrangements antagonistic to the manifest spirit of the system'.[37] Employment relationships and communal ties in which 'an acceptance of heightened mutual vulnerability overtakes the punctilious reckoning of tit for tat'[38] exemplify this tension. Moreover, the central core of classical property and contract law is continuously eroded by doctrinal exceptions which leave little for the central conception to operate on.[39]

The current organization of government is also criticized for the manner in which it stultifies any movement for real change, as opposed to interstitial tinkering with the system. The institutional arrangements which protect the citizen from the state also serve to ensure that the basic structure of societal ordering remains unchanged; they prevent the alteration of the formative context of power, even when this constitutes the electoral programme of a particular party. Any attempt to weaken the restraints on the reconstructive capacities of the state is challenged because of the dangers which this poses for the individual's security against his rulers.[40] Checks and balances on government increase, which also multiply the number of 'independent centres of power that must be captured, or persuaded to consent, before state power can be effectively mobilized behind any transformative objective'.[41]

The consequence is that party conflict tends to centre around promises of marginal advantage to a particular group rather than any serious attempt to reconstitute the actual formative context of power.[42]

> The practices of party politics in the advanced Western democracies belong to a distinctive style of governmental organization and partisan rivalry. Rather than embodying, together with the market, a pure method for the combination of free wills, this style helps reproduce a distinctive organization of society, rich in particular divisions and hierarchies and committed to a particular scheme of possible and desirable association.[43]

The *positive* aspect of Unger's analysis is the depiction of an alternative form of social ordering which diminishes the distinction between context-preserving routine and context-transforming struggle, and which more truly empowers the individual to be the master of his or her own life.

[37] *False Necessity*, p. 200.
[38] Ibid. 201.
[39] Ibid. 204–7.
[40] Ibid. 72.
[41] Ibid.
[42] Ibid. 72–3, 207–8.
[43] Ibid. 219.

The vision offered by this program is that of a society in which people are more fully empowered through the development of institutional arrangements that both diminish the gap between framework-preserving routine and framework-transforming conflict and weaken the established forms of social division and hierarchy. It is a program of empowered democracy because it promises to serve a range of forms of individual and collective empowerment, in part by empowering democracy itself: that is, by extending the subjection of social life to democratic participation and conflict.[44]

Unger then presents a detailed picture of the form which such an empowered democracy would assume. The picture describes the style of government and economic organization that would subsist within such a democracy and depicts the regime of rights which would exist therein. These elements must be briefly reviewed in order to comprehend and assess the theory as a whole.

The objective of *governmental organization* within an empowered democracy is to provide a system which will both prevent any faction from gaining lasting ascendancy over state power, and will also provide the maximum opportunity for transformative activity.[45] To achieve these ends Unger moves away from the classical techniques of separating state power into executive, legislative, and judicial branches. Such an organizational pattern stifles innovative activity and entrenches the established order.[46] The central theme of Unger's governmental organization is one in which the number of branches of government is multiplied, while attributing overlapping functions to differing state agencies.[47]

The decisional centre of government includes the traditional executive and legislature, but they are said not to operate in the traditional manner. The legislature itself is to perform two functions: to ensure that the party in power implements its programme, and to operate as the agency responsible for settling conflicts among other branches of government. Legislation itself is devised by the executive, and the 'cabinet and council govern subject to the restrictions imposed' by the legislature and other powers in the state.[48]

The most novel aspect of the scheme is the establishment of a branch of government which will possess a major role in transforming society in the manner envisioned by the programme of

[44] Ibid. 362.
[45] Ibid. 450.
[46] Ibid. 444–8, 456, 457.
[47] Ibid. 449–51.
[48] Ibid. 460.

empowered democracy. The precise nature of this branch is not entirely clear, but its rationale and nature would appear to be as follows. It has already been seen that the twin objectives of governmental organization are the need to prevent the state becoming hostage to a particular faction, and the desire to enhance all the possible forms of transformative activity. These objectives are said to require the establishment of an agency charged with enlarging access to 'the means of communication, information and expertise', and with the capacity 'to intervene in all other social institutions and change their operations, by veto or affirmative initiative'.[49]

Both the judiciary and the legislature are felt to be unsuited to this major task, with the consequence that the job is allocated to a new branch of government. The officers of such a branch are to be selected by 'joint suffrage of the other powers in the state, the parties of opinion, and the universal electorate'.[50] Those who serve on such a body should be drawn from 'activities that have acquainted them with the different modes of normative thought important in the society'.[51] This new governmental organ is to have broad powers to reorganize major institutions, and to reconstruct society. The more traditional branches of government can, it seems, resist the imperatives of this new agency,[52] but there is much left unexplained as to how these branches of government would interrelate.[53]

Not surprisingly, the structure of government also emphasizes decentralization, but the two forms which this is to assume are somewhat different from the normal suggestions which are advanced.[54] One approach is to allow a conditional right to opt out of norms established by higher authorities, provided that the parties who do so are relatively equal, and provided that the relationship does not result in casting one of them into a 'relation of enduring subjugation'. The other approach is more traditional and seeks to reallocate power from higher to lower governmental authorities, provided that such devolution does not serve to buttress a 'local citadel of hierarchy'. Suggestions for decentralization are complemented by those directed towards the encouragement of voluntary associations.[55]

49 *False Necessity*, pp. 450–1.

50 Ibid. 451.

51 Ibid. 453.

52 Ibid. 453, 457.

53 See below, ch. 11 sec. 4e for a discussion of some of these problems.

54 Unger, *False Necessity*, pp. 474–6.

55 Ibid. 476–80.

The *economic organization* within an empowered democracy involves a radical departure from existing arrangements. Existing forms of economic organization are criticized for the way in which they impair freedom by according a disproportionate influence over investment decisions to a small group of people. This reduces the 'plasticity' of economic arrangements, by reducing the opportunity for experimentation in social and economic life.[56]

The central theme of Unger's economic programme is that we should dispense with the absolute and consolidated conception of property rights which underpins existing economic arrangements, and substitute a rotating capital fund within which there are several tiers of capital-takers and capital-givers. The ultimate capital-giver is a social capital fund controlled by the party in power; the ultimate capital-takers are teams of workers, entrepreneurs, etc., who make 'temporary and conditional claims upon divisible portions'[57] of this fund. Capital is not to be allocated directly from the central fund; rather the fund allocates resources to a plethora of semi-independent investment funds which specialize in a particular type of investment. Central government exercises control by assigning them capital, by closing them down, and by setting the boundaries within which the more particular funds can allocate capital to the ultimate takers.[58] The particular investment funds can compete with each other for resources, and they can allocate capital either by auction or rotation. Capital auction connotes the idea that, within limits, the primary capital-takers can buy each other's resources by offering to pay the fund more for the use thereof than their current users. Capital rotation or rationing entails a far more direct role for the investment fund, which must take the initiative in redistributing capital to new takers, and bring prospective takers together.[59]

Capital-takers are limited in various respects, all of which relate to the dissolution of absolute property rights. Thus they do not acquire permanent rights to the capital which they receive; once certain limits of personal enrichment and economic investment are reached, the additional capital returns to the capital fund for reassignment. Nor are firms allowed to expand continuously either by internal growth or by merger.[60] The very dangers of hierarchy and domination, which are said to flow from absolute property

[56] Ibid. 483–4.
[57] Ibid. 491.
[58] Ibid. 491–2.
[59] Ibid. 495–6.
[60] Ibid. 492–3, 496, 497–500.

rights and the accumulation of wealth which this fosters, are to be countered by dissolving those rights and preventing the formulation of large financial empires. The difficulties with this economic framework, as with other parts of the scheme, will be considered below.

As Unger acknowledges,[61] the realization of the economic objectives presupposes a distinctive background *system of rights*, and it is to these that one must now term. The underlying idea is that rights should safeguard the security of the individual in ways 'that minimize both the immunity of institutional arrangements to challenge and conflict and the ease with which some individuals can reduce others to dependence'.[62]

Four types of rights are specified. Immunity rights protect the individual 'against oppression by concentrations of public or private power, against exclusion from important collective decisions that influence his life, and against the extremes of economic and cultural deprivation'.[63] Such rights encompass the traditional civil liberties, and also welfare rights.[64]

Destabilization rights protect the 'citizen's interest in breaking open the large-scale organizations or the extended areas of social practice that remain closed to the destabilizing effects of ordinary conflict and thereby sustain insulated hierarchies of power and advantage'.[65] Such rights possess both a negative and a positive quality. In negative terms such rights deny protection against destabilizing conflict to institutions when such immunity to conflict has produced stable ties of domination. In positive terms, the intervention precipitated by the exercise of the destabilization rights should alter the existing practice or institution. Such rights may be enforced through the distinctive arm of government adumbrated above which is concerned with social reconstruction, rather than through the ordinary courts.[66]

The regime of market rights serves to effectuate the scheme of economic organization outlined above.[67] There are two general aspects of such rights. On the one hand, there are rights which flow from the relation between the capital fund and the capital-takers. These reinforce the idea that access to capital is conditional and

[61] Unger, *False Necessity*, pp. 502, 509.
[62] Ibid. 513, 516.
[63] Ibid. 524.
[64] Ibid. 526–9.
[65] Ibid. 530.
[66] Ibid. 532.
[67] Ibid. 520–3.

provisional, by, for example, fixing the time for which capital may be available or the uses to which it may be put. On the other hand, there are rights which operate between capital-takers. Individuals are free to contract *inter se* within the limits prescribed by the political authorities, and the 'normal' rules of contract and property would operate within this context.[68]

Solidarity rights[69] complete Unger's depiction of the rights which would subsist within an empowered democracy. They are designed to give legal form to social relations of reliance and trust. Such rights are expressive of a communal ideal, not in the sense of presupposing a necessary identity of shared values, but rather as expressive of the mutual vulnerability and interdependence of individuals who subsist together within society. Such rights need not be enforced through the ordinary courts. Some may best be advanced through mediation; others may not be strictly enforceable at all.

3. NORMATIVE FOUNDATIONS

It is readily apparent that the views of Barber and Unger differ in many respects. These differences reside not merely in the details of the schemes but more importantly in the normative foundations which underpin them. Moreover the extent to which the two theories espouse communitarian objectives differs considerably as between them. It is only by revealing these foundations that their prescriptive plausibility can be assessed.

a. *Strong Democracy: Base without Base?*

For Barber, the theory of strong democracy is a theory of process. He continually reiterates this, and juxtaposes it to other democratic theories which rely on an independent ground such as justice, right, or freedom. What then is to prevent 'the right to community self-legislation from becoming a mask for majoritarian tyranny'?[70] If no appeal to prior standards is possible, then what is to prevent the imposition of harsh laws upon a weak minority? Barber admits the existence of this problem. His solution is not to retreat into the

[68] Ibid. 522–3.
[69] Ibid. 535–9.
[70] *Strong Democracy*, p. 158.

position of the extreme moral sceptic, who is unwilling to intervene because nothing can be adjudged for certain. It is to rely upon internal self-regulation. Reasonableness, commonality, participation, and citizenship provide the chief safeguards against such majoritarian action. Process protects substance, a substance which is capable of endless transformation and emendation.[71] The choice of internal self-regulation rather than any form of external control is made partly upon pragmatic and partly upon conceptual grounds. To admit of judicial review to protect against majoritarian tyranny could lead to the introduction by the back door of ideas of preordained rights which the theory is so eager to dispel. Such external constraints could, moreover, preclude the transformability and flexibility which is such a hallmark of the theory. Two comments are of relevance to this analysis.

First, despite Barber's constant denials, it would appear that he is operating from an independent ground upon which the remainder of the theory is then constructed. He appears to assume that the concept of an independent ground, external norm, or prepolitical truth must be of an explicitly substantive nature.[72] Thus Rawls and Nozick, whatever may be their considerable differences in approach, are jointly condemned for reliance on assertions relating to the original position/justice and to rights, respectively.[73] Process by way of contrast is regarded as self-contained and self-correcting. But, in the same way that Barber can challenge Nozick with 'why rights?', or 'why not obligations?', the question can also be posed 'why process?'

Now it is, of course, the case that all forms of democracy, as well as other types of decision-making, will entail some process. However, precisely because this is so, the particular vision of process with which one begins is crucial. The type of process from which one builds contains concealed premisses which are themselves essentially contestable. Process as envisioned within strong democracy reflects particular conceptions of community, autonomy, and transformability. The very dominance of process thus conceived, and the consequential denial of notions of abstract rights, encapsulate the view that such prepolitical notions of rights are built 'on sand'.[74] It is difficult to see why the entirety of this contentious proposition is any less an 'independent ground' for a political system than are the

[71] *Strong Democracy*, pp. 160–2.
[72] Ibid. 42, 156.
[73] Ibid. 135.
[74] Ibid. 43; see also p. 137.

ideas of Rawls or Nozick.[75] The kind of process which should be available, and the relationship between this process and other goals, forms one of the key distinguishing features of different types of democracy. A less direct, more representative conception of process, of the type commonly associated with liberal democracy, chooses to balance representative participation, the efficacious discharge of business, and the preservation of certain rights.[76]

Secondly, the direction which any form of constitutional review might assume within this vision of participatory democracy is none the less problematic. Judicial review is rejected in part because the existence of 'prepolitical norms', whether defined in terms of rights, justice, fairness, or whatever, are also rejected.[77] Thus, even if, as argued above, Barber's own thesis does have an 'independent ground' upon which the remainder of the theory is constructed, it is not akin to that of Dworkin or Rawls, and therefore any justification of review based upon such grounds is dismissed.

This enquiry into review should, however, be pushed a little further. Barber is keen to demonstrate that traditional democratic values of liberty, equality, and social justice will not be sacrificed by his theory. His central point is that we should not focus upon the 'prepolitical' roots or the 'epistemological status' of justice or right in the abstract. Participants put their own moral codes, interests, conceptions of the good, and principles to the test of politics itself.[78] Such values may well be drawn from systems of the kind offered by liberals. However, such values acquire their legitimacy from their 'acceptance into and transformation through' the democratic political process. Concepts such as justice are not treated in the abstract, but are regarded as symbols for competing ideas, which are constantly being challenged, modified, and reinterpreted. Participatory democracy is not therefore founded upon moral scepticism. Quite the contrary. 'The strong democrat wants to transform uncertainty into reasonable group action, not to protect the individual (in the name of uncertainty) against all group action.' There is no room for the idea that scepticism about moral truth justifies agnosticism concerning political choice.[79]

[75] The mere fact that strong democracy contains the idea of capacity for change and transformation does not meet this point. Although the particular results are capable of change, the framework of strong democracy remains constant.

[76] For a detailed discussion of this point within Rawls's theory, see above, ch. 8.

[77] Barber, *Strong Democracy*, pp. 130, 142–3.

[78] Ibid. 152, 156.

[79] Ibid. 161, 162.

This vision of politics could generate a constitutional role for the courts, notwithstanding Barber's own view to the contrary. The theory does possess a notion of the common good arising from conflict within society. Conflict is to be used as a means to achieve co-operation, not as an obstacle to all common endeavour. The prime object of strong democracy is to create a citizenry 'capable of genuinely public thinking and political judgement and thus able to envision a common future in terms of genuinely common goods'.[80] Constitutional review could be used to enhance this vision without necessarily relying upon 'liberal' conceptions of rights.

b. Empowered Democracy: Structure without Structure?

Unger's social theory is one of considerable complexity. No attempt will be made to address all of the important issues which it raises, many of which are outside the scope of the present work. The discussion will focus upon those aspects of the theory which are most directly relevant to the current project. Three such issues will be discussed. First, the limits which are set to the transformative enterprise will be considered. Secondly, the normative assumptions which underly these limits will be analysed. Thirdly, the tension which exists between the realization of the desired normative outcome, and the institutional mechanism whereby this is to be attained, will be assessed.

i. The limits of transformation

> The attempt to emancipate social life more fully from false necessity can succeed only if our ordinary social experience gives us the occasions and the means to challenge and revise every aspect of the basic institutional structure of society. To every major feature of this structure there must correspond a practical or imaginative activity that puts it up for grabs, and this activity must be available to us in the midst of our routine conflicts and concerns.

Quotations such as this by Unger[81] appear regularly throughout his recent work. The impression which can be conveyed is that empowered democracy operates without any confining structure. Everything must be up for grabs; no social ordering can be regarded

[80] Barber, *Strong Democracy*, p. 197; see also pp. 226, 232.
[81] *False Necessity*, p. 449; see also, e.g. pp. 572–5.

as sacrosanct; transformation is a continuous process in which options can be pursued, experiments tested, and the status quo, however ephemeral, can be shaken. The iconoclast, the destabilizer, is both the ideal citizen and the champion of empowered democracy.

This impression is misconceived. Everything is not up for grabs and the iconoclast is to be revered only on the condition that his disruption moves the system in the correct direction. Destabilization is itself asymmetrical, precisely because empowered democracy is premised upon a particular conception of the good which necessitates the placing of limits upon the direction of transformative activity. That this is in fact so is evident from a close reading of Unger's own reasoning. As Unger states: 'It should be clear that just as the program of empowered democracy does not depend upon perfectionist assumptions, so too it is not meant to remain neutral among competing conceptions of personality and society.'[82]

This point, once stated, may appear obvious or self-evident. The consequences which ensue therefrom concerning the limits of transformative activity which will be countenanced within empowered democracy are, however, quite drastic. They give the project an entirely different 'feel' from that conveyed by the many quotations of the same type as that which opened this discussion. Two related themes demonstrate the nature of the limits placed upon transformative activity within an empowered democracy.

On the one hand, there are those which flow from the socio-economic conditions which are regarded as the necessary pre-conditions for the establishment of empowered democracy. Unger's dislike of deep-structure theory has already been related. It is, however, also clear that certain types of socio-economic regime are not regarded as compatible with empowered democracy.[83] Thus, while one can deny that institutional orders stand or fall together as a single piece, this does not mean that 'all institutional arrangements and imaginative preconceptions can be combined with all others'.[84] Constraints exist upon the institutional elements which constitute a formative context, and historical experience 'suggests that some juxtapositions just do not work'.[85] Particular institutional arrangements cannot coalesce into a stable formative framework if they

[82] Ibid. 365; see also pp. 557–60.
[83] Ibid. 126, 134, 164, 166, 168, 169.
[84] Ibid. 126.
[85] Ibid. 166.

'embody very disparate measures of emancipation from false necessity'.[86]

The object of destabilization is, therefore, to help create the socio-economic conditions which offer, in Unger's terms, the optimum degree of empowerment. The destabilization branch of government does not treat everything as up for grabs, but only those institutional developments which reflect the sense of empowerment which underpins the thesis. The changes and 'revisions' which will be taken seriously are those which conduce to this end. A wide range of other suggested developments, whether relating to the forms of property-holding, the limits of corporate size, or the basis of entitlements, will fall upon deaf ears. Put more gently, they will be politely considered, and politely rejected.

On the other hand, the limits placed upon transformative activity are reflected in the rights which are recognized. Immunity rights are, as seen, protected within empowered democracy. The sense of immunity is however tightly circumscribed.

> Though the constitution of the empowered democracy requires an effective sense of immunity, it is not compatible with all possible views of security. The individual may, for example, feel that his vital sense of protection requires that he live in a quiescent polity and that he have at his disposal private wealth in the form of consolidated property rights. He may even feel he is secure only if he has a lifelong guarantee to occupy a particular job or to live in the manner customary to a certain caste. The constitution of the empowered democracy expresses a social and personal ideal incompatible with this version of the ideal of security.[87]

The nature of immunity rights will be considered more fully below. The object of the present discussion is simply to emphasize the scope of the limitations which this thereby places upon transformative action. Arguments for a species of contract and property right closely akin to the present regime cannot be accepted. Empowered democracy would be 'frustrated by a system of rights that effectively secludes a great deal of economic life from their influence and that drastically limits opportunities to innovate in the organizational settings of production and exchange'.[88] Rights are up for grabs no more and no less than the institutional settings within which they subsist. Experimentation and innovation with concep-

[86] *False Necessity*, p. 166.
[87] Ibid. 514.
[88] Ibid. 169.

tions of entitlement are tightly constrained. Transformation and destabilization are encouraged as steps *to* the desired democratic vision. Rights-based arguments cannot, however, be used to transform this into some other democratic view.

ii. Superliberalism It is clear that Unger regards his theory as a development of liberalism rather than republicanism. The object of 'classical liberalism' is said to be the empowerment of the individual within society and Unger perceives his own theory as one of 'superliberalism', which more completely realizes this underlying objective in a double sense. It more fully breaks down structures which allow domination, and it is premised upon the realization that one cannot be neutral as between differing conceptions of the good.[89] A sense of community does inform this vision, but it is founded upon the existence of conflict and the divergence of opinion. The core of this vision of community is 'the notion of a zone of heightened mutual vulnerability, within which people gain a chance to resolve more fully the conflict between the enabling conditions of self-assertion: between their need for attachment and for participation in group life and their fear of the subjugation and depersonalization with which such engagement may threaten them'.[90] Empowered democracy as thus conceived is participatory. Larger areas of social, political, and economic life are brought within the realm of collective decision-making, and there is considerable emphasis placed upon decentralization and citizen involvement. It is, however, not a communitarian vision in the sense of one based upon a sharing of ideals and exclusion of conflict.

The realization of such a communitarian society is perceived by Unger to be both empirically implausible and normatively undesirable.[91] Attainment of the classical republican ideal[92] is said to entail both material and spiritual costs. It entails the former in the manner in which it restricts innovation, *inter alia*, by restricting the scope for reconstituting the formative context of society. It entails the latter by entrenching a particular social form which is not desirable.

The adherents to this social doctrine have always claimed that the citizen of their desired republic can be expected to put the collective good over private

[89] Ibid. 557–60.
[90] Ibid. 562.
[91] Ibid. 556, 585–8.
[92] See above, ch. 10., for discussion of republicanism.

interest. But the content of this collective good is exhausted in the defense of the system of inviolable spheres of right against all domestic or foreign enemies. The sameness of different subjectivities must be ensured by their shared emptiness; any richness of subjective experience creates the danger of cumulative discord or hopeless self-absorption.[93]

Three comments on this normative frame are warranted. The first is a reiteration of the point made in the preceding section. Republicanism may or may not be open to the type of critique which Unger advances[94] concerning the constraints which such a doctrine places upon innovation and experimentation. It is, however, misconceived to envision empowered democracy as free from real constraints upon transformative activity for the reasons adumbrated above.

Secondly, the psychological assumptions which underpin 'super-liberalism' are contestable. Thus Dunn has asked why anyone should believe that a 'belligerently dissident opportunism really makes a benign contribution to human life', and concludes that 'the zest for interminable self-reconstitution appears as febrile at a personal level as it appears unpromising as a collective political project'.[95] Galston expresses a similar point more forcefully:

A world restructured to accommodate the iconoclastic cravings of modernist visionaries is a world from which everyone else would recoil in dread. Most human beings find satisfaction within settled contexts and experience the disruption of those contexts not as empowerment, but rather as deprivation. The everyday life that Unger holds in such contempt is not the imposition of the few on the many. It retains its customary form precisely because it is the mode of existence best suited to the overwhelming majority of the human race.[96]

The third comment on Unger's normative frame relates to the rights and the conception of distributive justice which inform the system. The previous discussion of liberalism and public law revealed that the precise content with which such concepts were to be imbued represented one of the more controversial aspects of the theory. While differing conclusions have been drawn on these issues,

93 Unger, *False Necessity*, pp. 587–8.

94 See above, ch. 10.

95 J. Dunn, 'Unger's *Politics* and the Appraisal of Political Possibility', 81 *Nw. U.L. Rev.* 732, 748 (1987).

96 W. A. Galston, 'False Universality: Infinite Personality and Finite Existence in Unger's *Politics*', 81 *Nw. U.L. Rev.* 751, 759 (1987).

the mode of argumentation possesses a certain common thread. Thus controversy would centre around the interests which warranted protection as rights; the relationship between the pursuit of rights and other social goals; and the extent to which an individual could be said to deserve certain of his attributes with consequential implications for the particular conception of distributive justice espoused by any commentator.

There is little direct reference to such ideas in Unger's own analysis. The justification for empowered democracy, with the species of rights recognized therein and the widespread redistributive role pursued by the state, proceeds in a rather different manner. The essence of this mode of argument is as follows.[97] Starting from the premiss of empowering the individual within society, the analysis seeks to demonstrate that the system of rights and distributive justice which currently exists, or which has existed hitherto, still allows society to be held hostage to a faction and tolerates domination through entrenched hierarchy.

This type of reasoning is problematic in the following sense. The *empirical fact* of power cannot in and of itself 'prove' that the existence of any resultant domination is *normatively* suspect. The fact that a parent can exercise hierarchical power over a child does not, within limits, invite criticism, precisely because we accept the normative reasons why such power is justified. Other areas are more controversial. Whether the factual power which an employer exercises over his employees is justified or not depends upon controversial normative assumptions concerning the relationship between capital and labour. This same point can be put in another manner. The existence of power may require justification. Other theories furnish such justification by a species of argumentation which seeks to show why a particular interest warrants recognition as a right, and by indicating why the possession of such a right should be interpreted *in the manner* proposed by the advocate of any such theory.

Now Unger does recognize this difficulty and seeks to respond to it in two related ways.[98] *On the one hand*, there is an implicit usage of reasoning based on an interest theory of rights.[99] Thus Unger states that the 'argument for empowered democracy depends on the belief

97 Unger, *False Necessity*, pp. 362–95.
98 Ibid. 365–8.
99 See above, ch. 6 sec. 3a, for a discussion of this concept.

that our ordinary demands for security, freedom, and connection do have the internal relations and the institutional implications invoked in my discussion of the aspects of empowerment and that there is little in our experience of longing that cannot be related to one of these varieties of empowerment'.[100] Unger thereby seeks to clothe the empirical hypotheses concerning empowerment with normative force by arguing that these interests are worthy of the protection accorded to them because we value them highly enough to interpret them *in the manner* he describes, with the consequences for institutional structure and rights which he articulates.

The response cannot resolve the problem, certainly when it is left at this level of generality. It is, for example, by no means self-evident that our demands for freedom should be interpreted in the manner which Unger articulates. The preceding discussion concerning the psychological assumptions underlying the theory reveals this clearly. Whether individuals really interpret freedom as the ability for constant self-revision and conflict, or whether such mutability would be treated as a species of deprivation, is highly contestable. It is, therefore, certainly not clear that 'our ordinary demands for freedom' do have the internal relations and institutional implications which he postulates. Nor is it any clearer that our 'ordinary demands for security' would necessarily be interpreted in the manner which he ascribes. For example, it may well be felt that the absolute system of property rights which Unger wishes to dismantle does afford greater protection for security than the regime which is to replace it, notwithstanding the fact that such absolute rights can lead in some factual sense to domination. A variety of reasons may combine to this conclusion. Individuals may believe in a Lockean conception of entitlement. Or they may feel that the encroachments by the state which are attendant upon the alternative rotating capital fund would produce a different type of domination with a correlative lack of security.[101]

On the other hand, Unger seeks to address the problem concerning the relationship between empirical claims of empowerment and normative argument by addressing the connections between the two styles of discourse.[102] He proposes an 'understanding of normative argument as a diverse and mutable series of historically located

[100] *False Necessity*, p. 367.
[101] See below, ch. 11 sec. 4e, for a discussion of this issue.
[102] *False Necessity*, pp. 367–8.

practices'. These practices change under the influence of an altered understanding of society, personality, thought, and language. Empirical ideas concerning 'the nature of institutional and imaginative contexts and the ways they change' may help to reshape the normative assumptions upon which we operate.

It is not clear that this resolves the problem under discussion. The proposition that normative argument can be perceived in some sense as grounded in a series of diverse, mutable, historically located practices has been accepted, albeit in varying degrees, by writers of differing persuasions.[103] It is the next stage of the argument which causes difficulty. This requires one to sustain the view that the outcome postulated by empowered democracy, with its particular specification of rights, institutions, and distributive justice, is indeed normatively justifiable, even using normative in the sense articulated above.

The fact, assuming it to be true, that such a regime might reduce domination as compared with other systems still leaves unexplained why such factual domination is normatively suspect. If a rotating capital fund is to be the substitute for absolute property rights then this must be defended not just on the contestable factual ground that the latter concept allows too much power to the holder thereof. To be convincing the argument must show why such power is unwarranted in normative terms.[104] This requires that one attend to the varying arguments as to why individuals have property rights at all. Regarding general normative argumentation as historically mutable does not, therefore, resolve the specific application of such arguments within a particular temporal frame. Further related difficulties will be considered when addressing the public-law implications which flow from empowered democracy.

iii. Institutional realization The discussion within this section will focus upon the tension which exists between attaining the objectives of empowered democracy, and the institutional mechanisms which are instrumental to these goals. The tension which exists between the desire for constant self-revision, and the centralizing, constraining

[103] e.g. Rawls; see above, ch. 9 sec. 4a; A. MacIntyre, *Whose Justice? Which Rationality?* (1988).

[104] Such arguments can, of course, be advanced in a variety of ways: e.g. R. A. Dahl, *A Preface to Economic Democracy* (1985); Pateman, *Participation and Democratic Theory*; J. Cohen and J. Rogers, *On Democracy: Toward a Transformation of American Society* (1983), chs. 3, 6.

conditions which follow from the proposed institutional structure, can be exemplified by focusing upon two aspects of this regime: the rotating capital fund and the destabilization branch.

The essential elements of the economic regime have been adumbrated above. If the new economic order is to be effective the powers of central government will have to be augmented in two related ways. On the one hand, central government will have to assume a wide range of controls over existing capital markets. The semi-independent investment funds which allocate capital must do so subject to the parameters laid down by the social capital fund. These investment funds are said to operate 'much like contemporary central banks'.[105] If, however, the economic scheme is to be effective then not only will central government have to set the framework within which the investment funds operate. It will also have to curtail any other institution, such as existing banks, from providing capital on terms other than those which it has stipulated. It may indeed have to prevent them undertaking any of their normal investment activity, if this is felt to be incompatible with the operation of the investment funds.

On the other hand, the investment funds themselves will have to be granted wide powers if they are to be able to perform their assigned tasks effectively. The dismantling of the system of absolute property rights is designed, *inter alia*, to prevent the permanent aggregation of large volumes of capital. Once certain limits of enterprise investment have been reached, the additional capital returns to the fund for reassignment. Corporate empires, whether evolving through internal growth or merger, are to be precluded. If this system is to be effective, the investment fund would have to be given extensive powers which it would use to monitor corporate size, to set limits to allowable capital potential (which would obviously have to vary from industry to industry), and to demand the original capital back for reassignment. Individuals operating within such a regime might be forgiven for thinking that the absence of security which is attendant upon such economic oversight is a high price to pay for empowerment and plasticity. They might even feel that the power thereby accorded to the investment funds produced a more ominous sense of domination than that attendant upon the absolute property right which had existed hitherto.

The wide powers which are exercised by the destabilization

[105] Unger, *False Necessity*, p. 495.

branch provide a further example of the dangers of central control which can arise in pursuit of the avowed objective of empowering individual citizens. The importance of the destabilization branch in breaking down established hierarchy is readily apparent from the earlier discussion. Its powers are indeed extensive: it has the ability to intervene in all other social institutions and change their operation, whether by veto or affirmative initiative. The legal problems to which this can give rise will be considered below. The very existence of such a power, the discretionary and uncertain nature of its application, and the fact that it perforce operates at a central level, are all factors which tend towards the centralization of initiative. The difficulties of rendering such an agency accountable, and of preventing it from becoming a novel form of oppressive domination, even when it is engaged in the very job of combating established hierarchy, may be very real.

Unger is aware of the perils of centralization which are apparent within his own scheme.[106] The antidote is the 'effort to achieve the maximum incitement to conflictual collective mobilization outside governmental institutions while obtaining the greatest permeability of governmental institutions to the results of this mobilization'.[107] The efficacy of this antidote may well be questioned. The institutions which subsist within an empowered democracy require the extensive powers accorded to them in order to effectuate the objectives of the system. This produces the dilemma evident in other democratic theories which have been discussed: the need for a strong central state to enable individuals to be 'free'[108] or 'empowered' in the manner desired by the system. It is precisely because Unger's sense of empowerment entails a commitment to constant transformation and revision that a strong centralized power, with all the attendant dangers thereof, is required to ensure that the conditions for such transformation are preserved. The dangers of Leviathan can assume many forms.

4. PUBLIC LAW WITHIN PARTICIPATORY DEMOCRACY

The analysis within this section will proceed in two stages. First, there will be a consideration of the more radical critics of traditional

[106] Ibid. 502–5.
[107] Ibid. 505.
[108] See above, ch. 5 sec. 4, ch. 6 sec. 2e.

constitutional and administrative law theory, who themselves often espouse some form of participatory democracy. Secondly, the nature of constitutional and administrative law within 'strong' and 'empowered' democracy will be considered in its own right. This analysis will consider, *inter alia*, whether the dilemmas which are said to beset traditional theory are not also present with participatory democracy itself.

a. *The Radical Critique of Constitutional Law Theory*

The work of Tushnet best exemplifies the radical critique of constitutional theory. He argues that such theory has been marked by an effort to reconcile three fundamental propositions about law and society.[109] The justification principle asserts that there are occasions when judicial review is justified to displace legislative decisions. The restraint principle affirms that judges cannot do whatever they choose, but must respect constraints on their behaviour. The principle of value-free adjudication states that in a pluralist society objective values are not available as criteria for ordering social institutions.[110] Tushnet argues that Ely's critique of then existing constitutional law theories failed to reconcile these principles. He then argues that Ely's own process theory has the very same problems: for example, by allowing judicial manipulation, thereby violating the restraint principle, and requiring the use of objective values which transgresses the principle of value-free adjudication.[111]

The conclusion reached is that this incoherence is itself reflective of internal tensions in liberalism.[112] The first two principles are responses to what Unger[113] has termed the principle of arbitrary desire, whereby every person is driven to satisfy desires for which no criteria of evaluation exists; these two principles assert the need to avoid 'the tyranny that can result when someone motivated by arbitrary desire occupies a position of power'.[114] Thus judicial

[109] M. V. Tushnet, 'Darkness on the Edge of Town: The Contributions of John Hart Ely to Constitutional Theory', 89 *Yale L.J.* 1037, 1038 (1980).

[110] In the sense that there is no consensus on objective values which might provide such a basis, not that it is necessarily impossible to discover philosophically valid principles of justice; ibid. 1038 n. 2.

[111] Ibid. 1045–47.

[112] Ibid. 1057.

[113] R. M. Unger, *Knowledge and Politics* (1975), 42–6.

[114] Tushnet, 'Darkness on the Edge of Town', p. 1061.

review exists to prevent majority tyranny, and judicial restraint is needed to preclude judicial tyranny. Liberalism is said to furnish no coherent mechanism for delineating the boundaries of review, and hence provides no method for determining the way in which the justification and restraint principles fit together. The rule of law may appear to fit the role. However, it is either defined in formal, neutral terms and becomes empty; or it is given substantive content which renders it the handmaiden of a particular political view and hence contradicts the principle of value-free adjudication. The conclusion is that the liberal tradition renders constitutional theory both necessary and impossible.

It is necessary because it provides the restraints that the liberal tradition requires us to place on those in power, legislators and judges as well. It is impossible because no available approach to constitutional law can effectively restrain both legislators and judges: If we restrain the judges we leave legislators unconstrained; if we restrain the legislators we let the judges do what they want.[115]

Constitutional theory would be possible under some form of republican regime in which shared values and civic virtue predominated. It would, however, be unnecessary, since 'the shared system, not the artificial design of our governing institutions, will constrain lawmakers'.[116]

b. The Critique of Traditional Administrative Law Theory

Frug's work exemplifies the radical critique of administrative law. His attack on interest-group pluralism as a method of justifying and regulating bureaucratic power is not simply to point to the difficulties of defining an interest, etc., which are addressed above. It is more radical. Frug's objection is that interest-group pluralism requires a combination of subjective and objective factors, the precise admixture of which cannot be justified.[117] All attempts to justify bureaucratic power are said to have undertaken two tasks. On the one hand, they have attempted to demonstrate that such power is constrained by some form of objectivity, some species of

[115] M. V. Tushnet, *Red, White and Blue: A Critical Analysis of Constitutional Law* (1988), 313.

[116] Ibid. 59; see also, e.g., p. 146.

[117] G. E. Frug, 'The Ideology of Bureaucracy in American Law', 97 *Harv. L. Rev.* 1276, 1286 (1984).

shared values. On the other hand, they have tried to show that bureaucracy does not stifle personal self-expression, that it does not negate the subjective values of individuality. Each of these terms is a 'dangerous supplement' to the other, which constantly threatens to encroach on the other's preserve. The tension which this produces for pluralism is captured in the following quotation.

> The problem of subjectivity in the pluralist vision is to ensure that all relevant subjective elements are included in the decision making process; otherwise the process would be illegitimate. The problem of objectivity is to ensure that the results of the conflict do not exceed the limits of the legislative framework . . . and do not engender wasteful protracted conflict; otherwise the decision making process would engender chaos.[118]

The strain between subjectivity and objectivity manifests itself in the choice of participants, the weight to be accorded to their views, and the rules within which such groups operate. For example, the choice of participants will involve a delicate balancing between the subjective claims of interest groups to take part in the decision-making process, and the objective needs of the administration to carry out its business. The weight which should be accorded to the views of participants depends upon whether one regards them purely as factions pursuing their own narrow sectoral interests, or as the collective embodiment of the 'public' which the bureaucracy should serve. If groups are perceived in the former subjective light, then more freedom should be afforded to the administrator to depart from the views which have been presented.

It is participatory democracy which is advocated by Frug as the way forward. Such a democratic model does not purport to 'solve' the problems of social life. Democracy is conceived as the process by which people 'create for themselves the form of organized existence within which they live'.[119] Interdependence and transformation are the hallmarks of human and social relationships, and the ability to transform institutions in order to prevent new forms of domination and hierarchy is the central organizational theme. The connection between this vision and that of Barber, who is cited with approval, is manifest.

The tension produced by the subjective/objective clash can itself be seen as a product of liberal democracy in a manner analogous to

[118] Frug, 'The Ideology of Bureaucracy in American Law', p. 1361.
[119] Ibid. 1295–6, 1386.

that described by Tushnet when reviewing constitutional theory. The argument would be as follows.

Barber identifies three dispositions which operate within liberal democracy, the anarchist, realist, and minimalist.[120] The anarchist disposition views the person as an autonomous being living in a condition of natural freedom. This very freedom possessed by all runs the danger of being self-destructive. Protection is required in order to ensure that the Hobbesian vision does not come to pass. The realist disposition posits the creation of the sovereign to forestall the battle of individual against individual. This very creation, while withdrawing one threat to liberty, merely substitutes another. How are the excesses of state power to be controlled? The tension between the anarchist and realist dispositions of democracy brings forth the third disposition, that of minimalism. Politics are viewed as relationships between autonomous beings who are incapable of living together peacefully. The dangers of intemperate state power are guarded against by ensuring that abdication of personal liberty is subject to qualifications, that certain rights are guaranteed. Pure majoritarian power is distrusted, and efforts are made to control such authority by checks and balances, and by the encouragement of pluralistic associations.

Viewed against this background, the difficulties produced by the subjective/objective dichotomy are a reflection of the competing tensions in liberal theory itself.[121] Thus our concern for protection of subjectivity is a reflection of the anarchist disposition within liberal democracy. The idea of subjectivity, of individuality, flows from the anarchic disposition which envisions the person as an autonomous individual to be subject to minimal constraints upon his independence. Bureaucratic power which imposes limits on this independence must be controlled. Objectivity is mirrored by a mixture of the realist and minimalist dispositions. The dangers of the state of nature necessitate the establishment of the sovereign. As the franchise broadens, the legitimacy of the sovereign increases, as does the cogency of the argument that the legislative will to be

[120] *Strong Democracy*, ch. 1. These dispositions are in substance recognized by J. Rawls, *A Theory of Justice* (Oxford, 1973), 228–30, 240–1, 497–8.

[121] For a philosophical treatment of the way in which liberalism is dependent upon the division between subject and object, see M. J. Sandel, *Liberalism and the Limits of Justice* (1982); M. J. Sandel, 'The Procedural Republic and the Unencumbered Self', 12 *Pol. Theory*, 81 (1984); cf. C. Fried, 'Liberalism, Community and the Objectivity of Values', 96 *Harv. L. Rev.* 960 (1983).

administered by bureaucratic delegates enshrines the objectively just result. This realist vindication of objectivity must itself be tempered by the minimalist disposition. Some constraints must be placed upon the guardians, in addition to the skeletal protection afforded by the vote itself. The belief that the enfranchised legislative will encapsulates an objective solution still leaves open the possibility that this might unduly impinge upon the subjective autonomy of individuals, and therefore requires mechanisms to limit this power.

c. An Assessment of the Radical Critique

The radical critique of public law has been examined earlier.[122] The essence of the argument presented can be briefly summarized, since it is of importance for understanding the discussion thereafter.

The strength of the radical critique of liberalism and its ramifications for public law depends upon an understanding of the structure of a political theory. When these structural features are revealed, the force of the preceding criticism diminishes.

Any political theory will have what Dworkin terms constitutive and derivative political positions.[123] A constitutive position is one valued for its own sake such 'that any failure fully to secure that position, or any decline in the degree to which it is secured, is *pro tanto* a loss in the overall political arrangement'. A particular political theory may be comprised of a number of constitutive positions, none of which is absolute, and such positions may well clash *inter se*. A derivative position is then a strategy for attaining the constitutive goals. Thus a theory might hold free enterprise to be valued, not in itself, but as a mechanism for attaining a constitutive position of efficiency. Three points of importance follow from this dichotomy.

First, it is obviously crucially important to ensure that the constitutive positions attributed to a particular political theory really are held by advocates of that theory. For example, it is highly questionable whether liberalism is in fact committed to value-free adjudication in the sense used by Tushnet. The deontological liberalism of Rawls and Dworkin certainly stresses the idẹa that the state should not exalt a particular conception of the good at the

[122] See above, ch. 9 sec. 2.

[123] R. Dworkin, *A Matter of Principle* (1985), 185, 408 n. 1.

expense of other possible conceptions thereof. However, in so far as the courts *are* accorded a role in protecting and furthering the principles of justice which have been agreed upon in the original position, this role will necessarily entail them in value judgements as to, for example, the relative importance of two liberties when they clash.[124]

Secondly, disagreement as to the best way to effectuate the constitutive positions will be endemic in *any* political theory. The strategies, or derivative positions, which can best attain the central objectives of liberalism, republicanism, or 'strong' democracy will always be a matter of contention and debate. A constitutive position which comprises the core of a political theory will not inexorably dictate one particular derivative strategy, although it might well rule out certain options. Even where a particular political theory possesses, or may be said to possess, only one constitutive position, there may still be considerable disagreement as to the best derivative strategies to attain the desired end.

Thirdly, the precise derivative strategies which actually emerge will themselves reflect competing tensions or dispositions within the constitutive objectives. It has already been seen that a political theory may have a number of constitutive positions, which will have to be balanced when determining more concrete strategies. Each of these abstract positions may itself be the product of competing dispositions. The particular rules which emerge will depend upon the blending of these dispositions. Barber's depiction of three dispositions which operate within liberalism—the anarchist, the realist and the minimalist—exemplifies this idea. There are doubtless some who would disagree with the particular meaning accorded to these labels. It is, however, the idea of competing dispositions which is of importance, and, for example, Rawls, while not explicitly employing these labels, makes the same type of point.[125] *Any* political theory will have a constitutive position or positions, and any such theory will have competing dispositions in the preceding sense, which operate to shape the more concrete strategies which emerge. Decisions concerning the derivative strategies will reflect the balancing of those dispositions.

The radical critique of liberalism and public law must, therefore, be based upon one of two assumptions. One presupposition might

[124] See above, ch. 8 sec. 3a (i), ch. 9 sec. 4c.
[125] *A Theory of Justice*, pp. 228–30, 240–1, 497–8.

be that a different political theory would not suffer from competing dispositions in the same way as liberalism. This argument will not withstand examination. A different political theory, such as strong democracy, which has been supported by both Tushnet[126] and Frug,[127] possesses its own constitutive positions, and is permeated by its own competing dispositions. Decisions as to particular derivative strategies will be affected by the precise blending of the dispositions which inhere within such a theory. The nature of this balancing or blending process will be contentious, and no less complex than that which arises within liberalism itself, as will be demonstrated below.

The other presupposition underlying the radical critique might be that the particular dispositions which operate within liberalism are 'flawed' in certain ways, and that these defects would not be present within some alternative theory. Now this may or may not be correct, but the issue is simply never addressed in these terms. To sustain any such contention requires detailed analysis of the philosophical basis of liberalism *and* of some alternative theory. It requires one to examine the substance or content of such theories in a manner which is not undertaken.

The radical critique *does* none the less have value. It helps us to perceive the breadth of the derivative strategies which are at our disposal when constitutive principles are translated into more concrete legal terms. The very process of deconstructing traditional legal doctrine and exhibiting the tensions within it is instructive and beneficial. Liberalism is not however 'responsible' for this in the sense that other political theories would render our choice less complex. Any political theory will have constitutive positions; any such theory will have competing dispositions which shape that theory. The precise balancing of these dispositions will mould the choices we make concerning derivative strategies, including particular legal doctrines.

d. Strong Democracy and Public Law

i. Constitutional law Barber's rationale for rejecting constitutional review has been given above, and that rationale has been criticized.[128]

[126] *Red, White and Blue*, p. 315.
[127] 'The Ideology of Bureaucracy in American Law', pp. 1295–6, 1386.
[128] See above, ch. 11 sec. 3a.

It might, as argued above, be possible to delineate a role for constitutional review within this theory, but such an enterprise would be highly artificial given Barber's own expressed disavowal of such an approach. Moreover any such conjecturing would run counter to his own dismissal of rights-based argumentation. Emphasis will, therefore, be concentrated upon the implications of Barber's analysis for administrative law, and the light which this sheds on the radical critique outlined above.

A brief comment on the absence of constitutional adjudication within Barber's scheme is, however, of importance in relation to the radical critique of constitutional law considered above. The essence of the point may be presented as follows. The disavowal of constitutional review by strong democrats does not serve to remove the problem which is said to beset liberal democracy, but to shift its institutional focus.

It is necessary to distinguish the rationale for restraints upon majoritarian action from the institutional medium through which this restraint is to be accomplished. Liberal democratic theory is founded on the belief that the present majority should not be able to interfere with certain rights, and accords the judiciary a role in helping to prevent this. Boundaries to this judicial role must then be devised to preclude judicial tyranny. Strong democratic theory is also based upon the assumption that there should be limits set to the scope of majority action. Advocates of such theory eschew reliance upon an external agency, such as the courts, to achieve this, and pin their hopes upon internal self-regulation and the transformation of conflict. There are, notwithstanding the various techniques which are intended to diffuse conflict, bound to be situations in which disagreement subsists as to whether the majority should be entitled to pursue certain action. It may be argued, for example, that the legislative outcome discriminates against minority interests.

Strong democracy may succeed in avoiding the problems of defining the proper boundaries of the judiciary's constitutional role in such situations, by declining to accord the courts any such function. The result is not however to avoid 'judgements' being made concerning the legitimate scope of legislative action, but rather to shift the institutional focus of any such critique. Criticism will emanate from a group within, and/or external, to the legislature, who will offer reasoned argument as to why they believe the outcome is open to criticism.

Two features of this process are worthy of note by way of comparison with the liberal democrats' reliance on external control attained through the courts. One such feature is that the criticism within strong democracy also emerges from a 'group' which is *external* to the current majority. Now it is, of course, true that any such group will not possess the formal powers of a court. That is obvious. However, courts do not possess a monopoly over constitutional dialogue, and that is exactly what our postulated critical group is engaged in. The practical impact of such a critical exercise will depend upon the circumstances, and may be greater or less than the power wielded by the judiciary depending upon the situation. The other noteworthy feature of this process is that *boundaries* as to the *legitimate* scope of any such external critique will necessarily have to be drawn, either implicitly or explicitly. Some assessment will have to be made concerning the type of majority action which can be subjected to such a critique (for example, whether the matter is of constitutional significance); the motives of the external group (for example, to determine whether they are prompted by concern for the public interest or whether they are seeking to buttress their own narrow self-interest); the manner in which their claims can be advanced (for example, can they be pursued by persuasion, civil disobedience, etc.); and the substantive correctness of the claim being advanced.

The rejection of constitutional review by the strong democrat may enable one to avoid difficult problems concerning the rationale for and boundaries of the judiciary's role. It cannot, however, prevent the same type of problems being raised when the appropriate scope of majoritarian action is raised by other institutions within society.

ii. Administrative law How then, in the light of the above, does strong democracy legitimate institutional power? What would administrative law 'be like' within such a system? The answer to the question of legitimacy might appear to be self-evident. After all, are not citizen participation and direct self-legislation the key to the whole enterprise? Citizen action, self-legislation, and process provide the validation for the general theory and also for particular exercises of institutional power within it.

It will be argued that the issue is more complex than this for three interconnected reasons. First, there are stresses within strong democracy which must be made explicit. The dispositions which interact within liberal democratic theory have already been examined. It will be suggested that strong democracy has its own competing dispositions, which will be described as the individualist, the mediatory, and the communitarian. Secondly, certain bureaucratic structures will subsist within strong democracy in which direct, general citizen participation may not be possible. How decision-making by these institutions should be legitimated is not self-evident. It will be argued that the response will depend upon which interpretation of the three dispositions is to be preferred. Thirdly, it will be argued that even within those institutional structures in which more direct, citizen self-legislation is possible the tensions of the competing dispositions will still be present. The existence of this tension will produce significantly different interpretations of what citizen self-legislation actually entails.

Let us turn to the three dispositions which are inherent within strong democracy. The individualist element may be depicted as follows. While the individual is conceived as a social being who interacts with his fellows and with society, it is also recognized that he comes with his own interests and concerns. These are not formulated in purely economic or material terms, and they may well be partially the result of the individual's previous interaction with other citizens in society. None the less at any particular stage of the process the individual will have a set of views and values which he wishes to impart. Because strong democracy maintains that there is no general independent ground to validate the entire enterprise, particular emphasis is placed upon the 'equalization of inputs'. Each person's views are accorded an equal starting-place, irrespective of their prior epistemological status.[129] Within Barber's own terms the functions of democratic talk which serve what I have termed the individualist end are the articulation of interests, the maintenance of autonomy and self-expression, and persuasion.[130]

The mediatory disposition bears the following connotation. One element is what Barber terms the exploration of mutuality.[131] Conversation is viewed as a dialectical process in which common ground is fashioned. The aim is to find language to bridge conflicting perceptions, while still sufficient to withstand the testing enquiry of the subscribing parties. Another such mediatory element

[129] Barber, *Strong Democracy*, pp. 134, 135, 190, 192.

[130] Persuasion may, of course, serve communitarian goals.

[131] *Strong Democracy*, pp. 182, 183.

is what Barber refers to as affiliation.[132] This embraces the ability of conversation to enhance empathy and thereby promote consensus and commonality. The setting of the agenda for the political debate itself performs a mediating function. The agenda is not to be regarded as fixed and immutable in advance. Nor is it to be arrogated by a powerful élite. It is open and flexible, a mechanism through which widely disparate individual ideas can be subject to analysis. In sum, the mediatory disposition functions to facilitate the expression of options, to help bridge differences of view, and to build a common ground.

The communitarian disposition represents the resolution of the two preceding strains. The ultimate aim for Barber, is, the building of community, the development of a citizenry 'capable of genuinely public thinking and political judgement and thus able to envision a common future in terms of genuinely common goods'.[133] The communitarian disposition is also expressive of the need for choice and action in the face of conflicting views as to what form that action should take.[134] Strong democracy is directed towards transforming this conflict through citizen participation, but recognizes that decisions will be necessary where something less than a universal common vision prevails. The very emphasis upon constant challenge, reinterpretation, and revaluation is designed to prevent any particular common vision from becoming ossified and immunized from the participatory process.

The way in which these dispositions interrelate will depend partly upon the types of organizational structure which exist under strong democracy. It appears probable that certain public bureaucratic structures will continue to exist. Barber, as we have already seen, insists that the institutionalization of strong democracy must be seen in the context of the modern world, with its attendant problems of scale and technology. Certain new bureaucracies, such as the Civic Communications Co-operative, are indeed regarded as central to the project of strong democracy. Other existing structures, such as the Federal Communications Commission and the Federal Trade Commission, would continue to fulfil an important role. These examples do not exhaust the range of bureaucracies which would continue to operate within participatory democracy. The precise

[132] *Strong Democracy*, pp. 182, 187–90.
[133] Ibid. 197.
[134] Ibid. 134–5.

function of such institutions within strong democracy may well be different from their role within a liberal democratic order.[135] It is this which forms the next stage of our enquiry.

Given that some agencies will continue to exist in which direct participation is not feasible, there must be some regime which tells one who is entitled to participate in the agency proceedings, whether the agency will be subject to external controls, what type of controls these will be, the nature of the relationship between agency and government, and between different agencies. These and a plethora of other issues will require resolution. Any such resolution will reflect an underlying political theory, or an interpretation of such a theory. What form are the rules likely to assume, given the framework of strong democracy? One is, of course, in the realm of hypothesis, but some calculated guess might be made.

At the general level a premium would be placed upon securing citizen participation within the decision-making of the agency. This follows both from the centrality of citizen action to the theory, and also from the insistence that there are no independent grounds to validate political decisions. None the less some power would have to be reserved to the agency itself. Considerations of practicality would dictate limits upon the scope of citizen participation. There would, moreover, be problems of ensuring that the result of the dialogue was consonant with existing regulations, and with the general scheme dictated by the legislation.

It is readily apparent that the divergent interpretations of the three dispositions could be combined to produce differing visions of administrative law within strong democracy. Three such interpretations can be briefly sketched. *One option* would be to place principal emphasis upon the maximum preservation of citizen participation and self-legislation within the confines of the agency structure. Rules which optimize citizen access will result, and there will be considerable opportunity for dialogue within the agency prior to any action being declared to be the common end. A high premium is, therefore, placed upon the individualist disposition, the mediatory process is likely to be protracted and polycentric, and the communitarian end reached relatively slowly.

Advocates of a *second option* might be less willing to assume that the common vision will always best be served by those appearing before

[135] See also G. E. Frug, 'Why Neutrality?', 92 *Yale L.J.* 1591 (1983).

the agency on a particular issue. Disparities of power might unduly tilt the agency towards a particular conclusion. They might feel, therefore, that greater discretion should be accorded to those running the agency to depart from the opinions proffered, and/or that there should be some aid given to less powerful groups in order that inputs into the decision-making process can be truly equalized. It may also be felt that the need for public action means that the agency must have considerable control over the length and format of meetings. The blend of the three dispositions is thus different from option one. The communitarian element, in so far as this represents the necessity for public action, is given a higher status, and in so far as it represents the actual substantive outcome, is a blend of the participants' beliefs, and the opinions of the agency officials themselves. The shape of the mediatory process will also alter, with the agency officials being granted greater power to stipulate limits to the discursive pattern.

Advocates of a *third option* begin from a somewhat different premiss. Bureaucratic legitimacy is the result of 'delegation from the top', combined with 'delegation from the bottom'. The former flows from the establishment of the agency by the national legislature, perhaps buttressed by a referendum; the latter from the existence on the agency of citizens chosen by lot, neighbourhood assemblies, and the like. The primary guardian of the common good becomes the agency itself. The communitarian disposition is interpreted accordingly, and, while citizen involvement with particular decisions is accepted, both the individualist and mediatory dispositions of strong democracy are interpreted against this background. It would, moreover, be possible to prefer different options within the context of different agencies, depending upon the nature of the task which is being performed.

It may be felt that the divergent interpretations of the three dispositions within strong democracy would only affect the public bureaucracies which continued to subsist therein, and that the more directly self-governing institutions would not be subject to such tensions. This would be mistaken. The same issues would have to be resolved. A glimpse at the past can help to illuminate the future.

Participatory democracy was one of the central themes of the Students for a Democratic Society (SDS) in the 1960s.[136] Their

[136] See, e.g., R. L. Hanson, *The Democratic Imagination in America: Conversations with our Past* (1985), 298–309.

vision bears considerable analogy to that propounded by Barber. Politics should be quintessentially discursive in nature. Decision-making which had social consequences should be carried on by public groupings; politics was to be the manner of collectively creating an acceptable pattern of social relations; it was to bring people out of isolation and into community; opposing views should be organized so as to illuminate choices and facilitate the attainment of goals; work should encourage independence, a respect for others, and a sense of social responsibility; and there should be industrial democracy.

The SDS experimented with community-action projects as a way of transforming US society. These projects were directed at concrete goals which would help and mobilize the poor. In order to maximize their impact, it was felt that links should be forged between such community unions, and alliances made with other radical groups. The dilemma became readily apparent. Participatory democracy and self-governing institutions presume the absence of organizational structures dominated by élites. However, organizational imperatives seemed to require a 'division of labour in which organizers enjoyed a privileged position of power and information'.[137]

> the major organizational problem of SDS grew out of the fact that it recruited on the basis of participatory rhetoric and then attempted to do its political work as if the rhetoric were sufficient to create the nonrepressive society of equals. In the operation of local chapters this usually meant the avoidance of an elected leadership (in the name of antielitism), the reliance on long, formless mass meetings (in the name of individual participation), and the absence of careful strategic thinking (in the name of spontaneity). The real results of this mode of operation were the following: elitist manipulation by individuals or cliques, which operated freely because there was no defined leadership responsibility; the disillusionment of large numbers of new recruits who found it impossible to participate in the manipulated mass meetings and who were given no opportunity to develop politically through other structural forms of participation; and the frustration of serious activists because neither serious organizational forms nor long range programs were developed.'[138]

The tensions between the three dispositions of strong democracy are manifest in this quotation. The original aspiration is proximate to option one described above. A high premium is placed upon the

[137] Ibid. 305.
[138] Ibid. 306.

individualist/participatory element; the mediatory process is protracted and open-textured, with the consequence that the communitarian goal is reached only slowly, or perhaps not at all. The quotation also reveals the dysfunctional consequences which can ensue when the aspiration becomes distorted in its actual operation.

This example cannot easily be dismissed as the product of particular historical circumstance. It exemplifies the types of choice which would have to be made within any self-governing institution. Barber himself is aware of this.[139] He addresses the problematic character of leadership within strong democracy, recognizing that it is opposed to self-government and encroaches upon the autonomy of individuals. Leadership is none the less recognized as both inevitable and necessary. It is inevitable because of the inescapability of natural leadership rooted in human differences of experience, articulateness, and personality which characterize even the most egalitarian of communities. Leadership is necessary for the 'transitional' role which it can play in guiding people towards greater self-government; for its facilitating role which can make participatory institutions 'work well despite the skewing effects of natural leadership'; and for the moral role which it affords by fostering social cohesion and community.

The operation of our putative neighbourhood assemblies and the like is therefore not self-evident. The role of leadership, inevitable and necessary, but also dangerous because of its potential for élitism and foreclosure of discussion, must be addressed. So too must the form of the discursive process which takes place therein. The degree of structure which should be imposed, and the ordering of the discourse, would have to be considered. The extent to which the resultant communitarian goal should be perceived in isolation, or as part of a broader plan of action, would have to be thought through. The answers to these and many other such questions will depend ultimately upon how one perceives the interrelationship of the individualist, mediatory, and communitarian dispositions which comprise strong democracy.

The preceding discussion has tried to evaluate the role and direction of administrative law within a participatory democracy. Certain conclusions emerge. Liberal democratic theory may well be beset by the anarchic, realist, and minimalist dispositions therein, which lend themselves to differing interpretations and thereby

[139] *Strong Democracy*, pp. 238–9.

produce a variety of alleged justifications for bureaucracy and administrative law. It would, however, be mistaken to see strong democracy as free from its own inner tensions. General themes such as citizen action, self-legislation, transformation, interdependence, and participatory process do not furnish any single, self-evident answer to the manner of organizing and ordering institutional power. They provide a framework for analysis, the resolution of which will depend upon contestable assumptions as to how the three dispositions within strong democracy should be interpreted and balanced. This is not, of course, to deny the real differences which permeate the liberal and the participatory models of democracy. It is, however, to argue that distinctive problems, which are no less intractable than those which beset liberal democracy, may await us if we follow the path of participatory democracy.

e. *Empowered Democracy and Public Law*

i. Constitutional law and immunity rights The general system of rights which subsists within an empowered democracy has been described above.[140] Four important issues concerning the nature and application of immunity rights arise.

First, the existence of constitutional review itself is not entirely clear. Immunity rights are 'required'[141] by the reformed constitution, and the implication is that they can be utilized to invalidate governmental action which infringes them. This is not, however, stated unequivocally, and, as will be seen below, there is a latent tension between the exercise of such rights and the commitment to transformation which underpins the whole system. It will be assumed in the subsequent discussion that such rights can be protected through some species of constitutional review.

Secondly, the ranking or priority of the differing types of immunity rights is unclear. The earlier discussion of liberalism and public law revealed that the relationship between the protection of traditional civil liberties and other 'primary goods' was one of the most complex issues within that theory.[142] The reasons for regarding civil liberties as having a higher priority than claims to welfare is still a difficult aspect of Rawls's thesis.

[140] See ch. 11 sec. 2b.

[141] e.g. Unger, *False Necessity*, pp. 514, 516, 524.

[142] See above, ch. 8 sec. 2c.

Unger, by way of contrast, provides little guidance as to the priority between the two principal species of immunity rights: traditional civil liberties and welfare entitlements. This is particularly problematic, because the nature of Unger's thesis renders the possibility of such clashes quite high. The activities of the destabilization branch might well encroach on particular civil liberties, but enhance the welfare of individuals. Such a situation is not difficult to imagine.

Those who operate the destabilization branch may seek to break down established power orders as part of the continuing movement to, and preservation of, empowered democracy. They decide that it is necessary to divest certain large financial empires of part of their holdings. Such divestiture will facilitate the operation of the economic goals of empowered democracy, and this will itself facilitate the provision of the welfare entitlements which form part of the immunity rights.[143] They also decide that the success of this operation requires some limitation upon the speech and association rights of those who are opposed to such a move. The fear is that those who currently possess financial power will use this to mount costly campaigns which seek to persuade people of the wisdom of current arrangements. Can civil liberties be restricted in this manner in order to enhance welfare entitlements?

It might be argued that there is in fact no clash between the two species of immunity rights in the above example. Unger makes clear that such rights cannot be used as instruments of subjugation, or as means to protect the social order against revision.[144] It might be argued that those who are opposed to the activities of the destabilization branch are seeking to do just that, and therefore cannot in fact use their civil liberties in this manner.

This retort does not resolve the tension adumbrated above. Those who are opposed to the activities of the destabilization branch, whether in the example proffered above or many others which could be offered, may genuinely believe that the transformation being espoused will reduce the empowerment of individuals. They may honestly wish to convince others of this position and desire to utilize their civil liberties to this end.

There are then two possible outcomes. *Either* one seeks to argue that any attempt to use one's civil liberties to oppose the changes

[143] Unger, *False Necessity*, pp. 528–9.
[144] Ibid. 516.

advocated by the destabilization branch are illegitimate, in the sense that one is attempting to entrench established hierarchy. The destabilization branch can therefore restrict such liberties without thereby infringing constitutional guarantees. Such a conclusion would, however, truly render this branch of government all powerful, and would drastically limit the scope of immunity rights. *Or* one has to determine the priority between civil liberties and welfare entitlements, assuming that the change which has been advocated will enhance the latter.

The preceding discussion leads naturally on to the third issue concerning immunity rights. This is the relationship between such rights (whether civil liberties or welfare entitlements) and the destabilization process. That a tension exists between immunity rights and the destabilization process is a fact which is recognized by Unger; it is not, however, clear that this is ever resolved.

The *existence* of the tension between the two aspects of empowered democracy is clear. On the one hand, immunity rights are to some extent 'not open to revision'.[145] They are defined 'as rigidly as possible at the time of their initial formulation', and there is no 'more latitude for their redefinition at the moment of exercise than inheres, inevitably, in the interpretive freedom of the law applier'.[146] The consequence is that a 'bright line circumscribes the boundaries of each immunity right', and the rightholder can 'expect to distinguish confidently between the factual circumstances in which the law protects him in the asserted exercise of such an entitlement and those in which it does not'.[147] On the other hand, immunity rights must satisfy two negative standards: they must not supply instruments of subjugation, and they must not protect the social order against revision.[148] If immunity rights produced either result they would render the destabilization process impossible. It is readily apparent that the attainment of the clarity, certainty, and specificity spoken of above exists in uneasy tension with the mutability which is required if the transformation process is to be successful.

The *purported resolution* of this tension is as follows. The essence of the argument is directed towards a redefinition of what is meant by the sense of security which underpins immunity rights. Thus, at one extreme, such security may consist of the 'intangibility of a

145 Ibid. 515.
146 Ibid. 530.
147 Ibid.
148 Ibid. 516.

particular way of life, defined by the position a group occupies within a well-defined communal and hierarchical order'.[149] At the other extreme, such security may be interpreted as a set of rights whose main demand on other parts of the social order is that they are open to constant challenge and revison.[150] There may, however, be various points along 'the spectrum defined by these two poles'. The immunity rights of empowered democracy possess the same relation to consolidated property that property has to caste. They allow the individual the background confidence of his own position to enable him to participate fearlessly in the conflicts and transformations which characterize community decision-making in an empowered democracy.[151]

This does not, however, resolve the tension outlined above. It can be accepted that the sense of security which underlies constitutional rights can be defined in different ways. The tension none the less remains unresolved, precisely because of the role given to immunity rights within Unger's own system. These are intended to protect the individual against oppression and the extremes of economic deprivation. They are designed to achieve this with some sense of certainty and specificity. However, they must not be a mask for subjugation nor impede revision. Yet, the more certain and specific they become, the more they will necessarily impede transformation. The greater the power accorded to the destabilization branch, the weaker will the immunity rights become, and the less will they be capable of serving the function assigned to them. No longer will the individual be certain of the bright line which circumscribes the boundaries of his dealings with others; and no longer will he be sure of the circumstances in which the law will protect him in the exercise of his entitlement.[152]

The final issue concerning immunity rights is in some ways the most important. The *content* to be ascribed to such rights will, as seen above, be closely circumscribed by the structure of the desired regime. An individual will not be successful in arguing that his sense of security requires that he possess consolidated property rights, or the right to a particular job; nor can he argue that he would feel more empowered by living in a quiescent polity which possesses the attributes associated with the rule of law, such as stability and predictability. Everything is not up for grabs within an empowered

149 Unger, *False Necessity*, p. 515.
150 Ibid.; see also pp. 525–8.
151 Ibid. 524, 530.
152 Ibid. 530.

democracy, and the individual will not succeed in addressing rights-based arguments which are inconsistent with the sense of empowerment which lies at the core of the theory.

ii. Constitutional law, administrative law, and destabilization rights It is clear from the preceding analysis that the destabilization branch and destabilization rights occupy an important place within empowered democracy. Two difficult issues are raised by the activities of this new branch of government.

The first issue concerns the *structural constitutional* position of this agency in relation to the other more traditional branches of government. The destabilization branch is to possess wide powers to reorganize major institutions, and to reconstruct society. These functions are accorded not to the established judiciary, but to a new agency specifically designed for these purposes.[153] If the other government organs could 'not resist and invade the jurisdiction of this corrective agency, it would become the overriding authority in the state'; yet the resistance of these other powers must not 'exemplify the rigid distribution of functional competences, the checks and balances, of the tradition inherited from the eighteenth century'.[154]

The precise nature of the relationship between the destabilization branch and the other organs of government is not, however, clear. Nor is it easy to imagine how they coexist, given the broad powers possessed by the new branch, and given the necessity for some control thereof set out above. There are two differing types of scenario in which such conflict may arise.

On the one hand, it may occur because the destabilization branch is acting on its own initiative to combat existing hierarchy. There may be no legislative authorization for such an initiative, and it is clear that the new governmental agency is intended to be able to operate in this way. Indeed the very rationale for its establishment is that the ordinary legislature would not be well suited to the task; legislatures concentrate on short-term marginal adjustments to the existing power order and partisan rivalries, rather than longer-term systematic intervention.[155] Yet if the destabilization branch is to operate in this fashion it will encounter the traditional arguments

[153] See above, ch. 11 sec. 2b (ii).
[154] Unger, *False Necessity*, p. 453.
[155] Ibid. 452–3.

which have been directed towards the legitimacy of constitutional review and of interventionist policy by the judiciary.[156] These problems may be exacerbated by the very fact that the new agency is not a court. At least when such action is undertaken by a court there is the possibility of adversarial argument as to the desirability of the proposed change. Whether the destabilization branch would be subject to any such procedural imperatives is unclear, and they would not sit easily with the structure of this agency.

On the other hand, conflict between the destabilization branch and the traditional governmental organs can occur, when the former believes that the latter is being subverted by particular power orders which wish to entrench their position. The objective of the new agency is 'to rob the nascent prerogatives of their defenses'.[157] The mode of fulfilling this objective is not, however, clear. It appears that the constitution will provide for a referendum in some instances. On other occasions, the exercise of power by the destabilizing branch only takes effect when 'confirmed by the electorate or by a broad range of intermediate representative bodies'. This will be so when the new agency's activities clash with legislative decisons.[158]

The very decision by the destabilization branch that the legislature is being subverted, its choice of 'remedies', and the legal methods to effectuate them are bound to cause considerable problems. These stem ultimately from the attempt to create a body with broad, autonomous powers of action which is intended to be free of the vices of normal partisan politics and yet subject to some control by these very political organs. This is not an easy mix, and it may not be a plausible one.

The second issue which is relevant to the present discussion concerns the *nature and limits* of destabilization rights. Both points are of considerable importance for an understanding of public law within an empowered democracy.

The *nature* of destabilization rights differs somewhat from the ordinary meaning attributed to the word 'right'. Destabilization rights do not generate straightforward correlative duties such as exist within other spheres. The basis of such rights is neither the result of a fully articulated agreement, nor the unilateral imposition of a duty by the state; it arises rather from the interplay between a

[156] See also Unger, *False Necessity*, p. 451, where Unger draws analogies with the judiciary's role in awarding injunctive relief against bodies such as schools, hospitals, etc.

[157] Ibid. 533.

[158] Ibid.

basic commitment to the constitutional plan, and the emergence of practices which place that commitment in jeopardy.[159] Moreover, no bright line surrounds the area of such rights.

> The point of destabilization rights is not to demarcate a fixed zone of discretionary action, with which an individual rightholder may do whatever he pleases, but to prevent recurrent, institutionalized relationships among groups from falling into certain prohibited routines of closure and subjugation. So the controlling image is the mandated, context-specific disruption of complex collective arrangements rather than the vigilant defense of a zone of untrammeled individual discretion.[160]

The preceding description helps to clarify the nature of such rights. They are rights which are to be exercised *by an institution*, the destabilization branch, in the pursuit of *its* reconstructive activities. Certain central features of this system are, however, still unclear. It is not apparent whether an individual can complain to the agency; whether he can suggest that it take certain action; whether he can oppose its activities; or whether he can demand that it provide a reasoned basis for its proposed interventions.

The *limits* of destabilization rights are of considerable importance. The existence of these limits is itself a reflection of the limits of transformative activity considered above.[161] Certain socio-economic conditions are regarded as necessary for the establishment of an empowered democracy, and a certain regime of rights is required if the system is to be effective. Destabilization is designed to move the social system towards these goals. It is to remove entrenched hierarchy which prevents the realization of these aims, and to monitor the new regime to ensure that new forms of domination do not become impervious to change. Destabilization rights cannot, however, be used as the basis for arguing that the polity would prefer a sense of empowerment associated with some previous socio-economic regime or with some previous ordering of rights. Even if such an argument could technically be put to the destabilization branch or the courts, it would be rejected. The citizenry will be told that they, and if not they then their children,[162] will in time appreciate the sense of empowerment which the new system engenders. Yearnings for atavistic conceptions of security should be

[159] Ibid. 535.
[160] Ibid.
[161] See ch. 11 sec. 3b (i).
[162] Unger, *False Necessity*, p. 514.

cast aside. They will receive no succour from the system of immunity or destabilization rights.

iii. Administrative law and the economic regime The institutions which will administer the economic regime which is central to empowered democracy have been considered above.[163] The earlier discussion also revealed the extensive powers which such institutions must possess in order to effectuate their avowed purposes.[164] Space precludes any full analysis of the problems of an administrative-law nature which are thereby created. Some indication of the type of issues which would have to be resolved can none the less be given.

There will clearly have to be decisions as to the scope and nature of any *procedural rights* for individuals or firms who are subject to the operations of the investment funds. These will have to cover varying situations. Thus, the issue of procedural rights will arise in the process of auctioning and rotating the capital. It will also occur when decisions are made that a firm's size warrants the reassignment of capital to the fund itself.

There will also have to be decisions as to the scope of *substantive control* over the operations of the funds themselves. Will a firm be able to argue that a court should, for example, take a hard look at the allocational decision made by such a fund? How intensively should the judiciary review such complex allocational decisions, in order to ensure that they are consonant with the parameters laid down by the central capital fund? These, and a plethora of other such questions, will have to be resolved if the agencies which are at the vanguard of empowered democracy are not to become new sources of domination.

5. CONCLUSION

No attempt will be made to summarize the entirety of the preceding arguments. Three points should however be emphasized.

First, there is little point in incanting the phrase 'participatory democracy' as if it possessed a self-evident meaning. Republicanism, strong democracy, and empowered democracy all entail an increased commitment to participation, but the nature of this varies consider-

[163] See ch. 11 secs. 2b (ii), 3b (iii).
[164] See ch. 11 sec. 3b (iii).

ably precisely because the theories differ from each other in important respects. It is only by revealing the detailed normative foundations of such theories, and by paying close attention to the conditions for their institutional realization, that any judgement can be made as to their desirability or plausibility. Conclusions as to the shape of public law within such regimes are only possible when this has been accomplished.[165]

Secondly, the idea that one can develop a democratic regime in which mutability is central, in which everything really is up for grabs, does not withstand examination. This theme, which is apparent albeit in different ways within both Barber's and Unger's work, is belied by closer attention to their own reasoning and the dictates of their own theory. Both theories are based upon a particular conception of the good which generates limits to the transformative enterprise. The psychological and normative assumptions which provide this foundation are themselves contestable.

Finally, a point of more general concern for legal doctrine may be perceived. The manipulability of doctrinal form is a standard theme within the Critical Legal Studies critique of other areas outside the public-law context.[166] The preceding discussion, and that in the previous chapter, may, however, serve to demonstrate that any democratic theory will, upon closer examination, have its own internal dispositions which can be combined in a plethora of ways to reach a variety of distinctive conclusions. Legal doctrine will represent a particular conclusion reached at a distinctive point in time. If, therefore, we are to pursue one of the more radical options, we should not do so under the pretence that any such participatory vision will spare us the types of doctrinal conflict which are said to beset liberal democracy. The conflicts will not be the same as those

[165] Other conceptions of participatory or deliberative democracy can be found in, e.g., Cohen and Rogers, *On Democracy*, and J. Cohen, 'The Economic Basis of Deliberative Democracy', 6 *Social Philosophy and Policy*, 25 (1988). Space precludes a detailed examination of the views of J. Habermas, *Legitimation Crisis*, trans. T. McCarthy (1976), and *The Theory of Communicative Action*, trans. T. McCarthy (1984). Any such examination would have to involve a detailed scrutiny of the normative content of the theory, the socio-economic conditions necessary for its institutional realization, and a careful depiction of the public-law consequences which were said to ensue therefrom.

[166] e.g. M.Kelman, 'Trashing', 36 *Stan. L. Rev.* 293 (1984); J. Singer, 'The Player and the Cards: Nihilism and Legal Theory', 94 *Yale L.J.* 1 (1984); C. Dalton, 'An Essay in the Deconstruction of Contract Doctrine', 94 *Yale L.J.* 997 (1985); J. Boyle, 'The Politics of Reason: Critical Legal Studies and Local Social Thought', 133 *U. Pa. L. Rev.* 685 (1985).

which are said to exist within liberalism. They will turn instead on the contrasting interpretations given to the differing dispositions which subsist within the particular view of participatory democracy which is being espoused.

BIBLIOGRAPHY

Ackerman, B., 'The Storrs Lectures: Discovering the Constitution', 93 *Yale L.J.* 1013–72 (1984).

—— 'Beyond *Carolene Products*', 98 *Harv. L. Rev.* 713–46 (1985).

Allen, C. K., *Law and Orders* (3rd edn., London, 1965).

Agger, R., Goldrich D., and Swanson B., *The Rulers and the Ruled* (New York, 1964).

Alexander, K. J. W., 'The Economic Case against Independence', in D. N. MacCormick (ed.), *The Scottish Debate* (Oxford, 1970), chs. 10, 11a.

Almond, G. A., and Verba, S., *The Civic Culture* (Boston, 1965).

Aman, A. C., 'Administrative Law in a Global Era: Progress, Deregulatory Change and the Rise of the Administrative Presidency', 73 *Corn. L. Rev.* 1101–247 (1988).

Anson, W. R., *Law and Custom of the Constitution*, ed. M. L. Gwyer (5th edn., Oxford, 1922).

Appleby, J., *Capitalism and a New Social Order: The Republican Vision of the 1790s* (New York, 1984).

Arblaster, A., *The Rise and Decline of Western Liberalism* (Oxford, 1984).

—— *Democracy* (Milton Keynes, 1987).

Arnold, R. D., *Congress and Bureaucracy: A Theory of Influence* (New Haven, 1979).

Areeda, P., *Antitrust Analysis* (3rd edn., Boston, 1981).

Arnull, A., 'The Single European Act' (1986) 11 *E.L.R.* 358–63.

Arthurs, H. W., 'Rethinking Administrative Law: A Slightly Dicey Business' (1979) 17 *Osgoode Hall L.J.*, 1–45.

—— *Without the Law: Administrative Justice and Legal Pluralism in Nineteenth Century England* (Toronto, 1985).

Asimow, M., 'Delegated Legislation: United States and United Kingdom' (1983) 3 *O.J.L.S.* 253–76.

Austin, J., *The Province of Jurisprudence Determined*, ed. H. L. A. Hart (London, 1955).

Bachrach, P., *The Theory of Democratic Elitism: A Critique* (London, 1967).

—— and Baratz, M. S., 'Two Faces of Power', in W. E. Connolly (ed.), *The Bias of Pluralism* (New York, 1969), ch. 3.

Bagehot, W., *The English Constitution*, ed. R. H. S. Crossman (Glasgow, 1963).

Bailyn, B., *The Ideological Origins of the American Revolution* (Cambridge, Mass., 1967).

—— *The Origins of American Politics* (New York, 1970).

BALDWIN, R., 'A British Independent Regulatory Agency and the "Skytrain" Decision' [1978] *P.L.* 57–81.

BALDWIN, R. 'The Next Steps: Ministerial Responsibility and Government by Agency' (1988) 51 *M.L.R.* 622–8.

—— and HAWKINS, K., 'Discretionary Justice: Davis Reconsidered' [1984] *P.L.* 570–99.

—— and HOUGHTON, J., 'Circular Arguments: The Status and Legitimacy of Administrative Rules' [1986] *P.L.* 239–84.

—— and MCCRUDDEN, C., *Regulation and Public Law* (London, 1987).

BARBER, B., *Strong Democracy: Participatory Politics for a New Age* (Berkeley, 1984).

BARENDT, E., *Freedom of Speech* (Oxford, 1985).

BARKER, A. (ed.), *Quangos in Britian* (London, 1982).

BARKER, E., *Reflections on Government* (Oxford, 1942).

BARRY, B., *Sociologists, Economists and Democracy* (London, 1970).

BEATSON, J., 'Legislative Control of Administrative Rulemaking: Lessons from the British Experience', 12 *Corn. I.L.J.* 199–226 (1979).

BEITH, A., 'Prayers Unanswered: A Jaundiced View of the Parliamentary Scrutiny of Statutory Instruments' (1981) 34 *Parliamentary Affairs*, 165–73.

BELL, D., *The Coming of Post-Industrial Society* (New York, 1973).

BELLAH, R. N., MADSEN, R., SULLIVAN, W. M., SWIDLER, A., and TIPTON, S. M., *Habits of the Heart* (Berkeley, 1985).

BELOFF, M., and PEELE, G., *The Government of the United Kingdom: Political Authority in a Changing Society* (2nd edn., London, 1985).

BELSEY, A., 'The New Right, Social Order and Civil Liberties', in R. Levitas (ed.), *The Ideology of the New Right* (Cambridge, 1986), ch. 6.

BENTLEY, A. F., *The Process of Government* (Cambridge, Mass., 1908; repr. 1949).

BERELSON, B., *et al.*, *Voting* (Chicago, 1954).

BERLE, A. A., *Power Without Property* (New York, 1959).

BERNSTEIN, R., *Beyond Objectivism and Relativism: Science, Hermeneutics, and Praxis* (Oxford, 1983).

BERTHOFF, R., 'Independence and Attachment, Virtue and Interest: From Republican Citizen to Free Enterpriser, 1787–1837', in R. L. Bushman, N. Harris, D. Rothman, M. Solomon, S. Thernstrom (eds.), *Uprooted Americans: Essays to Honor Oscar Handlin* (Boston, 1979), 97–124.

—— and MURRIN, J. M., 'Feudalism, Communalism and the Yeoman Freeholder', in S. G. Kurtz and J. H. Hutson (eds.), *Essays on the American Revolution* (Chapel Hill, 1973) 256–88.

BERTRAM, C., 'Decision-Making in the EEC: The Management Committee Procedure', (1967–8) 5 *CML Rev.* 246–64.

BEVIER, L., 'Money and Politics: A Perspective on the First Amendment and Campaign Finance Reform', 73 *Cal.L.Rev.* 1045–90 (1985).

BICKEL, A. M., *The Least Dangerous Branch* (New Haven, 1962).
—— *The Supreme Court and the Idea of Progress* (New Haven, 1978).
BIRCH, A. H., *Representative and Responsible Government* (London, 1964).
—— *Political Integration and Disintegration in the British Isles* (London, 1977).
BIRKENSHAW, P., HARDEN, I., and LEWIS, N., *Government by Moonlight: The Hybrid Parts of the State* (London, 1990).
BOGDANOR, V., *Devolution* (Oxford, 1979).
—— *The People and the Party System* (Cambridge, 1981).
BORK, R. H., 'The Rule of Reason and the Per Se Concept: Price Fixing and Market Division I', 74 *Yale L.J.* 774–847 (1965).
—— 'The Rule of Reason and the Per Se Concept: Price Fixing and Market Division II', 75 *Yale L.J.* 373–475 (1966).
—— 'Neutral Principles and Some First Amendment Problems', 47 *Ind.L.J.* 1–35 (1971).
BOTTOMORE, T., *Elites and Society* (London, 1964).
BOURN, J., *Management in Central and Local Government* (London, 1979).
BOYLE, J., 'The Politics of Reason: Critical Legal Studies and Local Social Thought', 133 *U.Pa.L.Rev.* 685–780 (1985).
BRAYBROOKE, D., and LINDBLOM, C. E., *A Strategy of Decision* (New York, 1963).
BREBNER, J. B., 'Laissez-faire and State Intervention in Nineteenth-Century Britain' (1948) 8 *Jnl. of Econ. Hist.* 61.
BRENNAN, G., and BUCHANAN, J. M., *The Reason of Rules* (Cambridge, 1985).
BREST, P., 'The Misconceived Quest for the Original Understanding', 60 *Boston U.L.Rev.* 204–38 (1980).
—— 'The Substance of Process', 42 *Ohio St.L.J.* 131–42 (1981).
—— 'Constitutional Citizenship', 34 *Clev.St.L.Rev.* 175–97 (1986).
—— 'Further Beyond the Republican Revival: Toward Radical Republicanism', 97 *Yale L.J.* 1623–31 (1988).
BREYER, S. G., 'Vermont Yankee and the Courts' Role in the Nuclear Energy Controversy', 91 *Harv.L.Rev.* 1833–45 (1978).
—— *Regulation and its Reform* (Cambridge, Mass., 1982).
—— and STEWART, R. B., *Administrative Law and Regulatory Policy: Problems, Text and Cases* (2nd edn., Boston, 1985).
BRILMAYER, L., '*Carolene*, Conflicts and the Fate of the "Inside–Outsider" ', 134 *U.Pa.L.Rev.* 1291–334 (1986).
BRITTAN, S., *The Role and Limits of Government* (London, 1983).
BROWN, R. G. S., and STEEL, D. R., *The Administrative Process in Britain* (2nd edn., London, 1979).
BRYCE, J., *Modern Democracies* (New York, 1921).
BUCHANAN, J. M., *The Limits of Liberty: Between Anarchy and Leviathan* (Chicago, 1975).
—— 'Comment', 18 *J.L.E.* 903–5 (1975).
—— *Freedom in Constitutional Contract* (Texas, 1978).

BUCHANAN, J. M., *Liberty, Market and State: Political Economy in the 1980s* (Brighton, 1986).

—— and TULLOCK, G., *The Calculus of Consent* (Ann Arbor, 1962; repr. 1965).

BURNHAM, J., *The Managerial Revolution* (London, 1942).

BYSE, C., 'Vermont Yankee and the Evolution of Administrative Procedure: A Somewhat Different View', 91 *Harv.L.Rev.* 1823–32 (1978).

CALVERT, H. (ed.), *Devolution* (London, 1975).

CAMPBELL, A., 'The Single European Act and the Implications' (1986) 35 *I.C.L.Q.* 932–9.

CAMPBELL, C. (ed.), *Do We Need a Bill of Rights?* (London, 1980).

CAMPBELL, T., *The Left and Rights: A Conceptual Analysis of the Idea of Socialist Rights* (London, 1983).

CANE, P., 'Standing, Legality, and the Limits of Public Law' [1981] P.L. 322–39.

CARR, C. T., *Delegated Legislation* (Cambridge, 1921).

—— *Concerning English Administrative Law* (Oxford, 1941).

CARSON, G. D., *Group Theories of Politics* (London, 1978).

CAWSON, A., *Corporatism and Welfare* (London, 1982).

—— *Corporatism and Political Theory* (Oxford, 1986).

—— and SAUNDERS, P., 'Corporatism, Competitive Politics and Class Struggle', in R. King (ed.), *Capital and Politics* (London, 1983), ch. 1.

CHAYES, A., The Role of the Judge in Public Law Litigation', 89 *Harv. L.Rev.* 1281–316 (1976).

CHESTER, N., *The English Administrative System (1780–1870)* (Oxford, 1981).

CLARK, T. N. (ed.), *Community Structure and Decision Making: Comparative Analysis* (San Francisco, 1968).

COHEN, J., 'The Economic Basis of Deliberative Democracy', 6 *Social Philosophy and Policy*, 25 (1988).

—— and ROGERS, J., *On Democracy: Towards a Transformation of American Society* (New York, 1983).

CONNOLLY, W. E., 'The Challenge to Pluralist Theory', in W. E. Connolly (ed.), *The Bias of Pluralism* (New York, 1969), ch. 1.

—— (ed.), *The Bias of Pluralism* (New York, 1969).

—— 'Legitimacy and Modernity', in W. E. Connolly (ed.), *Legitimacy and the State* (Oxford, 1984), introduction.

—— (ed.), *Legitimacy and the State* (Oxford, 1984).

CORNFORD, J. (ed.), *The Failure of the State* (London, 1975).

COSGROVE, R. A., *The Rule of Law: Albert Venn Dicey, Victorian Jurist* (London, 1980).

COURTNEY, L., *The Working Constitution of the United Kingdom* (London, 1901).

COWLING, M. (ed.), *Conservative Essays* (London, 1978).

CRAIG, P. P., 'Discretionary Power in Modern Administration', in M. Bullinger (ed.), *Verwaltungsermessen im modernen Staat* (Baden-Baden, 1986), 79–111.

—— *Administrative Law* (2nd edn., London, 1989).

CRAIG, P. P., 'Bentham, Public Law and Democracy' [1989] *P.L.* 407–27.

CRAMTON, R. C., 'The Why, Where and How of Broadened Public Participation in the Administrative Process', 60 *Geo. L.J.* 525–50 (1971–2).

—— 'A Comment on Trial-Type Hearings in Nuclear Power Plant Siting', 58 *Va.L.Rev.* 585–99 (1972).

CRAVEN, E. (ed.), *Regional Devolution and Social Policy* (London, 1975).

DAHL, R. A., *A Preface to Democratic Theory* (Chicago, 1956).

—— *Who Governs?* (New Haven, 1961).

—— *Polyarchy: Participation and Opposition* (New Haven, 1971).

—— *Dilemmas of Pluralist Democracy* (New Haven, 1982).

—— *A Preface to Economic Democracy* (Cambridge, 1985).

—— and LINDBLOM, C. E., *Politics, Economics and Welfare* (New York, 1953).

DAINTITH, T. C., 'Kilbrandon: The Ship that Launched a Thousand Faces?' (1974) 37 *M.L.R.* 544–55.

—— 'Regulation by Contract: The New Prerogative' (1979) *C.L.P.* 41–64.

—— 'Legal Analysis of Economic Policy' (1982) 9 *Jnl. Law and Soc.* 191.

—— 'The Executive Power Today: Bargaining and Economic Control', in J. L. Jowell and D. Oliver (eds.), *The Changing Constitution* (2nd edn., Oxford, 1989), ch. 8.

DALTON, C., 'An Essay in the Deconstruction of Contract Doctrine', 94 *Yale L.J.* 997–1114 (1985).

DANIELS, N., 'Equal Liberty and Unequal Worth of Liberty', in N. Daniels (ed.), *Reading Rawls* (Oxford, 1975), ch. 11.

—— (ed.), *Reading Rawls* (Oxford, 1975).

DAVIES, A., 'Patronage and Quasi-Government: Some Proposals for Reform', in A. Barker (ed.), *Quangos in Britain* (London, 1982), ch. 10.

DAVIES, K. C., *Discretionary Justice: A Preliminary Inquiry* (Urbana, 1969).

DE SMITH, S. A., 'The Prerogative Writs' (1951) 11 *C.L.J.* 40–56.

—— 'Wrongs and Remedies in Administrative Law' (1952) 15 *M.L.R.* 189–208.

—— *Judicial Review of Administrative Action* (4th edn., London, 1980).

DEUTSCH, J. G., 'Neutrality, Legitimacy, and the Supreme Court: Some Intersections between Law and Political Science', 20 *Stan. L. Rev.* 169–261 (1968).

DICEY, A. V., *Lectures on the Relation Between Law and Public Opinion in England During the Nineteenth Century* (London, 1905).

—— 'The Development of Administrative Law in England' (1915) 31 *L.Q.R.* 148–53.

—— *An Introduction to the Study of the Law of the Constitution* (10th edn., London, 1959).

DIGGINS, J. P., *The Lost Soul of American Politics: Virtue, Self-Interest and the Foundations of Liberalism* (Boston, 1984).

DIVER, C. S., 'Policymaking Paradigms in Administrative Law', 95 *Harv.L.Rev.* 393–434 (1981).

DOWNS, A., *An Economic Theory of Democracy* (New York, 1957).
DREWRY, G. (ed.), *The New Select Committees: A Study of the 1979 Reforms* (Oxford, 1985).
DRUCKER, H. and BROWN, G., *The Politics of Nationalism and Devolution* (London, 1980).
——, DUNLEAVY, P., GAMBLE, A., and PEELE, G., (eds.), *Developments in British Politics 2* (London, 1986).
DUNCAN, G. (ed.), *Democratic Theory and Practice* (Cambridge, 1983).
—— and LUKES, S., 'The New Democracy', *Political Studies*, 11 (1963) 156.
DUNLEAVY, P., and HUSBANDS, C. T., *British Democracy at the Crossroads: Voting and Party Competition in the 1980s* (London, 1985).
DUNN, J., 'Unger's *Politics* and the Appraisal of Political Possibility', 81 *Nw. U.L.Rev.* 732–50 (1987).
DWORKIN, R., 'The Original Position', in N. Daniels (ed.), *Reading Rawls* (Oxford, 1975), ch. 2.
—— *Taking Rights Seriously* (London, 1977).
—— 'Liberalism', in S. Hampshire (ed.), *Public and Private Morality* (Cambridge, 1978), 113–43.
—— 'What is Equality? Part 2. Equality of Resources' (1981) 10 *Phil. & Pub Affairs*, 283–345.
—— *A Matter of Principle* (Cambridge, Mass., 1985).
—— *Law's Empire* (London, 1986).
—— 'What is Equality? Part 4. Political Equality', 22 *Univ. of San Francisco L. Rev.* 1–30 (1987–8).
DYE, T. R., and ZEIGLER, L. H., *The Irony of Democracy* (7th edn., Pacific Grove, 1987).
EASTERBROOK, F. H., 'Foreword: The Court and the Economic System', 98 *Harv.L.Rev.* 4–60 (1984).
EHRLICH, S., *Pluralism On and Off Course* (Oxford, 1982).
EISENBERG, M. A., 'Participation, Responsiveness and the Consultative Process', 92 *Harv.L.Rev.* 410–32 (1978).
ELLIOTT, M., 'The Control of Public Expenditure', in J. L. Jowell and D. Oliver (eds.), (2nd edn., Oxford, 1989), ch. 7.
ELY, J. H., *Democracy and Distrust: A Theory of Judicial Review* (Cambridge, Mass., 1980).
EPSTEIN, D. F., *The Political Theory of the Federalist* (Chicago, 1984).
EPSTEIN, R. A., *Takings: Private Property and the Power of Eminent Domain* (Cambridge, Mass., 1985).
FARINA, C. R., 'Statutory Interpretation and the Balance of Power in the Administrative State', 89 *Col. L. Rev.* 452–528 (1989).
FAYOL, H., *General and Industrial Management* (London, 1949).
FENNO, R. F., *Congressmen in Committees* (Boston, 1973).

FERGUSON, R. B., and PAGE, A. C., 'Pay Restraint: The Legal Constraints' (1978) 128 *N.L.J.* 515.
FIGGIS, J. N., *Churches in the Modern State* (London, 1913).
FINER, S. E., *Anonymous Empire* (2nd edn., London, 1966).
—— *Adversary Politics and Electoral Reform* (London, 1975).
FINNIS, J., *Natural Law and Natural Rights* (Oxford, 1980).
FIORINA, M. P., *Congress: Keystone of the Washington Establishment* (New Haven, 1977).
FISS, O., 'Free Speech and Social Structure', 71 *Iowa L.Rev.* 1405–25 (1986).
FRASER, D., *Power and Authority in the Victorian City* (Oxford, 1979).
—— *Evolution of the British Welfare State* (London, 1973).
FRIED, C., 'Liberalism, Community and the Objectivity of Values', 96 *Harv. L.Rev.* 960–8 (1983).
FRIEDMAN, M., and FRIEDMAN, R., *Free to Choose* (New York, 1980).
FRUG, G. E., 'The Ideology of Bureaucracy in American Law', 97 *Harv. L.Rev.* 1276–388 (1984).
—— 'Why Neutrality?', 92 *Yale L.J.* 1591–601 (1983).
FULLER, L. L., 'Mediation: Its Forms and Functions', 44 *S.Cal.L.Rev.* 305–39 (1971).
—— 'The Forms and Limits of Adjudication', 92 *Harv.L.Rev.* 353–409 (1978).
GALLIGAN, D. J., 'The Nature and Function of Policy within Discretionary Power' [1976] *P.L.* 332–57.
—— *Discretionary Powers: A Legal Study of Official Discretion* (Oxford, 1986).
GALSTON, W. A., 'False Universality: Infinite Personality and Finite Existence in Unger's *Politics*', 81 *Nw.U.L.Rev.* 751–65 (1987).
GAMBLE, A., 'The Political Economy of Freedom', in R. Levitas (ed.), *The Ideology of the New Right* (Cambridge, 1986), ch. 1.
—— *The Free Economy and the Strong State* (London, 1988).
GANZ, G., *Government and Industry* (Abingdon, 1977).
—— *Quasi-Legislation: Recent Developments in Secondary Legislation* (London, 1987).
GELLHORN, E., 'Public Participation in Administrative Proceedings', 81 *Yale L.J.* 359–404 (1971–2).
GEWIRTH, A., *Reason and Morality* (Chicago, 1987).
—— *Human Rights* (Chicago, 1982).
GIERKE, O. VON, *Political Theories of the Middle Ages*, ed. F. W. Maitland (Cambridge, 1900).
—— *Natural Law and the Theory of Society (1500–1800)*, ed. E. Barker (Cambridge, 1950).
GIRVETZ, H. K., *Democracy and Elitism* (New York, 1967).
GOLDTHORPE, J. H. (ed.), *Order and Conflict in Contemporary Capitalism* (Oxford, 1984).

GORDON, D. M., 'The Relation of Facts to Jurisdiction' (1929) 45 *L.Q.R.* 459–93.
—— 'Observance of Law as a Condition of Jurisdiction' (1931) 47 *L.Q.R.* 386–410, 557–87.
—— 'Jurisdictional Fact: An Answer' (1966) 82 *L.Q.R.* 515–24.
GRAY, J., *Liberalism* (Milton Keynes, 1986).
GREEN, L., *The Authority of the State* (Oxford, 1988).
GRIFFITH, J. A. G., *The Politics of the Judiciary* (3rd edn., Manchester, 1977).
GUTMANN, A., 'Communitarian Critics of Liberalism' (1985) 14 *Phil. & Pub. Affairs*, 308–22.
HABERMAS, J., *Legitimation Crisis*, trans. T. McCarthy (London, 1976).
—— *The Theory of Communicative Action*, trans. T. McCarthy (London, 1984).
HAGUE, D. C., MACKENZIE, W. J. M., and BARKER, A. (eds.) *Public Policy and Private Interests: The Institutions of Compromise* (London, 1975).
HALÉVY, E., *The Growth of Philosophic Radicalism* (London, 1928).
HANSON, R. L., *The Democratic Imagination in America: Conversations with our Past* (Princeton, 1985).
HARDEN, I., and LEWIS, N., *The Noble Lie: The British Constitution and the Rule of Law* (London, 1986).
HARLOW, C., and RAWLINGS, R., *Law and Administration* (London, 1984).
HARRINGTON, J., 'The Commonwealth of Oceana', in *The Political Works of James Harrington*, ed. J. G. A. Pocock (Cambridge, 1977).
HARRISON, M. L. (ed.), *Corporatism and the Welfare State* (London, 1984).
HARRISON, R. J., *Pluralism and Corporatism* (London, 1980).
HART, H. L. A., *The Concept of Law* (Oxford, 1961).
—— 'Rawls on Liberty and its Priority', in N. Daniels (ed.), *Reading Rawls* (Oxford, 1975), ch. 10.
—— 'Bentham on Legal Rights', in A. W. B. Simpson (ed.), *Oxford Essays in Jurisprudence* (2nd ser.; Oxford, 1973), ch. 7.
—— 'Are there any Natural Rights?', in J. Waldron (ed.), *Theories of Rights* (Oxford, 1984), ch. 3.
HARTER, P. J., 'Negotiating Regulations: A Cure for Malaise', 71 *Geo. L.J.* 1–118 (1982).
HARTLEY, T. C., *The Foundations of European Community Law* (2nd edn., Oxford, 1988).
HARTZ, L. B., *The Liberal Tradition in America: An Interpretation of American Political Thought since the Revolution* (New York, 1955).
HAYEK, F. A., *The Road to Serfdom* (London, 1944).
—— *The Constitution of Liberty* (London, 1960).
HENDERSON, E. G., *Foundations of English Administrative Law* (Cambridge, Mass., 1963).
HEUSTON, R. F. V., *Essays in Constitutional Law* (2nd edn., London, 1964).
HOBBES, T., *Leviathan*, ed. M. Oakeshott (Oxford, 1946).

HOFSTADTER, R., *The Idea of a Party System: The Rise of Legitimate Opposition in the United States, 1780–1840* (Berkeley, 1970).

HOLME, R., and ELLIOTT, M., *1688–1988: Time for a New Constitution* (London, 1988).

HORWITZ, M. J., 'Republicanism and Liberalism in American Constitutional Thought', 29 *Wm. & Mary L.Rev.* 57–74 (1987–8).

HOVENKAMP, H., *Economics and Federal Antitrust Law* (St Paul, 1985).

HUME, D., *David Hume: Writings on Economics*, ed. E. Rotwein (Edinburgh, 1970).

HUNTER, F., *Community Power Structure* (Chapel Hill, 1953).

IPPOLITO, D. S., and WALKER, T. G., *Political Parties, Interest Groups and Public Policy: Group Influence in American Politics* (New Jersey, 1980).

JACOBSON, A., 'The Private Use of Public Authority: Sovereignty and Associations in the Common Law', 29 *Buffalo L.Rev.* 599–665 (1980).

JACOBSON, G. C., *The Politics of Congressional Elections* (2nd edn., Boston, 1987).

JACONELLI, J., *Enacting a Bill of Rights* (Oxford, 1980).

JAFFE, L. L., *Judicial Control of Administrative Action* (Boston, 1965).

—— and HENDERSON, E. G., 'Judicial Review and the Rule of Law: Historical Origins' (1956) 72 *L.Q.R.* 345–64.

JENNINGS, I., *The Law and the Constitution* (London, 1933; 5th edn., 1959).

JERGESEN, A. D., 'The Legal Requirement of Consultation' [1978] *P.L.* 290–315.

JESSOP, B., 'Corporatism, Parliamentarism, and Social Democracy', in P. C. Schmitter and G. Lehmbruch (eds.), *Trends toward Corporatist Intermediation* (Beverly Hills, 1979), ch. 7.

——, BONNETT, K., BROMLEY, S., and LING, T., *Thatcherism* (Cambridge, 1988).

JOHNSON, N., *In Search of the Constitution: Reflections on State and Society in Britain* (Oxford, 1977).

—— 'Editorial: Quangos and the Structure of British Government' (1979) 57 *Pub.Adm.* 379.

—— 'Accountability, Control and Complexity: Moving Beyond Ministerial Responsibility', in A. Barker (ed.), *Quangos in Britain* (London, 1982), ch. 12.

JOWELL, J. L., *Law and Bureaucracy* (New York, 1975).

—— 'Bargaining in Development Control' (1977) *J.P.L.* 414–33.

—— 'Limits of Law in Urban Planning' (1977) *C.L.P.* 63–83.

—— and LESTER, A., 'Beyond *Wednesbury*: Substantive Principles of Administrative Law' [1987] *P.L.* 368–82.

—— and—— 'Proportionality: Neither Novel nor Dangerous', in J. L. Jowell and D. Oliver (eds.), *New Directions in Judicial Review* (London, 1988), 51–72.

JOWELL, J. L., and OLIVER, D. (eds.), *New Directions in Judicial Review* (London, 1988).

—— —— (eds.), *The Changing Constitution* (2nd edn., Oxford, 1989).

KARIEL, H., *The Decline of American Pluralism* (Stanford, 1961).

—— (ed.), *Frontiers of Democratic Theory* (New York, 1970).

KAVANAGH, D., 'Political Behaviour and Political Participation', in G. Parry (ed.), *Participation in Politics* (Manchester, 1972), ch. 5.

—— *Thatcherism and British Politics: The End of Consensus?* (Oxford, 1987).

KEELING, D., 'Beyond Ministerial Departments: Mapping the Administrative Terrain: Quasi-Governmental Agencies' (1976) 54 *Pub. Adm.* 161–75.

KELLAS, J. G., *The Scottish Political System* (3rd edn., Cambridge, 1984).

KELMAN, M., 'Trashing', 36 *Stan L.Rev.* 293–348 (1984).

—— *A Guide to Critical Legal Studies* (Cambridge, Mass., 1987).

—— 'On Democracy-Bashing: A Skeptical Look at the Theoretical and "Empirical" Practice of the Public Choice Movement', 74 *Virg. L.Rev.* 199–273 (1988).

KETCHAM, R. (ed.), *The Anti-Federalist Papers and the Constitutional Convention Debates* (New York, 1986).

KIMBER, R. H., and RICHARDSON, J. J. (eds.), *Pressure Groups in Britain: A Reader* (London, 1974).

KING, R. (ed.), *Capital and Politics* (London, 1983).

KORNHAUSER, W., *The Politics of Mass Society* (London, 1960).

KRAMNICK, I., 'Republican Revisionism Revisited', 87 *Am.Hist.Rev.* 629–64 (1982).

KROUSE, R. W., 'Classical Images of Democracy in America: Madison and Tocqueville', in G. Duncan (ed.), *Democratic Theory and Practice* (Cambridge, 1983), ch. 5.

KYMLICKA, W., *Liberalism, Community, and Culture* (Oxford, 1989).

LANDES, W., and POSNER, R., 'The Independent Judiciary in an Interest-Group Perspective', 18 *J.L.E.* 875–901 (1975).

LASKI, H. J., *Studies in the Problem of Sovereignty* (New Haven, 1917).

—— *Authority in the Modern State* (New Haven, 1919).

—— *The Foundations of Sovereignty* (London, 1921).

—— *A Grammar of Politics* (4th edn., New Haven, 1938).

LATHAM, E., *The Group Basis of Politics* (Ithaca, 1952).

LESTER, A., 'Fundamental Rights: the United Kingdom Isolated' [1984] *P.L.* 46–72.

LEVITAS, R., 'Competition and Compliance: The Utopias of the New Right', in R. Levitas (ed.), *The Ideology of the New Right* (Cambridge, 1986), ch. 3.

—— (ed.), *The Ideology of the New Right* (Cambridge, 1986).

LEWIS, N., 'IBA Programme Contract Awards' [1975] *P.L.* 317–40.

LINDBLOM, C. E., *The Intelligence of Democracy* (New York, 1965).

—— *Politics and Markets* (New York, 1977).

LINDSAY, A. D., *The Essentials of Democracy* (London, 1929).
LIPSET, S., *Political Man* (London, 1960).
LIVELY, J., *Democracy* (Oxford, 1975).
LLOYD OF HAMPSTEAD, LORD, *Introduction to Jurisprudence* (4th edn., London, 1979).
LOUGHLIN, M., *Local Government in the Modern State* (London, 1986).
—— GELFAND, M. D., and YOUNG, K. (eds.), *Half a Century of Municipal Decline 1935–1985* (London, 1985).
LOW, S., *The Governance of England* (London, 1904).
LOWELL, A. L., *The Government of England* (New York, 1908).
LOWI, T. J., *The End of Liberalism: Ideology, Policy and the Crisis of Public Authority* (New York, 1969).
—— *The End of Liberalism: The Second Republic of the United States* (2nd edn., New York, 1979).
—— (ed.), *Legislative Politics U.S.A.* (3rd edn., New York, 1973).
LUBENOW, W. C., *The Politics of Government Growth: Early Victorian Attitudes to State Intervention (1833–1948)* (Newton Abbot, 1971).
LUCAS, J., *The Principles of Politics* (Oxford, 1966).
—— *Democracy and Participation* (Harmondsworth, 1976).
LUKES, S., *Individualism* (Oxford, 1973).
LYONS, D., *The Forms and Limits of Utilitarianism* (Oxford, 1965).
—— 'Constitutional Interpretation and Original Meaning', 4 *Social Philosophy and Policy*, 75 (1986).
MAASS, A., *Congress and the Common Good* (New York, 1983).
MCAUSLAN, J. P. W. B., *The Ideologies of Planning Law* (Oxford, 1980).
—— 'Administrative Law, Collective Consumption and Judicial Policy' (1983) 46 *M.L.R.* 1–20.
—— and MCELDOWNEY, J. (eds.), *Law, Legitimacy and the Constitution* (London, 1985).
MACCALLUM, G. C., 'Legislative Intent', 75 *Yale L.J.* 754–87 (1960).
MCCLUSKEY, LORD, *Law, Justice and Democracy* (London, 1987).
MACCORMICK, D. N., 'Independence and Constitutional Change', in D. N. MACCORMICK (ed.), *The Scottish Debate* (Oxford, 1970), ch. 4.
—— (ed.), *The Scottish Debate* (Oxford, 1970).
—— 'Rights in Legislation', in P. M. S. Hacker and J. Raz (eds.), *Law, Morality and Society* (Oxford, 1977), ch. 11.
—— *Legal Right and Social Democracy* (Oxford, 1982).
MACCORMICK, I. S. M., 'The Case for Independence', in D. N. MacCormick (ed.), *The Scottish Debate* (Oxford, 1970), ch. 7.
MCCORMICK, R. E., and TOLLISON, R. D., *Politicians, Legislation and the Economy: An Inquiry into the Interest-Group Theory of Government* (Norwall, Mass., 1981).
MCCOY, D. R., *The Elusive Republic: Political Economy in Jeffersonian America* (Chapel Hill, 1980).

MacDonagh, O., 'The Nineteenth-Century Revolution in Government: A Reappraisal', *Historical Journal*, 1/1 (1958) 52.

MacDonald, R. A., 'Judicial Review and Procedural Fairness in Administrative Law: II', (1980–1) 26 *McGill L.J.* 1–44.

Macey, J. R., 'Promoting Public-Regarding Legislation through Statutory Interpretation: An Interest Group Model', 86 *Col. L.Rev.* 223–68 (1986).

—— 'Transaction Costs and Normative Elements of the Public Choice Model: An Application to Constitutional Theory', 74 *Virg. L.Rev.* 471–518 (1988).

McGrew, A. G., and Wilson M.J. (eds.), *Decisionmaking: Approaches and Analysis* (Manchester, 1982).

MacIntyre, A., *After Virtue* (2nd edn., London, 1984).

—— *Whose Justice? Which Rationality?* (London, 1988).

McKechnie, W. S., *The New Democracy and the Constitution* (London, 1912; repr. 1971).

McLean, I., *Dealing in Votes* (Oxford, 1982).

—— *Public Choice: An Introduction* (Oxford, 1987).

MacPherson, C. B., *The Political Theory of Possessive Individualism: Hobbes to Locke* (Oxford, 1962).

—— *Democratic Theory* (Oxford, 1973).

—— *The Life and Times of Liberal Democracy* (Oxford, 1977).

Maine, H. S., *Popular Government* (London, 1885).

Maitland, F. W., *Collected Papers* (Cambridge, 1911).

Makielski, S. J. *Pressure Politics in America* (New York, 1980).

Mandeville, B., *The Fable of the Bees*, ed. J. P. Harth (Harmondsworth, 1970).

Marquand, D., 'The Paradoxes of Thatcherism', in R. Skidelsky (ed.), *Thatcherism* (London, 1988), ch. 9.

Marshall, G., *Constitutional Theory* (Oxford, 1971).

—— *Constitutional Conventions* (Oxford, 1984).

Mashaw, J. L., *Bureaucratic Justice* (New Haven, 1983).

—— *Due Process in the Administrative State* (New Haven, 1985).

Mayhew, D. R., *Congress: The Electoral Connection* (New Haven, 1974).

Mercer, J., *Scotland: The Devolution of Power* (London, 1978).

Michelman, F. I., 'In Pursuit of Constitutional Welfare Rights: One View of Rawls' Theory of Justice', 121 *U.Pa.L.Rev.* 962 (1973).

—— 'Formal and Associational Aims in Procedural Due Process', in J. R. Pennock and J. W. Chapman (eds.), *Due Process: Nomos 18* (New York, 1977), ch. 4.

—— 'Politics and Values or What's Really Wrong with Rationality Review?', 13 *Creighton L.Rev.* 487 (1979).

—— 'Foreword: Traces of Self-Government', 100 *Harv. L.Rev.* 4–77 (1986).

—— 'Possession vs. Distribution in the Constitutional Idea of Property', 72 *Iowa L.Rev.* 1319–50 (1987).

MICHELMAN, F. I., 'Law's Republic', 97 *Yale L.J.* 1493–537 (1988).
MICHELS, R., *Political Parties: A Sociological Study of the Oligarchical Tendencies of Modern Democracy*, trans. E. and C. Paul (New York, 1962).
MIDDLEMAS, K., *Politics in Industrial Society* (London, 1979).
MILBRATH, L. W., *Political Participation: How and Why do People get Involved in Politics?* (Chicago, 1965).
MILIBAND, R., *Capitalist Democracy in Britain* (Oxford, 1982).
MILL, J. S., *Utilitarianism, On Liberty, and Considerations on Representative Government*, ed. H. B. Acton (London, 1972).
MILLER, A. S., *The Modern Corporate State: Private Governments and the American Constitution* (New York, 1976).
MILLER, D., 'The Competitive Model of Democracy', in G. Duncan (ed.), *Democratic Theory and Practice* (Cambridge, 1983), ch. 9.
MILLS, C. W., *The Power Elite* (New York, 1956).
MITCHELL, J. D. B., *Constitutional Law* (2nd edn., Edinburgh, 1968).
MOODIE, G. C., and STUDDERT-KENNEDY, G., *Opinions, Publics and Pressure Groups* (London, 1970).
MORAWETZ, T., 'Persons without History: Liberal Theory and Human Experience', 66 *Boston U.L.Rev.* 1013–37 (1986).
MOSCA, G., *The Ruling Class* (New York, 1939).
MUELLER, D., *Public Choice* (Cambridge, 1979).
NAGEL, T., 'Rawls on Justice', in N. Daniels (ed.), *Reading Rawls* (Oxford, 1975), ch. 1.
NEWMAN, O., *The Challenge of Corporatism* (London, 1981).
NICHOLLS, D., *Three Varieties of Pluralism* (London, 1974).
—— *The Pluralist State* (London, 1975).
NISKANEN, W. A., *Bureaucracy and Representative Government* (Chicago, 1971).
NOWAK, J. E., ROTUNDA, R. D., and NELSON YOUNG, J., *Constitutional Law* (3rd edn., St Paul, 1986).
NOZICK, R., *Anarchy, State, and Utopia* (Oxford, 1974).
NUTTALL, R. L., SCHEUCH, E. K., and GORDON, C., 'On the Structure of Influence', in T. N. Clark (ed.), *Community Structure and Decision Making: Comparative Analysis* (San Francisco, 1968), 349–400.
OFFE, C., *Contradictions of the Welfare State*, ed. J. Keane (London, 1984).
OLSON, M., *The Logic of Collective Action: Public Goods and the Theory of Groups* (Cambridge, Mass., 1965).
THE OMEGA FILE (Adam Smith Institute, 1985).
OSTROGORSKI, M., *Democracy and the Organization of Political Parties*, trans. F. Clarke (London, 1970).
PANITCH, L., 'The Development of Corporatism in Liberal Democracies', in P. C. Schmitter and G. Lehmbruch (eds.), *Trends toward Corporatist Intermediation* (Beverly Hills, 1979), ch. 5.
PAREKH, B. (ed.), *Jeremy Bentham: Ten Critical Essays* (London, 1974).
PARETO, V., *The Mind and Society*, trans. A. Livingston (New York, 1935).

PARKER, R. D., 'The Past of Constitutional Theory—and its Future', 42 *Ohio St. L.J.* 223–59 (1981).

PARRIS, H., 'The Nineteenth-Century Revolution in Government: A Reappraisal Reappraised', *Historical Journal*, 3 (1960) 17.

—— *Constitutional Bureaucracy: The Development of British Central Administration since the Eighteenth Century* (London, 1969).

PARRY, G., *Political Elites* (London, 1969).

—— 'The Idea of Political Participation', in G. Parry (ed.), *Participation in Politics* (Manchester, 1972), ch. 1.

—— (ed.), *Participation in Politics* (Manchester, 1972).

PATEMAN, C., *Participation and Democratic Theory* (Cambridge, 1970).

PENNOCK, J. P., and Chapman, J. W. (eds.), *Due Process: Nomos 18* (New York, 1977).

PERRY, M. 'Substantive Due Process Revisited: Reflections on (and beyond) Recent Cases', 71 *Nw. U.L.Rev.* 417–69 (1977).

—— 'Interpretativism, Freedom of Expression, and Equal Protection', 42 *Ohio St. L.J.* 261–317 (1981).

—— *The Constitution, the Courts and Human Rights* (New Haven, 1982).

PHILIP, A. B., *The Welsh Question: Nationalism in Welsh Politics, 1945–1970* (Cardiff, 1975).

PIERCE. R., '*Chevron* and its Aftermath: Judicial Review of Agency Interpretation of Statutory Provisions', 41 *Vand. L. Rev.* 301–14 (1988).

POCOCK, J. G. A., *Politics, Language and Time* (New York, 1971).

—— *The Machiavellian Moment: Florentine Political Thought and the Atlantic Republican Tradition* (Princeton, 1975).

—— *Virtue, Commerce and History* (Cambridge, 1985).

POLSBY, N., *Community Power and Political Theory: A Further Look at Problems of Evidence and Inference* (2nd edn., New Haven, 1980).

POSNER, R., 'Economics, Politics and the Reading of Statutes and the Constitution', 49 *U.Chi. L.Rev.* 263–91 (1982).

—— and EASTERBROOK, F. H., *Antitrust* (2nd edn., St Paul, 1981).

POTTER, A., *Organized Groups in British National Politics* (London, 1961).

PRESTHUS, R., *Men at the Top* (New York, 1964).

PROSSER, T., 'Towards a Critical Public Law' (1982) 9 *Jnl. Law & Soc.* 1–19.

—— *Nationalized Industries and Public Control* (Oxford, 1986).

—— *The Privatization of Public Enterprises in France and Great Britain: The State, Constitutions and Public Policy* (EUI Working Paper No. 88/364; 1988).

QUELLER, D. E., *The Venetian Patriciate: Reality versus Myth* (Urbana, 1986).

RAWLINGS, H., *Law and the Electoral Process* (London, 1988).

RAWLS, J., *A Theory of Justice* (Oxford, 1973).

—— 'Fairness to Goodness' (1975) 84 *Philosophical Review*, 536–54.

—— 'Kantian Constructivism in Moral Theory' (1980) 77 *Journal of Philosophy*, 515–72.

—— 'Social Unity and Primary Goods', in A. Sen and B. Williams (eds.), *Utilitarianism and Beyond* (Cambridge, 1982), ch. 8.
—— 'Justice as Fairness: Political not Metaphysical' (1985) 14 *Phil. & Pub. Affairs*, 223–51.
—— 'The Basic Liberties and their Priority', in S. M. McMurrin (ed.), *Liberty, Equality and Law* (Utah and Cambridge, 1987), 1–87.
—— 'The Idea of an Overlapping Consensus' (1987) 7 *O.J.L.S.* 1–25.
—— 'The Priority of Right and Ideas of the Good' (1988) 17 *Phil. & Pub. Affairs*, 251–76.
—— 'The Domain of the Political and Overlapping Consensus', 64 *N.Y.U.L. Rev.* 233–55 (1989).
RAZ, J., 'The Rule of Law and its Virtue' (1977) 93 *L.Q.R.* 195–211.
—— 'Legal Rights' (1984) 4 *O.J.L.S.* 1–21.
—— *The Morality of Freedom* (Oxford, 1986).
—— 'Facing Up: A Reply', 62 *S. Cal. L.Rev.* 1153–235 (1989).
REDLICH, J., *The Procedure of the House of Commons: A Study of its History and Present Form* (London, 1908).
—— HIRST, F., and KEITH-LUCAS, B., *The History of Local Government in England* (2nd edn., London, 1970).
REICH, C., 'The New Property', 73 *Yale L.J.* 733–87 (1964).
RESNICK, D., 'Due Process and Procedural Justice', in J. R. Pennock and J. W. Chapman (eds.), *Due Process: Nomos 18* (New York, 1977), ch. 7
RICHARDSON, J. J., and JORDAN, A. G., *Governing under Pressure* (Oxford, 1985).
RIDGES, E. W., *Constitutional Law of England*, ed. S. E. Williams (3rd edn., London, 1922).
ROBBINS, C., *The Eighteenth-Century Commonwealthman: Studies in the Transmission, Development and Circumstance of English Liberal Thought from the Restoration of Charles II until the War with the Thirteen Colonies* (Cambridge, Mass., 1959).
ROBERTS, D., *Victorian Origins of the British Welfare State* (New Haven, 1960).
ROBINSON, A., 'The House of Commons and Public Expenditure', in S. A. Walkland and M. Ryle (eds.), *The Commons Today* (London, 1981) ch. 7.
ROBSON, W., *Justice and Administrative Law: A Study of the British Constitution* (London, 1928).
ROSSITER, C. (ed.), *The Federalist Papers* (New York, 1961).
RUBINSTEIN, A., *Jurisdiction and Illegality* (Oxford, 1975).
RYLE, M., 'Supply and Other Financial Procedures', in S. Walkland (ed.), *The House of Commons in the Twentieth Century* (Oxford, 1979), ch. 7.
SALISBURY, R., 'Why no Corporatism in America?', in P. C. Schmitter and G. Lehmbruch (eds.), *Trends toward Corporatist Intermediation* (Beverly Hills, 1979), ch. 8.
SANDEL, M. J., *Liberalism and the Limits of Justice* (Cambridge, 1982).

SANDEL, M. J., 'The Procedural Republic and the Unencumbered Self', 12 *Pol. Theory*, 81–96 (1984).
—— (ed.), *Liberalism and its Critics* (Oxford, 1984).
SAPHIRE, R. B., 'Specifying Due Process Values: Toward a More Responsive Approach to Procedural Protection', 127 *U.Pa. L.Rev.* 111–95 (1978).
SARTORI, G., *Democratic Theory* (New York, 1965).
SAX, J. L., 'The (Unhappy) Truth about NEPA', 26 *Okl. L.Rev.* 239–48 (1973).
SCARMAN, Sir L., *English Law—The New Dimension* (London, 1974).
SCHATTSCHNEIDER, E. E., *The Semi-Sovereign People: A Realist's View of Democracy in America* (New York, 1960).
SCHAUER, F., *Free Speech: A Philosophical Enquiry* (Cambridge, 1980).
SCHINDLER, P., 'The Problems of Decision-Making by Way of the Management Committee Procedure in the European Economic Community' (1971) 8 *C.M.L.Rev.* 184–205.
SCHMITTER, P. C., 'Still the Century of Corporatism', in P.C. Schmitter and G. Lehmbruch (eds.), *Trends toward Corporatist Intermediation* (Beverly Hills, 1979), ch. 1.
—— 'Modes of Interest Intermediation and Models of Societal Change in Western Europe', in P. C. Schmitter and G. Lehmbruch (eds.), *Trends toward Corporatist Intermediation* (Beverly Hills, 1979), ch. 3.
SCHMITTER, P. C., and LEHMBRUCH, G. (eds.), *Trends toward Corporatist Intermediation* (Beverly Hills, 1979).
—— —— *Patterns of Corporatist Policy-Making* (London, 1982).
SCHUMPETER, J., *Capitalism, Socialism and Democracy* (London, 1942).
SCRUTON, R., *The Meaning of Conservatism* (2nd edn., London, 1984).
SELF, P. J. O., *Administrative Theories and Politics: An Inquiry into the Structure and Process of Modern Government* (2nd edn., London, 1977).
SELZNICK, P., *T.V.A. and the Grass Roots: A Study in the Sociology of Formal Organisation* (New York, 1949).
SHALHOPE, R. E., 'Republicanism and Early American Historiography', 39 *Wm. & Mary Q.* 334–56 (1982).
SHAPIRO, D. L., 'The Choice of Rulemaking or Adjudication in the Development of Administrative Policy', 78 *Harv. L.Rev.* 921–72 (1965).
—— 'Some Thoughts on Intervention before Courts, Agencies, and Arbitrators', 81 *Harv. L.Rev.* 721–72 (1968).
SHONFIELD, A., *Modern Capitalism: The Changing Balance of Public and Private Power* (London, 1965).
SIMMIE, J., *Power, Property and Corporatism: The Political Sociology of Planning* (London, 1981).
SIMON, H., *Administrative Behaviour* (2nd edn., New York, 1957).
SIMPSON, A. W. B. (ed.), *Oxford Essays in Jurisprudence* (Oxford, 1973).

SIMPSON, D., 'Independence: The Economic Issues', in D. N. MacCormick (ed.), *The Scottish Debate* (Oxford, 1970), chs. 9, 11b.

SINGER, J., 'The Player and the Cards: Nihilism and Legal Theory', 94 *Yale L.J.* 1–70 (1984).

SKIDELSKY, R. (ed.), *Thatcherism* (London, 1988).

SMITH, B. L., and HAGUE, D. C. (eds.), *The Dilemma of Accountability in Modern Government* (London, 1971).

STEWART, R. B., 'The Reformation of American Administrative Law', 88 *Harv. L.Rev.* 1667–813 (1975).

—— 'Vermont Yankee and the Evolution of Administrative Procedure', 91 *Harv. L.Rev.* 1805–22 (1978).

—— 'Regulation, Innovation and Administrative Law: A Conceptual Framework', 69 *Calif. L.Rev.* 1256–377 (1981).

—— 'Regulation in a Liberal State: The Role of Non-Commodity Values', 92 *Yale L.J.* 1537–90 (1983).

—— and SUNSTEIN, C. R., 'Public Programs and Private Rights', 95 *Harv. L.Rev.* 1193–322 (1982).

STIGLER, G., 'The Theory of Economic Regulation', 2 *Bell J. of Econ. & Mgmt. Sci.* 3 (1971).

STORING, H., *What the Anti-Federalists Were For* (Chicago, 1981).

—— (ed.), *The Complete Anti-Federalist* (Chicago, 1981).

STOURZH, G., *Alexander Hamilton and the Idea of Republican Government* (Stanford, 1970).

STREECK, W., and SCHMITTER, P. C. (eds.), *Private Interest Government: Beyond Market and State* (London, 1985).

SULLIVAN, E. T., and HOVENKAMP, H., *Antitrust Law, Policy and Procedure* (Charlottesville, 1984).

SULLIVAN, L. A., *Antitrust* (St Paul, 1977).

SUNSTEIN, C. R., 'Public Values, Private Interests, and the Equal Protection Clause' (1982) *Sup. Ct. Rev.* 127–66.

—— 'Deregulation and the Hard-Look Doctrine' (1983) *Sup. Ct Rev.* 177–213.

—— 'Naked Preferences and the Constitution', 84 *Col. L. Rev.* 1689–732 (1984).

—— 'Interest Groups in American Public Law,' 38 *Stn L. Rev.* 29–87 (1985). (1985).

—— 'Legal Interference with Private Preferences', 53 *U.Chi. L.Rev.* 1129–74 (1986).

—— 'Constitutionalism After the New Deal', 101 *Harv. L. Rev.* 421–510 (1987).

—— 'Beyond the Republican Revival', 97 *Yale L.J.* 1539–90 (1988).

—— 'Disrupting Voluntary Transactions', in J. W. Chapman and J. R. Pennock (eds.), *Markets and Justice: Nomos 31* (New York, 1989), ch. 10.

Taylor, A. J., *Laissez-faire and State Intervention in Nineteenth Century Britain* (London 1972).

Taylor, C., 'Hegel and Politics', in M. J. Sandel (ed.), *Liberalism and its Critics* (Oxford, 1984), ch. 9.

Tribe, L. H., *American Constitutional Law* (2nd edn., New York, 1988).

—— 'The Puzzling Persistence of Process-Based Constitutional Theories', 89 *Yale L.J.* 1063–80 (1980).

—— *Constitutional Choices* (Cambridge, Mass., 1985).

Truman, D. B., *The Governmental Process* (New York, 1951).

—— 'The American System in Crisis', *Pol. Sci. Quart.* 481 (1959).

Tsoukalis, L. (ed.), *The European Community: Past, Present and Future* (Oxford, 1983).

Tullock, G., *The Politics of Bureaucracy* (Washington DC, 1965).

Turpin, C., *Government Contracts* (London, 1972).

Tushnet, M. V., 'Darkness on the Edge of Town: The Contributions of John Hart Ely to Constitutional Theory', 89 *Yale L.J.* 1037–62 (1980).

—— 'Following the Rules Laid Down: A Critique of Interpretivism and Neutral Principles', 96 *Harv. L.Rev.* 781–827 (1983).

—— *Red, White and Blue: A Critical Analysis of Constitutional Law* (Cambridge, Mass., 1988).

Unger, R. M., *Knowledge and Politics* (New York, 1975).

—— *Law in Modern Society* (New York, 1976).

—— 'The Critical Legal Studies Movement', 96 *Harv. L.Rev.* 563–675 (1983).

—— *Social Theory: Its Situation and its Task* (Cambridge, 1987).

—— *False Necessity: Anti-Necessitarian Social Theory in the Service of Radical Democracy* (Cambridge, 1987).

—— *Plasticity into Power: Comparative Historical Studies on the Institutional Conditions of Economic and Military Success* (Cambridge, 1987).

Van Alstyne, W. W., 'The Demise of the Right-Privilege Distinction in Constitutional Law', 81 *Harv. L. Rev.* 1439–64 (1968).

Vickers, J., and Yarrow, G., *Privatization: An Economic Analysis* (Cambridge, Mass., 1988).

Vining, J., *Legal Identity* (New Haven, 1978).

Wade, H. W. R., 'The Basis of Legal Sovereignty', (1955) *C.L.J.* 172–97.

Waldron, J., *Nonsense upon Stilts: Bentham, Burke, Marx and the Rights of Man* (London, 1987).

—— 'Autonomy and Perfectionism in Raz's *Morality of Freedom*', 62 *S. Cal. L.Rev.* 1098–152 (1989).

Waldron, J. (ed.), *Theories of Rights* (Oxford, 1984).

Walkland, S. (ed.), *The House of Commons in the Twentieth Century* (Oxford, 1979).

—— and Ryle, M. (eds.), *The Commons in the Seventies* (London, 1977).

WALLINGTON, P., and McBRIDE, J., *Civil Liberties and a Bill of Rights* (London, 1976).
WASS, SIR D., *Government and the Governed* (London, 1984).
WECHSLER, H., 'Toward Neutral Principles of Constitutional Law', 73 *Harv. L.Rev.* 1–35 (1959).
WELLINGTON, H. H., 'Common Law Rules and Constitutional Double Standards: Some Notes on Adjudication', 83 *Yale L.J.* 221–311 (1973).
—— 'The Nature of Judicial Review', 91 *Yale L.J.* 486–520 (1982).
WELLMAN, C., *Welfare Rights* (Totowa, 1982).
WESTON, C. C., *English Constitutional Theory and the House of Lords* (London, 1965).
WILLS, G., *Explaining America: The Federalist* (New York, 1981).
WILLSON, F. M. G., 'Ministries and Boards: Some Aspects of Administrative Development since 1832' (1955) 33 *Pub.Adm.* 43–58.
WILSON, G. K., *Interest Groups in the United States* (Oxford, 1981).
WOLFF, R. P., *The Poverty of Liberalism* (Boston, 1968).
WOLL, P., *Congress* (Boston, 1985).
WOOD, G. S., *The Creation of the American Republic, 1776–1787* (Chapel Hill, 1969).
—— (ed.), *The Rising Glory of America, 1760–1820* (New York, 1971).
WOOTTON, G., *Interest Groups, Policy and Politics in America* (Englewood Cliffs, NJ, 1985).
WRIGHT, C. A., *Law of Federal Courts* (4th edn., St Paul, 1983).
WRIGHT, Judge Skelly, 'Beyond Discretionary Justice', 81 *Yale L.J.* 575–97 (1972).
ZANDER, M., *A Bill of Rights?* (3rd edn., London, 1985).

INDEX

Lightning Source UK Ltd.
Milton Keynes UK
31 January 2011

166688UK00004B/2/A

9 780198 256373